Cape York
The Savage Frontier

by
Rodney Liddell

© Copyright Rodney Liddell, 1996.

1st Edition: 1996

2nd Edition: 1st Printing 1997
              2nd Printing 1999
              3rd Printing 2002

3rd Edition: 1st Printing 2004
              2nd Printing 2024

All rights reserved. No part of this publication may be reproduced or transmitted in any form or by any means, electronic or mechanical, including photocopying, recording or any information storage and retrieval system, without permission in writing from the copyright holder.

ISBN: 978-0-646-89632-8

Cover Photo - Artist's impression of a castaway clubbed to death at Cape York.

ACKNOWLEDGEMENTS

Whilst researching the history of Cape York, various sources had to be checked and rechecked for their accuracy.

I am therefore indebted to the following for their assistance in providing documents, photographs and recorded evidence used in this book.

- **Queensland State Archives** – Brisbane [Q.S.A.]

- **John Oxley Library** – Brisbane [J.O.L.]

- **Hibberd Library** – Weipa [H.L.]

- **Mitchell Library** – Sydney [M.L.]

- **Hubert Hofer** [Marine Photographer, Bamaga, Cape York]
  for the following coloured photographs: (5)
  "Raine Island"
  "Raine Island Beacon"
  "Yedthu Beach, Prince of Wales Island"
  "Under-water wreck of the Quetta"
  "Albany Island graves"

- **Grahame Jardine-Vidgen** for photographs from the "Jardine-Vidgen Collection", of Somerset and the Jardine family.

- **Betty Pamela Ivey** for photographs of the "Sheldon Family, Pulau Babi and Dobo in the Aru Islands" and permission to publish the coloured photographs of the "Silver Fish Knife Service". The time she gave for 3 tape recorded interviews on her life in the Aru Islands is also appreciated.

- **John Hore-Lacy** for family photographic portraits of Emily Lacy.

- **Ian Hore-Lacy** for the narrative written by Emily Lacy, on the sinking of the R.M.S. Quetta.

- **Arthur Tillett** – Queensland Maritime Museum – Brisbane, for the photograph of the "QGSY Merrie England" and valuable information on the "R.M.S. Quetta".

- **Mrs M Lawrie**.

- **Bill Kitson** – Department of Lands – Brisbane, for the maps of the Jardine Cattle Drive to Cape York.

- **Tom Moss** for photographs of Lizard Island.

- **John Gray** for the photograph of the caretakers cottage at Somerset.

All other coloured photographs excluding the front cover were taken by the author.

INTRODUCTION

When aborigines murdered a sailor from the Dutch ship "Duyfken", on the west coast of Cape York in 1606, it was the beginning of Australia's "Race War". This was the first recorded murder in Australia.

Within weeks, another 9 "Duyfken" sailors were murdered by aborigines near Cape Keerweer. This was Australia's first recorded massacre.

The contents of this book portray history as it really happened, rather than the many fictionalised accounts that academics have inserted in recent years.

During my 10 years of research into original documentation held in libraries and archives, it became very obvious that many of them particularly anthropologists and sociologists were promoting what they personally wanted the public to believe, rather than write an accurate historical record. In effect they have included a mass of fiction into the history books, that is now taught in schools and universities as fact.

In the process they effectively covered up the aboriginal invasion of Australia and extermination of the "Original Indigenous Australians" [Papuans] less than a thousand years ago.

"The Savage Frontier" exposes the raw savagery that existed amongst the native tribes of Cape-York and the Torres Strait Islands in the 19th century.

Many of the lies and deceptions published by academics are also exposed and where possible, copies of the hand written reports of last century are included as evidence of academic deceit and naivety.

This narrative commences with the Aboriginal Invasion of Australia and exposes the "False Aboriginality" of the 40,000 year myth.

It progresses through the violent confrontations of the native tribes and the massacres of hundreds of Europeans, including men, women and children who were cast ashore from the numerous shipwrecks along this hostile coastline of the Cape York Peninsula and the Torres Strait Islands.

They were slaughtered by club and spear and in many cases, beheaded.

One castaway who survived was 16 years old Barbara Thompson, who was held captive for nearly 5 years by a tribe of headhunters and witnessed the eating of human heads and the murders of their own babies. [1844-1849]. Her testimony totally refutes statements made by academics.

As you journey through these pages you will read of the incredible settlement of Somerset, at Cape York, established as a "Harbour of Refuge" where shipwrecked castaways found sanctuary from the constant massacres perpetrated by "Islanders and Aborigines at Cape York".

Read of the unbelievable Jardine Cattle Drive, in which 10 men fought against all odds, to drive 250 head of cattle over a thousand miles to Somerset. In spite of the savage aboriginal attacks, they made it.

Continuing through the 1800's you will read of the River of Gold [Palmer River] where men died from starvation, disease and savage attacks by aborigines.

This is followed by the traumatic death of "Lizzie Watson" who fought off aboriginal spears on lonely Lizard Island, only to die of thirst with her baby.

When the Quetta sank in 1890 at Cape York, 133 people drowned. Many of the survivors owed their lives to the quick actions of Frank Jardine of Somerset.

What of the Jardine Silver Treasure found embedded in a coral reef in 1891. Was it really buried with the Jardine Journals on an Indonesian Island.

In 1899 Cyclone Mahina struck Cape York killing over 300 people and sank 61 vessels.

This is the history that many authors were afraid to write for fear of being branded as racist by a biased and prejudicial press.

Now at last, the truth can finally be told.

During Australia's pioneering history, distances were measured in miles, yards, feet and inches. Whilst weights were in tons, pounds [LBS] and ounces and the currency was in Pounds, Shillings and Pence. [£.S.D.] These have been retained as the only valid Currency, Weights and Measures of their day.

Notes in square brackets [ ] are author's comments.

AS DISTANCES WERE CALCULATED BY VISUAL OBSERVANCE, THEY WERE OFTEN OVERRATED.

ISLANDS OF THE WESTERN TORRES STRAIT

EUROPEAN NAME	NATIVE NAME	ABBREVIATED NAME	TRIBE
Banks	Moa	–	Moa-Ita
–	–	–	Moa-Laig
Booby	Neungu	–	–
Cape York Is	Wamalaga	Wamalug	Gudang [Ab]
Friday	Gialaga	Gialug	Kaurarega
Goode	Palilaga	Palilug	Kaurarega
Hammond	Keriri	–	Kaurarega
Horn	Nurapai	–	Kaurarega
Jervis	Mabuiag	–	Gamalega
Mt Ernest	Nahgi	–	Kulkalega
Mulgrave	Badthu	Badu	Badulega
Possession	Tuined	–	–
Prince of Wales	Muralaga	Muralug	Kaurarega
Talbot	Saibai	–	Saibili
Thursday	Waibene	Waiben	Kaurarega
Tuesday	Kudalaga	Kudalug	Kaurarega
Entrance	Juna	–	Kaurarega
Wednesday	Maurarura	Marwai	Kaurarega

THE 6 ABORIGINAL TRIBES NORTH OF THE JARDINE RIVER

CORRECT NAME	ABBREVIATION	TRIBAL BOUNDARIES	COAST
Gudanga	Gudang	Cape York to Fly Point	East
Induyumu*	Duyam	Fly Point to Newcastle Bay	East
Yadagana	Yadagan	Newcastle Bay to Escape River	East
Gumukudinya	Gumukudin	Peak Point to Cowal Creek	West
Ambagana	Ambagan	Cowal Creek to Jardine River	West
Korkarega	–	Albany Island	East

* Also called "Unduyumu"

CONTENTS

CHAPTER 1
The Aboriginal Invasion of Australia – Exposure of the 40,000 year myth
and the extinction of the original Papuan Indigenous Australians 1

CHAPTER 2
Corsairs of the Coral Sea – Massacres of shipwrecked castaways who
were speared, clubbed to death, or beheaded. [Charles Eaton Massacre] 9

CHAPTER 3
Giom of the Kauraregas – The capture of 16 years old Barbara Thompson,
enslaved for nearly 5 years by headhunters and her amazing escape 19

CHAPTER 4
The Lost Expedition – The ill fated Kennedy Expedition to Cape York in 1848
and the murder of Edmund Kennedy by the Yadagana aborigines 37

CHAPTER 5
Somerset – A Refuge for Castaways – The settlement of Somerset was
a sanctuary for shipwrecked castaways only to have aborigines attack and
try to wipe it out... 47

CHAPTER 6
The Jardine Cattle Drive – 10 men drove 250 head of cattle over 1000 miles to
Somerset. They fought their way through swamps, jungle and aboriginal attacks 75

CHAPTER 7
Debil-Debil Jardine – The colourful life of Frank Jardine who tamed the
warring tribes with a peace settlement. He was a cattleman, Police Magistrate and
Pearler who fought and protected aborigines and Torres Strait Islanders 83

CHAPTER 8
The Sperwer Massacre – The massacre of the crew of the Sperwer
in which the victims were beheaded by the Kauraregas in 1869 99

CHAPTER 9
Pearl Fever – The arrival of the pearlers in the Torres Strait
and the kidnapping and murder of the natives 93

CHAPTER 10
The Battle of Somerset –
The aboriginal attack against Somerset and the battle that followed 97

CHAPTER 11
Fate of the Magistrates – The Police Magistrates who held office at
Somerset after Frank Jardine. The extinction of the Gudang aborigines 99

CHAPTER 12
Palmer Gold – The gold rush of the Palmer River where men became
wealthy overnight or died from starvation, disease or aboriginal spears 103

CHAPTER 13
Thursday Island – The pearling industry and the transfer from Somerset
to Thursday Island, as the new settlement 113

CHAPTER 14
Lizzie Watson – The poignant story of Mary Watson [Lizzie] who fought
off aboriginal attacks on lonely Lizard Island only to die of thirst with her baby......117

CHAPTER 15
Wreck of the Quetta – The tragic sinking of the Quetta,
which cost the lives of 133 people...125

CHAPTER 16
The Deadly Cyclone – The destruction of the pearling fleets at
Princess Charlotte Bay by Cyclone Mahina in 1899 which cost over 300 lives..........137

CHAPTER 17
Occurrences on Cape York – The construction of the Overland Telegraph to
Cape York and the discovery of the Jardine treasure. The death of Frank Jardine....145

CHAPTER 18
The Jardine Vidgen Era – The Jardine Vidgens and their life at Somerset.
Proposal that Somerset and Albany Island be proclaimed a
"Sacred and Historical Site of European Settlement"...171

CHAPTER 19
Jardine's Diary – The truth of the Jardine Diaries and silver treasure.
Pulau Babi and the execution of Major Sheldon..183

CHAPTER 20
Academic Blunders – Some of the many statements made by academics
which were later found to be false..193

CHAPTER 21
The Political Aftermath – The political consequences of a false
aboriginality, and the solution to the land rights issue by a
Citizens Initiated Referendum across Australia..197

CHAPTER 22
Historical Statements – Some of the important statements written last
century that make a mockery of academic evidence on the history of Cape York....207

CHAPTER 23
Fact Versus Fiction – The facts are compared to some of the fallacies
that have been inserted into history..215

CHAPTER 24
Extracts of Official Somerset Reports – Some of the Somerset Reports
that totally refute much of the evidence promoted by academics.........................221

CHAPTER 25
Sequence of Events: British Ships – Naval Surveys of the ships:
"Fly", "Bramble", "Rattlesnake", and "Prince George"......................................229

CHAPTER 26
Sequence of Events: The Kennedy Expedition –
A daily account of the Kennedy Expedition to Cape York in 1848........................233

CHAPTER 27
Sequence of Events: The Jardine Cattle Drive –
A daily account of the cattle drive to Cape York. 1864-1865...............................243

CHAPTER 28
Sequence of Events: Cape York – A guide to events on
Cape York Peninsula and the Torres Strait Islands. 1597-1986............................265

CAPE YORK PENINSULA INCLUDING THE MAJOR HISTORICAL EVENTS

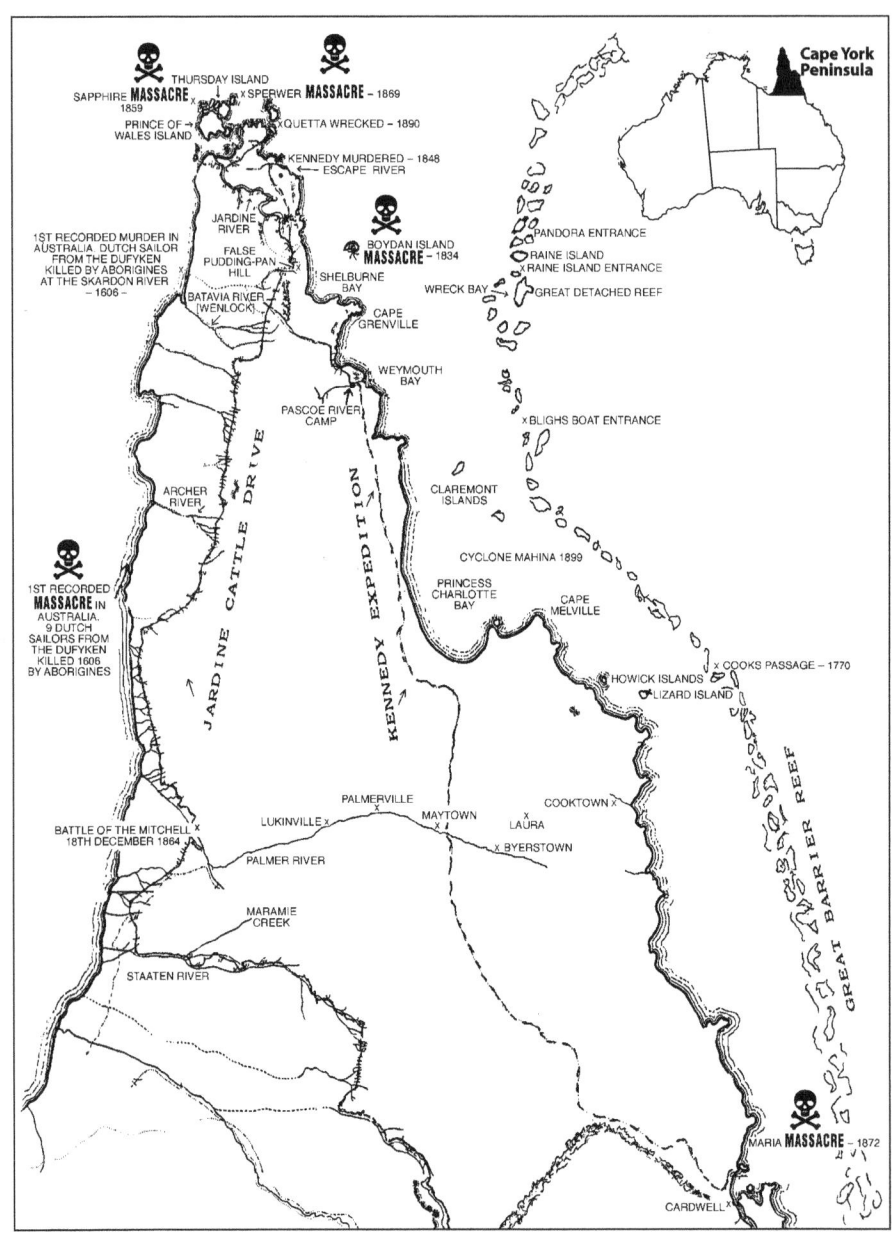

Chapter 1
"THE ABORIGINAL INVASION OF AUSTRALIA"

Whilst researching the history of Cape York, I found it necessary to re-trace the "ORIGINS OF MAN" on the Australian Continent.

It soon became apparent that the "ORIGINAL AUSTRALIANS" were definitely "NOT" the people we now refer to as aboriginals.

For over 200 years, Australians have been constantly indoctrinated into accepting the dark skinned natives that Captain Cook saw in 1770, as being the original Australians.

Yet, truth is stranger than fiction. For all the latest anthropological evidence shows very clearly that the original Australians were "PAPUANS", who came down from New-Guinea when both countries were connected by a natural land bridge estimated to have been 100 miles wide [160km], consisting of vast lowlands and undulating hills.

The final separation was caused by rising seas which flooded the lowlands, leaving only the highest parts above water, thereby, creating 200 islands within a shallow sea now known as the Torres Strait.

The breaching of this land bridge is generally believed to have occurred around seven thousand years ago. [6500-8000].

Prior to the separation, the Papuans had access all over the continent, including Tasmania.

It is a point of fact that the Tasmanians were positively identified last century as being of a Papuan race.

In 1930 a book titled "ARTISTS IN STRINGS" was published. The author was Kathleen Haddon [Rishbeth]. She was the daughter of one of the worlds most highly acclaimed anthropologists in his day [Alfred Cort Haddon].

She had travelled the world with her famous father and in reference to the Australian aborigines she stated:

> "Long headed, broad nosed people of 'Pre-Dravidian' stock, they are connected racially with the 'Veddah' and certain jungle tribes of South India, rather than the neighbouring Papuans and Melanesians.
> These 'Pre-Dravidians' appear to have displaced an earlier, woolly haired people, who had come into Australia via New-Guinea and who survived until recent times only in Tasmania."

This statement is but a portion of a mass of evidence which proves that the original Australians were "Papuans", who were brutally massacred by the Pre-Dravidian invaders, whom we now erroneously refer to as the "Aborigines of Australia", but who in fact were the "Aborigines of South India and Ceylon".

In April 1898, Professor Haddon led the Cambridge Anthropological Expedition to the Torres Strait, and later carried out further research in Australia.

He clearly identified the Australian aborigine as being of the same Pre-Dravidian race as the following:

INDIA	Gond, Bhil, Kurumba, Irula, Veddah.
CEYLON	Veddah.
MALAYA	Sakai.
CELEBES	Toala.

In 1909 Haddon published "THE RACES OF MAN" and exposed the invasion of Australia by the aborigines [Pre-Dravidians].

He states:
> "Australia was originally inhabited by Papuans or Negritoes, who wandered on foot to the extreme south of that continent. When Bass Strait was formed, those who were cut off from the mainland formed the ancestors of the Tasmanians.
> Later a Pre-Dravidian race migrated into Australia and overran the continent and absorbed the sparse aboriginal population.
> The latter being driven off, "EXTERMINATED", or even partially assimilated, but the formation of Bass Strait prevented the entry of the Australians [Pre-Dravidians] into Tasmania."

Further evidence that the aborigines invaded Australia comes from Professor A. P. Elkin, Emiritus Professor of Anthropology, University of Sydney, during the 1950's.

Professor Elkin was said to be the leading authority in his day on this vital subject.

He also claimed that the aborigines were the early aborigines of South India and classified all the Pre-Dravidians as "Australoids".

In his book "THE AUSTRALIAN ABORIGINES", he states:
> "Was there a preceding race in Australia, namely the Tasmanians? The latter were a Negroid group related to the Melanesians and Papuans.
> If the Tasmanians were living in parts of Australia at the time the aborigines commenced their invasion, they must have been either conquered and absorbed, or extinguished.
> It is also possible that the Tasmanians were already in their island home as well as on the mainland at the time of the Australoid Invasion."

Still further evidence comes from E. R. Gribble who wrote "A DESPISED RACE". He states:
> "The first inhabitants were a negroid race being curly haired. Later came the "Dravidians" [Pre] A straight haired race driven from Egypt, through the north of India.
> In both these places indications of the use of the boomerang have been found.
> In Tutankahamen's tomb [The boy king of Egypt] there were two model boomerangs wrought in silver.
> These "Dravidians" [Pre] were huntsmen and brought the dog with them. They conquered the "Negroids" and intermarried.
> These two types of hair were found as far as the southern portions of Australia, showing the intermixture of the two races. On the other hand, in Tasmania, only the curly haired were found, and no dingoes.
> Another difference was the status of the women in a tribe. In Tasmania they were well treated, but on the mainland they were regarded merely as goods and chattels, i.e. slaves."

When the invaders left India, in their canoes and rafts small groups dropped off along the way and settled in Malaya and the Celebes where they are known as the "Sakai" and "Toala." The main groups are believed to have landed on Cape York Peninsula and other areas of Northern Australia.

Professor Elkin states:
> "We may picture them reaching Australia finally by raft or canoe, bringing with them the dog (dingo) which is not indigenous and had to rely on man for its transport to its new home.
> The aborigines landed in Northern Australia, probably on Cape York Peninsula."

Throughout Australia's 200 years of European civilisation, various academics had tried to speak out against the false "Aboriginality of Australia".

They had a mass of evidence which clearly indicated that the native race generally referred to as the "Aborigines of Australia", were in fact the "Aborigines of India", and that they invaded Australia in recent times and were accompanied by the Indian native dog now known as the dingo and which early mariners referred to as the "Indian Jackal".

These genuine academics wanted nothing more than to speak the truth, but are silenced or ridiculed by those in authority, who have too much to lose if the truth were accepted by the public.

It is no coincidence that many anthropologists involved in promoting this false aboriginality are amongst the most highly paid academics in Australia.

Their task is to continually feed the public with a constant flow of false and misleading information that cannot be proved or disproved by the general public.

A prime example is the forty thousand year myth of occupation by aborigines in Australia.

In 1961 it was claimed that they had been in Australia for eight thousand years [8000]. Then it climbed rapidly during the 1980's to thirty thousand years [30,000]. By 1990 the academics were claiming forty thousand years [40,000] and by 1996 it had peaked at fifty thousand years [50,000].

So what is the truth?

One of the earliest reports written in English describing the Australian aborigines was from the English navigator William Dampier, who had visited Northern Australia in 1688 and returned in 1699-1700. He described the aborigines as having *"Hair curled like the Negroes"* [Papuans] [Western Australia].

Obviously these must have been the original Australians and not the Pre-Dravidians [aborigines]. [This was 70 years before Captain Cook arrived.]

By the time European man had arrived most of the Papuans had already been exterminated by the Australoid invader.

These eye-witness reports add further credibility to the evidence that the Papuans were the traditional owners of Australia.

The fact that Dampier had seen the Papuans less than 300 years ago, spread over a thousand miles of the West Australian coastline, clearly shows that large numbers had survived the onslaught up to that time and that the invasion by aborigines may have been of a very recent occurrence.

Professor Elkin states:
> *"One or two thousand years gives scope for many changes. The point is, that we do not yet know whether the aborigines have been in Australia, one or many thousands of years."*
> *"Some years ago Professor J. W. Gregory came to the somewhat surprising conclusion that the aborigines had only been in Victoria for four hundred years."*

CARBON DATING

In order to prove that the aborigines have occupied Australia for thousands of years, a system of dating "ancient artifacts", such as skeletal remains, shell fragments and rock paintings is used, called Carbon 14 Dating.

This method of dating by radio active carbon, was invented by Professor Libby in the 1940's. The system is so erratic that it has been condemned by scientists world wide as being "unreliable and highly inaccurate". In fact even Professor Libby acknowledged that the system was only good for dating material between 5,000 and at the very most 10,000 years old.

Carbon 14 [14C] occurs naturally in the atmosphere. It combines with oxygen to form carbon dioxide [CO_2] which is absorbed by vegetation [Photosynthesis] which in turn is eaten by animals and humans.

After death the amount of Carbon 14 in the remains will hopefully decrease. The difference between a live specimen is compared to the amount of Carbon 14 in a dead one and an age assigned to it by guess work.

Because the original Carbon 14 content in the specimen can only be a wild guess, then the results are given in thousands of years rather than individual years.

The system is so faulty that many researchers have rejected it as it tends to add too many zeros to most specimens.

For example: A seal that had only just been killed gave a carbon 14 dating of 1300 years.

The shells of live snails showed they had been dead for 27,000 years.

The shells of living mollusks were dated at 2300 years.

ROCK PAINTINGS

One of the most controversial issues of Carbon 14 dating are native rock paintings.

A small number are known to have existed last century and are therefore authentic. However in recent years they have suddenly appeared like stars in the universe. Hundreds of paintings have miraculously been "found" in areas where they did not exist prior to world war 2. Yet, many of these sites have been carbon dated at anywhere between 5,000 to 40,000 years old???

At one of these sites it was found that the colour "blue" was used. As blue is rarely used in rock paintings, it aroused suspicion. When tested it was identified as "Reckitts Blue", a detergent used in washing machines.

Incredibly these paintings where supposed to be thousands of years old, or so the academics would have the public believe.

In the 1950's a white man and 2 aborigines were seen painting their own rock paintings on Cape York Peninsula. These paintings have been carbon dated at over 14,000 years old. [More paintings were added after 1970.]

Perhaps some of the most recent exposures of rock paintings took place in Western Australia, where enamel paint was identified as the main colouring agent.

A number of other sites had already been exposed as frauds at the Kimberleys in Western Australia and Kakadu in the Northern Territory.

There was a time when scientists used to say that a theory must have a lot of evidence before it becomes a fact.

Yet, in respect to Carbon 14 dating, this statement appears to have been overlooked. Suddenly a little guess work can replace evidence in order to balance the theory.

What the anthropologists did not want the public to realise is that there are numerous substances containing Carbon 14 including oil and coal.

One only needs to add some oil or coal dust to a batch of clay and create your own 40,000 year painting. I suspect that something like this has been happening all over Australia to promote these new "ancient paintings".

This may have been the case during the early 1950's when a group of natives accompanied by an East European immigrant were observed painting all kinds of rock art across the Northern Territory.

Access to many of these sites is now cut off, to prevent the public from getting too close and thereby learn the truth.

At other sites a rope barricade is erected at a considerable viewing distance from the paintings to prevent a close inspection.

Commonsense dictates that a number of rock paintings are genuine. However, statements made by various academics that they are up to 40,000 years old is incorrect. There is no scientific evidence to support their claims other than the highly inaccurate carbon 14 dating.

Although many sites were painted within the last 200 years, little mention is ever made of them. It is only after personally inspecting them that the reason becomes obvious.

These paintings are so badly faded that they would not last longer than 300 to 400 years. So if they are already faded within 200 years, how could they ever last to 40,000 years.

With this evidence now available, the more accurate guide to the age of rock paintings would be to remove the last 2 digits. This would make an overrated 40,000 year dating into a more accurate 400 years.

Due to the constant criticism levelled against Universities for continually using a dating system that was proven to give false readings, a new system was "invented". This was called MASS ACCELERATOR SPECTROMETRY [MAS].

The system was no better than carbon dating and gave similar overrated results for the simple reason that it was nothing more than a refined version of carbon dating.

The most recent dating disaster is called "CATION RATIO DATING".

This technique is supposed to measure minuscule fragments of calcium and potassium deposits by ratio to titanium on rock paintings.

When it was tested by a geologist from the Australian National University it failed miserably and the poor results were similar to carbon dating.

When "Geo Australasia", [Vol 15, No. 4. 1993] published the article, "THE DATE DEBATE", the following statement was made:

"Some scientists, have raised continued concerns over accuracy after endeavouring to duplicate some of the cation ratio work without success."

In recent years the Australian public have been subjected to a massive indoctrination campaign, designed to "Mentally Program" Australians, into accepting a mass of false and misleading information relative to the occupation of Australia by aborigines.

Almost daily the public are swamped with this false advertising through television, newspapers, radio and magazines.

Even school children cannot escape this web of academic deception, for the Education Department is controlled by the very people who promote it.

All the evidence clearly identifies the Papuan as being the original Australian. Numerous anthropologists have acknowledged that fact, but are ignored by Universities who are paid millions of dollars to force feed the public with a false pre-history of Australia.

This "false aboriginality" is believed to be the greatest academic cover up the world has ever witnessed.

In the past the word of an academic was accepted by the general public almost without question. They were assumed to be the foremost authority on the subjects they wrote or lectured on.

Today, that is not the case, for the public have lost the faith they once had in them.

In recent years, numerous books have been written by academics to promote the myth of aboriginality. Many of these books have proven to contain a mass of false and misinterpreted information, intermingled with factual accounts so as to appear as an accurate historical record, which of course it is not.

In one of these books, the author was so vindictive against our early pioneers, that her own credibility has now been questioned by the very University she worked for.

In some cases only the first name of an informant is used, whilst in others an artificial native name is used.

This system is used to prevent their sources from being checked. In too many cases the information has been found to be incorrect and the informant did not even exist.

Another point of contention is the native population at the time of European settlement.

Most authorities place the figure from 250,000 – 300,000.

Professor Elkin states:

"The Australian aborigines took possession of Australia, spread over its surface and by 1788 numbered, as far as we can calculate, about 300,000."

Even this figure could be excessive when one considers the thousands that died each year from disease and thousands more from their savage tribal warfare in which entire tribes were massacred by their more powerful opponents.

The belief that they lived in a lotus land of plenty, free of violence and disease is the romanticised dream of individuals who are unable to relate to the violent realities of the times.

The truth of the matter is that the aborigines lived in a very harsh and dangerous environment. To drop ones guard in the day or night, could mean instant death. This was not just from their tribal enemies, but also from their own witch doctors.

Likewise, should a 13 year old girl refuse to marry a 50 year old man, she could be speared to death and if any female attempted to dance in a corroboree she could suffer a similar fate. [Corroborees by coloureds are a farce.]

Another important issue relates to the discovery of human skeletal remains throughout Australia. Some of the more recent finds were at "LAKE MUNGO" in Western New South Wales, "ROONKA" in South Australia and "COOMA" in New South Wales.

Their physical structure clearly identified them as being of a Papuan race [Ulotrichi] and like many earlier finds were erroneously classified as aborigine [Cymotrichi].

In early 1993, the Cooma find, was written up with glossy pictures in a magazine. The remains included an old woman and a young man. All the evidence clearly identified them as being of a short stocky build of a Papuan race and carbon dated at seven thousand years [7,000].

In spite of the fact that they were known to be Papuan, this information was withheld from the public.

Another vital issue of contention are rock carvings or engravings carved into the rock face by the Papuans and in later years duplicated by the aborigines. Many sites can be found on the walls of overhanging rock shelters and even on open rocky ground.

A number of these sites face the sea and portray sailing ships. They are said to have been carved by aborigines centuries ago?

One of these sites can be found at Hook Island in the Whitsunday Islands off the Queensland coast.

Year after year unsuspecting tourists have been told the same story, that they were carved by aborigines hundreds of years ago.

In fact, they were engraved by the sons of a fisherman who anchored there in 1963 [I interviewed 2 of the witnesses].

This illustrates the stupidity of many academics who automatically assume that if something even remotely appears to have been made by natives, then it is credited to Aborigines.

During the thousands of years that the Papuans lived in Australia, they had made many artifacts from stone. These included weapons such as stone headed clubs and axes.

Many of these stone age weapons have been found in recent years but instead of being classified as Papuan weapons, they have been falsely credited to aborigines.

At a number of these sites the Papuans had quarried tons of rock from which they had made thousands of stone axes and clubs, which were traded to the surrounding tribes.

Although commonsense dictated that these sites were Papuan quarries which demanded heavy manual labour, they were credited to aborigines [who avoid heavy manual labour].

In fact the media even publicised one of these sites as a quarry made by Aborigines, never realising that they were being used by the academics to promote their false pre-history of Australia.

Shell Middens are piles of crustaceans [shell fish] where aborigines had once feasted on this abundant sea food. They are often referred to as native rubbish dumps.

The existence of these mounds has often been used as evidence of great antiquity of aborigines in Australia.

However, the real evidence shows the exact opposite to be the case.

Professor Elkin states:

> *"The formation of such a heap does not imply thousands of years. A few score natives spending a few weeks occasionally in the locality would make a large refuse heap in the course of a century."*

Some of the oldest middens are found on the west coast of Cape York near Weipa. When tested by the inaccurate carbon 14 dating they only measured 800 years [average].

All this evidence clearly points to the aborigines as being a very recent arrival. After all, if they had been in Australia for 40,000 years, then surely the middens would have been here for a similar period.

One of the most controversial issues in Australia today is "LANDRIGHTS".

On the one hand, the race of people whose early ancestors, [Pre-Dravidians] slaughtered the original Australians [Papuans] claim that all of Australia belongs to them, whilst the White majority claim it belongs to all Australians.

In order to seize vast tracts of Australian territory, the issue of imaginary sacred sites was invented as a spring board to what could only be classified as a highly discrimatory form of "Legalised Land Theft".

It is no coincidence that most of these non existent sacred sites just happen to be within areas containing vast mineral resources or tourist attractions.

Yet, the most important point in relation to Land Rights, that has been conveniently overlooked, is that at no time in their short history, did aborigines own land.

This was made very clear by an Anthropologist researching "native occupancy" during the early 1970's. He stated:

"Land ownership is totally alien to aboriginal thinking."

As Cape York Peninsula was believed to be one of the major landing sites by the invading aborigines, it made sense to investigate old native campsites at the top of Cape York and hopefully prove they had been here for thousands of years.

In 1973, an anthropological research team, collected various samples from these ancient camp sites, such as fragments of cooking shells. These were then carbon dated.

The result was catastrophic for the academics, for all they could show was between 600 to 1100 years of occupation by Aborigines.

The Native almond or Sea almond can be found growing all over Northern Australia. It is also known as the Indian Almond and was probably a vital food source carried by the Pre-Dravidians in their canoes on their long sea journey to Australia.

When they invaded Australia, and massacred the Papuans, the surviving women became the spoils of war.

As food was difficult to find in a strange land, it is almost certain that they ate their victims.

For, contrary to the image of him being a docile native, he was in fact a savage individual of cannibalistic tastes, who gave no mercy to his victims.

Although it is now virtually impossible to calculate the full number of Papuans slaughtered, by the Aborigines it was probably in excess of 150,000. In today's world that is classified as genocide.

When explorers traversed the coastline of Cape York Peninsula, they witnessed the "Negritos" [Papuans] being hunted down like kangaroos by the taller Aborigines.

The Negritos were some of the last survivors of the Papuans, who fought with broad wooden swords, in close combat in the confines of the rainforest. By the time the white man had arrived, they were almost extinct.

Throughout the centuries the Aborigines branched out into separate tribal communities. They were natural hunters of both man and beast and were soon involved in tribal wars with each other.

Wherever the Papuans were found they were pushed further back and finally liquidated. "This was the HOLOCAUST that no one knew.

A number of small groups did survive. Some of these were known to have lived along the Murray River in South Australia and in the vicinity of Cairns in Northern Queensland last century.

The Papuans living in Tasmania were relatively safe from the invader as the Aborigines were unable to cross Bass Strait.

With the demise of the Tasmanians last century, the Authorities later brought mainland Aborigines to the island as labourers and in some cases, prisoners.

Today, many of the offspring of these imported aborigines have claimed to be the traditional owners of Tasmania, which of course they are not.

Over the past decade a massive indoctrination campaign has been orchestrated by the Australian Broadcasting Corporation to literally brainwash the public into accepting the aborigine as the Original Australian. He is often painted as a timid native who lived in harmony with the environment, when in fact the exact opposite is the case.

Is it any wonder that many Australians now refer to the A.B.C. as the "Aboriginal Broadcasting Corporation".

The available evidence now shows that many birds and animals were hunted to extinction before the arrival of Europeans, and that thousands of square miles of forest was deliberately burnt out to attract game to open grassland that replaced the forest.

Even today in many areas of Northern Australia, turtles are ruthlessly hunted down by the Aborigines and cut open whilst still alive.

All this evidence clearly contradicts the statements that they lived in harmony with the environment.

How long they occupied Australia has never been accurately assessed other than by the inaccurate carbon dating, which is rapidly being rejected world wide.

When one considers that the dingo arrived with them and it has been carbon dated at only 4,000 years, then take into account the inaccuracy of carbon dating, then it is very possible that they may have been here for less than 1,000 years.

By the time Europeans had arrived, the aborigines had massacred tens of thousands of their own people in their savage tribal conflicts in which the weaker tribes were totally annihilated.

With numerous shipwrecks around the Australian coastline they now turned their attention to easier targets.

As castaways from these wrecks rowed ashore they were often set upon by hordes of savages. Hundreds of helpless men, women and children were brutally slaughtered by club and spear. Many of these were eaten, whilst others were beheaded in Northern Australia and the nearby Torres Strait Islands. Still, others more were kept as slaves and slowly worked to death, whilst subsisting on starvation diets.

Numerous young children, were incarcerated into various tribes, after witnessing their mothers being clubbed to death. Although a small number of castaways were fortunate to escape, after many years of captivity, the majority were never seen again. It was inevitable that violence would be fought with violence, and that the spear was no match for the gun.

Chapter 2
"CORSAIRS OF THE CORAL SEA"

The Torres Strait Islands nestle serenely between Cape York, "the most northerly point of the Australian mainland" and New Guinea. The Strait is only 110 miles long by 100 miles wide, yet, within these tranquil waters lie 200 islands of which only 17 were permanently inhabited.

With the establishment of free settlement in Australia early last century, ships of all types and sizes began moving up the east coast to Cape York and through the Torres Strait on journeys to Singapore, India and England, thereby avoiding the notorious Cape Horn of South America.

The seeming tranquillity of the Torres Strait belied the treacherous nature of the passage and the savagery of the island inhabitants. For, hidden beneath the shallow waters of the Strait were coral reefs waiting to tear our the hearts of unwary vessels. Within the past 200 years, hundreds of vessels have been wrecked in these waters.

The Torres Strait Islanders were acknowledged as some of the most savage headhunters of the South Seas, and were known by British seamen as the "Black Corsairs" of "Terror Strait". They sailed the Strait in large war canoes up to 70 feet long, fitted with Pandanus matted sails and carrying up to 40 warriors.

Shipwrecked castaways became floating targets of the Islanders. They had a long boat journey of over a thousand miles to the nearest white settlement, which was either Timor to the west, or Moreton Bay [Brisbane] to the south.

Castaways, dying of thirst, were no match for the war canoes and entire boatloads of up to 20 people were caught and beheaded by the headhunters of the Strait.

Those who made it to "Booby Island" at the western end of the Strait were generally safe from further attacks from the Corsairs. This was the most acceptable route to civilisation and food and water was left in casks, in a cave on the island by passing ships. Ironically the same island the mariners chose as a refuge was generally feared by the Islanders, who believed it to be haunted by demons and would give up the chase within a few miles of it.

A large sign was later erected on Booby Island which read "POST OFFICE". It was indeed the mariners Post office where ships would deposit and collect mail for the various destinations around the world faster than through the official channels.

So many ships were wrecked in or on the approaches to Torres Strait, that the list read like a who's-who of a daily shipping column. It was a common sight to see a wreck sitting high on a reef with its masts intact until it was finally claimed by a tempestuous Coral Sea. In one incredible case 3 large sailing vessels following in convoy, were wrecked side by side, on the same reef.

In some cases their cargo was horses destined for India. Hungry sharks soon found their way through the broken hull and attacked the helpless animals. The screams of the dying horses echoed through the wreck until finally it was all over in a blood red sea around the stricken vessel.

Life boats were often smashed as ships struck the reef and castaways had little choice but to swim for the nearest island. Survivors who made it to shore were often captured by the Islanders and suffered a grizzly fate.

Held down by a number of warriors, their eyes were prized out of their sockets and eaten raw amid the agonising screams of the victims. The warriors believed that by eating the eyes of their victim they were receiving the energy of the person they were killing or had killed. The death blow came when the head was cut off with a bamboo beheading knife called an "upi".

Once the heads were cooked and the flesh eaten, the skulls were sun dried and eventually taken to New-Guinea as trade items. A sufficient number of heads could pay for a large war canoe.

The canoes were hollowed out from a single tree trunk at the mighty Fly River estuary on the New-Guinea coast and later fitted with out riggers on either side with detachable floats. This created a large fighting platform with a hut built in the middle for shelter. With their Pandanus sails and stout oarsmen they could easily capture unarmed castaways in open boats.

The savagery of the Torres Strait Islanders was recorded as far back as 1792, when William Bligh of "Mutiny on the Bounty" fame was attacked by 12 large war canoes and only stopped them by blowing the stern off the lead war canoe from his warship, the "Providence". In honour of their bravery, Bligh named their island home "Warrior Island" [Tutu].

In July of 1793, the ships "Hormuzeer" and "Chesterfield", were anchored off Darnley Island in the eastern Torres Strait.

When 8 men went ashore they were ambushed and 5 of them brutally murdered by the natives. The 3 survivors [of whom 2 were wounded] managed to escape in the whaleboat but could not reach the ships, so they headed west towards Booby Island and then on to Timor.

On board the ships they waited for the return of their men and after 3 days sent in a search party in 2 boats. As they approached the island, 80 armed natives were seen on shore in hostile array.

As the searchers rowed around the island, the natives followed on shore. A man, who appeared to be the chief, held a small axe that had belonged to one of the missing men. [Chief Mate-Mr Shaw].

When the boats arrived at a bay on the northwest side of the island, most of the natives disappeared, excepting about 30 who were trying to entice the men to land. Instead they rowed on and suddenly the beach became crowded with warriors who had been waiting in ambush to kill them.

They now realised that the missing men had probably been murdered and after circumnavigating the island, they returned to the ships.

As some of the men may still be alive, then an attempt would have to be made to rescue them. The ships headed around the northern reefs and anchored in the bay on the north west side of the island, and named "Treacherous Bay" [9th July].

The next day an armed search party of 44 men was landed and upon entering the abandoned huts, they found clothing and belongings of the missing men and concluded correctly that they had been murdered. They also found 2 skulls and several strings of skeletal hands in each of the huts.

The Darnley islanders [Erubians] retreated to the hills in the centre of the island, rather than confront such a large force of armed men. This did not stop them from being punished, for although they were safe, their livelihood was not.

The searchers were outraged at the senseless killings of their men and in retribution they burnt 135 huts in a dozen villages that dotted the shore line and destroyed 16 large canoes from 50 to 70 feet in length. When their plots of sugar cane were set alight, a pall of smoke engulfed the island that could be seen for miles at sea.

They paid a heavy price for their violence.

THE CHARLES EATON MASSACRE

When the "Charles Eaton" [a 3 masted, 300 ton vessel] was wrecked at the Raine Island Entrance, south of Cape York, 24 passengers and crew were clubbed to death and beheaded at Boydan Island near Cape Grenville. 2 Years later 2 boys were found alive on Murray Island in the Eastern Torres Strait. They were 4 year old William D'Oyley and 16 year old John Ireland of the "Charles Eaton". Ireland later related the full horror of the massacre.

The "Charles Eaton" struck the Great Detached Reef [GDR] near Raine Island at 10am on the 15th August 1834. She hit with such force that her keel and rudder were torn away as the ship was pushed high onto the reef.

Several miles away another wreck could be seen sitting on the reef with her masts still standing. This part of the reef was a ship's graveyard containing the wrecks of the "Pandora", the "Furguson" and the "Martha Ridgeway" and many others, all within 50 miles of Raine Island.

As well as her 24 crew the "Charles Eaton" also carried 7 passengers. These were Captain D'Oyley of the Bengal Artillery, his wife Charlotte, their sons, George [7] and William [2] with their Indian servant, Dr Grant and Mr Armstrong.

Of the 4 boats carried by the ship, a long boat and the dinghy were smashed on impact and a cutter was swamped and sank when launched, drowning a sailor [James Price]. The remaining cutter was launched with 3 seamen aboard. They stayed near the ship all that day and night. The next day 2 other sailors swam through the rough seas and joined them. They sailed away leaving the passengers and crew to their fate.

Fortunately, the wreck still remained firm on the reef and the crew set to work building a raft which was later found to be too small. It was launched and tied to the wreck. Overnight, 9 people stayed on board, but by morning, the rope had been cut and the raft was gone.

Those on board the raft were Captain Moore, the D'Oyley family and servant, Dr Grant, Mr Armstrong and at least one sailor.

Undaunted, the remaining crew constructed a larger raft which took 7 days to complete and finally as the ship was starting to break up they all boarded it and floated away from the wreck.

Over the next 3 days the raft drifted towards the coast at about one mile an hour with its occupants half submerged in sea water. Then they sighted a large war canoe with a dozen Torres Strait Islanders aboard.

They often sailed as far south as Cape Grenville, 100 miles south of Cape York on their fishing trips hunting turtle and dugong. They instilled a deadly fear into the aborigines who occasionally came into conflict with them which resulted in the Islanders taking home many heads.

As the canoe stopped beside the raft, the Islanders appeared to be very friendly and coaxed the helpless castaways aboard the canoe.

They were taken to the Boydong Cays and landed on the island called "Boydan" about 40 miles north west of the wreck site. Here they were allowed to walk around the island in search of water. The natives of course knew that it was a waterless island and had planned a terrible finale for the thirsty castaways.

When the whites returned to the beach totally exhausted, they were greeted by the most hideous laughter from the grinning natives. Realising they were to be killed, they all knelt and prayed on the beach and now, resigned to their fate, they collapsed into sleep never to see another sunrise.

John Ireland was 14 at the time and had worked as a cabin boy on the "Charles Eaton". That night he awoke to the screams of his companions as the savages clubbed them to death. A naked savage fell upon Ireland trying to cut his throat with a carving knife. He grabbed the blade and refused to let go cutting his finger to the bone.

Breaking free, young Ireland raced for the sea and swam out but realising there was no escape he returned awaiting his fate, when the infuriated savage fired an arrow into his right chest, near the shoulder and dragged him up the beach, thus sparing his life.

A short distance away the natives had lit a large fire with the victims heads lined up in front of it. Ireland and another survivor, William Sexton [14] watched them dance around the heads screaming hideously as the headless corpses were washed by the surf.

During the massacre, Sexton had struggled desperately with a savage and bit out a piece of his attackers arm after which his life was spared.

The last to die was the Chief Officer, Claer, who had earlier led everyone in prayer before the slaughter. He raced for the canoe only to be captured and clubbed to death.

At dawn the heads were put in the canoe together with Ireland and Sexton and taken north to the island of Pullan. Here they met 2 other children, George and William D'Oyley from the first raft. He learnt from George D'Oyley that everyone from the first raft had landed on Boydan and were also beheaded. His mother was holding little William in her arms as she was clubbed to death.

Pullan was a temporary fishing village inhabited by 60 natives. All 4 boys were kept here for 2 months and saw the heads of their fellow whites being cooked and eaten.

The natives later separated with one party taking little William and Ireland to Aureed Island in the Eastern Torres Strait. The other 2 boys, William Sexton and George D'Oyley were later murdered by their captors.

Meanwhile on Murray Island [Mer] a native named Duppar heard of the 2 white captives on Aureed and sailed with his wife Pamoy to the island where he bought the boys for a bunch of bananas each.

Upon returning to Murray Island, Duppar and Pamoy kept Ireland and gave baby William to a native called Oby. Ireland was named "Wak" and William was "Uass".

The following year [1835] the trading vessel "Mangles" skippered by Captain Carr, anchored at Murray Island. The crew noticed a light skinned boy of about 15 years of age who yelled out from a canoe that he was from the "Charles Eaton".

By now a large number of natives in canoes were near the "Mangles" wanting to trade and Carr decided against trying to rescue the boy by force.

Instead he sailed out of the Straits and reported what he had seen to the Authorities.

Meanwhile the 5 sailors who left the wreck in the only remaining cutter had only just arrived in Batavia. After leaving the "Charles Eaton" they reached Timor Laut [Tenimber Islands] 300 miles north of Darwin.

Here they were attacked and captured by several proas and taken to the village of "Olilet" which was built on a cliff overlooking the sea.

To reach it you had to climb up a flight of log steps cut into the hillside after which one had to ascend the last 50 feet up 2 movable ladders secured against the cliff face. At the top was a gateway leading into the village. In the event of attack the ladders would be removed preventing any access from the shore.

After 12 months captivity the sailors managed to convince the 2 major chiefs "Pabok" and "Lomba" that if they let them go they would bring back plenty of arms and ammunition to help them defeat their enemies further north at "Laourau".

In 1823 the natives of "Laourau" had attacked the schooner "Stedcombe" and massacred all the crew except 2 boys. One of these had died but the other had been held captive for the past 12 years. He was later rescued.

At "Olilet" Pabok and Lomba finally allowed the 5 sailors to leave on a proa, in the belief that they would return with the promised arms.

The sailors arrived at Batavia [Djakarta] in December. One of them [George Piggott] died of fever in a Dutch hospital. The remaining 4 survived and made a statement to the authorities claiming that once they were in the cutter, they could not get close enough to rescue anyone else from the "Charles Eaton". This statement was later contradicted by John Ireland.

When the news reached Sydney that survivors were held captive on Murray Island, the Colonial Schooner "Isabella" was made ready for a rescue mission.

As Captain D'Oyley had been a soldier of the British East India Company, they also sent their armed Brig of War "Tigris" to search for survivors, which departed Bombay in March 1836.

The 116 ton "Isabella" left Sydney in June 1836 under the command of Captain Charles Lewis with a heavily armed crew of 5 Officers and 25 men.

When she arrived at Murray Island, a large number of natives gathered on shore and among them, a white teenage boy was clearly seen. As the natives launched their big war canoes, the cannons were loaded, but kept out of sight with most of the crew.

The natives came out to trade, not to fight. They rubbed their bellies and yelled out "Powad Powad" [Peace Peace], and called out "Tooruk" [Iron-axes and knives].

Lewis displayed some axes, but would not allow any trade until the white man [John Ireland] was brought to the ship. They finally relented and sent a canoe back to shore and after a tense wait of over an hour they returned with a naked John Ireland.

The natives had by now become a noisy excitable people shouting for "Tooruk". In this hot humid climate, Lewis stood on deck and called for silence and instantly all was quiet. Neither the natives or the whites made a sound as Lewis looked down onto Ireland, who was now standing on the platform of the canoe.

What Ship were you wrecked on? asked Lewis.

The "Charles Eaton" he replied.

Are there any more survivors? asked Lewis.

Only one, a boy about 4 years old replied Ireland.

As Lewis told him to step forward on the platform, the natives allowed him to do so, but instantly grabbed him and would not allow him on the ship, till a ransom had been paid.

The atmosphere was electric. Although the natives would gladly trade one of their own kin for an axe, they did not wish to lose their captive.

Finally common-sense prevailed as Lewis held out the axe and John Ireland climbed aboard the "Isabella".

No sooner had Lewis given permission to trade, and the natives were exchanging bananas, yams, mats and turtle shells for knives and axes.

As Duppar had been so kind to John Ireland he was allowed on board and showered with gifts including a fine linen gown and clothes which were known to be highly prized by the natives.

Lewis now requested that little William D'Oyley be handed over. However, the natives balked at this suggestion, claiming he was on the other side of the island and could not be produced that day. It was clear they did not want to part with him. Lewis instantly stopped all trade until he was brought to the ship.

The next day a number of canoes came out to trade but still did not bring the boy and Lewis refused any bartering. After waiting several hours with no sign of them bringing the child, Lewis had little choice but to threaten to use force. His face portrayed a countenance of intense anger and he ordered his men to open the ports and run out the guns.

Now they realised he meant business and sent a canoe ashore for the boy.

When the canoe returned, the child was not aboard. Instead, the Islanders agreed to trade him for an axe, to be given in advance, which Lewis refused to agree to.

Finally at 4pm little William was put on the canoe and taken to the "Isabella" where he was handed over to Lewis.

Just as Duppar had been rewarded for looking after Ireland, so "Oby" was also invited on board and dressed in fine clothing for sheltering and protecting the young child.

The Murray Islanders were so impressed with Lewis, that they invited him ashore to visit their village. He gladly consented and took toys for the children and various items for the women.

When he landed he left 2 boatloads of armed sailors at the beach, but they were not needed for the natives treated him like a king. They were intensely grateful to him for sparing their village when he could have so easily resorted to violence had he chosen to. The large crowd gathered round him just to shake his hand and when he left they followed him to the beach, crying out "Lewis! Lewis!"

Before leaving Murray Island, Lewis left 2 letters with the tribe, just in case anything should happen to the ship or its crew. The natives were instructed to deliver them to the master of any visiting ship.

Lewis still felt that there may be other survivors in the islands and after bidding farewell to Murray Island set sail for Darnley, with Ireland as a guide and interpreter. [NNE 30 miles].

Over the past 2 years Ireland had forgotten much of his English but had an excellent grasp of the native language. Captain Lewis initially had great difficulty in trying to understand him due to the intermixture of native and English words. After several days on the ship his English was returning and now he was to be indispensable as an interpreter in assisting Lewis to communicate with the various island tribes.

Upon arrival at Darnley the canoes came out to trade, but Lewis would not permit it until any whites held captive were handed over.

Ireland instantly identified 2 of the warriors involved in the massacre of his companions. It was clear they were not Darnley Islanders, but visitors from another island. As Lewis still refused to trade, the canoes headed back to the shore.

The next day more canoes came out and the natives recognised Ireland and William, calling them "Wak" and "Uass". When questioned about the 2 suspects identified by Ireland, they claimed they were of another tribe and had gone back to their own island [Aureed].

Lewis' main concern was to find survivors of the massacre rather than punish the murderers. Although the natives claimed they had no whites on the island, Lewis was not convinced and landed armed sailors who searched the huts. In one of them they found part of the ship's sail that had come from the first raft.

When questioned, the natives claimed it had been given to them by the Aureed Islanders.

After intense questioning by Lewis the natives gave the names of some of the murderers from Aureed and the identity of some of their victims. These were "Abooyu" [William Sexton] "Cut Cut" [Mrs Charlotte D'Oyley] and "Mayam" [George D'Oyley].

They also acknowledged that the killers had eaten the eyes and cheeks and made their own children do likewise so that they would be as brave as their fathers.

Lewis now learnt that the victim's skulls were at Aureed and that each morning and evening the natives entertained themselves by dancing around them screaming and shouting with the most horrid gestures.

Before leaving Darnley, Lewis wrote 2 more letters and gave these to 2 natives who had befriended John Ireland during his early captivity with the Aureed Islanders, when they visited Darnley. They were also told to give them to the first visiting ship.

Convinced there were no survivors on Darnley the "Isabella" sailed west to Stephens Island and then south to an island where John Ireland had once seen the victims skulls. He believed it was Keats Island, but may have been Yorke Island as Keats was only a small uninhabited islet.

Upon landing here, Lewis ordered the natives to hand over any white captives, upon which they assured him, there were none. When questioned about the skulls of the whites, they became agitated and explained that the Aureed natives had only brought them here to show them and then left with the skulls.

Suspecting these natives may not be telling the full truth, Lewis ordered 18 of his armed men to come on shore from the boats. With cutlasses by their sides and bayonets fixed to their guns, the sailors covered the natives, as Lewis again demanded they hand over any captives or skulls.

The terrified natives pleaded with him, saying they had nothing to do with the murders and that the Aureed natives knew a "man-o-war" was searching for them to punish them and so had left Aureed Island.

After checking the huts and searching the island, Lewis concluded that there were no captives or skulls here. Bidding farewell to the natives, the "Isabella" continued south, as Lewis searched every island along the way. Suddenly, an island appeared that matched the description given by the Murray Islanders. At last he had found the mysterious Aureed Island.

As they anchored there was no sign of any natives. Their normal habit of canoes coming out to trade was now totally absent. With the exception of some dogs barking, all else was quiet.

Lewis went ashore with a group of armed sailors and walked towards a small coconut plantation. He noticed a track lined by shells painted red which led him to a thatched hut. As he entered, he froze at the horrifying sight before him.

A huge tortoise shell mask measuring almost 5 feet long by 3 feet wide had 45 human heads tied around it confronted him.

In order that the figure should not be damaged, the roof was removed and the entire mask with the skulls intact was lifted out in one piece.

Among this collection of skulls were the passengers and crew of the "Charles Eaton". The skull of Mrs D'Oyley was easily identified, by her blonde hair, much of which was still embedded in the skull where the savages had clubbed her to death whilst trying to shield her little child.

The mask like figure was taken aboard and Captain Lewis was so enraged at these senseless and horrific murders that he burnt down the skull house and set fire to the island. All night the fire raged out of control, yet the coconut plantation still survived.

The next day he took his men back on shore and cut down every coconut tree, completing the destruction on this island of evil. After one final search, they discovered 2 more European skulls, that had been badly scorched by the inferno.

These were also taken on board the ship and as they pulled away from Aureed, Lewis renamed it "Skull Island".

As the "Isabella" headed south west, Lewis searched various islands along the way and anchored at Double Island. The following day [31st July] the "Thomas Harrison" anchored nearby and Lewis learnt from her skipper that the "Tigris" was also in the Straits searching for survivors.

After leaving India, she had been badly damaged in a storm and was held up for a month in Sydney undergoing repairs. She finally arrived at Murray Island on the 29th and was given one of the letters written by Lewis.

Suddenly the "Tigris" also arrived at Double Island and Captain Iggledston and the ships surgeon [Tigris] went aboard whence the surgeon examined the skulls and concluded that 17 were European.

All the skulls and mask were taken to Sydney and the 17 European skulls were buried at the Sydney Cemetery, [17th November 1836].

As the site later became the Central Railway Station, the skulls were removed with the large monument depicting the disaster to the Bunnerong Cemetery at Botany Bay, in 1904.

Due to the large number of ships wrecked in the vicinity of Raine Island and particularly at the entrance, the authorities decided to construct a large beacon on the island as a warning to shipping, alerting them to the existence of the Great Detached Reef.

At the centre, a reef strewn arm protruded for several miles from the GDR east into the Pacific. It was on this arm that the "Charles Eaton" is believed to have struck.

In May 1844, "HMS Fly", her tender, the "Bramble" and the revenue cutter "Prince George" arrived at Raine Island to construct the beacon, using convict labour.

The island was a popular breeding place for sea birds and on a previous visit, the naturalist Jukes [HMS Fly] stated:

*"The whole island stank like a fowl hen roost and we were covered
in bird-lice and ticks."*

Some material, including a water tank and timber were salvaged from the nearby wreck of the "Martha Wridgway" [1841], whilst the rock had to be quarried from other islands and the mainland.

For months the convicts laboured in the humid heat and finally it was completed in September.

The reward for the months of toil and pain was their freedom.

Although the beacon warned many mariners of the dangers of the reef, there were still many casualties and in later years, 9 ships anchors were found embedded in the coral by Frank Jardine of Somerset.

Today, the beacon still stands on this small coral rim, minus its roof, which collapsed with age. It is a fitting tribute to the convicts who built it.

As the shipwrecks increased, so did the massacres and it was into this savage arena that the "America" arrived in December 1844.

The monumental gravestone at the Bunnerong Cemetery in Sydney in memory of those beheaded from the "Charles Eaton". [Mitchell Library – Sydney]

TOMB OF THE "CHARLES EATON" MASSACRE

WITHIN THIS TOMB WERE INTERRED ON XXVI NOVEMBER, MDCCXXXVl, THE REMAINS OF SEVENTEEN HUMAN BODIES.

DISCOVERED, AFTER THE MOST DILIGENT RESEARCH, IN THE ISLAND OF AUREED, IN TORRES STRAIT, BY MR C.M. LEWIS, COMMANDER OF H.M. COLONIAL SCHOONER "ISABELLA" AND BY SATISFACTORY EVIDENCE IDENTIFIED AS THE MORTAL REMAINS OF CERTAIN OF THE OFFICERS, CREW AND PASSENGERS OF THE BARK "CHARLES EATON", WHO, AFTER ESCAPING FROM THE TOTAL WRECK OF THAT VESSEL, ON XV AUGUST, MDCCCXXXIV, WERE SAVAGELY MASSACRED BY THE NATIVES ON THE ISLANDS ON WHICH THEY LANDED.

HIS EXCELLENCY SIR RICHARD BOURKE, K.C.B. GOVERNOR IN CHIEF OF THIS COLONY, BY WHOSE COMMAND THE EXPEDITION TO ASCERTAIN THE FATE OF THESE UNHAPPY PERSONS WAS UNDERTAKEN, CAUSED THE LAST OFFICES OF PIETY TO BE DISCHARGED TOWARDS THEM, BY DIRECTING THE INTERNMENT OF THEIR REMAINS WITH THE RITES OF CHRISTIAN BURIAL, AND THE ERECTION OF THIS MONUMENT TO RECORD THE CATASTROPHE BY WHICH THEY PERISHED.

"AND THEY TOLD DAVID, SAYING, THAT THE MEN OF JABESH-GILEAD WERE THEY THAT BURIED SAUL"; AND DAVID SENT MESSENGERS "TO THE MEN OF JABESH-GILEAD, AND SAID UNTO THEM BLESSED BE YE OF THE LORD, THAT YE HAVE SHOWN THIS KINDNESS".   11.SAM.11-IV,V.

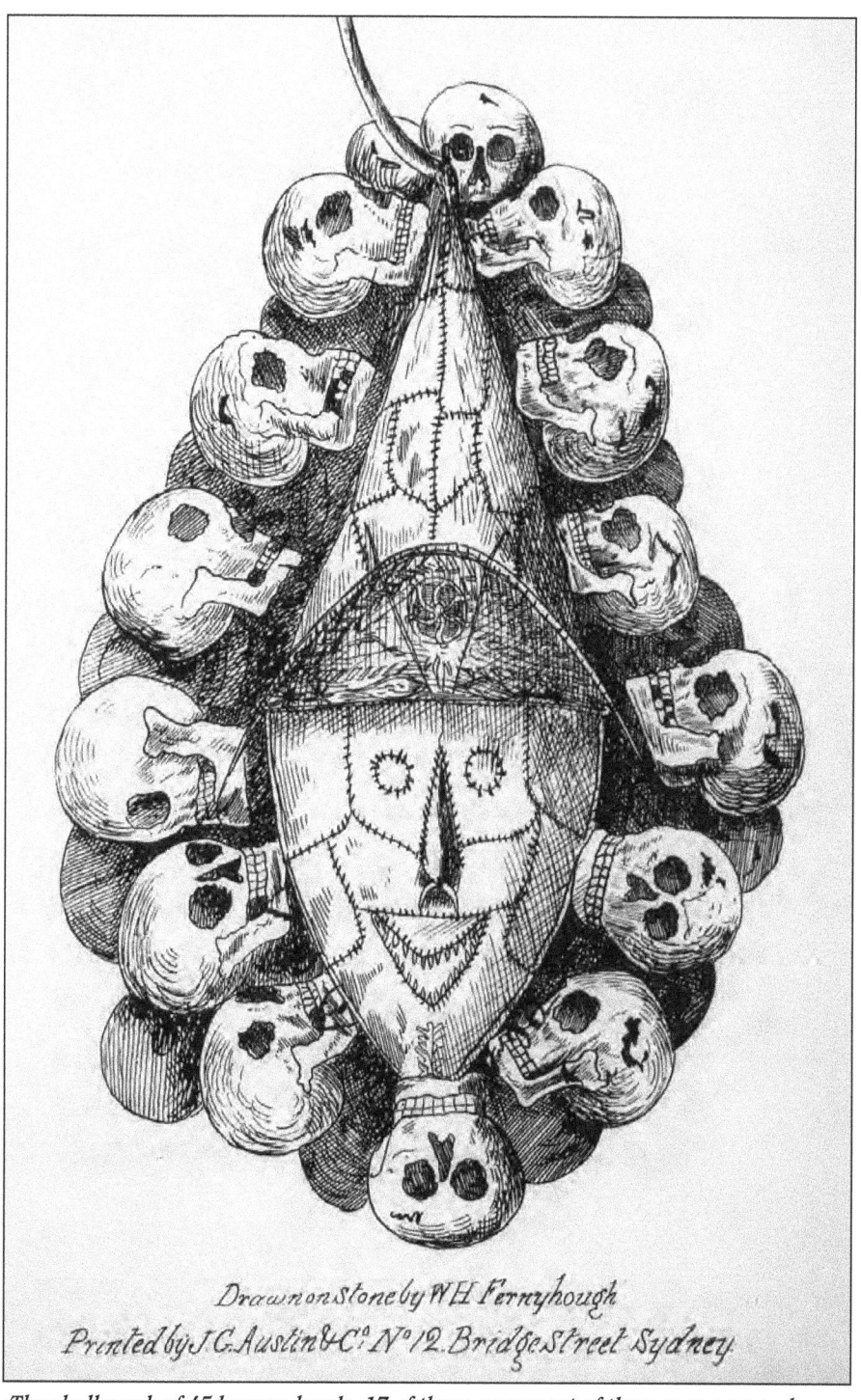

The skull mask of 45 human heads. 17 of these were most of the passengers and crew of the "Charles Eaton", beheaded by Torres Strait Islanders at Boydan Island in 1834. [Mitchell Library – Sydney]

CAPE YORK AND THE TORRES STRAIT ISLANDS

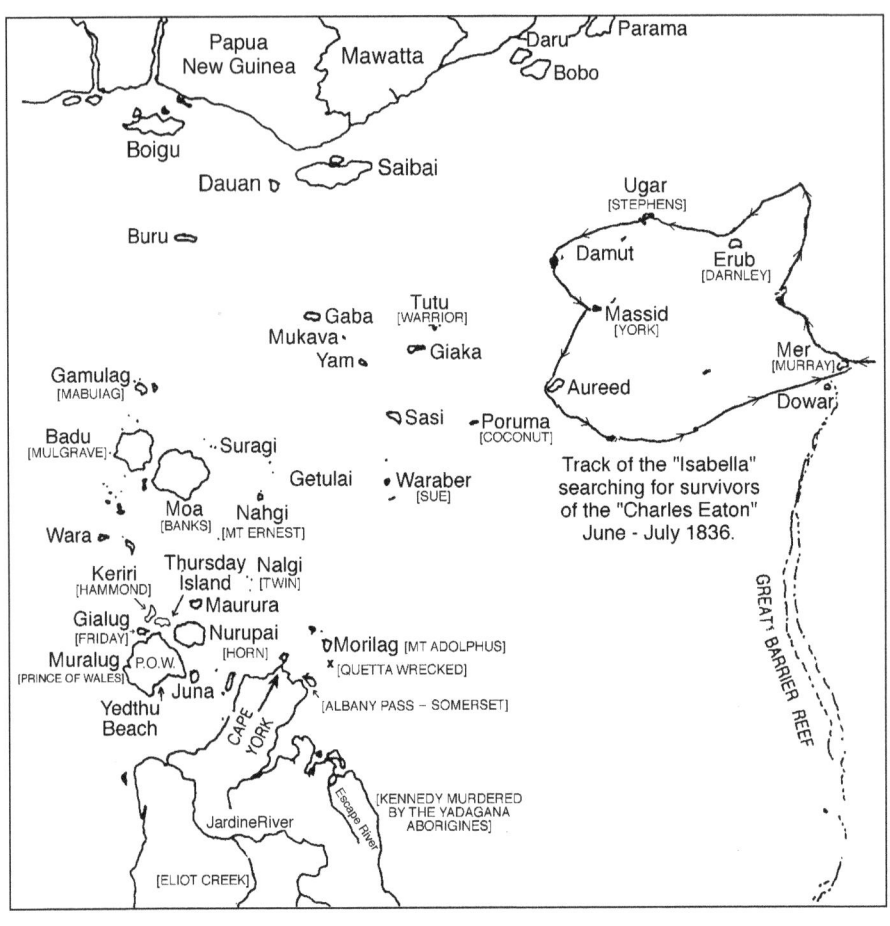

CHAPTER 3
"GIOM OF THE KAURAREGAS"

The "America" was a small 12 ton cutter, skippered by a young Australian adventurer named William Thompson. In Sydney he fell in love with a young Scottish girl named Barbara Crawford, who had migrated with her family from Aberdeen 7 years earlier [1837].

The Crawfords lived next door to a popular drinking house in Kent Street Sydney, known as the City Inn. It was here that sailors often relaxed when in port and where Thompson probably met Barbara.

As she was barely 15 years old, there was no way her parents would allow them to marry. So she eloped with him and the couple sailed to Moreton Bay [Brisbane] where they were married.

They stayed here for the next 18 months when Thompson met an old sailor who claimed to have been shipwrecked on a whaler in the Torres Strait. He believed the ship must still be sitting high on the reef with a fortune of whale oil in casks, stacked in her holds. At £150 a ton, it was worth a fortune.

At this same time Thompson had been asked to join Leichardt's last expedition but declined after meeting the old sailor.

He wasted no time in preparing the "America" for the long trip ahead, and in September 1844 they headed north in search of this liquid gold.

On board was a total crew of 6, including Thompson, Barbara, the Mate, 2 additional sailors and the old salty who was to be their guide.

2000 Miles and 3 months later they arrived in the Torres Strait, where a constant lookout was kept for the notorious war canoes. Sighting an island, Thompson and the 2 deck hands rowed ashore to collect wood, but overloaded the dinghy which swamped on the return journey and sank.

Only Thompson had the strength to swim a mile back to the "America", where Barbara and the Mate helped him aboard, when she quickly prepared some soup, as the old sailor tried to get his bearings.

Next morning they headed west past a cluster of islands, when the old salty again tried to get his bearings, but by now Thompson suspected he was a fraud, and an argument broke out as the sailor tried to convince them to continue going west.

When no sight of a wreck could be found, Thompson was satisfied he had led them on a false trail, and as punishment they left him stranded on a sandbank to drown on the incoming tide.

They now headed south west past a cluster of islands and finally reached the Prince of Wales group of islands including Wednesday, Thursday, Friday, Hammond, Horn and Prince of Wales.

The wet season broke with a vengeance as sheet lightning lit the sky and thunder echoed through the Strait. The "America" headed south to escape the storm sailing down the east coast of Horn Island, as waves broke across the bow, pounding the small vessel. As they rounded the bottom of Horn, Barbara noticed a small island. This was little Entrance Island which sits at the southern entrance of Boat Channel.

With only half his crew left, Thompson anchored on the south side of the island, knowing it was impossible to fight against the gale force winds, and here they sheltered overnight for the duration of the storm, only to be pushed onto a submerged patch of rocks and wrecked at midday the next day.

As water flooded into the shattered hull, Thompson and the Mate tried to swim to shore as Barbara was left clinging for her life on the wrecked "America".

They never made it and a broken hearted Barbara watched in agony as torrential seas claimed the love of her life.

By now the "America" lay on its side with Barbara grasping her arms tightly around the broken mast as the vessel was pounded by a raging sea. Tears rolled down her cheeks at the memory of her husband drowning before her very eyes. How long she lay there weeping for him she did not know, but finally the storm was gone.

She was now alone in a hostile sea ruled by some of the most savage head hunters in the south seas. The nearest white settlement was at least 1000 miles away.

Lifting her head, she looked out to sea and what she saw filled her with dread, for heading directly for her was a canoe. It had outriggers on either side and a hut in the centre. This gave every indication of a war canoe and in her demented state she knew it would soon be over.

As it came closer she could make out a number of naked warriors yelling out in a babble of words she could not understand. The large canoe stopped some distance from the wreck so as to be clear of the rocks and she could distinctly hear the same repetitive babble over and over again as they threw their arms into the air, crying out "Toomah-Toomah".

One of them, much taller and darker than the others, jumped into the sea and swam towards her, she shivered with fear and clung ever so tightly to the broken mast.

The others were still crying out "Toomah-Toomah" as he climbed onto the wreck, but instead of a fearsome approach, he seemed somewhat friendly and upon sighting her up close noticed something familiar about her, as if he had seen her somewhere before. He gently enticed her off the wreck, even helping her into the water.

This strong wiry native was not an islander at all. His name was Tomogugu, the chief of the Gudang tribe of aborigines at Cape York. At 6 feet 2 inches tall there were few who would challenge him.

Once in the water he helped her swim to the canoe, when an islander named Alika jumped in the sea to assist them, whilst another man named Boroto lifted her onto the platform of the canoe. She noticed his face was horribly scarred by burns.

As she lay exhausted, a chatter of excitement broke out among them, as they discussed their strange find. They looked at her more closely, causing her to shudder with fear. They continued to stare at this frightened creature convinced they had seen her somewhere before.

To the Islanders, all Europeans were seen, not as humans, but as spirits in human form, which they called "Markai". However, this particular Markai was special, because not only was she female, but they believed there was something very important about her, judging by their excited conversation.

Rather than take her head, they took her to nearby Entrance Island where they had a temporary fishing camp. Here they boiled up some turtle soup for her and gave her a pandanus mat to sleep on.

Barbara could not understand why they were treating her so kindly, for by all accounts of tales from shipwrecked survivors, she should have been beheaded.

Finally, they again boarded the canoe and took her across to Prince of Wales Island. This was "Muralug", home of the dreaded Kauraregas.

The village was situated on the fringe of a large beach at the extreme base of the island, on the eastern side of Cape Cornwall. This was "Yedthu" beach, which was more commonly known as the "Yedt". It was so named due to the large number of Casuarina trees that dotted the beach and appeared to the Kauraregas as a beard. [Yedthu].

The sea was so shallow here that one could wade up to their knees for half a mile off shore. For this reason their large canoes could not be anchored in shore. Instead, they were taken up the estuary of a mangrove fringed creek which ran behind the camp and where they could be hidden from their enemies.

It was here that Barbara stepped ashore and was taken along a well used track to the Kaurarega campsite. Upon entering the village, all eyes were upon her.

The commotion caused Chief Peaqui to emerge from his hut and upon seeing Barbara, cried out in exhilaration; "Giom-Giom", setting off a chorus from the tribe, who joined in the chanting, "Giom-Giom". Peaqui's 3 wives followed after him and threw their arms around her and now she realised they were not crying out for her blood, but were welcoming her.

As incredible as it sounds, Chief Peaqui,* saw Barbara Thompson as the spirit of his dead daughter "Giaoma" whom they all called "Giom". She had died a few weeks earlier and had now returned as a markai. So Barbara was taken in as the spirit daughter of a chief. [Giom – Pronounced with a "G" as in geese – Gee-om].

By now she was aware that all eyes were upon her, for the entire village had gathered around her, amazed that Giom had come back from a vengeful sea. The very fact that the ghost ship had deposited her so close to Muralug was evidence that she had been there before and so knew where to come. So they believed.

The resemblance of Barbara to the real Giom was quite remarkable. Her physical attributes such as height, chin, nose, eyes and slim body were almost identical.

To the Kauraregas she could only be Giom and the entire tribe referred to her by that name.

The Kauraregas were a potent mixture of the advanced island culture and the savagery of the mainland aborigine. They are often referred to as Island Aborigines. In earlier years they had gone to war against the Gudang at Cape York and won. When the Gudang sued for peace, they became allies. This was why the Gudang chief Tomogugu was with them when the "America" was wrecked.

As with most native tribes the women worked for their survival. Giom was no exception and she spent her days digging yams in the rocky hills behind Cape Cornwall and carrying her heavy loads back to camp.

Peaqui realised she did not have the strength of the native women and she was relegated the task of looking after the children in the camp.

When her dress eventually disintegrated, she reverted to wearing the island grass skirt called a dadje. To protect her wedding ring, she wrapped it in her only handkerchief, which she tied around her neck.

When ever she took it out from its hiding place, she would remember the death of her love and was unable to stop the tears from falling.

The natives believed the ring held a strange power over her. To them it was evil. So they removed it whilst she slept and threw it into the camp fire so it would never torment her again.

Although her life had been spared under incredible circumstances, she was virtually a captive of the Kauraregas, and forced to live the life of a primitive on a forested island covering 75 square miles. As Cape Cornwall was well clear of the shipping lanes then there was little chance of escape.

As the days went by she learnt about the crude realities of this culture that was so alien to her own. One day she witnessed a horrifying event as a young girl gave birth on the sand.

No sooner was the baby born, and another woman took the infant away from its mother and dug a small hole in the sand. She then placed some tea tree bark on the bottom with the baby on it and put more bark over the child, and buried it alive.

It was a rule of the tribe that although young girls could have all the sex they wanted, any babies born out of wedlock were to be *"marramatised"*, which literally means buried alive.

Living the life of a native woman, Giom's feet blistered so badly she could barely walk and with only a short grass skirt to protect her from the hot tropical sun, she burned like a lobster.

* Also pronounced: Piaquai, Paquee.

Through pain and suffering she slowly adjusted to this primitive lifestyle, but never lost her determination to escape from this nightmare.

Although the tribe only numbered 150 people all told, they were a deadly foe. Giom was soon to bear witness of their incredible savagery.

Across Endeavour Strait, only 13 miles east of Muralug, lay Red Island Point on the Australian mainland. Here lived the wild Gumukudin aborigines, the enemies of the Kauraregas.

Their territory embraced over 12 miles of coastline along the western side of Cape York, from what is now Peak Point to as far south as Cowal Creek. The Kauraregas held them in such contempt that they referred to them as "Yegille's", meaning "ugly nose" of the kangaroo.

From their lookouts at night, the Gumukudins spotted a lone campfire on Muralug, and headed across in their canoes to attack what they thought was the main Kaurarega camp, but which was only a small fishing camp.

They found only one old man, and in their rage, forced a spear up his nostrils, into his brain. He had been crab hunting and was named Eengah, the father of Boroto, one of the warriors who had rescued Barbara from the "America".

The next day his body was found a mile from the main camp. Boroto and his brother, Gunahgi, threw themselves onto the body weeping. After placing it on a makeshift ladder, they mounted it on 4 stout poles, 5 feet above the ground at the site where he died. He was then left to rot under the blazing sun on this "sara" [stage], under which the remains would later be buried and this would be his "Kaga" [grave].

The death of Eengar sparked war between the Kauraregas and the Gumukudins. It was customary for the islanders to let their enemies know they would soon be at war by lighting bonfires on a beach or headland.

The Kauraregas stoked their fire to let the Gumukudins know they would soon be over to teach them a lesson and the Gumukudins replied by daring the Kauraregas to come across and fight. The Kauraregas waited for several days for their enemy to lose their vigilance and then they were ready.

Before setting out for war, they feasted on a concoction of turtle fat and yams called Marbouchie. Next they tied a strong vine belt [wakau] around their waist and dressed to kill with vines around their ankles and shell finery hanging off their ears. Then they applied their war paint for the more grotesque they appeared to their enemy, the better.

The warriors would not be permitted to eat again, until they returned with the heads of their enemy. The old man's sons, Gunahgi and Boroto, would lead the attack at midnight, promising to strike with all the savagery that they could muster. Every warrior carried his Upi [bamboo beheading knife] and Singa [head carrier]. This device had a detachable vine that was passed through the severed neck and out through the mouth and reconnected to the Singa. To sharpen the Upi for the kill, they simply bit into one end and peeled off a single strip, making it sharp enough for one beheading, when it would be resharpened. A tally of heads taken was cut into the handle.

6 Large war canoes headed across Endeavour Strait to do battle and the rest of the tribe moved close to the mangroves for protection in case they should be attacked whilst their warriors were away.

On the second night Giom could hear noises off the coast. Fearing an attack by their enemies the tribe moved deeper into the mud and slush of the mangroves with the women and children, and total silence fell.

When it was established that it was their own warriors returning, they left the mangroves and excitedly rushed down to the beach to greet them. In the shadows, Giom watched horrified as 6 heads were thrown onto the sand. A large fire was soon blazing and the warriors grabbed the heads and danced in a circle around it. They threw the heads down onto the sand again and again, and soon some of the women also joined in with the warriors, shouting and screaming as they worked themselves into a frenzy.

Their bodies glistened with sweat, and saliva dribbled from their mouths as they screamed in unison, celebrating their victory.

Giom was so frightened by the "Death Dance" that she hid herself under a mat watching the whole proceedings. She was nauseated to see the heads of 2 females, one an adult and the other a teenage girl, amongst the collection. The dancing and screaming lasted for over an hour until the revellers dropped exhausted and hungry.

Stones had been heated during the celebrations to make 2 ahmais [ah-my]. These were their stone ovens. The ahmais were made by heating the stones and placing the meat on the top. This was covered with Pandanus leaves and more heated stones and so layered until finally a turtle shell [Ahgu] was placed on top and covered with Pandanus leaves and sand to keep in the heat. In this manner, the heads were placed in 2 ovens and left to cook for 30 minutes.

The feast began. The flesh was cut off the heads, including the cheeks, nose, ears and neck. The Kauraregas also ate the eyes of their victims, although they preferred them cooked. The women sat a short distance away as the warriors ate their fill, for only men could eat human flesh.

It was customary that the eyes be eaten first as a kind of tidbit before the main course, although the warriors also believed that it would give them extra strength and warriorship in their battles with their enemies.

Giom watched in disbelief as a warrior held a piece of flesh above his mouth, and called out to the women through a mouthful saying how delicious it was.

The tongues were never eaten, but were tied to poles and sun dried. Later they were wrapped in bark and carried with the warrior who had cut off the head. They were kept as a magical item and whenever the warrior went turtle hunting the tongue would be tied to the bow of the canoe and the owner would actually talk to it, telling it to entice the turtle closer so he could catch it.

A fortnight after Eengar's death, the "Marragatali" [funeral men] returned to the body still decomposing on the Sara [stage] and removed the head from the cadaver as well as some bones which were later distributed to family members. The remains were then buried between the 4 poles and this became the "kaga" [grave], which was decorated with dugong skulls. Coconut fronds were then placed over the grave and sara to shelter it.

It was another 6 weeks before the funeral commenced. In the days leading up to the dugong moon [full moon], when the women returned each afternoon with their heavy loads of yams, they would tear off their dadje's and throw themselves down on the ground, severely lacerating themselves on the rocks and stones. At night the tribe would moan and groan, lamenting and talking about the deceased Eengar. This was the "Mai" and it continued night after night till the funeral took place.

At last, the wake concluded with the "Marragaeta" [leading funeral man] carrying the head that had now been rotting for 8 weeks in a basket decorated with cockatoo feathers.

In a special celebration, he presented it to the dead man's wife, thrusting it into her face again and again, so as to make her cry, when it was finally given to her as a keepsake.

As wet season followed dry, Giom observed their strange lifestyle. She took seriously the warning that should she ever escape, she would be hunted down and only her head brought back to camp. Yet, even these threats did not stop her trying to escape, but her attempts were often thwarted, for as a "Garsarmigi" [captive] she was watched day and night. As they knew all about telescopes then they hid her in the scrub when a ship passed within several miles.

One day Boroto excitedly rushed into camp and showed her his latest acquisition, some European tobacco. She learnt a ship was anchored off the beach and that several armed sailors had landed. This was the chance she had been waiting for. Telling Peaqui, she was going to the waterhole, she picked up her 2 "kusus", [hollowed coconut shells for carrying water] but headed instead to the beach, to arrive as the boats were being hauled back on board.

In desperation she stood on a rock on shore waving a green branch. As they were only half a mile off shore she yelled and screamed for them to return for her, but her pleas were in vain. For, she was now so dark from the constant exposure to the tropical sun, that from the ship she looked like a native woman. Her heart almost fell apart as she watched the vessel slowly disappear from view.

With tears in her eyes, a heart broken Giom staggered to the waterhole and broke down into an avalanche of tears as she wept uncontrollably.

As the sun slowly set she could hear the natives calling for her, but would not answer. As darkness approached, she became frightened and headed along the track to the camp. She could not be comforted and did not eat for 2 days.

The Kaurarega camp was situated at Yedthu Beach for many reasons. One of these was protection from the driving north west monsoonal winds and rain. Another was security from a surprise attack due to the extreme shallow water which prevented enemy raiders storming ashore except on a good high tide. In addition, their large war canoes could be hidden up "Muddy Creek" which was well camouflaged by mangroves at its mouth.

One particular type of mangrove that had edible seed pods was called "Beeyu", which grew in profusion around Cape Cornwall and was the major vegetable component of their diet. However the "Beeyu" was highly toxic and could not be eaten in its natural state. It would first have to be roasted and then slit open with a shell. The flesh would be scraped out and then soaked in fresh water for 24 hours to extract the poison. Then it could be eaten.

The other major vegetable food was "Coti" a particular yam that grew in the rocky hills behind the camp. This was a dry season food whilst the "Beeyu" was mainly eaten in the wet season, and then, only due to necessity, when food was scarce.

The major disadvantage of the camp site, was the scarcity of fresh water. The "Marrum" [well] was almost a mile from the camp. This meant that the women would have to take their kusus to the well and fill them. They would then drink as much water as possible before returning to camp with their kusus full of water.

WITCH DOCTORS OF MURALUG

The 4 chiefs of Muralug were Peaqui, Queequi, Manu and Baki. These men were the most powerful individuals within the tribe, and owned the largest of their war canoes.

They decided whether a life should be taken or spared, even from their own people. For they were also the "Maidalaig" – that is the witch doctors and sorcerers.

Giom soon learnt the amazing power they held over the tribe. If they had a grudge against a particular individual then an ambush would be planned.

The Maidalaig would paint himself up with clay so as not to be identified and hide behind a large "Moogu" [termite mound] which could be over 15 feet high beside a track leading to the well. He would then spear any man, woman or even a child who may have offended him in the past.

After killing his victim, he would collect the blood from the bleeding nose into a shell and drink a portion of it. Then he would dig a little hole in the sandy ground and after laying the base with tea tree bark, pour the blood into it so it soaks into the bark. Later he will carry a piece of the dried bark in his dilly bag as a memento of the occasion.

If he was unable to kill his proposed victim in the daytime, then he would try it at night.

After painting himself, he would crawl on his belly throughout the camp whilst everyone slept and search out his victim. As everyone's footprints were known then the only alternative to avoid being identified was to crawl.

After locating his victim, he would squeeze poisonous juices over the face and body, causing the skin to erupt later in blisters and ulcerate. In some cases the poison was so toxic, the victim died in excruciating pain.

Giom soon realised that escape from the Kauraregas was near impossible unless she could get closer to the main shipping lanes. So when 20 canoes of the Kulka-legas arrived from Nahgi [Mt Ernest Island] she jumped at the chance of going back with them. As they were a friendly tribe then she felt this would be her only chance to escape from Muralug.

Early one morning, she carried her kusus, as if going to the well, but once she was out of sight, she switched towards the beach to meet up with the Kulkas and hopefully get away as they were going back to Nahgi.

Within minutes, the Kauraregas stormed onto the beach and prevented her wading out to the canoes. They were well armed with axes, spears and bows and arrows and were prepared to attack the Kulkas even though they were allies. They later told her they would have killed her rather than let her escape.

Throughout her captivity, Giom was to bear witness to the incredible customs and beliefs of the Kauraregas. They actually believed that the babies of Markai's [whites] must be put into a bag to prevent them from going black and asked her how often they were taken out to be washed.

When she asked why so many of their babies were born with hair on their backs they claimed it was because of the dogs looking at them when they were pregnant.

Giom noticed that whenever a woman was about to give birth, they seemed to have no pain. An older woman would kneel beside her and rub the belly and in a short time the baby was born.

3 Days after the birth she observed a rather peculiar operation being performed on the baby. This was called "Luwai Adtha" [press flat].

With the baby asleep, the mother would place it on her lap whilst seated on the sand, with its head resting on her knees. She now gently pressed and kneaded the baby's forehead with the palm of her hand. This would continue for several hours each day until finally the crown of the forehead becomes flat.

Their reasons for carrying out this strange custom were twofold. First, they believed it made their baby a "Kopi Kidje" or pretty child and secondly they had an immense amount of admiration for a particular fish they called "Gapu", better known as the Remora or Sucker fish. This fish had a flat head where the sucker is located and to identify with it they flattened their own babies heads.

Giom had often accompanied them in their turtle hunting expeditions and was fascinated by their method of catching turtle with the Gapu. It was mainly used for hunting a turtle called "Gapu Warroo" or what we know today as the Flatback Turtle.

A string made of coconut fibre was tied through a hole in the lip and another through the tail and joined to form a triangle which was connected to a long line from the canoe.

The Gapu would then be released into the sea and finally, as the string went taught they knew it had attached to a turtle whence a native would dive into the shallow bottom and bring both the "Gapu" [fish] and "Warroo" [turtle] to the surface and hauled onto the canoe.

Giom learnt that different types of turtles were caught at certain times of the year. As one turtle season finished another would start. One of the most favoured was a large turtle called "Soolah" [Green Turtle] which was plentiful early in the dry season. It was easily caught by jumping off the canoe onto its back and quickly tying its flippers with a vine.

Giom was quite shocked to see the turtles were cut open whilst they were still alive and soon realised that the natives had little concern with the environment. In one year she observed 300 turtles were caught and for the next 3 years they were very hard to find.

WINI – THE WHITE SAVAGE

When word spread through the islands that Peaqui's daughter had returned as a spirit, many tribes visited Muralug just to see her. Among her many visitors was a powerful individual who lived on the island of Badu, nearly 40 miles to the north.

He knew she was not a spirit, and when he arrived at the Kaurarega camp, she instantly realised he was not a native. He was a white man who claimed to have been shipwrecked. He had been with the Badus for such a long time he could not speak his European language and now conversed in the native tongue.

He told her he was a captive like herself and was owned by 2 brothers and asked her to come to Badu with him as his bride.

She was not fooled by his tale of captivity, for she had heard many horrifying stories about him.

This was "Wini", the white chief of Badu. He stood close to 6 feet tall, of average build with long fair hair. His face was pockmarked from an earlier attack of smallpox and lumps were growing out of his skin. The 2 brothers seemed to be with him at all times and were almost certainly his bodyguards.

He was in every respect a "White Savage", who murdered any shipwrecked castaways who were unfortunate enough to land near his island fortress of Badu.

Wini had taught the Badus the white man's way of war. They should strike without lighting fires and beating drums. Surprise was the tactic he employed and this gave them victory. He was the major cause of the Badu attacks against innocent tribes who were annihilated by his warriors.

Giom rejected his proposal and he sailed back to Badu to bide his time.

There are 2 major seasons in the tropics – the "wet" and the "dry".

During the wet the Kauraregas camped at the Yedt at Cape Cornwall and in the dry they ventured to the northern islands of Waiben [Thursday], Keriri [Hammond] and Gialug [Friday] to hunt turtle and dugong, setting up temporary camps for the season.

One of their favourite camps was on the north western side of Keriri. Here was a large bay with several fresh water creeks running into it and an abundance of fish in the region. To the north were miles of reefs where turtle and dugong were hunted.

One day whilst looking out to sea she noticed 2 canoes approaching. She yelled out in alarm and the natives responded with fear in every syllable, "Badthu Gooli-Badthu Gooli" [Badu canoes].

The Badus now knew where she was and 3 days later sent an entire fleet towards Keriri.

The alarm was raised by an old man looking towards Badu. Giom observed the sea was alive with 16 large war canoes and 200 warriors converging on Keriri.

As most of the Kauraregas were turtling on the reef, the rest of the tribe were extremely vulnerable. In a panic, the children and old people left at the camp, were bundled onto the only remaining canoe and taken up a mangrove creek further south.

Fearing the canoe would be captured by Wini's warriors Giom chose to run along the beach towards the safety of the mangrove creek. The lead war canoe was gaining fast as she desperately tried to outrun it. Her way was barred by a creek but she fearlessly plunged into it regardless of crocodiles and swam across. Ahead she saw the Kaurarega canoe head for the shore and almost exhausted, she caught up with it as it disappeared into the protection of overhanging mangroves at the mouth of the creek, and joined them in their hiding place.

From her vantage point on the bank, Giom could see the Badu war canoe slowly gliding past the entrance with warriors peering up the creek in search of her.

Not a whisper or movement could be heard as all eyes watched the entrance. Meanwhile Gunahgi held an axe above Giom ready to split her head if they had been seen. If the Kauraregas could not have her neither could the Badus.

Meanwhile the Badu's checked all along the shoreline listening for voices that might betray her position. Finally they gave up and headed for the Kaurarega camp where the rest of their fleet was anchored.

With the canoe gone, Gunahgi took Giom through the scrub to where several women were cooking the Beeyu. From their high position they could observe any strangers approaching along the track, giving her ample time to flee further inland if necessary.

That night the Badu's camped with the Kauraregas making out that they were only on a friendly visit but always carried their weapons with them. The Kauraregas had an uneasy truce with them and were constantly on guard. The fact that they did not bring any women with them clearly showed they had ulterior motives.

Throughout the night they tried to get information about Giom's where-abouts and one of them finally took Peaqui's son [Adi] aside to extract information from him, but still Adi would not talk. So the Badu slept beside him all night hoping to break him down. As the suns rays welcomed a new day, Adi finally yielded and offered to search for her, knowing that if he refused someone in the camp would die.

The 4 women constantly watched the small track leading to their hideout. Suddenly, Giom saw 2 men approaching and the women instantly ducked behind some boulders. As the men called out to Giom the women watched in deadly silence through a cleft in the rocks.

Giom was not taking any chances with the Badu warrior, who's ferocity was evident in the bone through his nose and the shells hanging from his ears. Around his waist was a "wakau" [plaited belt of vines] and over his shoulder he carried his beheading knife and head carrier [upi and singa]. Not a rustle or whisper could be heard as they called out for Giom, hoping she would betray herself, until they gave up and returned to the camp.

From her hideout, Giom could later see the canoes leaving and counted each one as they passed her lookout. All 16 were decorated and painted a bright red on the bow, signalling war. The warriors became aggressive and yelled out to Peaqui, threatening revenge for failing to capture Giom for Wini.

During this attempt to kidnap Giom, no sign of Wini was seen on shore. He is believed to have kept under cover on the lead war canoe so Giom would not connect him with her attempted abduction. Although, one authority believes he may have remained at Badu, waiting for the arrival of his bride to be. Whatever the truth it was the last chance he had of capturing her alive. Disappointed, the warriors sailed back to Badu singing a melancholy song.

GIOM PLANS HER ESCAPE

With the wet season approaching in December, the Kauraregas once again headed south through Boat Channel, rounded Entrance Island and then west to their camp at Yedthu Beach near Cape Cornwall at the bottom of Muralug where they settled into another long wet season, called the Kuki [pronounced Cook-ee].

The Kuki was the worst time of the year. Food was scarce, tropical storms swept the islands and malaria was prevalent each wet season. Giom suffered terribly from this disease in their mosquito ridden camp.

Apart from this affliction she was also the victim of malice from other women in the camp who did not like her. One day whilst putting some beeyu in the Ahmai, she neglected to invite a woman called Yuri to put hers in as well. This infuriated Yuri, for it was customary for everyone to share the same oven.

An enraged Yuri picked up a large boo shell [conch shell] and threw it at Giom stirring her into a fighting mood. Filling the shell with water, Giom threw it back. Yuri saw red and being much older and larger than Giom, she raced for a long pole intending to batter her head with it. She had under estimated Giom's hot Scottish blood and the brawl dissolved into a real cat fight, as Giom lunged for Yuri before she could reach the pole.

The ruckus had caused the tribe to gather around the fighting women, and they joined in a circle yelling for blood, and urging Giom on with cries of "Perkee Giom Perkee", meaning "Kill Giom Kill". Chief Peaqui was drawn by the noise and when he saw Yuri actually fighting his daughter, he grabbed his Upi in a rage intending to cut off Yuri's head when the men held him back.

He need not have worried, for as small as Giom was, she was more than a match for Yuri. She had grabbed Yuri by the hair and was slapping her face when she begged for mercy and Giom let her go. They later became the best of friends.

This incident proved that Giom had adjusted well to her pitiful life as a native woman. Yet, just as she was fitting into the tribal life, she was being carefully watched as she walked to the waterhole. After filling her kusus she strolled back along the track when a savage grabbed her from behind and dragged her screaming into the scrub and forced her to the ground.

Fortunately other women going to the well heard her terrified screams and rushed to her aid. When their men arrived they grabbed the intending rapist and thrashed him.

Yet disaster was about to strike in a manner she could never have imagined.

One night, whilst sleeping on her dry pandanus mat near the warmth of the fire, the mat ignited. She was in such a deep sleep that she awoke only when the flames were licking at her body.

The camp awoke as one to her screams as warriors grabbed their weapons fearing an attack. Instead they saw Giom writhing in pain as they rushed to help her.

The burns were horrific, extending from the breast to the thigh on one side. She would carry the scars for the rest of her life.

It was to be many months before the wounds healed and whilst bedridden during those first few weeks, it was a period of daily agony for her.

The natives had lived for centuries with the laws of nature and knew the best cure for illness was plenty of water and little food. Slowly she recovered although many times she begged for more food.

As wet season followed dry, she constantly observed their strange beliefs and customs. She noticed that the native women eagerly collected native plums [mee] that fell to the ground and were infested with grubs. The grubs were placed in their ears to eat out the wax. If they failed to emerge after 5 minutes, they were floated out with water.

Whenever they had malaria, they would stand near a blazing fire, then throw water over them and sweat the disease out. Ironically it also cured their other diseases.

When their babies reached 4 months they suddenly broke out in sores and became sickly. As this only happened to the Kauraregas, then it may have been caused by a vitamin deficiency.

Babies often died from disease and most were buried without a funeral. One of the most pitiful sights she ever witnessed was to see a young mother who's baby had died, holding a little mat in her arms and rocking it as if her baby was still on it.

By 1849, Giom had been held captive for over 4 years. In that time she had witnessed the savagery of aborigines and islanders unfold before her eyes. Then one day her right eye started fading. As the days went by it became worse and finally she could barely see from it. The maidalaig tried to cure her with various concoctions, to no avail.

A distraught Giom sought the courage to survive and above all the hope that she would be rescued before the eye failed.

With only one good eye, she soon met with another disaster, when she tripped on the rocks whilst collecting shellfish, turning her nose into a blooded mess and tearing her knee to the bone.

Now she pined more than ever to escape from this nightmare, when suddenly, one day she saw smoke signals at Cape York, 18 miles to the east.

The message was sent by Tomogugu, inviting the Kauraregas to come over, as a large war canoe of the Markais had arrived at Cape York and they should bring Giom with them.

The Kauraregas had no intention of taking Giom to Cape York, fearing that she would escape and refused to go. Tomogugu then set sail in his own canoe for Muralug. As he had a wife among the Kauraregas he could come and go as he pleased. She was the young girl, Sibi, whose baby was buried alive 4 years earlier and whom Tomogugu later married.

Shortly after landing at Muralug, he went to Giom and told her to go to his canoe. His action prompted an outcry in the camp as the warriors refused to let her go. He reminded them that as he captured her from the wreck, then he had first claim to her and effectively owned her. Despite this privilege they would not let her go.

At this point Giom spoke to her friend Urdzannah, the wife of Gunahgi and assured her all she wanted was "Uperi" [medicine] for her nose and knee and at the same time she would get all the "maleel" [knives and axes-iron] they wanted.

The mere mention of "maleel" changed the entire situation and now they all decided to go to Cape York on their best war canoes.

In nearly 5 years of captivity she had never been permitted to go on visits to Cape York. They questioned her repeatedly as to why she wanted to go to the Markai ships. She replied each time that all she wanted was medicine. They were finally convinced and asked her to get plenty of knives, axes and things made of Maleel. The Islanders valued iron more than any other commodity and even burnt the wrecks in the Strait to extract iron from them.

Giom was only too willing to get anything they wanted, but she was very careful not to show any excitement, even in her eagerness to please them, as they could easily change their mind.

Tomogugu had always promised that one day he would get her back to her people. This was the first step.

At least half the tribe boarded the canoes up Muddy Creek for the trip to Cape York and at last they set out to sea on the incoming tide. It was 8am on the 13th October 1849.

Her heart beat rapidly with excitement at the prospect of being rescued. She sat on the stage of the largest canoe searching in all directions for a boat or ship, but all she saw was a calm sea.

It took all day to cross to Cape York as there was little wind, but finally it loomed ahead at dusk beneath a setting sun. The Gudang aborigines had lit large fires on the rocky promontory of Cape York to guide them in the dark and let them know it was safe to land.

Always cautious, the Kauraregas remained off shore for fear of attack from the hostile Gumukudins further to the west.

Soon the Gudangs were crowding around the canoes in the shallow water. In an excited babble they told them of all the presents they had received from the friendly Markais. For as well as knives and axes, they had also been given "domawaka" [clothes] such as shirts and singlets which were highly prized.

The Kauraregas, being islanders would not camp on the Australian mainland, but chose instead to stay on the small island of Wamalug [York Island] only 100 yards off the western side of the Cape. The island to the east is Eborac.

Fire carried on the canoes was taken ashore and fire sticks used to search for wood. Soon a large fire was blazing and a turtle caught was cooked and eaten.

The next day as the warriors went turtle hunting, Giom climbed the hill and spotted not one ship but 3. The largest was "HMS Rattlesnake", a 500 ton British warship with 28 guns and 180 marines and sailors. Nearby was her tender the "Bramble". Both these ships had been charting the waters to New Guinea to map out a safe shipping passage through the Strait to avoid further shipwrecks. From her position she could see them anchored about a mile or so to the south at Evans Bay. A much smaller vessel was also anchored nearby. This was the supply ship "Sir John Byng". The "Rattlesnake" had arrived here on the 1st October 1849, to meet her and take on mail and stores.

The warriors returned later that day with turtles and Giom obediently made an ahmai to cook them under the blazing sun. That night in the camp, Tomogugu's wife [Sibi] showed Giom a tobacco pipe that a sailor had given to her. As it had a warship engraved into it she suddenly realised that the big ship must be a Man'o'War and now new hope surged within her.

The men promised to take her to the ships next day, telling her all the things she must get for them. But once again they let her down, for they had no intention of letting her get anywhere near the ships, although they badly wanted the knives and axes. When they went turtling the next day they left her in tears. She had come all this way hoping to be rescued, only to be trapped on a small island, so near and yet so far from freedom.

Devastated, she climbed the hill and looked across the water wondering in frustration how she could get to those ships. The little passage between Cape York and Wamalug was home to sharks and crocodiles and its strong rip was treacherous, so swimming across was out of the question.

DELIVERANCE

The 16th October 1849, was a warm sunny day. When the warriors returned as usual for lunch, they ate turtle and rested in the shade. Their peace was suddenly disturbed by the sound of gunfire from the beach opposite [Frangipani] on Cape York.

Leaping up, they ran to their canoes and poled across the passage to meet the whites.

It had been agreed that there would be no killing at Cape York. Even Tomogugu had warned the Kauraregas not to murder. This arrangement worked well and peace reigned between the natives and Europeans. Both whites and natives joined together in hunting for food. The sailors had been shooting birds for dinner when the Kauraregas joined them, and headed inland.

Giom saw this was her only chance to reach the ships and was very hesitant. The warriors had all crossed over to join the whites and only Tomogugu, Sibi and a few old people were left on the island. They boarded a small Gudang canoe and rowed across to the mainland where Tomogugu helped her ashore.

Giom's knee was extremely painful after climbing the hill on Wamalug and every step was agony. Yet she knew she must make this last effort or perish. Slowly she moved off the beach with Tomogugu and their small group. They followed a native track through thick rainforest at the northern base of Mount Bremer and headed towards the eastern side of Cape York. Turning south they walked above the rocky shore and came to a tiny beach.

This little beach is only a mile or so from the tip of Cape York and is the most northerly beach on the east coast of Australia. Just as they stepped onto it, they saw several sailors approach with a group of Gudangs, who almost always guided the sailors around the area, in return for some reward [biscuits].

The Gudangs had noticed Giom and were gesticulating to the sailors, trying to explain who she was. Unable to fathom the language, the sailors shook their heads, uncomprehending. Giom tried to interrupt the babble, but the English words would not come to her and all the sailors heard was a cacophony of native words. Incredibly she was so used to speaking in the Kaurarega language she had lost the ability to speak English. Desperately she tried to remember her forgotten tongue.

Unable to communicate with her they walked away. Then in a panic she cried out in the native language;

"I am a white woman – Why do you leave me – I am a Christian".

The sailors stopped in their tracks, unable to believe what they had just heard. The accent was rather peculiar although that last word sounded very much like English.

Then again she cried out; "I Christian".

Now they knew they were not hearing things and returned to her to take a closer look at this dark haired creature, so weather beaten from almost 5 long years of captivity. They noticed the horrible scars from her burns and the inflamed eyes, the right one almost blind. Her knee was ulcerated to the bone and her nose lacerated so badly, that she looked like a worn out native woman.

Fortunately for her, there is no native word for "Christian" and this came out in English.

The sailors now realised she was indeed a white woman. Whilst questioning her they detected a Scottish accent and yelled out to another man a short distance away; "Hey Scotty! Come here, we've found a Scotch girl."

Scott was the Captain's coxswain of the "Rattlesnake". He instantly rushed up and taking her hands in his looked into her face. Giom broke into uncontrollable tears.

The sailors gave a shirt to Tomogugu for his young son. Had it not been for this man she may have died among the Kauraregas, or even worse been captured by Wini of Badu.

Taking her by the hand Scott led her off the beach [Deliverance Beach] and across the grassy flat of Evans Cape to Evans Bay. By now her knee was so painful, she could barely walk, but she slowly made her own pace. She was so overcome with emotion that she cried all the way to the waterhole. Here, the Kauraregas were gathered around the sailors fascinated by them washing clothes and sheets.

Suddenly, all eyes turned to Giom, both black and white, as an armed guard was placed around her preventing any violence from the Kauraregas. She was then taken into the forest to be washed and scrubbed. For the first time in 5 years she could once again use soap to wash her hair and body. Assisting her was Scott and Sergeant Mew of the Marines. Next, she was given a white shirt to cover her chest and a blue one to wrap around her waist and cover her nakedness.

Finally, she emerged from the forest, not as Giom, but as a new Barbara Thompson, only to be confronted by the Kauraregas who demanded to know why she wanted to go aboard the ship. The armed sailors watched closely in case of violence.

To waylay their suspicions she told them that there were some Markai women on board whom she wanted to talk to. For the time being they believed her.

The "Rattlesnake" had on board a number of distinguished academics including the Scottish naturalist, John Macgillivray, the assistant surgeon Thomas Huxley who later became a world famous botanist and the ships artist, Oswald Walters Brierly.

Brierly was at the south end of the beach when he heard of the rescue of Barbara Thompson. He raced up to find her sitting on a sandbank with white guards and aborigines close by. The sandbank is a natural formation of the Evans Bay foreshore with rainforest trees growing on it.

The Kauraregas were now planning to take her back by force but Barbara overheard them saying there were too many guns. She managed to translate it into broken English, and to avoid any violence, Sergeant Mew was ordered to put her in the boat and take her to the "Rattlesnake".

In order that friendly relations continue with the natives, several of them were permitted to come aboard. Brierly also accompanied her in the boat and tried to question her but got little response. The rescue had overwhelmed her and she kept lapsing into periods of shock. Brierly later stated that she appeared like someone coming out of a deep sleep. She answered in the language of the Kauraregas interspersed with snatches of English, making it extremely difficult to understand her.

Upon boarding the "Rattlesnake", the natives with her were given gifts of biscuits and Captain Owen Stanley came on deck to meet her. He later wrote that he could not believe this pitiful creature had once been a white woman. He took her to his cabin and ordered food. She sat there almost motionless staring at him with her one good eye, trying desperately to remember her forgotten tongue. She frequently hit her forehead with frustration, trying to remember the words to thank him for her rescue. All that came out was a chatter of Kaurarega mixed with a few English words.

The "Rattlesnake" being a warship, was never designed for carrying passengers other than military personnel. However Stanley's workroom was previously used by his sisters as a cabin when the ship was in England. It was made ready for her with a bed, cupboard and mirror.

The transition was difficult for Barbara for only a few hours earlier she had been cooking turtle over a hot ahmai under the midday sun, and now she had all the comforts of civilisation. Over the next few days she spent hours in her cabin unable to comprehend it all, until finally she readjusted to the civilised world.

As there were no clothes available for her, a collection was taken from some of the crew. Their hearts went out to her and soon curtains of different colours, flannel and calico were gathered together, and with needle and thread, was soon making her own clothes, or in the words of Huxley, was making "mysterious feminine toggery".

From their canoes, gathered off the starboard side, the Kauraregas were stirring and yelling out for her to come back.

The last thing Captain Stanley wanted was a confrontation with them. He preferred a peaceful communication with all the tribes around Cape York, in case a settlement should one day be established in the area. He therefore permitted small groups of natives to come on the ship and see her. Once aboard, they tried every conceivable trick to entice her back.

Barbara, of course, could not go ashore and she explained to Stanley that if she did so she would be beheaded for violating the rules. A "Garsimigi" who had escaped must be caught and her head brought back to camp.

Even when she was in her cabin, the natives would bring their canoes alongside and reach through the porthole with their long black arms trying to touch her and lure her back.

All of their attempts to woo her ashore failed, until one day a savage Boroto confronted her on deck and demanded she return with him to the Kauraregas. When she refused, he threatened that if he or any of his tribe were to catch her on shore, they would cut off her head and carry it back with them to Muralug.

In their final attempt to woo her back, they stood on their war canoes, with spears pointing to the sky, their tall naked bodies glistening in the sun, with voices raised in unison, crying out "Giom Giom".

All hands watched in disbelief at this incredible and moving sight. Defeated, they turned their canoes and sailed back to their camp at Wamalug.

Barbara could not be expected to eat with a rough crew of sailors and soldiers, and was invited to have her meals at the Captain's table. As dinner was served it was realised that she had great difficulty using cutlery, for they seemed so heavy and cumbersome. The officers ignored her re-adjustment rather than cause acute embarrassment for her.

As her English improved daily, she told Captain Stanley of the existence of Wini, the white chief of Badu.

The tender, "Bramble" was due to continue the survey of the New Guinea waters and her skipper was instructed to check around Badu and if possible to capture him.

However, Wini already knew of the ships at Cape York and when the "Bramble" arrived there was no sign of him or the Badus. He is believed to have moved the entire tribe, temporarily, to an island further north called Mabuaig [Jervis] that had previously been conquered by the Badus.

The naturalist Macgillivray later wrote the "Voyages of the Rattlesnake" and exposed Wini's true nature. He related;

> *"He had reached Mulgrave Island [Badu] in a boat, after having by his own account, killed his companions, some three or four in number. In the course of time he became the most important*

person in the tribe having gained an ascendancy, by procuring the death of his principal enemies, and intimidating others; which led to the establishment of his fame as a warrior; and he became in consequence the possessor of several wives and canoes and some property in land, the cultivation of which last he pays great attention to. Wini's character appears from the accounts I have heard – for others have corroborated part of Giom's statement [natives] to be a compound of villainy and cunning, in addition to the ferocity and headlong passions of a thorough savage. It strikes me that he must have been a runaway convict, probably from Norfolk Island. [off New South Wales] It is fortunate that his sphere of mischief is so limited for a more dangerous ruffian could not easily be found. As matters stand at present, it is probable that not only during his life, but for years afterwards, every European who falls into the hands of the Badu people will meet with certain death."

Unable to locate Wini and the Badus, the Bramble later returned to Evans Bay. Lieutenant Sweatman of the "Bramble" remembered the report in Sydney, of the massacre of 4 sailors off Badu. This was the incident of June 1846, whilst Giom was held on Muralug and which she had also heard from the natives.

The murdered sailors were from the 70 ton schooner the "Thomas Lord". There were 6 men in a whale boat, 4 of which had camped on an island, one mile off Badu, whilst the other 2 stayed in the boat. Around midnight, the Badus attacked and murdered 3 of the men. Another man was seriously injured when one of his hands was completely severed and the other held together by only a few tendons. The sailors in the boat opened fire and dragged the wounded man to safety. He later died on the "Thomas Lord".

The "Thomas Lord" arrived in Sydney on the 6th August 1846, and a report was published in the "Australian Journal" on the 8th August 1846. A later report claimed the warriors were led by a tall lighter tanned man with long fair hair wielding a cutlass.

2 Years later in 1848, a ship was wrecked and 18 helpless castaways were believed to have been beheaded near Badu. A large horde of cutlasses were retrieved and later used to conquer Wini's enemies on Moa.

It was a further 20 years before this mad white savage met his end.

On her journey back to Evans Bay, the "Bramble" stopped off at "Booby Island" and stocked the refuge with casks of water and salted meat. They learnt that the crew of an American whaler, wrecked on the northern Barrier Reef, had made it safely to the island and were rescued by a passing ship.

Before the "Rattlesnake" left Evans Bay, a corroboree was danced on shore at night in honour of the European visitors. The event almost ended in violence, when an old woman, nicknamed Queen Baki was given biscuits which were a favourite trading item. She in turn gave them to the children. The warriors were outraged, for although they wanted them, they would never accept anything from a woman.

They suddenly emerged with weapons and the whites were quickly escorted to the waiting boats by friendly blacks.

After 9 weeks at Evans Bay, the "Rattlesnake" weighed anchor, her sails filled with wind and followed by the "Bramble" she sailed past Cape York.

In the eyes of the Kauraregas the ships were taking Giom back to "Ke-Buka" where all spirits dwell near the setting sun in the land of darkness.

As the "Rattlesnake" passed Cape York Barbara stood on deck and observed the Kauraregas campsite on Wamalug. Within minutes they were behind it and she imagined herself fetching water from the rock holes that never went dry. In the hazy distance she could see the ghostly outline of Muralug and now tears filled her eyes as she thought of those 5 long years of captivity and the terrifying violence she had witnessed amongst the indigenous people of the region.

The "Rattlesnake" continued the survey up to New Guinea and during this time the artist Oswald Brierly wrote down everything she could remember of her life among the Kauraregas. To this day no one has been able to improve on the information she gave.

The "Rattlesnake" could not sail down the east coast against the prevailing winds, so continued down via Western Australia.

Barbara Thompson, "Giom of the Kauraregas" arrived in Sydney on the 5th February 1850, when she was re-united with her parents.

Captain Owen Stanley had a seizure and died on board the "Rattlesnake" within weeks of his arrival. He is buried in Sydney.

Barbara settled back into civilised life and on the 27th November 1851 married James Adams in Sydney and lived till over 84 years of age.

"WHERE WAS THE AMERICA WRECKED"

This question has puzzled writers and researchers for almost 150 years. For although the approximate area was known, that is in the south western part of the Torres Strait, the island that Barbara Thompson referred to as the site of the wreck, had not been accurately identified by those who questioned her on board "HMS Rattlesnake", after her rescue in 1849.

The following are those who questioned her and the island they claimed where the "America" was wrecked.

Captain Owen Stanley claimed the site was "Possession Island".

Thomas Huxley, the assistant surgeon, claimed the site was "Possession Island".

Oswald Brierly, the ship's artist, claimed the site was "Horn Island".

John Macgillivray, the naturalist, claimed the site was the eastern "Prince of Wales Island", which could have been either "Horn" or "Entrance Island".

Possession Island must be eliminated due to its close proximity to the Gumukudin aborigines on the mainland, who were the enemies of the Kauraregas.

The Kauraregas would not have been hunting turtle so close to their enemies in an under-manned canoe at the break of the wet season.

Horn Island [Nurapai] must also be excluded due to its large size.

Barbara Thompson stated that they had sailed down past "Nurapai" [Horn] and were wrecked near a "small island".

Brierly concluded that the island she referred to must be Horn Island.

Her statement was written down on the 17th October 1849, when Captain Stanley claimed: "She could barely speak 3 words of English".

It would appear therefore, that Brierly wrote what he thought she meant and not necessarily what she was trying to say, due to the difficulty in communication.

Horn Island [Nurapai] is not a small island. It is in fact the second largest island in the Prince of Wales group and therefore, it could not have been the island she referred to.

Secondly, whilst questioning aircraft pilots and ships captains in the region, they all agreed that there are no reefs shallow enough to sink a small cutter off Horn Island.

However just south of Horn Island is little Entrance Island. So named, because it sits at the southern entrance to Boat Channel, between Horn and Prince of Wales Islands.

To the south west of this small island are rocks hidden below the high tide. This may have been the site where the America sheltered for the night whilst outrunning the storm. With a change to a low tide the next day, they would almost certainly have been on the rocks.

Barbara Thompson stated very clearly that they were on the "rocks". No mention is made of being on a reef. She was very meticulous in her descriptions and this applied especially to rocks and reefs.

Although Horn Island has often been described as the site where the America was wrecked, it has to be incorrect.

The most logical site must be close to Entrance Island. [Juna].

CHRONOLOGY OF BARBARA THOMPSON

Name at Birth	Barbara Hill Crawford
Year of Birth	1829.
Date of Christening	1st June 1829
Place of Birth	Aberdeen, Scotland
Religion	Presbyterian Church of Scotland
Date Departed Scotland	27th March 1837
Place of Departure	Dundee, Scotland
Name of Vessel	John Barry
Place of Arrival	Sydney, Australia
Date of Arrival	13th July 1837
Deaths on Board During Voyage	22 Children, 3 Adults – Total 25
Cause of Deaths	Typhus
Number of Migrants on Board	312 left Scotland
Married William Thompson	1843
Place of Marriage	Moreton Bay (Brisbane)
Departed Moreton Bay on America	September 1844
Wrecked in the Torres Strait	December 1844
Rescued at Cape York	16th October 1849
Arrived Sydney, Australia	5th February 1850
Married James Adams	27th November 1851
Church married in	St Andrews Presbyterian Church
City where married	Sydney, Australia
Died at Sydney, Australia	1912, aged 84 [not confirmed]*

Names of Crawford family, showing their relationship to Barbara Thompson and their age upon arrival in Sydney, Australia on the 13th July 1837.

Charles Crawford	Father	30 years
Jane Crawford [Morrison]	Mother	29 years
Alexander Crawford	Brother	14 years
Charles Crawford	Brother	12 years
Mary Crawford	Sister	10 years
Barbara Crawford		8 years
Anne Crawford	Sister	6 years
Jane Crawford	Sister	4 years
Andrew Crawford	Brother	2 years
Baby born during voyage. Sex unknown.		6 weeks

*One source claims she died in 1916

CHAPTER 4
"THE LOST EXPEDITION"

Cape York Peninsula is that part of Queensland that extends from its base at Cardwell, west to the Gulf of Carpentaria and all the land north to the rocky top of the Peninsula, originally called "York Cape" but later changed to Cape York.

The Peninsula is a hot, humid and unforgiving land. In some areas it is covered in lush rainforest, but for most the terrain is dry and scrubby and only seems to breathe life when the rains arrive in December.

It was into this country that Australia's most disastrous exploratory expedition was launched last century.

"HMS Rattlesnake" anchored in Rockingham Bay in company with the "Tam-O-Shanter" at a point 18 miles north of what is now the town of Cardwell on the 23rd May 1848. On board the ships was all the equipment needed for an amazing expedition in which 13 men would traverse 600 miles of the Peninsula. It was planned to re-supply the expedition at Port Albany, near the top of Cape York and then journey west from there. The expedition would then travel down the west coast to Fort Bourke at the base of the Peninsula.

On the 24th May 1848, the expedition was landed in unknown territory where no white man had ever trod. Leading the expedition was 6 foot tall Edmund Besley Court Kennedy. At 30 years of age he was fit and full of confidence that he would succeed in his mission of exploration.

For food, they carried: 600 pounds of sugar, 1 ton of flour, 90 pounds of tea. For meat they took along 100 live sheep and even a shepherd. 2 Light carts and one heavy cart were to carry the mass of equipment. Among the 28 horses were 9 draught horses to pull them. One horse drowned on landing leaving, 27.

A reconnaissance to the north showed the way was barred by an impenetrable 4000 foot mountain range, so they headed south on the 5th June. For mile after mile they forced their way through jungle swamps and crocodile infested rivers. As carts bogged down to their axles in mud they could only cover a few miles each day.

Weeks later on the 15th July, Kennedy had to abandon the carts, whilst tackling the steep terrain. Dingoes howled in the surrounding jungles and crocodiles surfaced in the rivers near their camp sites, waiting for the sheep to come and drink. In the humid heat, they cut their way through the jungle covered ranges that were so steep, that a horse slipped 30 feet down an embankment. Once clear of the swamps, they continued cutting their way through almost impenetrable rainforest. Many were soon weakened by the Ague, or what was later called Malaria and all of them were constantly plagued by leaches.

Now they could turn north and pushed their way across the ranges reaching the highest point of the ascent across the Great Dividing Range on the 9th August.

After months of toil and sweat they hacked their way through to open country. By now their food supplies were dwindling, and horses too weak to continue, were killed and eaten. By early September the expedition was well inland on a parallel with Cape Tribulation, and by the middle of the month had crossed the Palmer River, later to be the site of one of Australia's largest goldfields.

During their trek, aborigines had made several unprovoked attacks on their camps, forcing Kennedy to order his men to open fire in self defence. They again attacked the camp and set fire to the grass to try and burn out the explorers, but the flames failed to reach the camp.

The expedition had lost more than 60 days through the range. By now most of the remaining sheep and horses are skin and bone. The blood from a weak horse is extracted and made into a pudding and when the horse died the next day, its flesh was cut up and dried for food. This became a common practice as the horses weakened or died.

By October several of the men were too weak to walk and suffered from diarrhoea. They were Douglas, Costigan and Taylor. One week later Luff was unable to walk. 2 Round tents were burned to enable him to ride the horse that had carried them.

By mid-November the expedition was camped at a creek adjoining the Pascoe River and most were too ill to travel further. Kennedy realised they would never make it to Cape York in their weak condition to rendezvous with the "Bramble". He decided to divide his party.

He now planned to make a dash for Cape York and hopefully bring relief to his 8 sick companions camped at the Pascoe River near Weymouth Bay, 140 miles south of Cape York. He left Carron, [botanist] in charge with Wall, Niblett, Taylor, Goddard, Carpenter, Mitchell and Douglas.

Kennedy left most of the food supplies with them and of the 9 horses still alive, 2 were left as emergency food. If he could not bring a rescue party within 2 weeks, then the horses were to be eaten.

On the 13th November, Kennedy and his faithful native tracker, Jackey Jackey [Galmarra] left with Costigan, Dunn and Luff taking the remaining 7 horses. A week later on the 19th November, Costigan, the tough blacksmith accidentally shot himself under the right armpit, whilst removing his gun from the saddle.

Meanwhile Luff was extremely ill and could go no further. Dunn had little choice but to remain with them at their camp [False Pudding-Pan Hill].

The men left at these camps were slowly dying of disease [malaria] and starvation and Edmund Kennedy knew he must make it to Cape York where a supply ship would be waiting. It was now just the 2 of them "Kennedy and Jackey" – one white, the other black and both dependent on each other.

Further up the track, Jackey's horse went down whilst crossing a bog, trapping him by his leg. Kennedy, although himself ill and weak managed to go to his aid and freed him. Just as Kennedy assisted Jackey, so Jackey helped Kennedy when he became so weak that he had to be carried up to 2 miles at a time until too exhausted they both rested for several days to recoup their energy.

By early December [3rd] they arrived at the mouth of the Escape River and could barely see Port Albany, less than 20 miles away. After forcing their way through miles of swamp, jungle and creeks they were disappointed to find that the river mouth was too wide and deep to cross in safety. In fact the whole area was a myriad of swamps and creeks stretched over an area of 15 square miles.

They now ventured about ½ a mile up the river only to be confronted by a tribe of aborigines. Jackey immediately sensed they could not be trusted. Kennedy however, believed they were friendly and gave them gifts and ordered Jackey to hand over his knife. He did so reluctantly.

Kennedy's concern, even at this stage was the salvation of his men left at the 2 camps in the remote wilderness of Cape York Peninsula. If he and Jackey were killed by these people, then all the others would also die, for there would be no one to inform the ship of their helpless plight. Rescue was at hand, if only they could make it.

Kennedy was not to know that Jackey's suspicions were correct. They had met with the "Yadagana", the most savage and largest tribe in the Cape York region, who in later years [1867] would annihilate 2 other tribes [Gumukudin and Ambagana].

When the aborigines first saw Kennedy they rubbed their bellies and cried out "Powad Powad". This was the sign of peace acknowledged throughout the area.

For this reason Kennedy believed they were peaceful, but in fact they were disguising peace with treachery.

After Kennedy gave them fish hooks, they parted peacefully and Kennedy and

Jackey camped.

The next morning as they left their camp, Jackey looked behind and saw the aborigines with spears in their hands rifling the camp. He warned Kennedy that they would soon be following them, but Kennedy still believed they were friendly.

After 3 miles they camped, but knowing they were being followed, did not light a fire. Throughout the night they took it in turns to keep watch. Suddenly Jackey could see scores of aborigines searching for them in the bright moonlight that filtered through the trees after midnight.

By day break the natives had disappeared, so they saddled up and continued their hazardous journey, knowing the aborigines would soon be tracking them.

Late in the afternoon, they were spotted and Jackey warned Kennedy to watch his back. The Yadagana advanced through the scrub with their 9 foot spears ready to impale their prey.

The warning came too late. A spear cut through the humid air and struck Kennedy in the back. Crying out in anguish, he shouted, "Shoot em, Jackey! Shoot em!".

As he spoke, a spear struck Jackey a glancing blow on the forehead, but fortunately hit side on and ricocheted off. With blood pouring down his face, Jackey opened fire hitting one of them in the face with buckshot. Spears rained down as Kennedy grabbed his gun, but it failed to fire and he was speared in the leg.

The war cries of the Yadagana sounded a death knell for Kennedy. Dying horses were falling about him when he was again speared in the side. An enraged Jackey fired again and again until finally the savages retreated.

Kneeling over his dying friend, Jackey cut the barbed spears out of Kennedy's body. Propping him against a termite mound, he went and retrieved the saddle bags.

Returning with the saddle bags, he saw the blacks stealing Kennedy's watch and hat, whence upon seeing him they made a hasty retreat. He now picked up his friend and carried him to a nearby creek to wash his wounds even though he knew, he could not possibly survive.

The mortally wounded man rasped out a plea for Jackey to get a pencil and paper to write a message, and then died suddenly in his arms.

Holding Kennedy's body tightly, a heart broken Jackey wept over his friend for a full hour. His tears were still falling when he buried his white brother amongst a copse of tea trees, several hundred yards away from the creek where he had washed Kennedy's wounds.

By now the savages had regrouped and attacked Jackey with a barrage of spears as he made his escape to the creek and waded neck deep in the water for half a mile and finally got clear of them by nightfall.

For the next 18 days Jackey struggled north, living on a small native fruit called nonda and the large fruit of the pandanus palm. At times he was so exhausted, he could travel no further and rested for 2 days at a time. At last he stumbled out of the swamps into an open area now known as Jackey Jackey airfield [Higgins Field]. The country was much easier to traverse than the morass he had left behind, but Jackey's strength was failing him and he became weaker by the day. He knew he must keep going if the others were to be saved.

Then, on the 23rd December 1848, he clambered onto a rock on the shore at Port Albany and Coo-eed to an anchored ship.

The ship was the "Ariel" which had been posted at Port Albany in place of both the "Rattlesnake" and the "Bramble", to await any news of the "Lost Expedition".

On board the "Ariel" a lookout had spotted him on the rock and called Captain Dobson. They agreed it must be Jackey considering he was a native wearing trousers.

A boat was immediately sent to fetch him, but once aboard the ship, he fainted. Revived, by a tot of wine, Jackey was able to relate the whole horrifying saga of Kennedy's brutal murder to the authorities. This was written down word for word by Dr Vallack on board the "Ariel".

Ironically, Barbara Thompson was also able to corroborate Kennedy's death as she had heard about his plight even before the Authorities knew of it when she was held captive on Prince of Wales Island. After her rescue in 1849, she was able to tell them the reason for Kennedy's murder.

Over the years there have been many interpretations of why he was murdered in such a brutal manner. One of the most recent do-gooder theories is that he stumbled onto a burial ground of the Yadagana. This is clearly nothing more than a blatant attempt to justify the cold blooded killing of a man who befriended aborigines. This excuse has been rejected, as the Yadagana did not bury their dead in areas prone to heavy flooding. The Escape River catchment is highly flood prone during the wet which is why they did not bury their dead near the river.

Barbara Thompson stated:

> "He was with a blackman named Jackey and that he had been murdered because the warriors had wanted his 'domawaka' the clothes he wore and any material he had."

With Jackey safely on board preparations were being made to rescue the others from the 2 camp sites at Cape Grenville [3 men] and the Pascoe River at Weymouth Bay [8 men]. Of the 13 men who set out on the expedition, only Jackey reached Port Albany. He was the hero of the day, and the lives of the other sick and dying men depended on his ability to locate the camps.

The "Ariel" was not a military vessel, but a 70 ton schooner hired by the government to carry supplies to Cape York for the presumed 2nd stage of the expedition down the west coast.

The flock of live sheep grazing on Albany Island were brought back on board, but a large bullock could not be caught and was shot. As there was no time to butcher it and bring the meat on board it was left behind.

The "Ariel" finally got under way [24th December] and headed south for Cape Grenville near where Costigan, Dunn and Luff had been left. That night they anchored near Shadwell Point and the next day a native canoe approached.

One of the natives was allowed on board, and Jackey instantly recognised him as the native to whom he had given his knife, and the others in the canoe had all been connected with Kennedy's murder. He was immediately arrested, and found on his arm was a piece of dried horse flesh tied on with a segment of bridle.

Seeing their comrade captured, the other natives headed for the shore but were overtaken by the long boat from the "Ariel". the aborigines dived into the sea to escape, except one, who turned and speared Barratt in the arm, before the crew shot him. They later found various items of clothing and part of a saddle iron in the canoe.

The next day the "Ariel" anchored at Shelburne Bay. 6 Miles inland, Costigan, Dunn and Luff had been left to await relief, over a month earlier on the 21st November.

On the beach, 2 natives could be seen wearing blue clothing and a canoe was found the next day with clothing in it, which Jackey identified as belonging to the 3 men.

At day break an attempt was made to reach the camp, but Jackey, although eager, had still not recovered from his ordeal, and after travelling 2 miles inland returned exhausted. He decided the party would need to go further south.

A new landing was made at the southern end of Shelburne Bay, and once again Jackey, Captain Dobson, Dr Vallack, Barratt and a sailor, Tom, trudged inland for almost 6 miles, but failed to find any trace of the 3. Their remains were never found. Rather than spend any more time searching for them, it was decided to sail for Weymouth Bay and hopefully find the party of 8.

Once again it was Jackey who led the way. Although still weak, he refused to slow down and constantly urged the others to reach the explorers as quickly as possible.

The camp at the Pascoe River at Weymouth Bay, was by now a death camp. Of the 8, only 2 survived. The others had all died from malaria and starvation.

When Kennedy had struck out for the Cape to bring speedy relief to his comrades, most of them were too ill even to walk.

He had left Carron in charge, and it was this man who wrote the story of the group's tragic sufferings from notes he kept whilst awaiting the rescue party.

The feeble group had been constantly attacked by aborigines, who pretended friendship in order to get close enough to launch their spears, but always stayed out of range of the guns [60 yards].

Occasionally, they would hold up a dried smelling fish to try and entice the starving survivors towards them in order to spear them. At other times they would walk within a short distance from the camp with an obvious limp. They were trying to bluff the survivors into believing they had no spears with them. In fact they were dragging them along the ground with their toes.

At one time there were several different tribes in the surrounding bush, just waiting for the right moment to kill the sick and starving men. When food ran out they ate their horses, but with no salt to preserve it, were forced to eat the horse meat in a putrid rotting state.

When 60 warriors surrounded the camp, the men refused to be tempted by a fish offered by a native. So they acted out a charade of torture, putting their spears to their necks and sides, mimicking agony, to let the explorers know what a horrible fate awaited them when the spears struck. On this occasion they threw 11 spears, forcing Carron to retaliate with gun fire, which wounded one of them.

The most disheartening experience was the appearance of the "Bramble" in Weymouth Bay only 3 miles from their camp, on the evening of the 1st December.

The ship had anchored for the night in the bay and Carron tried desperately to attract the crew's attention, by lighting a large fire and setting off 3 rockets as well as firing his gun in the hope they would see the flashes.

Convinced of certain rescue the next day, the survivors slept well and awoke in the morning to see a boat on shore. They were positive it had come to collect them, but by the afternoon the crew had failed to reach the camp. By mid-afternoon, Carron again climbed the hill only to see the "Bramble" in full sail heading south until it disappeared over the horizon.

To this day it is not known how the ship's crew failed to see the signals of fire, rockets and gun flashes. One explanation is that the fire was lit on a hill, [later named Barrett Hill] which was several miles inland to the west and the light of the fire was blocked by another hill closer to shore. [Simpson Hill].

This hill may also have prevented the gun flashes from being seen at sea level, but it does not explain why the rockets were not seen.

Defeated by the hostile environment, the explorers slowly succumbed to death. Douglas died on the 16th November, followed by Taylor on the 20th November. They were buried side by side in a shallow grave.

On the 26th November, Carpenter also passed away. By now the survivors were so weak they did not have the strength to dig his grave, and instead, rolled his body into the creek. Mitchell expired on the 13th December. He was found in the morning with his feet in the creek. His body was wrapped in a blanket with stones and sunk beneath the water. Finally Wall and Niblett drew their last breaths on the 28th December. The remaining 2 survivors were so weak by this stage they could only manage to cover the bodies with branches in the nearby gully.

Ironically, the "Ariel" anchored off the mouth of the Pascoe River at Weymouth Bay on the following day, the 29th December.

Meanwhile, the aborigines prepared for their final onslaught on the camp, after failing to tempt the last 2 survivors away with some rotting fish. At this stage, the only remaining animal was a starving sheep dog, who had managed to survive by eating the bones of pigeons, shot for food. He was being primed by the frail survivors for their next meal.

Suddenly, things were about to change, for the next day [30th December] several natives approached the camp forcing Carron to fire his pistol in the air to warn Goddard, who was trying to shoot a pigeon in the scrub. One of the natives held up his hand with a note in it and gave it to Carron. The long awaited rescue party was on its way.

Carron was overjoyed and writing a note in reply handed it to the aborigine to take back to the "Ariel", together with a gift of a shirt. However, the native, had no intention of passing the message on, and tearing the shirt from his back, he rejoined the other warriors in the scrub. Over 100 of them had now surrounded the camp preparing for their final attack.

Fortunately, for the survivors, Jackey was unable to rest knowing that his friends were in danger, and had guided Captain Dobson, Barrett and Dr Vallack to the camp. As the rescue party approached, the aborigines saw they were armed and retreated to the safety of the scrub, realising, that if they attacked now, they would pay a high price.

Jackey, had observed them hiding behind the trees and cautioned Dr Vallack, who later applauded the bravery of this faithful aborigine; he later stated:

> "Whilst here we were considering what was best to be done, when natives in great numbers were descried watching our movements. Jackey said, "Doctor!" calling me aside, "Now I tell you exactly what to do. You see these black fellows over there" (and in pointing to them I saw a great number, some 800 yards away, peeping from behind trees), "You leave him tent, everything, altogether there and get the two white fellows down to the boat quick." Jackey was exceedingly energetic, and grave as well. "Get away as quick as possible" was resounded by all, but what was to be done? Two men almost dead, to walk 2 or 3 miles! We looked over the tent, asked Carron for what important things there were, and each laid hold of what appeared to be of most value, the Captain taking two sextants, other parties, firearms, etc. etc. "Come along," again and again Jackey called out, and the Captain too, whilst they were half-way down the creek, and Barrett and I loaded ourselves. I took a case of seeds, some papers of Carron's, a double gun and brace of pistols, thermometer and my pockets full of powder and shot, was as much as I could manage. Seeing Carron could not get along, I told him to put his hands on my shoulders and in this way he managed to walk down, as far or nearly through the mangrove swamp, towards the water's edge, when he could not in that way get any further, and Barrett, with his disabled arm, carried him down to the edge of the water. Goddard, the other survivor, who was just able to walk down, spoke and looked exceedingly feeble. They were brought on board at noon, and attended to according to my instructions. Carron's legs were dreadfully swollen, about three times their normal size, from oedema. In the afternoon both reviving and thanking God for their deliverance. I was for some time afraid of Carron. At 10pm they are both doing well, and I trust will be enabled to tell us their tale, which will render it unnecessary for me to write it down here. I told the Captain to proceed direct on to Sydney, Jackey, Carron, and Goddard, and the Captain stating it would be running too great a risk to go to recover anything from the tent. Moreover, with so small a party as the Captain, Jackey and myself (Barrett really being unfit to go and the sailors all refusing to go), I consider the Captain deserves considerable credit for his action throughout in exerting himself to rescue the survivors."

With the 2 men safely aboard they sailed directly for Sydney and Carron later wrote of the bravery of his rescuers when he stated:

"I and my companion who was preserved with me, must ever be grateful for the prompt courage with which these persons, at the risk of their own lives, came to our assistance, through the scrub and mangroves, a distance of about three miles, surrounded as they were all the way by a large number of savages."

So ended the "Kennedy Expedition" to Cape York.

"THE VOYAGE OF THE FREAK"

The "Ariel" arrived in Sydney on the 5th March 1849, and the following day an official investigation was held. At this enquiry, Carron presented his own journals of the expedition and their ordeal at the "Camp of Death" at the river later known as the Pascoe River, at Weymouth Bay. The account of Kennedy's death related by Jackey and written down by Dr Vallack on board the "Ariel" was also submitted in evidence.

The verdict was, that those who had planned the expedition were to blame.

A mural tablet made of white marble was erected at Saint James Church of England [near St James station] in Sydney, in memory of the ill fated Kennedy Expedition. It included recognition of the hero of the saga "Jackey Jackey". It reads:

"Jackey Jackey, an aboriginal of merton district, who was Mr Kennedy's sole companion in his conflict with the savages, and though himself wounded, tended his leader with a courage and devotion worthy of remembrance, supporting him in his last moments and making his grave on the spot where he fell."

One of the greatest tributes to Jackey, was paid to him by one of the last of the old time explorers, Robert Logan Jack, who in his book "Northmost Australia" wrote:

"Though tawny was his hide, he was white, clear white inside, and in courage, prudence, resourcefulness and loyalty, he could not be surpassed by the whitest of men".

It was established at the enquiry, the names of the explorers who died at the **"PASCOE RIVER CAMP".**

JOHN DOUGLAS	Labourer	Died: 16th November 1848
EDWARD TAYLOR	Carter	Died: 20th November 1848
EDWARD CARPENTER	Shepherd	Died: 26th November 1848
THOMAS MITCHELL	Labourer	Died: 13th December 1848
THOMAS WALL	Naturalist	Died: 28th December 1848
CHARLES NIBLETT	Storekeeper	Died: 28th December 1848

"CAPE GRENVILLE CAMP"

WILLIAM COSTIGAN	Blacksmith	Died: Date Unknown [accidentally shot]
JAMES LUFF	Carter	Died: Date Unknown
DENNIS DUNN	Labourer	Died: Date Unknown

These 3 were not seen alive again after the 21st November 1848.

With the enquiry over, the Government of New South Wales chartered a brig called the "Freak", under the command of Captain T. Beckford Simpson. He was instructed to locate the camps at Weymouth Bay [Pascoe River] and Cape Grenville [False Pudding-Pan Hill] and inspect them for any remains, and if possible locate the documents that Jackey hid in a hollow log at the Kennedy Inlet, after Kennedy's death.

The "Freak" anchored at the mouth of the Pascoe River, on the 3rd May 1849. Jackey led a party of whites and 2 aborigines from his own tribe, [Jemmy and Tommy] who had sailed from Sydney with him, to Carron's campsite.

They found the camp had been rifled by the natives and books, tins, leather harness etc, were scattered around the camp.

A tree was found nearby engraved with letters carved by Kennedy, "KLXXX". This was the 80th camp.

The searchers now concentrated on looking for the remains of Wall and Niblett. These were the last 2 to die and had not been buried. Simpson checked around the scrub and found them in a gully, submerged beneath 2 feet of water. Their remains were taken aboard the "Freak" and later buried further north on Albany Island.

Leaving the Pascoe, the "Freak" headed north and anchored at Shelburne Bay [4th May]. In the morning the crew started searching the coastline of this large bay and occasionally fired a gun as they went. They landed at 3 different sites and at the 2nd one saw a native canoe and a camp. In the canoe they found a leather pistol holster with number 34 engraved on it.

Jackey instantly identified it as belonging to one of the missing men. They surmised that the men were all dead, although they could not ascertain whether they had been murdered or had died from other causes.

During the search, the base of a mast from a 400 ton vessel with wreckage was found. The fate of her crew was never solved.

On the evening of the 6th May the "Freak" anchored at the Escape River and sighted another vessel. This was the "Coquette", with Captain Elliott at the helm. The following morning a whaleboat from the "Coquette" joined the search for Kennedy's remains.

As the boats headed up the river, Jackey pointed out where the various incidents had occurred. After 12 miles they landed at a site free of mangroves where the river was now only 30 yards wide. It was here that Jackey had told Kennedy to swim the river knowing the natives would track the horses easier than if they walked without them. Nearby he pointed to a tree where he tied the horses whilst he searched for oysters.

Boarding the 2 boats the searchers of 11 men continued for another 3 miles upstream when the river narrowed to a fresh water creek. The searchers landed on the western bank [left] near a large open plain with numerous termite mounds. During their search Jackey pointed out where "horse tumble down creek" after being speared and to substantiate his claim, horse dung was found after months of rain.

The site where Kennedy lay mortally wounded was marked by 3 termite mounds. Jackey had propped his dying leader against the middle one.

He led the searchers through the scrub to 3 young pandanus trees, near the creek where he had washed Kennedy's wounds. It was here that Kennedy died. Next, he led the way to a tea tree scrub several hundred yards away where he buried him in a shallow grave.

The men searched the area for hours, pointing their ramrods into the ground trying to locate the body, without success. Nearby they found a prismatic compass clearly showing they had hit the right spot. The valuable saddle bags were also missing and had obviously been taken by the natives.

The search continued until late in the afternoon, and since night was approaching they gave up and headed back to the boats. Rowing back to the river mouth they camped at 11pm near Shadwell Point.

The next morning at 10am, the boats reached their ships and were taken aboard. After lunch, the ships left the Escape River and anchored that night at Albany Island.

At dawn [11th May] Mr Macnate, the Chief Officer of the "Freak" took Jackey and his 2 aboriginal companions [Tommy and Jemmy] in the whaleboat, south to the Kennedy Inlet, to search for Kennedy's important papers of charts and diaries, that Jackey had hidden in a hollow log after escaping from the Yadagana. After rowing 11 miles up the inlet, Jackey led them inland for 2 miles through the scrub to the hollow log.

Some of the papers were found on the ground, where a rat had removed them from their hiding place. They were saturated with water and badly damaged. They were carefully collected and taken to the "Freak" at Albany Island.

On Sunday, the 13th of May 1849, the remains of Wall and Niblett were taken to the highest rise on the southern part of Albany Island and buried after a funeral service read by a passenger, Christopher Hay D'Oyley Aplin.

It is ironic, that 26 years later, this same man was buried beside them after he died across the pass at the future site of Somerset.

Before leaving Albany Pass, Captain Simpson completed his report on the search for Kennedy's remains and in reference to Jackey, he stated:

> *"Jackey Jackey was very quiet, but felt and felt deeply during the day. When pointing out the spot where Mr Kennedy died, I saw tears in his eyes, and no one could be more indefatigable in searching for the remains. His feelings against the natives were bitter and had any of them made an appearance at that time, I could barely have prevented him from shooting them."*

The Kennedy Expedition, had cost the lives of 10 men, which made it the most tragic exploratory expedition in Australian history. Kennedy, however, was remembered for his great leadership qualities by Carron, who wrote:

> *"I am confident that no man could have done more for the safety of the party than was done by Mr Kennedy, nor could any man have exerted himself more than he in the distressing circumstances of our perilous journey. He walked by far the greater part of the distance, giving his one horse for the use of the weak man and the general use of the expedition... The unfortunate death of our brave and generous leader, deeply and extensively as I know it has been lamented, can have no more sincere mourner than myself. The tale of his sufferings and those of his party has already been read and sympathised over by hundreds and it would ill become me to add anything to the artless narrative of the faithful and true hearted Jackey who having tended his last moments and closed his eyes, was the first and perhaps the most disinterested bewailer of his unhappy fate."*

In memory of the explorers, various plants have been named in their honour on Cape York. These include the Pitcher plant or "Nepenthes Kennedyi". a wild plant named after William Carron called, "Bauhinia Carroni" and a native grass that is highly durable called "Galmarra", Jackey's native name.

On Jackey's return to Sydney, he was feted as the hero of the expedition, although he could not understand what all the fuss was about. A bank account was opened in his name with a deposit of £50 and he was highly decorated with a brass medal presented to him by the authorities.

In his later years he went droving, and is believed to have fallen into a campfire whilst drunk and died from the burns.

Although William Carron survived the expedition, the ordeal had taken a toll on his health and he died at the age of 50 on the 20th February 1876.

In 1973, an army patrol attempted to find the site of Kennedy's grave. With the use of 4 wheel drive vehicles and outboard motor boats, they made it to the Escape River and claim to have found the site where Kennedy was murdered. Even the termite mounds were said to be still there although diminished in size.

Flanked with this success, a second patrol later ventured in on foot. Trudging through the slime of the swamps, they appreciated the incredible journey that Kennedy and Jackey had undertaken. They finally dragged themselves out of the bog and left it to the dead.

*The pioneers created their own entertainment.
Eric Foxton on a dead crocodile at Somerset.*

*Chum Jardine
Frank Jardine's eldest son.*

Chapter 5
"SOMERSET – A REFUGE FOR CASTAWAYS"

THE SAPPHIRE MASSACRE

By 1854, 70 shipwrecks were recorded within 100 miles of Cape York and the Torres Strait, with the loss of over150 lives.

In that same year the French had established a colony at New Caledonia.

Once again the subject of a station at Cape York was raised only to be shelved.

Then, on the 23rd September 1859, the 700 ton "Sapphire", was wrecked near the notorious Raine Island.

As the ship was in danger of breaking up, supplies were put into the 2 boats and launched.

The life boat held 18 men including Captain Bowden, whilst the covered boat [Pinnace] held the remaining 10, under the charge of the Mate, William Beveridge.

They headed for Booby Island refuge, where they stayed for over a week in the hope of being picked up by a passing ship, to no avail.

Finally, they left Booby Island and headed east to Friday Island at the northern end of Prince of Wales [Muralug].

Here, the pinnace anchored and sent 5 men ashore to trade with the Kauraregas, whilst the lifeboat continued a mile north towards Hammond Island [Keriri].

Meanwhile, on the Pinnace, Beveridge suspected treachery, as he observed the natives being reinforced with heavily armed warriors preparing to attack his men.

The crew instantly yelled out to them to swim for the boat. 3 Of them made it safely. The last 2 were not so fortunate.

One of these was speared in the back, whilst the other was wounded and dragged aboard. The crew now opened fire and hit 2 warriors, killing one instantly.

With one man dead [Schmallfuss] and another wounded they left in search of the lifeboat.

As they headed towards Hammond Island, they heard a yell from the water and rescued Richard Law.

He now related the horrifying massacre of the crew in the lifeboat.

"Captain Bowden had come across 25 Kauraregas in 3 canoes. They offered to trade some turtles, as a pretense to friendship.

A trade was made for 2 turtles, that lay on the stage of an empty canoe. The natives having left it and joined their comrades on the other canoes. It all seemed safe enough as the sailors boarded the empty canoe to collect the turtles.

In the meantime, the Kauraregas manoeuvred their canoes into position and suddenly attacked the unarmed sailors. Spear after spear rained into the crowded whaleboat, impaling the sailors through the head, heart and stomach.

Richard Law instantly threw himself out of the boat the moment the savages commenced their attack, and was not seen by them as he swam away and observed the whole horrifying massacre".

Now safely on board the Pinnace, he saw the lifeboat bearing down on them, rigged with pandanus sails and manned by over a dozen warriors.

Instantly, the sail on the Pinnace was hoisted and Beveridge urged his men to row with every ounce of energy in their bodies as the savages screamed for their blood.

For 2 hours the chase continued until finally, hungry and exhausted, the Kauraregas dropped back and gave up the chase.

That day they took home 18 human heads, whence they were cooked and eaten after the death dance to celebrate their victory over the helpless castaways.

Meanwhile Beveridge and his crew headed back to the wreck site at Raine Island and arrived within a few days, when they noted a wreck which they thought was the "Sapphire", but on a close inspection it turned out to be the 500 ton "Marina" which was wrecked on the 5th October 1859 [Captain Jamieson].

She had been wrecked during their absence to Booby Island and abandoned by her crew, who headed south in the life boats.

Beveridge and his crew boarded the wreck and realised there was little danger of it sinking as its cargo of timber had buoyed it up, keeping it afloat.

They decided to sail the water filled wreck as far south as possible. Again and again she was reefed as she refused to sail a straight course and each time the sailors coaxed her back into deeper water.

For 12 weeks they sweated day and night, living off the ships water logged supplies, until finally after a thousand miles they reached Port Curtis [Gladstone] on the 17th February 1860.

"John Jardine", the first Police Magistrate of Somerset.

The "Jardines" from the left: Charles Lennox, Frank Lascelles, Captain John Jardine, John Robert and Alexander William [taken 1866].

Inside the verandah of the Somerset Homestead.

SOMERSET

Of all the settlements established during Australia's colonial era, none could surpass the violence and isolation of Somerset, only 5 miles south of Cape York.

Its very existence was necessitated by the constant massacres of helpless castaways from the countless shipwrecks of this cannibal infested region.

For over 20 years during the early 1800's the issue had been discussed but nothing was done about it. Even after the rescue of Barbara Thompson in 1849, there was still no sign of the authorities making a decision about establishing a settlement in the area.

Then, on the 10th December 1859, Queensland seceded from New South Wales and became an independent state.

With the massacre of 18 men from the "Sapphire" still fresh on their minds, the Queensland Government was jolted into doing something positive on the issue.

Queensland's Governor, George Furguson Bowen, believed that a settlement at Cape York, would provide a "Refuge for Castaways", as well as a coaling station for steamers and a trading post that would eventually become the Singapore of Australia.

As Queensland could not afford to establish such an outpost, the British Government came to the rescue and donated £5000 towards its cost and to protect the new settlement they would send a detachment of Royal Marines and a naval doctor.

On the 29th July 1864, "HMS Salamander", a British navy steamsloop, arrived at Albany Pass with 20 British Marines aboard. The following day [1st August] the barque "Golden Eagle" arrived. On board were 96 sheep and the prefabricated buildings to be erected by the marines. A small band of civilians were also aboard including, the Police Magistrate of the new settlement, "John Jardine", his 17 year old son "John", the Works Foreman "J Halpin" with a carpenter, and the Surveyor "WCB Wilson" with 2 chainmen.

The site originally chosen was the bay known as Port Albany on Albany Island. However Jardine preferred a much better site across the pass on the mainland, where there was an abundance of fresh water, continually seeping from the fringing rainforest onto the beach at the south east end of the bay.

The sheep were landed on Albany Island and the 20 marines under the command of Lieutenant Pascoe of whom the Pascoe River is named, landed on the mainland at the new settlement site. It was named "Somerset", after the Duke of Somerset, First Lord of the British Admiralty.

The rainforest was cleared and the military establishment erected on the hill at the north western end of the bay, known as Somerset Hill [Point].

The Police Magistrate's residence was built on a rise overlooking the picturesque Albany Pass and several hundred yards south west of the marine camp on Somerset Hill. At a later date a hospital was erected near the barracks.

On the 21st August 1864, Somerset was officially proclaimed a settlement and harbour of refuge.

The "Golden Eagle" left Somerset on the 30th August and the "Salamander" departed a week later [7th September]. With the departure of the ships the new residents were on their own, surrounded on 3 sides by hostile aboriginal tribes. The "Salamander" was not expected back for another 3 months with supplies.

By the middle of September, the Police Magistrate's residence was partially completed, allowing Jardine and young John to move into the kitchen until the rest of the house was finished.

Whilst the marines were still busy clearing the scrub and erecting buildings, the entire area was being surveyed for building lots by the Surveyor Wilson and his chainmen. Their task was not made any easier by the aborigines who stole the pegs as fast as they could be replaced.

The first of numerous aboriginal attacks took place on the 13th September when 2 marines were speared. One of these was seriously wounded with a spear in his chest.

During the assault, Jardine identified 4 of the warriors involved. Returning to his residence he could see a large number of natives amassing in the surrounding scrub. A further bombardment of long barbed spears missed his son's head by an inch and one of them sunk deep into the hardwood corner post of the house.

Over the next few weeks there were many attacks against the settlement, causing everyone to be constantly on their guard.

Jardine patrolled around the settlement on foot every second day and noticed he had always been followed, by the aboriginal tracks he saw in the sand. On October 15th he rowed across to Albany Island and saw 6 natives in a canoe. Recognising them as the aborigines who had speared the marines, Jardine ordered the marines to pursue them. In the ensuing fight they were killed and later identified as the same warriors who had callously attacked the marines.

The natives made a repeated practice of raiding the settlement and stealing various items of value to them such as metal tools. A raid by the marines on the native camp at Evans Bay, 4 miles to the north, uncovered the metal fashioned into spear heads and knives. In retaliation, 2 horses were speared the next day and 2 others belonging to the Surveyor, Wilson were stolen. The horses, including the wounded ones, were later returned in reasonable condition. Fortunately the spears had only struck the fatty tissue and had not penetrated to the bone.

"Jaki"
Elizabeth Jardine poses on a crocodile killed at Somerset.
She was named after Dr Jack Hamilton of the Palmer River.

NAME AND RANK OF THE TWENTY BRITISH MARINES BASED AT SOMERSET 1864-1867

R.J. PASCOE	Lieutenant Commanding Officer
MORRIS GUIVER	Sergeant
DAVID DENT	Corporal
CHARLES JARVIS	Private
EDGAR BAXTER	Private
SAMUEL WILKINSON	Private
CHARLES COPELEY	Private
GEORGE TUCKER	Private
JOHN SAICH	Private
WILLIAM CARMICHAEL	Private
RICHARD WHELE	Private
THOMAS RICE	Private
JONATHON LAWTON	Private
JAMES BOSWORTH	Private
WILLIAM TIMMS	Private
THOMAS COLWILL	Private
JOHN SMITH	Private
WILLIAM O'REGAN	Private
EDWARD WALLIS	Private
JOSEPH BLAKE	Private

Corporal David Dent and Private John Saich were speared by Aborigines on the 13th September 1864.

Corporal Dent was wounded in the left shoulder by a barbed spear and survived.

Private John Saich was wounded by 2 spears, One 4 pronged spear struck his right arm and was easily extracted. However, the other, a normal pointed spear entered the lung.

His condition was so serious that he was removed to the Military Hospital in Sydney, where he died on the 21st April 1865.

Dr Richard Cannon, R.N. temporarily relieved Dr Timotheus J. Haran, who returned on board the Salamander to Brisbane, to bring back his wife and young daughter. [This daughter and their later baby died at Somerset. As no timber was available, a coffin was made from the door of one of the marine's cottages].

The Jardine Cannons were salvaged from a shipwreck.

Frank Jardine's home, rebuilt from the old Residency, with 2 of his children in the foreground. The rock garden on the left is still intact today.

— SOMERSET HOMESTEAD —

The Jardine home when it was rebuilt by Chum Jardine after Frank Jardine's death. A mango tree is now growing from the rock garden at left.

The Vidgen's home at Paira, 2 miles north of Somerset.

Alice Vidgen, Frank Jardine's eldest daughter with 2 of her 3 sons, "Gordon" and "Boy".

CAPE YORK AND THE WESTERN TORRES STRAIT ISLANDS

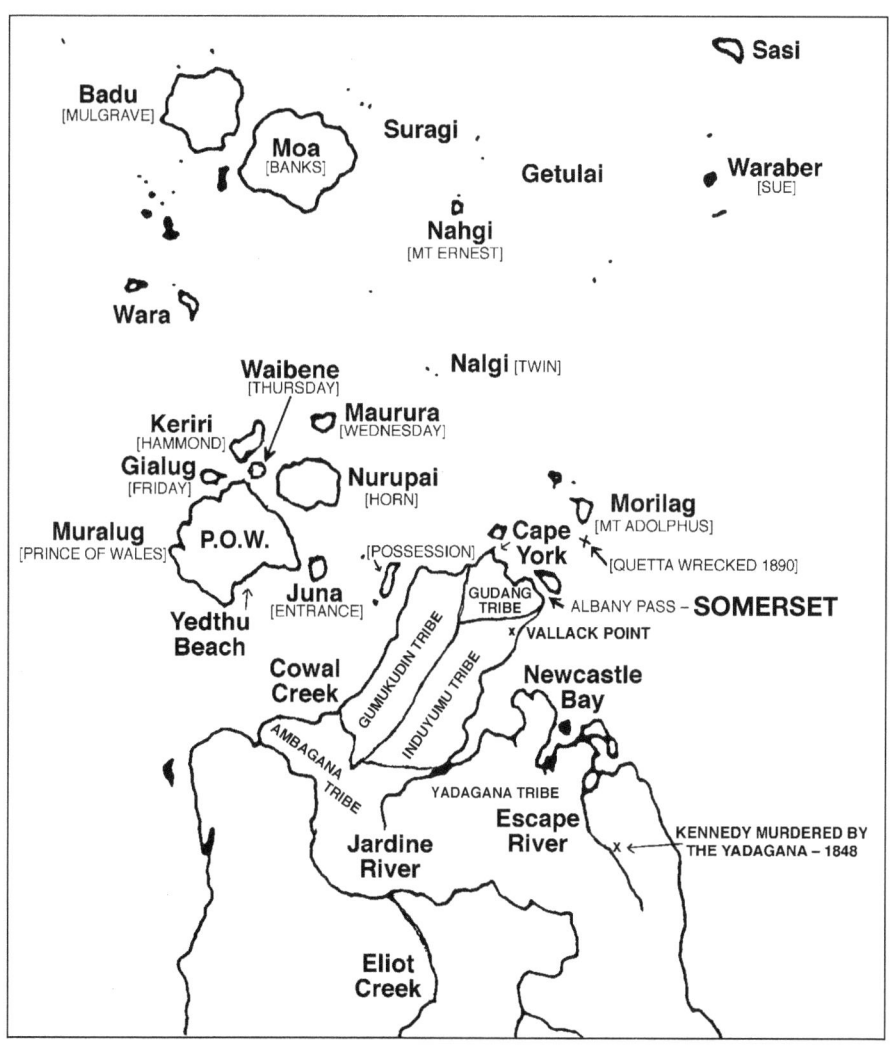

Police Magistrate Frank Jardine – eldest son of Police Magistrate John Jardine.

CORSAIRS OF THE CORAL SEA – *Boydan Island: Site of the Charles Eaton Massacre in 1834*

CORSAIRS OF THE CORAL SEA
The beacon on Raine Island still stands today [Credit H Hofer].

CORSAIRS OF THE CORAL SEA
Raine Island: Site of countless shipwrecks [Credit H Hofer].

KENNEDY EXPEDITION
Pascoe River: Where 6 explorers perished in 1848.

KENNEDY EXPEDITION
*Escape River: Kennedy was murdered further upstream by aborigines in 1848.
It is now a pearling station.*

BARBARA THOMPSON – *Prince of Wales Island where Barbara Thompson was held captive for 5 years. The "Serpents Head" is Yule Point. Arrow points to Yedthu Beach.*

BARBARA THOMPSON
Kaurarega Campsite: Corroboree ground. Yedthu Beach. P.O.W.

BARBARA THOMPSON
Kaurarega Campsite: Yedthu Beach. Shallow water prevented canoes landing close inshore [Credit H Hofer].

BARBARA THOMPSON – *Submerged ribbon reefs north of Hammond Island [Keriri].*

BARBARA THOMPSON
The N.W. coast of Keriri where Barbara Thompson [Giom] outraced Wini's war canoes.

BARBARA THOMPSON
The bay where Barbara Thompson escaped into the mangroves on Keriri [Hammond Island].

BARBARA THOMPSON – *Boat channel from Thursday Island, with Horn Island [Nurapai] on the left and Prince of Wales [Muralug] on the right.*

BARBARA THOMPSON – *Cape York from the north. Wamalug Island [right] and Deliverance Beach [tiny beach on the left], with Evans Bay behind it. In the background is Newcastle Bay where Kennedy was murdered at the Escape River.*

BARBARA THOMPSON – *Wamalug Island [Cape York Island] from where Barbara Thompson escaped to Cape York.*

BARBARA THOMPSON – *Cape York from the east [foreground].*
Prince of Wales Island [Muralug] in the hazy distance [right – below white cloud].

BARBARA THOMPSON – *Deliverance Beach – right [Author's title] where Barbara Thompson was rescued by sailors from HMS Rattlesnake on the 16th October 1849.*

JARDINE CATTLE DRIVE – *The mouth of the Jardine River.*

ALBANY ISLAND – *Albany Island is a "Sacred and Historical European Site" where 2 of the Kennedy explorers are buried as well as missionaries, pearlers and Police Magistrate Christopher D'Oyley Aplin [White Cross] [Credit H Hofer].*

SOMERSET – *The armoury and lookout on Somerset Hill.*

SOMERSET – *Somerset Beach: Looking towards Somerset Hill [Point] where the marine camp once stood, whilst the remains of the slipway pylons are still visible on the beach.*

SOMERSET – *The British Marine Camp on Somerset Hill with the 3 married mens cottages on the left, the barracks in the centre and the hospital far right. The slipway can be seen on the beach running from the boatshed*

THE JARDINE RIVER SECTION OF THE JARDINE CATTLE DRIVE 1864 – 1865

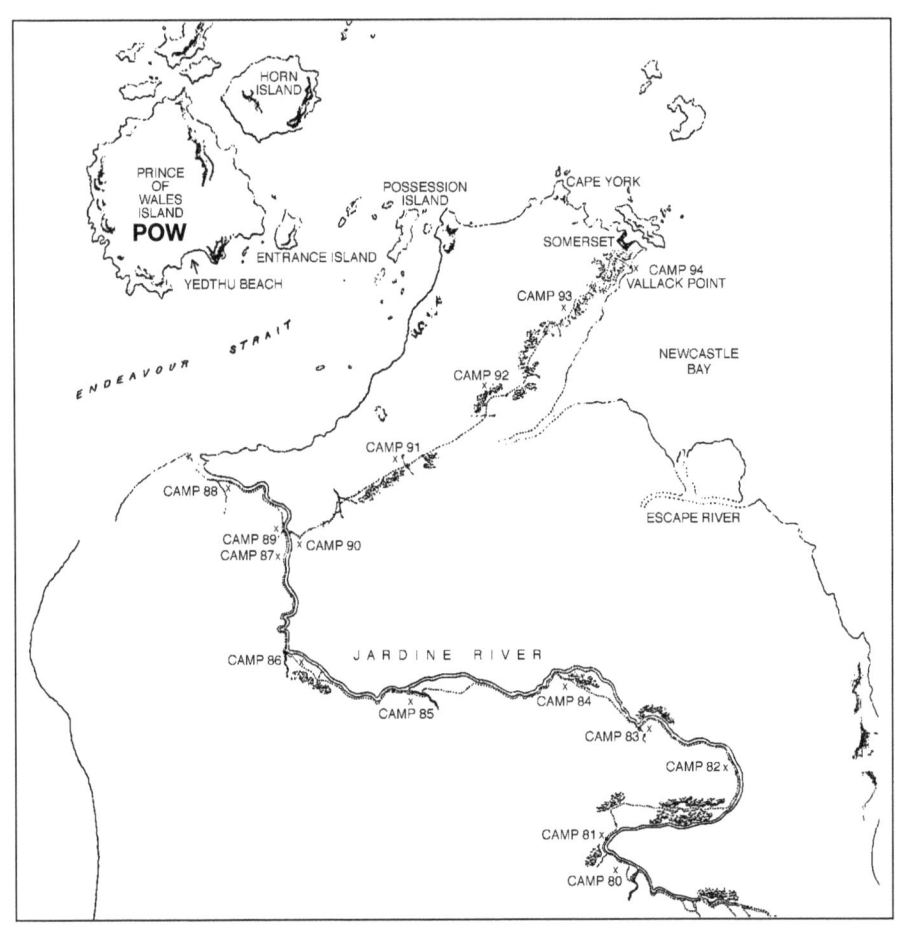

NOTE: The crossing point was Camp 89, not 87 as stated by some writers.
Drawn by A J Richardson 1865
"Reproduced with permission of the Department of Lands, Qld."

CHAPTER 6
"THE JARDINE CATTLE DRIVE"

Before Somerset was established, Captain John Jardine had suggested to the Authorities that his eldest son should bring 250 head of cattle overland to the new settlement to provide fresh beef for the residents of Somerset as well as future castaways. Beef could also be sold to passing ships calling in for supplies of coal.

The authorities accepted this suggestion and plans were made for the most amazing cattle drive in Australian history.

Captain Jardine's eldest son Frank Lascelles Jardine, aged 22 was the leader and his younger brother Alexander, aged 20, was second in command. They would be accompanied by a government surveyor Archibald J Richardson, and an additional 7 men including Charles Scrutton, a wiry character who had spent most of his life defying death in the lonely bush, Richard N Binney [Roy], Alfred Cowderoy and 4 trusted aboriginal stockmen.

One of these was "Black Eulah", who was Frank Jardine's closest and most reliable companion. The other 3 were Peter, Sambo and Barney.

These men were invested with the task of driving the herd of bulls and cows 1200 miles to Somerset at the top of Cape York, through some of the worst country imaginable in Australia.

The horses and cattle were collected and driven to the most northerly station at that time from Rockhampton to "Carpentaria Downs" near the Gulf of Carpentaria. In the meantime Frank and Richardson had collected additional horses and cattle and brought them through to Carpentaria Downs Station.

In preparation for the gruelling trip that lay ahead, the 41 horses and a mule were shod under a shade temperature of over 100 degrees fahrenheit. It took 3 long days before the animals were all shod [fitted with shoes].

At sunrise on the 11th October, the expedition was on its way and by the 16th they were already being tracked by 50 armed warriors painted for war. The cattlemen tried to ignore them so as to prevent any hostilities. Jardine had made it clear to all, that there would be no shooting unless it was absolutely necessary. Throughout the day the aborigines continued to trail them, waiting for the right moment to attack.

Jardine realised that sooner or later they would be at the mercy of the aborigines, and as they passed the western side of Cawana Swamp he gave the signal for the cattlemen to turn and face the warriors. They immediately fled into the surrounding scrub, frightened by the spectacle of the giant animals with strange men on their backs, who could soon crush them into the dust if they charged.

Within days, word of their fearlessness had filtered through to the surrounding tribes on the cape and many avoided them.

On the 19th they found freshly cooked human remains at an abandoned campsite. As the fire was still hot, the occupants must have fled at their approach. They were now in cannibal country, for the body was cut up ready for eating.

Several days later they found good grass and rested the animals. They had now travelled 100 of the 1000 miles and already some of the cattle were lame.

As the cows were calving, the weak calves were killed and their flesh dried for food.

It was a common practice for the Jardine brothers and Eulah to scout ahead and mark a treeline for the cattle to follow. Sometimes they could be up to 30 miles in front of the cattle searching for the most practical route.

Whilst on one of these treks, the dry grass caught fire during their absence at camp 16 on the 5th November. More than half their supplies of food were destroyed and nearly all their clothing, boots, blankets and assorted equipment.

What they did salvage was only saved by the quick actions of Charlie Scrutton, who grabbed several canisters of gun powder in his bare hands as the solder was melting at the seams. Although he severely burnt his hands he saved much of the camp in the process. Fortunately the cattle had been moved earlier in the day.

Moving on again, they entered the poison scrub. A young steer and cow were left behind poisoned, and a horse Marion also died from the poison bush or snake bite. By now they were moving along the Staaten River and the aborigines were mustering for a showdown as they kept constant watch over the cattlemen.

The country had now changed from a dry barren wasteland to a greener, more inviting landscape. On the 20th November, a thunderstorm broke overhead and the warriors bided their time as the cattlemen set up the camp. By dusk, the aborigines were in position with the sun behind them, ready to impale the men on their 9 foot spears.

More than 20 aborigines attacked from the setting sun. The shower of spears fell around the camp but the cattlemen escaped injury and retaliated with a fusillade of lead, scattering the warriors who remained out of range of the guns [Camp 27].

Throughout the night the natives returned to steal the horses and the next morning as they were moving camp, they discovered 13 were missing. It took them almost a week to locate them in the torrid climate, plagued by mosquitoes, sandflies and marsh flies. No sooner had they found them and 15 cattle strayed overnight, of which only 7 were ever found [Camp 28].

Frank Jardine often set out alone to reconnoitre the land ahead. On one such mission he was crossing a sandstone gully when he was attacked by a dozen aborigines. Without warning, a spear flew past his face. He retaliated instantly, firing 3 shots in succession and hitting 3 of his attackers. The others beat a hasty retreat, unable to believe the speed at which their comrades had fallen.

One annoying problem at Camp 28, were the flocks of crows and Kites [hawks] scavenging after any morsel they could grab. The kites would actually swoop down and grab the meat cooking on the fire. The aboriginal stockmen had a field day killing them with sticks and captured spears. Yet, for everyone killed another 20 took their place.

During the aboriginal attacks, old "Eulah" loved collecting the spears and throwing them back against his own countrymen.

As the cattle were moved further down the Staaten River, Jardine scouted ahead. As a spear passed within 6 inches of his face he whirled round and shot the man who threw it, when his 6 comrades instantly fled. Later, after meeting up with the cattlemen, he learnt that they had also been attacked in force but had fought a determined defence against their assailants who then retreated.

By now their food supplies were rapidly dwindling and the wet season would soon be on its way. The horses and cattle were all in poor condition and occasionally a weak steer or cow would be killed and the meat sun dried and salted to keep fresh.

For sometime now, the expedition had been travelling west along the Staaten River to the Gulf of Carpentaria. They noticed with horror the floodmarks on the tree trunks and realised if the wet season broke they would be in serious trouble. The Jardines named the river the "Ferguson" after Sir George Ferguson Bowen. They did not realise it was already named the "Staaten".

On the 3rd December they approached the mouth of the river which was now becoming salty. They camped in a thunderstorm which turned the ground into a quagmire, bogging cattle and horses upto their bellies. Alec Jardine took the opportunity to explore ahead and saw crocodile tracks. They must now prepare for the northern run.

By the 5th December the expedition was heading north across sandy ridges and tea tree flats. That evening they camped in a waterless wasteland [Camp 37].

The next morning, 28 horses were missing, They had strayed overnight in search of water and were now scattered over 100 square miles of the country side.

During the week it took to locate them, they lost 2 of their best hacks. One of these was "Deceiver" who died of thirst, and the other was "Lucifer" who was last seen galloping to his death, near camp 35. He was covered in a sweaty white foam and had gone mad from drinking salt water.

Their greatest loss was the mule which was never seen again. It had wandered away from the camp in broad daylight. Sambo had tracked him for 2 days all the way to camp 35 on the Staaten. He noticed that for some reason it had been galloping. [It may have been wounded by an aboriginal spear and galloped away in a panic].

Unable to find it, Sambo returned to camp delirious through not having had any water during the 2 day search. The mule had been carrying the Jardines spare pairs of boots, and more importantly a shovel which had been used to dig for water. During the horse hunt, Scrutton and Cowderoy became extremely ill from drinking stagnant water, the only water available.

By the 15th December, the expedition was approaching the Mitchell River and camped at Dunbar Creek, one of the many tributaries of the Mitchell. "Eulah" had found a paradise for them. The creek was crystal clear here, with grassy banks, shaded by tropical palms. There was plenty of wildlife in the surrounding forest, including scrub turkeys and wallabies. The creek was named Eulah Creek in his honour but was changed by Officialdom to "Magnificent Creek" [Camp 40].

Leaving behind this bountiful camp, they headed 6 miles in a north easterly direction and found jungle so dense they had to cut a track through it.

Once out of the forest into open country, the Jardine brothers moved ahead, but their ease of travel was short lived. Ahead of them was a band of tall solidly built warriors who dared the Jardines to come closer. As they did so the natives retreated across a creek, and leaving their women on the other side, swam back heavily armed and attempted to surround them. The brothers repelled the resulting volley of spears with lead and their defensive shots left 9 warriors dead.

Whilst travelling through this region, they noticed the natives expertise in creating small dams and weirs for trapping fish, which were plentiful in the streams.

BATTLE OF THE MITCHELL

On the 17th December, the cattlemen reached the Mitchell River. Their pleasure at the sight was shortlived. For, the next day [18th December] they experienced the most frightening confrontation of the entire trip. The incident was later known as the "Battle of the Mitchell".

Following along the river bank for 9 miles, they came to the major stream which was 100 feet wide. The cattle were halted here whilst the Jardines and Eulah searched for a good crossing.

About a mile downstream, they surprised some natives fishing, who immediately swam across the river. When the cattlemen retraced their path along the river, the natives swam back with spears and clubs with a determination to kill them. The men, as usual tried to avoid a fight and headed back to their camp.

Interpreting this move as whiteman's fear, the warriors yelled and screamed in hot pursuit as the horsemen tried to outrun them. The situation soon dissolved into a battle, with spears raining down thick and fast and gunshots reverberating in reply.

Back at the camp, the cattlemen heard the shooting and galloped to the scene. The full compliment of 10 men fired into the savage horde of 80 charging aborigines.

After expending all their spears, Frank halted the shooting, allowing the natives to retreat back across the river after leaving 30 of their comrades dead on the river bank.

As the cattlemen left the battleground, a warrior filled with a vengeful hate hid in the water near the river bank and threw a spear, missing Charlie Scrutton by a hairs breadth. He was instantly shot dead.

Although none of the cattlemen were killed, they had some very close shaves. Alec Jardine had a spear land between his legs and Scrutton received an arm injury.

The group took several days to leave the Mitchell Basin travelling through boggy melon hole country in pouring rain, that turned the land into a quagmire.

In the afternoon shadows of the 21st December, the natives were seen trying to stalk the cattlemen once again. They were using the eternal camouflage ploy of hiding behind portable branches and advancing on the camp. The sharp eyes of the native stockmen soon spotted them. The cattlemen now played a game of cat and mouse by moving towards them, slowly at first, then suddenly increasing their pace in short spurts, which caused the warriors to drop their weapons in their haste to get away. They repeated the game for 2 miles and as darkness approached they strolled back to camp, laughing at the humour of the situation and collecting the abandoned spears [Camp 47].

A week later whilst camped at a lotus lagoon at Thalia Creek, one of the native stockmen raced into camp yelling that he had been hunted by the aborigines and they were running the horses. The brothers and Scrutton grabbed their guns and prepared for another fight. Frank donned a short coat with a gun in each pocket and jumped onto the bare back of his horse as a thunder storm approached.

Alexander Jardine and Scrutton each wore a long mackintosh to protect their carbines from the rain. One wore black and the other white.

The warriors waited in the nearby mangroves for the men to come within range before throwing their spears. The men retaliated with their terry breech loaders as spears showered within 60 yards of them.

As the thunder cracked overhead amid brilliant lightning flashes the cattle went into a stampede and the natives retreated.

In these conditions, the cattle could not be rounded up in this dark stormy night. They were let go and recovered the next day. 10 Of them were never found (Camp 54).

By now the wet season had well and truly set in and there was still over 200 miles to cover. Along the route cattle were dying or lost themselves in the scrub.

The country changed almost daily from tea tree flats to turkey bush scrub – miles of matted vines which constantly impeded their progress.

For a thousand miles they had forced their way up the peninsula constantly tormented by hordes of mosquitoes and flies, harassed by violent aboriginal tribes and battling the elements. Now, like Kennedy they were running out of time, within reach of their destination. It was now a contest between man and nature as they struggled towards their goal.

The group was a sorry sight – with their clothes rotted away, leaving them naked except for the long shirts on their backs. Their boots had worn out long ago and they now wore bush sandals made of rawhide as they pushed through the slime of bogs and primeval jungle, where no white man had ever trod.

As they continued through the boxwood flats, they spent hours each day hauling cattle out of the bogs. They finally reached the Batavia River [Wenlock] and crossed in safety and camped 6 miles north of it [Camp 65].

The next day as they headed north through boggy tea tree flats, 40 cattle bogged to their bellies. They spent the day hauling them out with their horses, until 5 were left. As only their head and back were above the mire, they had to be abandoned.

The next day [11th January] they battled through more bogs and slush and after 2 miles reached a creek that was flooded from bank to bank, 80 feet wide and running like a mill sluice. Now their troubles were really just beginning.

To get the saddles and stores across, they felled a large tea tree over the river as a footbridge and carried everything over. Then the cattle were herded into the creek and swam across with only one drowning and finally it was the horses turn.

2 Of these became tangled by vines in the middle of the creek even though they were being pulled across with ropes.

Although Alexander Jardine managed to reach them he could not free them and was almost drowned himself when he was hit on the head by a log whilst trying to untangle his own horse "Jack" and Richardson's horse "Blokus". Both horses drowned.

They continued north leading the horses through more bogs and swamp under a constant deluge of heavy rain. After a mile of this, they were forced to turn back to the creek. The bogs were so bad that 5 horses were left behind stuck in the mire.

The camp was set up about ½ a mile from the creek crossing where there was good grass [Camp 67, 11th January].

It was decided to stay here for 24 hours to allow the horses to recuperate and dry out the packs. In the morning the horses left in the bog were pulled out and brought back to camp.

Upon arrival at the creek, it was found that 4 other horses were poisoned by some mysterious herb and another one was missing. Therefore all the horses were penned in a makeshift yard and any herbs dug up.

The precautions came too late as the 5 horses pulled from the bog also died and the missing horse [Rasper] was found dead in the creek after going blind from the poison.

The symptoms were described:
Profuse sweating, with a heaving of the flanks, the ears droop, the eyes glaze, set, and the horse finally turns stone blind. He then lies down, struggles fitfully for several hours, and never rises again.

With the loss of 10 horses poisoned and 2 drowned, there were now only 21 left. As there were not enough horses to carry their supplies, then all equipment not needed was buried in a cache beneath a tree on top of a ridge facing the creek and marked in a shield; FJ over LXVII over DIG in a heart.

The creek was aptly named "Poison Creek" [Nimrod Creek]. Frank Jardine wrote in his diary on the 12th January" *"Black Thursday-nil Desperandum"*. Finally on the 13th January they were glad to leave this fatal camp and continued north.

Torrential storms lashed the land each evening, turning it into an oozing swamp overnight. By day the strong Cape York sun dried the swamps to mud puddles.

By now all the best horses were either dead or missing, for the poison attacked the healthier ones more so than the weaker ones.

Day after day they forged their way through miles of swamps of the tea tree flats. To lighten the load, the horses packs had to be carried across the bogs. Yet, despite these trials and tribulations, they could not drop their vigilance. They were again tracked by aborigines, who were circling their prey, waiting to strike like hawks, when the men were at their weakest.

Frank Jardine had a policy of firing only if the natives were about to attack, for he did not wish to be the aggressor. So they waited for the strike, when finally, the stand-off erupted into conflict as the aborigines pitched their fishbone barbed spears at the cattlemen.

2 Shots were fired in retaliation and 2 warriors fell, and the others instantly retreated in a panic. Frank Jardine freely admits to wanting a "shine" with these wretched savages and rightfully so, for they had dogged their footsteps all through the thickest of their troubles, watching with cowardly patience for the right moment to attack them [Byerley].

As in all other confrontations along the route, it was the aborigines who commenced hostilities, even when the cattlemen went out of their way to avoid them.

This was the last battle between the aborigines and the cattlemen [14th Jan. 1865].

By now the men had become very disillusioned. Ahead of them lay miles of turkey bush scrub, which could only be penetrated by forcing the horses ahead and goading the cattle into following behind. Occasionally they would get their horns tangled in the matted vines and could only be freed, by hacking away at the wall of creepers.

At last they emerged from the thicket to a river they believed to be the "Escape", but it was not. This river flowed to the west, whilst the "Escape" flows to the east. It was the largest river on Cape York Peninsula and was later named the "Jardine".

Along the route horses were still dying from the poison and by the 17th January they only had 15 left.

Still they forged ahead under heavy rain, whilst the cattle floundered and bogged, at one stage almost every hundred yards. At a dry creek bed, the horses broke through the crust and they bogged down, but were easily pulled out by sliding them on their sides like a sled along the now, slippery crust.

Following the river they crossed a major tributary, which they named the McHenry River.

After battling their way through dense jungle, rain, bogs and swamp they set up a base camp on the river [Camp 82].

2 Days later the Jardines and Eulah, left to search for Somerset [30th January]. They followed the river to the north west, still believing it was the Escape and must therefore curve back to the east. They reasoned that if they could get around the bend then they could soon find a way to Somerset. They still did not realise that this was a completely different river and there was no bend.

They followed its windings through dense jungle and found a large tributary, which they named the "Eliot". After crossing it they continued for mile after mile, but were forced to turn back and returned to camp 82 on the 2nd February.

They now decided to explore the east coast and hopefully find a route to Somerset, from that direction.

Fashioning a raft from the hide of a slaughtered steer, the Jardines and Eulah floated saddles, guns and rations across the river, which was 130 yards wide at this point [5th February].

After pushing their way through dense jungle and creeks they found the mouth of the Escape River [7th February]. They followed behind their horses as they forced a track through this jungle maze. Alexander Jardine writes *"too bad to describe"*.

During this trek they burnt fires all night in camp to keep away the hordes of mosquitoes and sand flies and lived off the land eating turkey eggs and goannas.

Unable to penetrate the mangroves near the river mouth they finally turned back. Once again they forced their way through miles of bogs, swamp and jungle in pouring rain and were enmeshed in the swamps just as Kennedy had been before them. They finally made it back to the cattle camp on the 11th February.

As it was obvious, the cattle could not cross the river to the east, then, they had to follow the river to the north west. This they did, only to find their way barred by an impassable deep creek, 20 yards wide with boggy banks [20th February]. Unable to get the cattle across, they camped [Camp 88].

The next morning the Jardines and Eulah swam across and walked to the top of a ridge. Alexander and Eulah climbed the highest tree and from their lofty perch they could see where the river entered the sea. This was not the "Escape" and there was no "bend to the east". They had discovered a river that no one knew even existed.

From their position, they observed the river mouth only 3 miles away, whilst to the north they could clearly see Prince of Wales Island.

As the cattle could not cross the creek, they decided to take them back up river to their previous camp [87].

This camp was 9 miles back, and by dusk they only made 6 miles, so they set up camp 3 miles short of it [Camp 89]. This now became the main cattle camp from which another attempt would be made to reach Somerset.

Once again Frank, Alexander and old Eulah, crossed the river in search of the settlement. After several days they saw some aborigines. For the sake of precaution, they unslung their guns and as they approached, Eulah heard one of them speak some English words and called out: *"Hold on, you hearim, that one bin yabber English"*.

Sure enough they heard them say, "Alico, Franco, Dzoco, Johnie, Toby and other English words. Then pointing to the North East, they cried out "Kaieeby" [Somerset].

They were the Gudang aborigines and they now led them towards Somerset.

That night they all camped near where the natives had hidden their canoes and the Gudang put on a grand corroboree for their visitors dancing till the early hours of the morning. They were treated to the roasted eggs of the scrub turkey and the cooked pith of the mangrove seed.

The following day they were led to Somerset and finally after 10 long months, father and sons were re-united.

At the time of their arrival, Police Magistrate John Jardine was working in the residency and heard a loud commotion. Upon seeing the natives rushing towards the house he concluded that they were about to be attacked.

Grabbing his gun he rushed out to see instead, his sons surrounded by half the tribe all claiming to be their Kotaiga [brother]. From a distance he saw them with emu feathered caps on their heads and only a shirt and belt for their clothing.

After forcing his way through the excited crowd John Jardine embraced his sons and took them in the house for a well deserved lunch.

The brothers rested for several days while fresh horses were brought across from Albany Island, Then, they were guided back to the river to collect the cattle and remaining horses.

In order to help his sons find Somerset, John Jardine had cut a line of trees for 30 miles marking the way to the settlement. Coming from a different direction, they missed this path, but on their second trip from the river they were able to drive the cattle along the cut for 10 miles.

The cattle were herded across the flooded river on the 9th March and a camp erected on the other side [Camp 90]. Over the next few days they are driven towards Somerset.

As they were herded through the scrub at Woomerah Creek, 30 head of cattle went missing, but fortunately 25 of these were found the next day.

Camp 93 was at Lake Chappagnyah which was thick with crocodiles. The next day Police Magistrate Jardine met the party at Lake Boronto and guided them to Vallack Point, about 3 miles south of Somerset where they formed the Vallack Point cattle station on the 13th March 1865 [Camp 94].

The incredible cattle drive was finally over, but this expedition was only the start of Frank Jardine's rich adventurous life. Although it has often been said that they covered 1200 miles, that was only the length of the route covered. The Jardines had probably traversed an additional 1500 miles in their exploration of Cape York Peninsula, trying to find their way through this untamed land.

Alec Jardine had, with Eulah, also traversed an additional 300 miles before the expedition had left Carpentaria Downs in order to check the country ahead. All told they had probably covered around 3000 miles of hostile and unknown territory without losing a man, in spite of all the attacks from aborigines. During the last 250 miles they were subjected to extremely arduous conditions – weak, from living on a diet of beef, with virtually no vegetable component – almost naked, as their clothes fell off them from rot – and blistered feet for having no footwear except their rawhide moccasins they made from the hide of a slaughtered steer.

Huts were soon erected at the station and a track cut through the jungle, linking the station with Somerset, 3 miles to the north.

The cattle losses on the drive have often been overstated. Of the 250 head they started with, approximately 20% were lost, whereas most of the horses perished from eating poisonous plants or vines. Only 12 of the 41 horses that commenced the journey, made it to Vallack Point, and they were too weak to ride.

With the arrival of "HMS Salamander" the white members of the expedition left Somerset for Brisbane on the 24th May, leaving the cattle station under the care of their younger brother John with the 4 aboriginal stockmen.

*Map of the Cattle Drive: Staaten River section where the horse hunt took place.
Drawn by A J Richardson 1864.
"Reproduced with permission of the Department of Lands, Queensland".*

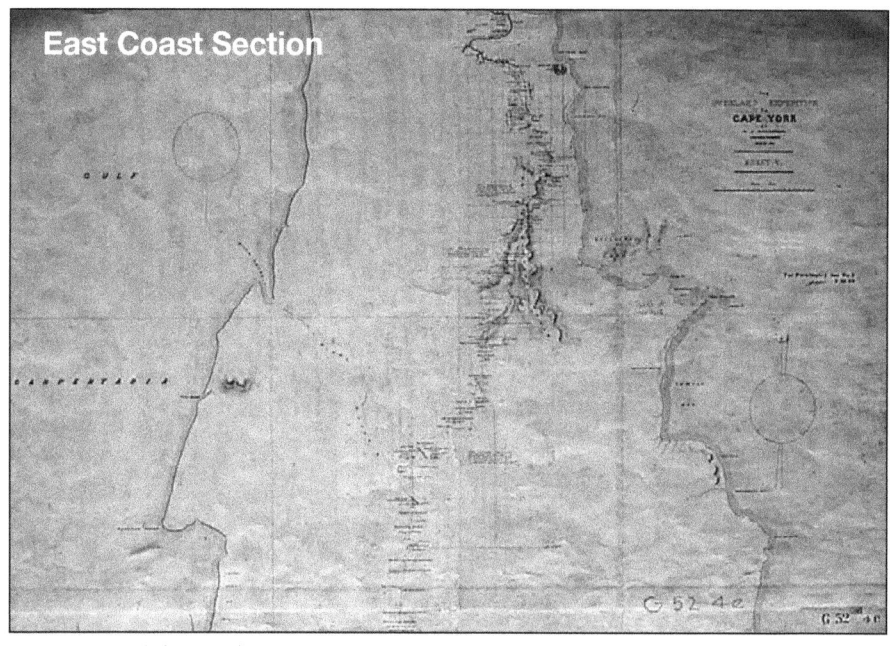

*Map of the Cattle Drive: Batavia River to the lower Jardine River Section.
Drawn by A J Richardson 1864.
"Reproduced with permission of the Department of Lands, Queensland".*

CHAPTER 7
"DEBIL – DEBIL – JARDINE"

Frank Jardine returned to Somerset, with his father on board the "Salamander" on the 6th October 1865. By then the hospital, painted white, could be seen on Somerset Hill from miles out to sea. Beside it, although not as visible were the marine barracks and married men's cottages.

Frank immersed himself in running the cattle station, providing beef when needed at the settlement. His father and younger brother John returned south in November on the "Salamander" and the settlement was left under the charge of Walter McLintock, the Customs Officer [young John later returned].

Of the 6 tribes near Somerset, it was the "Yadagana" from the Escape River who caused most of the violence amongst the various tribes.

The most timid and friendliest tribe were the "Gudang", who lived in the region from the top of Cape York, and south to Fly Point along the eastern side of Cape York. Somerset was built on their land. When the settlement was established, they moved to its outskirts for protection from their enemies, the "Yadagana" to the south and the "Gumukudin" in the west.

On the east coast, living between the "Gudang" and the "Yadagana" were the "Induyumu" [who could be friendly one day and enemies the next].

There were inevitable confrontations between Frank and the "Yadagana" and "Induyumu", who were constantly spearing the cattle. Between April and August 1866, they had speared 51 head.

In previous years, the "Yadagana" were able to attack the small "Gudang" tribe as often as they chose. But now the settlement was established it became a barrier to their murderous assaults. To make matters worse, they considered Frank Jardine as an advance guard who with his 4 native stockmen would soon alert the settlement and the "Gudangs" to any danger.

Therefore, he had to be eliminated.

He was soon targeted in several ambushes, but fortunately escaped the murder attempts. It was almost as if he knew of their intentions before hand. In one ambush a warrior tried to kill him with his bare hands. It was a fatal mistake as Frank came off the victor.

As they failed to kill him by daylight ambush, they changed their tactics and decided to murder him at night, whilst he slept.

On the night of the 7th July 1866, they crept up to the Vallack Point hut and silently opened the wooden shutter. Taking careful aim under a moonlit night, they launched their spears at the sleeping body of Frank Jardine.

It was not an easy shot, and the first spear missed by 6 inches, whilst the other passed within an inch of his chest. There was no time for a 3rd shot, for Jardine awoke in anger and opened fire with a double barrel shotgun, hitting 2 of his attackers, who were quickly carried away by their comrades.

Once again he had survived and the natives were convinced that he was a "devil spirit". They spread the story far and wide and all over Cape York he became known as "Debil Debil Jardine".

After failing to kill him by cunning and devious methods, they waited in the nearby scrub for him to relax his vigilance. They watched him digging a large strainer post hole, 4 feet deep by 3 feet wide. The "Yadagana" failed to see his snider rifle on the ground behind the large mound of earth from the hole, and decided to attack.

When the 9 foot spears started falling, Jardine immediately took cover in the post hole, and using it as a bunker, he blazed away with his snider, hitting 11 of the 12 attackers.

Between these murderous attacks, the aborigines also tried burning him out by setting his hut alight whilst he slept, but this also failed and his native stockmen rebuilt the hut.

Frustrated by their failure, they tried again to destroy the devil in his bed. By now he had a network of native spies who informed him of the happenings amongst the various tribes. From this bush telegraph he already knew when they would attack.

On the night in question, his younger brother, John, was staying with him and they waited patiently as midnight approached. They had packed their beds with decoys of pillows and blankets and hid in the adjoining room.

The floorboards creaked and a barrage of spears sunk into the beds. The assailants realised too late, that it was a trap. A death struggle ensued as the brothers grappled with the assassins.

At first clubs were used by the aborigines, with the Jardines fending them off with the butts of their rifles. In the semi darkness it was difficult to know who was friend or foe. The final combat was hand to hand until finally only the Jardines and one wounded aborigine survived.

He was in such a shocked state that the Jardines healed his wounds and employed him at the station. They showed him pity and kindness, but he was ostracised by his own people, who finally murdered him.

Frank Jardine realised that there must be a transit camp of the "Yadagana" nearby. In the morning he mounted his horse and searched the surrounding area. From the top of a wooded ridge he spotted them.

The aborigines believed their warriors had killed Jardine as there was no sound of shooting in the night. "The Devil must be dead".

With a revolver in one hand, and the reigns in the other, he spurred his horse down the ridge and into the camp, yelling out in latin, "Cave Adsum" [Beware I am here] and firing his gun into the air [Cave Adsum was the Jardine motto].

Before they could react to the intrusion, Jardine had ridden through the camp and disappeared in the scrub. In their eyes he was truly an apparition, "the dead man riding again."

Although the "Yadagana" represented the greatest threat to Jardine, he also had many running battles with the "Induyumu" who were constantly spearing the cattle.

Cape York was a savage untamed land, where no quarter was asked nor given among the native tribes, who seemed to be forever at war with each other, stealing women from their enemies to prevent relatives inter-breeding within the tribe.

WINI'S DEATH

Whilst Jardine was tackling his own problems at Vallack Point, the new Police Magistrate Henry Simpson was supervising the Somerset establishment which was now serving its intended purpose as a refuge for castaways.

In earlier years, Simpson had been the Lieutenant on "HMS Rattlesnake" during the rescue of Barbara Thompson, in 1849, so, was quite familiar with the area.

Now, 17 years later he was administering to 24 castaways from 3 different shipwrecks. They were all taken south on the 20th August 1866, aboard "HMS Salamander" on her return journey, after delivering stores to Somerset.

The following year the Reverend Frederick C Jagg arrived at Somerset [15th March 1867].

He had been directed by a missionary organisation [Society for the propagation of the gospel in foreign parts] with its headquarters in London, to take the gospel to the natives of Cape York and the adjacent Torres Strait Islands. The Rev. Jagg was a fiery gun toting cleric, who advised the natives, that it was wrong to kill women but acceptable to kill men.

When the hostile "Yadagana" attacked and slaughtered the "Korkarega" on Albany Island, Jagg had wanted Frank Jardine to arm his 4 blacks and attack the "Yadagana". Jardine refused [The "Korkarega" were a sub-group of the "Gudang"].

Ever since the establishment of Somerset, the existence of "Wini of Badu" was well known. John Jardine, during his time as Police Magistrate of Somerset, wrote that the white man "Wini" referred to in the "Journal of HMS Rattlesnake", was still on Badu. According to the "Gudang" he was a "great and savage warrior", who had been to Cape York on a number of occasions trading iron tipped spears for young Gudang girls.

It was no coincidence that shortly after Somerset was established, rumours started circulating that "Wini" had died. The missionaries at Somerset were happy to accept this story, as they believed most of what the natives told them, whether it be true or false.

School teacher William Turton Kennett, who assisted the Rev. Jagg, corroborated the myth by writing in his journal that "Wini" had died in 1866.

In fact, he was very much alive and well, and had no doubt circulated the rumour to deceive the authorities. After all, he knew of the regular visits to Somerset of several British steam powered warships [Salamander, Blanche, Virago] and the last thing he wanted was to see one of them anchored at Badu with the Somerset Marines aboard.

In recent years the subject of "Wini" the white savage of Badu, has been taken up by various writers. Some of these have tried to dress him in respectability and claimed he was just a helpless castaway and not the white savage he was painted as.

This line of thought was stated by various academics who obviously knew very little about the island language. The whole argument stems from a statement made by a chief of the Kauraregas named "Manu", just after the rescue of Barbara Thompson in 1849.

At that time, the artist, Brierly, asked "Manu" did he know about "Wini". His reply in the native language has caused the misinterpretation. "Manu" is recorded as saying; "Wini – Kopi Garki".

The only meaning that Brierly knew for "Kopi-Garki" was "Good-Man". However, what he did not know was that there were 5 meanings for the word "Kopi", and it would appear that a number of academics still do not realise this.

We know that "Garki" means man, but what of "Kopi". The following words all mean "Kopi": "Thigh – Seed – Good – Pretty – Light or Pale Colour".

It is clear from these meanings that the chief was inferring that "Wini" was a light coloured man, that is a white man and not a good man. After all, his atrocities were mentioned by Barbara Thompson when she informed Captain Stanley and MacGillivray that he was a white man who was involved with the murder of many whites.

Later, John Jardine corroborated this fact when he stated:

"Wini is the worst renegade ever to sail the south seas".

There is no official version of the death of "Wini". He is believed to have been shot dead from a police boat during the 1870's. The man credited with his death was Frank Jardine.

The academics counter this claim by stating that the man shot on a Badu beach from the police boat was a native mourning for a dead relative, who was whitened with clay for the mourning period. This argument again falls apart, as Wini was identified by his long fair hair, and not the colour of his skin, for he was by now almost as dark as the natives.

THE ABORIGINAL CIVIL WAR

In early 1867 the aborigines north of the Jardine River were involved in a series of devastating tribal wars, which eventually erupted into an "Aboriginal civil war".

The powerful "Yadagana" were constantly attacking the weaker tribes and stealing their women. If it continued they would be in danger of becoming extinct.

As a result the "Ambagana" and "Gumukudin", on the western side of Cape York, declared war against the "Yadagana". In so doing, these united tribes had signed their own death warrant, for they were virtually annihilated by the "Yadagana", and the few who survived [7 of them] with the women and children were inducted into the "Yadagana" tribe. This only left 3 tribes on the mainland, and the "Korkarega" on Albany Island.

The white population did not interfere in these battles, knowing such intervention would only attract trouble from the savage "Yadagana". Meanwhile, the "Gudang" moved even closer to the settlement, expecting the marines to help them if they needed assistance. When this was denied them due to the policy of non interference, they moved across to their relatives on Albany Island.

They had every reason to be afraid, as they had earlier retaliated against the "Yadagana" and killed 10 of them. Now it was their turn to feel the sting of retaliation.

The "Yadagana" moved north, giving Somerset a wide birth, so as not to be seen, then, swam across the pass at night, After landing on the northern end of Albany Island they moved south within range of the camp and waited till the Gudang fell asleep.

They hit the camp at midnight with spear and club, slaughtering as many as they could as quickly as possible. The casualties included a little 4 year old girl whose head was smashed in by a gaba-gaba [club] and a young boy who was speared through the heart.

During these tribal wars, 2 heads were bought by the servant who worked for Dr Haran, the marine's physician.

As a result of the massacre on Albany Island, the "Gudang" warriors approached Frank Jardine, when he was about to start mustering the cattle. They asked him and his 4 native stockmen to back them in an attack against the "Yadagana". He refused and sent them away.

Putting off his mustering for several days, Frank rode with his black stockmen to an outcamp, only to find 80 "Gudang" warriors about to make an attack on the "Yadagana", who were camped no more than half a mile away. Jardine realised that if the weaker "Gudang" attacked the more powerful "Yadagana", they would almost certainly be wiped out.

Frank Jardine's next move was completely unprecedented. He offered to talk peace to the "Yadagana". He knew only too well that they could impale him with spears, if they should see him near their camp. But, he also realised that if he did nothing the tribes would continue their senseless killings.

He now instructed the "Gudang" to go in the opposite direction and approach the camp from behind, and he would talk to their enemies.

Jardine then rode into the "Yadagana" camp without a gun in his hand. His carbine was slung over his shoulder and the revolver was in his belt. 3 Of his native stockmen rode behind him and did not display their arms.

The "Yadagana" instantly dived for their spears when they saw him, but stopped when he rubbed his belly with one hand and raised the other for peace. They could have turned his body into a pincushion of spears had they chosen.

Jardine rode right up to them and offered to mediate between the 2 tribes. He noted there were close to 400 warriors. If the "Gudang" had attacked they would almost certainly have been decimated.

In a simple ceremony, both tribes embraced each other and commenced dancing. That night Frank Jardine and his stockmen camped next to the ferocious "Yadagana", who spent the entire night in a huge corroboree [see page 222].

Although the tribes had reconciled their differences, the "Gudang" were still so frightened, that they camped close to Jardine. Then as he departed in the morning, the nervous "Gudangs" tailed him so closely back to his campsite, it became impossible for him to muster the cattle.

Police Magistrate, Henry Simpson was amazed that the tribes had finally made peace, thanks to the intervention of Frank Jardine. He hoped the peace would last at least till the end of the Green Turtle season, which was imminent. As the warriors rarely went to war during the season, the peace could last for 6 months, between August and the following March.

The green turtle [Soolah] was caught during the dry season until the end of December, when the wet started and the Flatback turtle emerged [Gapu Warroo].

On the 1st August 1867, "HMS Salamander" arrived on her final voyage to Somerset. When she left a week later she took with her the British Marines who were replaced with a Police Inspector W D Howe and 6 white policemen. As Dr Haran was a part of the military establishment of the Royal Navy, then he also left.

One of the major reasons for the withdrawal of the Marines, was the British Governments refusal to provide further funds. Queensland was obliged to pay for the future running of the settlement, which had previously been supported by England.

It was clear that in spite of 109 Somerset Town Lots sold to the public, no one was prepared to live there due to the constant violence of the aboriginal tribes.

These lots were sold at Martins' Auction Rooms in 2 separate auctions. The first was on the 4th April 1865 [70 lots] and the second was on the 2nd May 1866 [82 lots].

As a number of bidders failed to pay for their lots then the total count was reduced from 152 lots to 109.

The dream of a new Singapore with its streets marked out for building, soon dissolved.

If the settlement was to continue as a refuge, then cost cutting would have to be implemented. To this end, the position of Police Magistrate at £500 a year was replaced by the more economical Police Inspector which cost the State Government £300 a year. Henry Simpson refused the appointment, with its reduced salary and the offer was made to Frank Jardine.

POLICE INSPECTOR JARDINE

Jardine realised there was little future in the cattle station at Vallack Point unless markets were available. As Inspector of Police, he could have a good job, plus the Residency as his home and still run the station as a back up if necessary.

On the 27th January 1868, Frank Jardine took the oath of "Inspector of Police and Justice of the Peace", before Commander H M Bingham of HMS Virago anchored in Somerset Bay.

With Frank in residence at Somerset, his brother John, now 21 years old took charge of the Vallack Point cattle station with their 4 native stockmen to assist him.

Occasionally at weekends, John would ride over to Somerset and spend a night at the Residency with Frank. One such night was Saturday 9th May 1868.

It was usual for a number of the "Gudang" to be loitering around the Residency each morning doing odd jobs when it suited them. But on this Sunday morning [10th] there was no sign of them. All was deadly quiet. Something was obviously wrong. The Jardines saddled their horses and headed to Vallack Point to check that all was well.

On entering old Eulah's hut they were shocked to find him lying on the floor in a pool of blood. He had been shot from behind the right ear with the bullet passing through his head and blasting out his left eye. The right side of his face had been smashed with a solid object, and his cheekbones were crushed, leaving his jaw hanging in a grotesque form. A knife had sliced through the back of his neck.

Frank Jardine was enraged at the ruthless destruction of his best friend. The other 3 stockmen had disappeared with all the weapons and ammunition they could lay their hands on. The "Gudang" had assisted them in murdering old Eulah and ransacking the station, which was why Somerset was deserted that morning.

The devil exploded in Frank Jardine and he would not rest until Eulah's 3 murderers were hunted down and punished.

In a simple ceremony, the Jardines buried their old comrade at Vallack Point and returned to Somerset.

The missionary, Jagg, had taught many of the "Gudang" to shoot a gun, and now they were in possession of the weapons, the settlement itself could be in danger.

Jardine pursued the murderers in the rugged bush and in his search found many of the stolen weapons in the native camps. He had also offered a reward to the natives absolving them from punishment, if they caught the culprits. The "Gudang" sensed that if they did not co-operate they would bring trouble on themselves and would not have the protection of the settlement.

Within days, they sent word to Somerset, that the 3 were captured and bound at their main camp. As the penalty for murder was death, then the Jardines had little choice in the matter and upon arriving at the camp, Peter, Barney and Sambo were executed.

The missionaries considered Frank's action as brutal and yet, one of the murderers [Barney] had previously murdered a "Gudang" woman and had cut out her liver and heart, leaving the gutted corpse to rot on the beach. At that time Jardine could do nothing about the matter as black witnesses were not acceptable in court.

The government decided that Frank Jardine was eligible for promotion to Police Magistrate, [June 1868] although his salary would remain at £300 per annum. By making this deal they effectively employed a Police Magistrate on a Police Inspector's salary.

When "HMS Virago" arrived in December 1868, she had on board 2 white constables and their sergeant Tyrell, plus 3 native troopers. These replaced 4 white constables and acting Sub-Inspector Howe, who were returning south on the "Virago".

By now Vallack Point Station, was an expensive liability and a losing gamble for the Jardine Family, in both time and money. After a lengthy period of negotiation it was sold to the Queensland Government on the 11th January 1870 in exchange for land valued at £1200.

Frank Jardine with his favourite horse "RAMARAH".

Chapter 8
"THE SPERWER MASSACRE"

In April 1869, the cutter "Sperwer" under the command of Captain James Gascoigne was attacked by the Kauraregas [Muralug – P.O.W.] and the Kulkalegas [Nahgi – Mt Ernest Island]. The entire crew were massacred and beheaded.

It was another 2 months before Frank Jardine heard of the slaughter. He also learnt that another ship had been attacked several months before the "Sperwer" and again all were massacred.

As the schooner "Melanie" was anchored just up the coast at Charo, Jardine requested 2 long boats and their crews from Captain Archibald McAusland.

Taking 4 of his native troopers, he took the small force to the Kauraregas camp on "Muralug". The natives were found wearing the clothes of the murdered men and around their necks were watches and parts of revolvers worn as decorations. In the forks of the trees they found the decaying bodies of her crew, minus their heads.

Jardine had learnt that a white woman and her son had also been captured alive by the Kauraregas and believed she may have been Mrs Harriet Gascoigne, the Captain's wife.

The Kauraregas, watched the small group and guessed that their leader was the "Debil Markai" from Somerset who had deflected the spears of death even as he slept and destroyed those who tried to kill him. The Kauraregas were extremely superstitious, and fearful at his appearance on Muralug.

Frank sensed that all eyes were on him and realised that there was no way of removing the bodies with out inciting reaction from the tribe. Outnumbered by 10 to one, the small force backed away from the burnt out wreck, boarded the boats and headed back to Somerset.

It was later learnt that there was a woman and her 12 year old son captured alive by the Kauraregas, but it was not Mrs Gascoigne. She was later found alive in Prahan, a suburb of Melbourne and did not have a 12 year old son to Capt. Gascoigne.

The woman captured with her son was from the first ship and not the "Sperwer". At this stage she was still alive, but her exact where-abouts was not known, and until Frank could find out where they were holding her, he could do little.

On the 27th July 1869, "HMS Reconnaissance" arrived at Somerset with stores, and Frank Jardine took his leave. On board was an old sea dog of Her Majesty's Indian Navy, who was to take Jardine's place. His name was Henry Marjori Banks Chester.

Before leaving Somerset, Jardine had given Chester the details of the massacre and the location of the wreck. He had also gained additional information from the "Gudang", who were a good source of knowledge due to their alliance with the Kauraregas and to a lesser extent, the Kulka-legas.

Although the massacre was supposed to have occurred at Wednesday Island, the burnt out Sperwer wreck was found at the northern end of Prince of Wales, opposite Friday Island, over 6 miles to the west of Wednesday Island. Whether it drifted with the currents or was towed by the large Kauraregas war canoes is still one of the unsolved mysteries of the times.

The "Georgina Godfrey" was one of many vessels involved in collecting sea slugs [beche-de-mer] for the China market, where they could fetch £50 a ton. This vessel of 45 ton had anchored at Somerset and Chester arranged with its skipper, Captain George Godfrey to search the northern end of Prince of Wales [Muralug].

On the 2nd August, the schooner anchored off Friday Island. On board was Chester, 2 native troopers and 9 "Gudang" natives who acted as guides. Directly opposite their anchorage was the northern end of Muralug and only 400 yards away lay the burnt out hulk of the "Sperwer".

As they landed next to it, they were greeted by a sickening sight. Only 100 yards from the cutter, were the decomposed bodies of 2 white men. Even at this stage of decomposition, the spear wounds were quite visible in one body, whilst in the other, an arrow tipped with iron barbs was embedded in the thigh. The heads had been taken together with the arms, to be cooked and eaten.

Normally, they would only eat the flesh off the heads, unless there was a food shortage. This was probably the case as the attack took place at the end of the wet season, when food was usually scarce.

The wreck had been completely stripped of all its ironwork, which was why it had been captured and set alight in the first place. Burying the remains near the wreck, they returned to Somerset.

On the 30th August, the Georgina Godfrey found 8 castaways in an open boat, from the wrecked Barque "Tynemouth", which had struck a reef and sank 70 miles east of Raine Island. They were brought into Somerset and later put on a ship going south. Once again Somerset had served its purpose as a necessary "refuge for castaways". However the settlement was vulnerable to aboriginal attack, and only a week before the "Induyumu" natives, had raided the customs store and stolen supplies. A raid by the police on their camp resulted in some of the supplies being retrieved. Weapons found in the camp were destroyed.

On the 16th October the Georgina Godfrey found an 8 ton cutter near Cape Grenville. Captain Godfrey saw it anchored, with not a soul on board. He noticed the deck was covered in blood stains and learnt that the crew had been murdered by aborigines. The vessel was brought to Somerset, and Chester named it the "Alerte", and used it as a police boat.

By now there were 9 children at Somerset, with their mothers – the wives of serving officers of the Police Force, who were housed in the original marines married quarters on Somerset Hill.

A slave trade had been in progress now for many years to provide cheap labour for the Queensland sugar fields. Just as the natives had murdered helpless castaways by the hundreds, they were now suffering the same fate. They were captured at gunpoint, crammed into the ships humid holds and taken south. Those who tried to escape were shot. This blackbirding as it was then known was to last almost 60 years, before it was finally halted.

Meanwhile, Chester was still deeply pre-occupied with the "Sperwer" massacre. More importantly he had learnt that the Kauraregas still had a white woman on the island.

Then on the 13th December, 3 Kaurarega canoes arrived at Albany Island and camped on shore directly across the pass from Somerset. Hearing of their presence, he boarded the "Alerte" with the Police and anchored near the camp.

Chester managed to entice a minor chief, "Teapotti" and his son, to board the "Alerte" under the pretence of trade. Once on board they were taken across to Somerset for payment of trade goods, or so they thought.

Instead. "Teapotti" was wrestled to the ground and locked in chains. His son escaped, but that made no difference, for word was sent to the Kauraregas, that if the white woman and her son were not returned in 7 days, "Teapotti" would be killed.

After 12 days the Kauraregas still refused to give in to Chester's demands, knowing from the "Gudang" that this was an idle threat. They guessed right, for soon after he was released. But, they had under-estimated Henry Chester.

"HMS Blanche" arrived at Somerset on the 4th April 1870. On board she had additional water police and native troopers, as well as another 3 months supply of provisions for the settlement. The ship's commander, Captain Montgomerie was informed of the recent developments of the "Sperwer" and told about the white woman and her son held by the Kauraregas.

The following day Chester boarded the "Blanche" with 8 native troopers and 9 "Gudang" aborigines as guides. At midday, the "Blanche" left Somerset and anchored later in the day at Possession Island on the western side of Cape York.

From here, a force of 25 marines from the "Blanche", 9 natives, and the 8 troopers sailed in 2 boats at sundown to the northern end of Boat Channel and camped on shore. At dawn they sailed for Wednesday Island and landed at daylight.

The native scouts were sent out and soon returned with the news that they had seen a camp and 4 canoes on the other side of the island.

The heavily armed band of marines, native troopers and aboriginal guides, moved stealthily through the scrub for more than 2 miles until they sighted the camp on the edge of the mangroves.

The camp was quickly surrounded, taking the natives completely by surprise. The warriors instantly jumped up to defend themselves, with bows and arrows, clubs and beheading knives, but then realised the futility of their move against the power of the gun and dropped their weapons.

Disarmed, the warriors were forced to sit whilst the women and children moved to the canoes. The huts and canoes were searched and various items from a selection of wrecks was uncovered. Some of the booty proved conclusively that a ship had been attacked and the crew massacred before the "Sperwer" attack and that the kidnapped woman and boy were possibly from that ship.

The doctor, on board the "Blanche" confirmed that a bone Chester had found on Friday Island, was in fact a thigh bone from a 12 year old caucasian boy. The arrow was still embedded in the bone.

The time of reckoning was nigh. The encamped natives were not Kauraregas, but Kulkalegas from Nahgi [Mt Ernest Island], allies of the Kauraregas, who had participated in the attack on the "Sperwer". The "Gudang" guides pointed out the 3 most important people in the tribe and justice was done. They were shot by the native police.

A search of the canoes found additional ship's gear, pamphlets and school books. 2 Of these large canoes were destroyed and the other 2 left intact to permit the Kulkalegas to return to Nahgi.

THE RETURN OF FRANK JARDINE

Frank Jardine returned to Somerset on the 17th August, 1870 and took over his old post of Police Magistrate from Chester. The final episode of the "Sperwer" tragedy was about to be written in blood.

Shortly after his return, Frank learnt of the where-abouts of the mystery woman held by the Kauraregas. He realised they would not give her up and so he prepared a rescue mission.

In 1869, pearling had commenced in the Torres Strait and there were a number of vessels anchored in Albany Pass, opposite Somerset. Jardine hoped to enlist the services of these pearlers in the rescue operation.

To this day, no one really knows how many men were involved in the attempt to rescue this poor woman. A number of whites and their South Sea Island crews were believed to have landed with Frank on Prince of Wales Island. The rescue force was heavily armed with guns and revolvers and would not hesitate to use them if they were attacked.

Before leaving Somerset, Jardine informed everyone that the purpose of the expedition was purely to rescue the woman and get out. The Kauraregas were staunch warriors who had never been defeated in battle, but their superiority in warfare was about to be shattered by the might of the white man's fire power.

When the rescuers landed on Muralug, it was the end for the Kauraregas. What started as a rescue mission ended in the defeat of a proud and even endearing people, whose own violence was the cause of their destruction.

The woman they went to rescue was found dead in the now abandoned Kaurarega camp. They had brutally murdered her, before retreating into the surrounding jungle clad hills. For just as they were prepared to kill Barbara Thompson in 1847, rather than let anyone else have her, so they killed this young woman as the rescuers moved in to retrieve her.

Her name has evaded writers and researchers for over 120 years [From my research I believe she was a Mrs Mathids].

Frank Jardine took the woman's body to the top of a hill outside the camp and there she was laid to rest. It was many years later after Frank had died, that this information was passed on by his son, Bertie Bootle Jardine. In Frank's journal, reference was made to the incident:

"Yes poor soul, she was there, but dead when we found her. It could not have been long either. We buried her on a hill outside the village."

With the defeat of the Kauraregas, the name of "Debil Debil Jardine", took on an even greater significance. The headhunting tribes, who had attacked ships and castaways with impunity, and gone unpunished, now knew of the terrible retribution they would face, if caught by this Markai Devil. If he could defeat the mighty Kauraregas, what would he do to others who dared to slaughter the weak and helpless.

It was only after the Kauraregas devastating defeat on Muralug, that peace finally came to the islands, and attacks against shipping ceased. The Kauraregas were dispersed throughout their northern islands and were no further threat to foundering ships.

Bertie Bootle was Frank Jardine's youngest son. He fought in the Middle East in World War I. In World War II he guided American ships through the Torres Strait reef strewn waters. Note the American Eagle on his cap.

CHAPTER 9
"PEARL FEVER"

In 1869, Captain Banner, of the Schooner "Bluebell" arrived in the Torres Strait, and headed north towards New-Guinea to Warrior Island [Tutu]. It was here in 1792 that Captain Bligh was attacked by 12 war canoes, whilst in command of the "Providence".

Tutu's reputation was so bad that few vessels ever ventured near the islands reefs, knowing that they would almost certainly be attacked. Their chief was known as a powerful warrior named "Kebisu" and many referred to him as the "Cannibal Chief". He had a large navy of giant war canoes ready to attack any vessel that approached too close to his island domain.

When Banner anchored in the bay, he was prepared for "Kebisu". A 4 pound cannon on the deck of the "Bluebell" was trained on the village. Should "Kebisu" attack, the village would be the first to be hit. The attack never came, and instead of war, "Kebisu" offered friendship to this "Markai" who had the courage to land at his door and offer to trade.

Banner's intention had been to search for sea slugs, but he noticed the warriors wearing large pearl shells to protect their groins and others decorating their arms and foreheads.

After boiling the sea slugs, they were dried and loaded aboard and he headed for Sydney, leaving his assistant John Joseph behind to look after the station. Joseph was a 60 year old Tongan who had served on many British ships including "HMS Leopard" at the siege of Sebastopol. The Tutu's showed him the reef where they had found the pearl shell and collected all they could find for him.

When Banner returned some months later he was amazed to find that Joseph had collected 6 tons of pearl shell, which was loaded onto the "Pakeha", and sold in Sydney. Over the next few months an additional 50 tons was found.

The discovery of pearl shell in the Strait, triggered the founding of a lucrative industry. In Sydney and Brisbane, the news spread like wildfire, and in a short time, boats of every description sailed up the coast to Cape York and the Torres Strait.

Captain Banner did not live long enough to enjoy his new found wealth, but died on "Warrior Island" [Tutu] on the 22nd July 1871. Upon his death the South Sea Islanders who worked for him, broke into the store and stole all the rum and spirits, and drank themselves into a stupor. Whilst under the influence of alcohol, they distributed all the trade goods to the "Tutu's". It was considered the worst drunken rort in the history of the Torres Strait.

Banner was buried on "Tutu", but the sea washed away the grave and his remains were later reburied beside "Kebisu" on Stephens Island [Ugar].

Pearl fever, gripped the boatmen of the south, who decided they had nothing to lose by heading north. Many were almost penniless, whilst others were wanted by the law. They swarmed into the Strait, and brought with them their particular brand of civilisation. Some were involved in kidnapping Islanders and forcing them to work at the point of a gun.

Young females were violated by their abductors and when they fell pregnant, were abandoned on tidal reefs to drown or be eaten by sharks on the incoming tide.

Frank Jardine wrote to the authorities on numerous occasions reporting the recurring atrocities against the Islanders, but the offences were committed outside his jurisdiction and he was powerless to assist them.

Although Somerset was the official refuge for shipwrecked castaways, ships still dropped off food, water and mail at Booby Island. With the influx of reprobates from the south, casks of meat and water were stolen, as was the log book. This book had an incredible record of narratives about shipwrecks and massacres in the "Terror Strait".

The natives had now overcome their fear of "Booby Island" by this time and were also guilty of raiding the cave and stealing supplies.

Jardine decided to leave a new log book in the cave, with instructions directing castaways to Somerset, for surprisingly, many castaways were not aware of the existence of the settlement.

To ensure the continuation of Somerset was a backbreaking task for its inhabitants. Many of the buildings were being eaten out by white ants, and had to be continually repaired. The hospital was so bad it had to be closed down [1873].

By this stage the cattle had spread all over the top end of Cape York and many were drifting back down south. Jardine decided to build a 6 mile fence across the top from east to west and lock them in. It was an arduous job, but with the help of some of the aborigines, was completed in December 1870, only to rot out within a few years, from white ants.

Shortly after its completion, Frank learnt that the native troopers were planning to desert and make their way south by land. Sure enough, they made their break after robbing the Somerset store and taking Frank Jardine's guns, ammunition and tomahawks. Within a few days, they had returned to raid the store again, but this time the police were waiting. The ring leader was shot and 2 others captured, whilst the other 3 in the raiding party escaped into the bush.

Justice was Jardine's intent as he spent the next 5 weeks tracking the renegades across the grassy flats to the west of Vallack Point. He discovered dead cattle killed for food along the route. Finally he trapped all 3 and once again became the avenger of death, shooting them, when they refused to surrender.

BLACKBIRDING OUTLAWED

With the discovery of large pearl beds, the Strait had attracted all types of undesirable characters. Many a hard bitten slug skipper switched from sea slugs to pearl shelling, often kidnapping the Islanders and forcing them to dive for the shell.

If they didn't dive fast enough, they were shot in the water as a lesson to others.

Soon the Strait was inundated with some of the lowest types of human beings, from kidnappers to escaped convicts and blackbirders. Kidnapping vessels ranged far and wide raiding the Islands of the Torres Strait and the Solomons, in search of slaves for the sugar plantations, which needed 2000 labourers each year. When the Islanders resisted, they were shot and the survivors dragged aboard.

Over the years, Frank Jardine had laid numerous complaints against some of the pearlers known to be kidnapping Islanders but little could be done about it. Then the kidnapping act was passed by the British Authorities on the 27th June 1872. This was more correctly known as the "Pacific Islands Protection Act", and it was now an offence to allow Islanders on board without a licence. After this, the Queensland border was pushed 60 miles north of Cape York on the 24th August 1872.

To enforce the new act the authorities sent the British warship "HMS Basilisk" north to the Torres Strait.

Captain Moresby of the "Basilisk" arrived at Cardwell on the 2nd January 1873, and learnt from the Police Magistrate, Brinsley Sheridan, that the pearlers involved in kidnapping, had already heard he was heading north and were scattering from the Strait before the "Basilisk" arrived. A number of vessels managed to escape the intransigent Captain Moresby, but others were not quick enough to avoid his net.

On the 5th January, 2 vessels were sighted and boarded. These were the "Challenge" with 33 natives aboard and the "Melanie" with 55 natives.

Both vessels were taken to nearby Fitzroy Island [off Cairns] where an investigation was held, which resulted in the seized vessels being sent to Sydney and impounded. Many of the Islanders on board had been forced to work for 6 years with only food, clothing and tobacco as payment.

3 Days later, on the 8th January, the "Woodbine" was boarded and found to be carrying 20 tons of pearl shell which had been collected by Islanders without a licence. The barque was seized and sailed to Brisbane.

The next to go was the "Crishna". In her holds were 35 Islanders, who like many before them had been captured at gunpoint or run down whilst fishing in their canoes. She was captured on the 14th January.

Frank Jardine had raised complaints against 2 of these vessels on previous occasions and finally his concern was vindicated.

When Jardine's own 10 ton cutter arrived at Somerset [May 1872] he was in a position to patrol the Strait at his leisure. As his younger brother, Charles, was at Somerset with him. then he could also use the vessel for pearling. He called the cutter the "Vampyre" and to the kidnappers she was aptly named for she could strike without warning in the day or night.

Throughout the years, he had made many enemies amongst the pearling fraternity, who would have been only too glad to put him out of business. There was no love lost between Jardine and several known kidnappers, who he warned would be charged if caught in the act.

When he learnt that 3 longboats from the kidnapping vessel "Crishna", [previously seized but later released] were being used by natives with firearms in their possession, he ordered coxswain Brown of the water police to set sail in the "Vampyre" and seize the boats.

2 Of these boats were found at Coconut Island and brought to Somerset. Jardine learnt that the Coconut Islanders had visited Dugong Island, about 30 miles east of Cape York, and shot everyone on the island whilst all the young men were away hunting for turtle. The only people left on the island were old people with some women and children. The guns and boats had been left with the Coconut Islanders for their own protection, but used instead to massacre innocent people on nearby islands.

Prior to purchasing his own vessel, Jardine had made repeated requests for a cutter able to patrol the Torres Strait. The vessel finally arrived on the 25th May, 1873 and was named the "Lizzie Jardine" after Frank's sister, Elizabeth Jane.

"Sana"
The wife of Frank Jardine.
She was the niece of the Suzeraine of Samoa.
[King Malietoa.]

Chapter 10
"THE BATTLE OF SOMERSET"

Although the first attempt by missionaries to convert the aborigines was a failure, the second was more successful.

On the 11 July 1871, the schooner "Surprise" anchored in Albany Pass opposite Somerset, with 8 missionaries on board.

This was the beginning of an invasion of the Strait by the London Missionary Society [LMS]. From Somerset they were to be planted like seeds throughout the islands and further afield to New-Guinea.

Jardine accommodated them in the old marines married quarters and using this as a base they quietly went about their work. It was over 12 months later that the missionary boat "John Williams" also anchored at Somerset and this time there were 47 missionaries and native teachers aboard.

One of these mission teachers was to have a profound effect on Frank Jardine. Her name was Sana Solia, a princess of the royal house of Samoa and extremely attractive at 16 years of age. She was the niece of the Suzeraine of Samoa*, and as a child she is said to have been the Protege of the German Governor of Samoa and sent to Europe to be educated. Now as an attractive mission teacher she arrived at Somerset.

Frank Jardine fell deeply in love with Sana, and 12 months later, against the opposition of the missionaries and his own father, they were married at Somerset by the Reverend Murray, on the 16th October 1873.

Although the missionaries meant well, they were putting themselves in great danger. When the natives did revolt, their plight was very serious, for they were scattered on various islands in the Torres Strait. With insufficient boats to make their escape, the women and children had to be left on an isolated island.

Jardine arranged for their rescue by instructing the water police to take the Reverend Murray to the islands and rescue the stranded families before the natives found out about them.

Meanwhile at Somerset there was a serious threat to the community. The uprising in the islands was small in comparison to the general civil war on the Cape.

From the pearling station, 8 miles south of Somerset, Frank Jardine received a message from James Atkins, warning him by native messenger, that the "Yadagana" were preparing to march on Somerset and kill every man, woman and child at the settlement and burn it to the ground.

The missionaries, with their wives and children arrived safely at Somerset, followed by the pearlers, bringing the news that Atkins had been brutally murdered at his post, shortly after sending the message to Jardine.

When an advance guard of the "Yadagana" were spotted at the barracks, they cut the throat of one of the horses as they retreated. Frank realised that if the "Yadagana's" main force reached Somerset, there would be an outright slaughter of helpless women and children, including his own beloved Sana.

Rallying a force of Police, native troopers and volunteers from amongst the pearlers, he sent them out to confront the large force of warriors, marching on Somerset. They met the "Yadagana" force of several hundred strong, north of the Jardine River.

The aborigines immediately launched themselves into the attack, throwing their spears with fanatical zeal at the defending whites. The Somerset Brigade now retaliated

* King Malietoa of Samoa.

and a pitched battle ensued as the sound of gunfire tinged with the battle cries of the "Yadagana" echoed across Cape York.

They had hoped to conquer Somerset by club and spears, but instead were defeated by the Devil's Warriors. When there were no more spears to throw, they turned and fled to the Jardine River and never again had the courage to threaten Somerset.

Whilst the battle was being fought, Frank remained at Somerset with a number of armed fishermen and pearlers to protect the women and children, in case the "Yadagana" had split their ranks and advanced on the community from the opposite direction.

Many years later the "Yadagana" claimed they would have wiped out Somerset and killed every person in the settlement if it had not been for Jardine.

Although the aborigines suffered heavily from their attack, there were no serious casualties among the defenders. One native trooper was struck on the chest by a heavy spear, but fortunately was deflected by his rib cage, whilst others had spears pass through their loose shirts and trousers [see pages 199 and 226].

Meanwhile in Brisbane, allegations were made against Frank Jardine, in relation to his brother, Charles, pearling operations. The accusations incriminated Jardine himself, implying that he had used his position as Police Magistrate to obtain a licence to pearl.

On the 16th October 1873, Frank Jardine was notified from Brisbane that he was suspended as Police Magistrate.

The "Fly Point" airfield at Somerset.

CHAPTER 11
"FATE OF THE MAGISTRATES"

On the 5th November "H.M.S. Beagle" arrived at Somerset with stores. On board was Charles E Beddome, the new Police Magistrate who took charge of the settlement on the 7th November 1873.

One of his first tasks was to commence an inquiry into the false allegations made against Frank Jardine [see page 224].

This was held on the 10th November. The evidence from Coxswain E L Brown, of the Water Police clearly indicated that Jardine was innocent of the charges laid.

Meanwhile a Government "Board of Inquiry" in Brisbane had also found Jardine innocent as none of the charges could be proved.

Now that his name was cleared of any wrong doing, he resigned from the Government Service.

At last Frank and Sana could move away and start their life together. He had fought on the Cape for almost 9 years and now opted to move to "Nahgi" [Mt Ernest Island] in the Torres Strait to start a life of pearling. Over the past decade, he had tamed the savage tribes on Cape York, sheltered shipwrecked castaways and battled kidnappers and blackbirders in the dangerous seas off Cape York.

Over the next few years there were several Police Magistrates running Somerset at different times.

Beddome became ill and was replaced by George Elphinstone Dalrymple on the 1st May 1874. He was one of Queensland's great pioneers in earlier years.

Within 4 months Dalrymple also became extremely ill and as a result of partial paralysis and fever he authorised E L Brown who was now the Postmaster and Storekeeper to take over the running of the settlement from the 7th July 1874.

If there were any serious problems which required to be settled by a Police Magistrate, then he was to send the Government cutter "Lizzie Jardine" to Nahgi and request Frank Jardine to return to Somerset and sit at the bench.

Dalrymple was taken to Brisbane on board the Royal Mail Ship "Legislator" in July 1874 and replaced by Police Magistrate D'Oyley Aplin* who arrived at Somerset on the 25th August 1874.

3 Days later he took charge of the settlement from Brown on the 28th August, who reverted back to his normal duties as Postmaster and Storekeeper.

Throughout the chequered history of Somerset, the various Police Magistrates had witnessed and recorded one very important fact.

This was the incredible violence of the Aborigines against their fellow man which often resulted in a wholesale slaughter of men, women and children.

As a result of these savage conflicts their numbers were drastically reduced. Although the Gudang camped close to the settlement, they would not be spared.

They were seen as easy prey by their more powerful opponents, the Yadagana and Induyumu and slowly liquidated.

In April 1875 a mystery man was brought into Somerset. Although obviously a white man he could only speak in a native tongue. His right ear lobe was stretched down and there were many scars resembling cicatrices on his chest and stomach.

His name was Narcisse Pelatier who had just been rescued from the New Guinea coast by the slug boat "John Bell".

* His name was Christopher D'Oyley Aplin – not Charles D'Oyley Aplin as claimed by academics.

He was one of the few survivors from the wreck of the "St Paul" which struck a reef near Rossel Island, off the New Guinea coast in 1858.

All of the 327 chinese passengers and the French crew of 13 made it safely onto a nearby cay.

Although this little cay was a refuge from the sea, it was also a trap.

The next day the headhunters arrived from New Guinea and carried off several victims including a white man.

The Captain now left in the only boat with 8 of his crew including 12 year old Pelatier and headed for New Caledonia.

As they needed water they pulled into a small bay on the New Guinea coast and young Pelatier fell asleep under a tree. When he awoke the boat and crew were all gone.

He was captured by the natives and inducted into the tribe and named Anco. Although he was reasonably well treated he was not permitted to communicate in any way with passing vessels.

Finally, 17 years later, the crew of the "John Bell" landed on the New Guinea mainland for water and saw a white man with several natives at a waterhole. The crew returned to their ship which was anchored at Night Island just opposite the mainland.

They reported the news to their Captain, Joseph Fraser, who operated a Beche De-Mer [sea slugs] fishing station on the island.

The next day Frazer made contact with the natives and arranged to swap the man for a number of trade items.

D'Oyley Aplin later sent Pelatier to Brisbane on a visiting ship and he was handed over to the French Consulate and returned to France.

Pelatier was not the first survivor of the "St Paul" to arrive at Somerset. 10 years earlier in 1865, Captain Edwards of the Schooner "Blue Bell" had traded axes for 2 Chinese held captive at Piron Island to the north of Rossel Island.

He brought them to Somerset where they were handed over to Police Magistrate John Jardine.

He learnt their names were Pa-Qui and Tan-Tan and they related the full horror of the massacre of the "St Paul".

Whilst the passengers and crew were stranded on the coral cay, the savages would return each day and kill 9 people. These were loaded aboard their canoes and taken away to be eaten.

This continued for 10 days, until finally the remainder died of thirst, except 3 chinese who were taken to Rossel Island and forced to work in the native gardens.

Meanwhile the boat crew had made it to New Caledonia and in January 1859, the French ship "Styx" arrived at the scene of the tragedy.

As the ship anchored off Rossel Island she opened fire on the native camp. Whilst shells exploded in the surrounding bush one of the Chinese escaped and swam to the ship as sailors landed and set fire to the huts.

With the destruction of their camp, the entire tribe moved north to Piron Island where Pa-Qui and Tan-Tan were finally rescued by Captain Edwards in 1865.

They were later sent to Brisbane on board "HMS Salamander".

In July of 1875 measles entered the Torres Strait and killed hundreds of people. On Prince of Wales Island the Kauraregas died at the rate of 15 a week.

Within a short time it had spread to Somerset, where the survivors of the Gudang tribe were wiped out. Only 3 old men survived the epidemic and these died shortly after from old age.

On the 1st September 1875 D'Oyley Aplin wrote to the Authorities in Brisbane informing the Government that the **"friendly tribe of the Gudangs has become extinct."**

From Somerset the disease spread all over the top of Cape York wiping out young and old. The European children at Somerset also contracted the disease but all survived. The natives were not so fortunate, for they had no immunity to this deadly virus.

Now, every time they attacked their enemies they unknowingly spread the disease further.

Meanwhile, D'Oyley Aplin had been ill for several months and was slowly dying from Bilharzia Fever. He had earlier informed the Government that he could not continue much longer and that a new Police Magistrate would be required.

The Government ignored his request for a replacement and his condition worsened to the point that he was bedridden for days at a time.

When the "Chervert" anchored at Somerset, the doctor came ashore to assist him with medicine. This was of little help and he died at 6pm on the 9th September 1875.

It is ironic that 26 years earlier Aplin had been a passenger on board the "Freak" in 1849, when the remains of Wall and Niblett of the Kennedy Expedition were found and taken to Albany Island, where he assisted with their burial on the highest hill.

Now his body was taken across the water and laid to rest in this tiny graveyard next to Wall and Niblett.

The new Police Magistrate was once again Henry Chester, who arrived at Somerset on the 19th October 1875.

Shortly after his arrival he was offered a trip to New Guinea on board the missionary steamer the "Ellengowan".

The Reverend Macfarlane of the London Missionary Society had wanted to establish a mission station in the interior of New Guinea with access to the sea by the mighty "Fly River".

Chester jumped at the chance of joining the expedition and after arranging for Mrs Aplin's return to Brisbane the "Ellengowan" departed Somerset for the Cannibal Coast of New Guinea on the 29th November 1875.

Several months earlier Macfarlane and his crew had steamed 90 miles up the Fly and noted that the mouth of this river is over 40 miles wide.

Now they would go even further with a larger crew which numbered 14 people including the explorer Signor D'Albertis and 2 friendly New Guinea chiefs named Manio and Outa, who were picked up at Katow near the mouth of the Fly. They would be indispensable as guides and interpreters.

The "Ellengowan" entered the mouth of the "Fly" on the 6th December and 2 days later were attacked by 200 warriors, in 10 large war canoes. The warriors were decorated in fighting costumes of shells and feathers and screamed and yelled as they lunged into the attack.

For her defence the "Ellengowan" carried a small cannon as well as numerous sticks of dynamite which could be floated down stream in the path of attacking war canoes. Chester had also brought 3, well armed native troopers from Somerset.

With 5 attacking canoes on either side, a warning shot was fired across the bow of the lead canoe. They abruptly halted as if stunned when suddenly in a fit of vengeance continued to attack.

All hands now opened fire with an intense fusillade which caused the warriors to drop their weapons and paddle as fast as possible to escape the wrath of the "Ellengowan".

The following day they were again attacked by 120 warriors in 6 canoes further up the river. The crew opened fire and the natives beat a hasty retreat to the shore. This time Chester and some of the crew chased them in a whale boat. In their haste to escape, the warriors ran their canoes straight up the mud bank and fled into the forest.

To teach them a lesson, Chester chopped up one of their large canoes for firewood. In one of the canoes they found a number of weapons including some arrows with barbs of poisoned human bones and a dagger made from the thigh bone of the cassowary with knotches cut into it representing the number of people its owner had killed with it.

By the 15th December they had ascended the river for 150 miles and decided to turn back due to the approach of the wet season and the strong current which only allowed them to forge upriver for 15 miles a day.

They now commenced the long journey back down the river and 3 days later they were being followed by 21 canoes that were within 150 yards of them.

To avoid having to fight off such a large force of natives, D'Albertis threw a charge of dynamite towards them which exploded in front of the lead canoe.

Their reaction was incredible, for they instantly stopped paddling and ducked for cover in their canoes afraid of more explosions. Only when the "Ellengowan" was out of range did they sit up and row as fast as possible to the shore.

Later that day they grounded on a mudbank directly opposite a village that had previously attacked them on the journey upriver.

Using Manio as an interpreter, Chester offered to trade for pigs so that he could have some fresh meat. He was told to go ashore and shoot them himself.

Chester was no fool and suspecting treachery, took 7 men in a whaleboat and raced for the shore ahead of the canoes. He was mobbed by 100 men waiting to trade.

They soon became a noisy difficult people to deal with, so pointing to a target Chester fired a gun to let them see the accuracy of it.

Within seconds not a soul could be seen as they disappeared into the surrounding jungle. Just as quickly the canoes were run up the mudbanks as the warriors jumped ashore and raced for the sanctuary of the forest.

Suddenly 2 pigs appeared on the bank and were quickly shot and loaded onto the whale boat. Chester now took advantage of the disturbance and walked 50 yards away to the "Longhouse" which was an incredible 150 yards in length.

After placing several armed guards outside, he entered and found it partitioned into 3 parts. Human skulls were seen hanging from the rafters and an array of weapons including a bamboo beheading knife with 13 notches carved in the handle, representing the beheading of 13 people.

On the 21st December they finally reached the mouth of the "Fly", where Manio and Outa disembarked at a river camp.

With the expedition now over, the "Ellengowan" returned to Somerset and arrived on the 27th December 1875.

By 1876, pearl shell was still an attractive commodity, fetching over £100 per ton. A lot of Chesters time was now spent checking the licences and crews of pearling vessels, making sure that the skippers were not in violation of the Kidnapping Act.

Whenever the mail steamer arrived, the pearlers would converge on Somerset to receive fresh supplies and news from down south.

Chester would also take the opportunity to inspect any vessel that he suspected may have been pearling with an unlicenced crew and if necessary seize the vessel.

In July 1876, the native police deserted from Somerset and Chester forwarded warrants for their arrest to the Cooktown Police. They were captured 4 months later at Thornborough, after walking over 400 miles through enemy territory.

The large store at Somerset was operated by a Mr W Webb of Brown, Webb & Co.

In 1877 it was sold to Mr Raff, a businessman from Darwin who arrived at Somerset on his own leaving his wife in Darwin till he could arrange their accommodation and settle the agreement with Mr Webb.

Mrs Raff left Darwin on the steamship "William Mckinnon" in August 1877 bound for Somerset. During the voyage she was found murdered in her cabin. Her body had been stripped of jewellery and a large sum of money she was carrying with her was also missing.

Although the ship was searched, no trace of the murderer or her possessions was found. When the ship anchored in Albany Pass her body was taken ashore and buried at Somerset.

By now there were 16 pearling companies operating throughout the Torres Strait and Cape York. This was in spite of the fact that pearl shell had fallen in price from £150 per ton in 1875 to as low as £80 per ton by early 1877.

To bring the shell to the surface they employed 700 natives and 50 Europeans working from 109 vessels.

Chapter 12
"PALMER GOLD"

Throughout the 1870's countless shipwrecked castaways were still being slaughtered by the aborigines along the North Queensland coast, including men, women and children.

Occasionally a young white child would be kept alive, after killing the parents, if it had the slightest resemblance to a deceased child of the tribe.

The innocent toddler would grow up as an "Enslaved Child", knowing only the language, customs and violent warfare of the tribe.

In other cases young women of child bearing age were also captured and forcibly inducted into the tribe. Although some escaped, most were "Incarcerated for Life", and died amongst the aborigines as helpless captives.

When the "Maria" was wrecked off Cardwell at the base of Cape York Peninsula, on the 25th February 1872, many castaways made it to shore by rafts and boats, only to be speared and clubbed to death by the aborigines.

At one particular site, where several mutilated bodies were discovered on the beach, north of Cardwell it was appropriately named "Murdering Point" [Kurramine Beach].

With the discovery of gold on the Palmer River in July 1873, dozens of miners perished from the aggressive aboriginal attacks.

The first overland convoy of 100 miners was led by James Venture Mulligan, the discoverer of this rich gold field.

The convoy included hundreds of horses and bullocks pulling wagons loaded with every conceivable item needed including tools, explosives and food supplies. Many of the miners brought entire families with them in their hopes of finding their bonanza.

The less fortunate who could not afford a horse or wagon had to walk the entire distance and many were struck down by thirst and aboriginal attacks.

With the gold rush well and truly on, many established towns lost up to half their populations as men packed up and headed for this "River of Gold".

Within weeks, hundreds of men were mining the banks and bed of the Palmer River. It soon proved to be one of the biggest gold strikes in Australian history extending for 100 miles along the river. The authorities realised that a port would have to be established with access to the Palmer River. This would allow heavy equipment for the crushing plants to be landed and taken overland for a shorter distance.

There was also the fear that hundreds of people could eventually be trapped by the wet season if they continued to travel hundreds of miles overland.

The site chosen was the Endeavour River where Captain Cook had beached the Endeavour in June 1770 to make repairs to the ship.

On the 25th October 1873, the steamer "Leichhardt" arrived at Cooks Landing. On board were 96 miners, Government officials and mounted police.

Nearby was "HMSS Pearl" [Her Majesties Surveying Schooner] which had been surveying the river and the landing site.

Tents could be seen on shore opposite 2 vessels, the "Coquette" and "Flying Fish". These vessels had been hired by the Queensland Government to bring officials and equipment to the site.

They had been led up the coast from Cardwell by the explorer George Elphinstone Dalrymple [the founder of Cardwell].

On the journey north they explored various rivers and estuaries using the lifeboat from the wrecked "Maria" and were often attacked by aborigines.

Whilst exploring the North Johnston River a crowd of aborigines lined the river bank preparing to attack them when a tall burly savage, became over eager in his desire to kill the whites.

He swam halfway across the river when he was instantly taken by a crocodile and the attack suddenly abandoned.

Continuing up the coast they reached Trinity Bay [Cairns] where they were again attacked by the aborigines, who considered the whites as easy prey, but soon retreated when fired upon.

Finally, on the 24th October 1873, they reached the "Endeavour River" with the "Flying Fish" leaking badly and her stores wet from taking water in her hold.

Within days the horses and equipment were landed from the "Leichhardt" and over 100 tents were soon erected.

The site of this tent city was named "Cooks-Town", and later abbreviated to "Cooktown".

As the Palmer River was 150 miles south west of Cooktown it was decided that the Government horses should rest and feed on good grass for a few days, allowing them to recoup their energy after the trying sea journey.

These horses belonged to the Mounted Police and Government Officials, led by A C Macmillan [Surveyor and Engineer] who would mark a track to the Palmer for the miners to follow on foot.

One group of 5 men were too impatient and set off on their own through hostile territory, their greed overriding common sense.

The expedition finally left Cooktown on the 30th October led by Macmillan, Howard St George, [Gold Commissioner] and Inspector Dyas and his Mounted Police, who cut a tree line for the miners to follow.

Several days later they stumbled across the only survivor of the original 5 who had tried to make it on their own. The other 4 had been brutally murdered by aborigines.

The expedition continued on crossing numerous creeks and rivers, always on the alert in case of attack, knowing they were being watched all the way.

Finally at dawn on the 5th November, scores of painted warriors attacked the camp hoping to massacre the sleeping whites, only to be repulsed by a fusillade of lead.

Stunned by this vicious defence the savages retreated, only to regroup and attack in even larger numbers.

The defenders fired rapidly into this screaming horde as they hurled themselves like an avalanche against the miners.

Unable to assail the camp they finally retreated deep into the surrounding forest, after this "Baptism of Fire" from the deadly snider rifles during their attack at "Battle Camp".

As they continued the hard trek, following the horses over the range, the miners weakened and were soon spread out for miles along the track.

By nightfall of the 6th November, the first group of 25 men made it into the camp on the Deighton River, whilst the others, unable to see the marked tree line in the dark, fired their guns to keep in touch with each other and the last of the stragglers reached camp at 7am.

Finally on the 14th November, they reached the diggings at Palmerville on the Palmer River. Here they found a township of tents and bark huts with hundreds of diggers working the river banks, gullies and creeks.

Although many men found good payable gold, others were not so fortunate. Food was both scarce and expensive.

At this time a monopoly was held on the sale of flour by the Neil Family and they decided what they considered a pound of flour should be.

Neil's wife would sit on a cart and dip into the flour with a pannikan which was supposed to measure a pound of flour. If anyone so much as questioned the weight, they instantly went without.

Although Macmillan had blazed a track from Cooktown to the Palmer River, it could only be negotiated in single file by men and horses. It was therefore unsuitable at this time for carts and wagons.

Supplies were sent from Townsville to Georgetown where they were carted in wagons pulled by strong bullock teams 250 miles north to the Palmer River.

The tough bullocks ploughed through bogs and flooded rivers and creeks hauling their heavy loads with an ease that would have been near impossible with horses, although they were also used.

When Macmillan arrived at the Palmer River he noted that what little food was available was sold at extremely high prices. Unless a reliable supply could be maintained then starvation must ensue.

Within days of his arrival, Macmillan started the long journey back to Cooktown followed by 70 miners and over 150 horses, many of them carrying gold.

Upon reaching Cooktown he gave a full report of the terrible conditions on the Palmer, where men died from fever and starvation as well as aboriginal spears and there was not a single doctor on this rich Gold Field at this time.

A Government inquiry was also held in Cooktown, over the aggressive aboriginal attack at "Battle Camp" and the evidence showed that the Blacks intention, was to murder the Whites and under these circumstances the men had every right to defend themselves.

The incident was a clear message to anyone travelling on the Palmer track, to expect violence from the aborigines.

The food crisis on the Palmer was temporarily averted with the arrival of 40 wagons from Georgetown just before the onset of the wet season.

Many of these wagons were carrying miners and their families. They had earlier halted at the Mitchell River, when their horse teams could not pull the wagons across.

Fortunately, the bullock teams arrived hauling food to the Palmer and were able to help them get across.

With the start of the wet season, the access track from Georgetown was cut preventing any wagons from reaching the Palmer.

The food supplies were insufficient to last throughout the wet season and were soon consumed. Once again the threat of mass starvation loomed over the Palmer.

Many of the men now began shooting their horses for food. As the constant rain prevented the flesh from being sun dried, it was smoked in a makeshift enclosure, protected from the rain. Even the bones were cooked into a stew.

With the rain came millions of mosquitoes and a deadly fever that is often referred to as the "Palmer Pestilence" but which was probably malaria.

All along the river, men were dying from starvation, fever and aboriginal attacks.

Finally hundreds of starving miners abandoned the river and tried to walk back to Cooktown in both small and large groups in early 1874. This was at the height of the wet season and many drowned whilst trying to swim across flooded rivers and creeks.

In some cases the sheer weight of the gold strapped to their bodies, amounted to over 30 lbs, no doubt helped to pull them under.

Many also perished from starvation and disease, whilst others in 2's and 3's were ambushed and murdered by aborigines.

Yet, incredibly, whilst hundreds of sick and starving men had left the Palmer and were stumbling towards the sanctuary of Cooktown, a thousand others were heading to the Palmer with their spirits high in the hope of finding their El Dorado.

Few of them realised the full intensity of the tropical storms that lashed the land during the wet season, turning dry river courses into a raging torrent.

It wasn't long before hundreds of men were stranded between the flooded rivers, unable to move ahead towards the Palmer or return to Cooktown.

As it was extremely difficult for pack horses to be used with their heavy loads to cross flooded rivers and bogs during the wet season, then most men only carried a limited amount of provisions in their packs if they were walking, or on their horses if they were riding.

After running out of food, many of them were shooting their horses and eating them.

One enterprising group left Cooktown with planks of timber intending to build a boat to cross the flooded Normanby River.

After 3 days of trudging through mud and rain, they only covered 10 miles.

Ships were now arriving at Cooktown almost daily, crammed with men heading for the Palmer. Few of them had ever experienced a wet season and were unaware of the harsh conditions on the Palmer and the terrible trek that lay ahead.

It was now estimated that hundreds of pack horses would be needed to form a series of supply trains carrying food and essentials to the field once the track was widened.

Meanwhile a good by-pass off the Macmillan track was discovered by Sub Inspector Alexander Douglas, which shortened the journey by 60 miles.

This track passed between an outcrop of large rocks and was later named the "Hell's Gate Track", due to the rocky appearance and numerous savage attacks by aborigines, who brutally massacred scores of travellers as they passed through "Hell's Gates".

By May 1874, the Macmillan track had been widened sufficiently to allow wagon teams to head for the Palmer from Cooktown.

With the wet season now over, all manner of supplies and equipment could be brought onto the field much faster and in greater volume.

How many starving, fever ridden miners died during that first wet season, as they struggled to reach Cooktown with their gold, is inestimable.

Although many were murdered by aborigines, others perished from starvation, when they became trapped between flooded rivers.

At the Normanby River, a bag containing 1000 ounces of gold was found beside the skeletons of 3 men who had died of starvation during the wet season. They had made it to an island in the middle of the river and became trapped by rising flood waters and starved to death.

The first heavily armed gold escort party, left the Palmer with 6000 ounces of gold for Cooktown in May 1874. It was led by Sub Inspector Clohesy with his Mounted Police.

They followed the pack horse route via "Hell's Gates" constantly on their guard for treachery from marauding aborigines.

As they camped each night, they always kept their loaded sniders nearby in case of an attack.

Within days of leaving the Palmer, the aborigines attacked the camp at night, from the cover of the surrounding scrub.

As dozens of spears landed in and around the camp, the troopers retaliated by firing round after round into the fringing scrub from where their hidden adversaries had launched their cowardly attack.

All through that sleepless night, the troopers waited for another attack, which never came, for the aborigines had retreated in panic.

In the morning spears were found littering the ground where the aborigines had made their hasty retreat.

As blood was also found on the bushes, then they must have had a number of wounded.

By now Cooktown had grown into a thriving port, where ships of every description were arriving daily, with horses, drays, mining equipment and human cargoes of thousands of people heading for the Palmer.

The town was in a state of "constant activity" as masses of people jostled their way along the wide main thoroughfare of Charlotte Street with its wooden buildings of shops, hotels, houses and shanties.

With large numbers of men moving to and from the Palmer, the hotels did a roaring trade, as did the sly grog shanties and dens of iniquity.

As the new arrivals headed for the Palmer they stretched out for miles along the track, in the hundreds. In some cases entire families of men, women and children were making the trek.

Many were pushing wheelbarrows loaded with food and possessions, whilst others pulled small carts. Some even had wheeled boats for crossing rivers.

Amongst the throngs streaming to the field, were masses of Chinese coolies under the control of ruthless overseers.

They appeared as human "beasts of burden", carrying up to 70 pounds of merchandise at each end of a bamboo pole suspended across the back of their neck and shoulders. In some cases the combined weight of both ends was over 150 pounds.

They became easy targets for the cannibalistic aborigines who simply attacked from behind, clubbing the last man in the line and carrying him back to their camp.

The noisy Chinese made such a racket that they could also be grabbed from behind and dragged into the scrub, as their screams for help were deadened by the calamitous din of their merchandise.

If necessary, they could be kept alive as fresh meat for days and finally cooked and eaten.

The statement, written by journalists and authors, that the "aborigines preferred eating Chinese flesh to European", has little evidence to support it.

It is more probable that the timid Chinese, travelling unarmed in single file, were easily snatched from the rear of their long drawn out columns.

In contrast, Europeans were usually armed with revolvers or rifles and generally travelled in groups, making it difficult to attack them without sustaining casualties.

Yet, in spite of their superior weapons many whites were to be continually attacked along the route.

Among the casualties were 2 men transporting supplies by pack horses, through "Hell's Gates". They were knocked unconscious by flying clubs and carried to a nearby camp, where they were later cooked and eaten [McQuarrie Brothers – 1874].

Anyone travelling alone or in a small group along the Palmer road, ran an extremely high risk of being killed or captured by the aborigines.

One of the most vicious attacks recorded took place along Macmillans wagon track near the Battle Camp Range when a migrant family were ambushed near a lagoon [1874]. The victims were Johannes Strau, his wife Brigit and 5 year old daughter Annie.

He was found beneath the dray with a spear through his chest. Nearby was the mutilated remains of his naked wife and their little girl, who was horribly disembowelled.

William Corfield was a teamster carting supplies to Palmerville with his bullock wagons at the time of the Strau murders. He later gave the following account in his excellent book "Reminiscences of Queensland 1862-1899". He stated:

> *They found Strau's body beneath the dray. The dead body of his wife was a little distance away. A spear had been driven through her mouth, and had pinned her to the ground ... before being killed outright the woman was subjected to "horrible outrage" by the blacks ... In the scrub, they found the little girl, a large gash across her forehead, her stomach ripped up by the blacks wooden knives, and her eyes pecked out by crows. The body was buried with the father and mother ... The blacks dug up the grave and carried off the bodies.*

All along the Palmer track the aborigines laid siege to areas commonly used as overnight camping sites. One of these was at a crossing on the Laura River.

It was here that the Mounted Police found the bodies of a young couple who had only just been married in Cooktown. They had set out for the Palmer River on horse back.

When they reached the Laura, they hobbled their horses and camped. Within hours they were viciously attacked by aborigines.

The young miner fought back against hopeless odds, armed only with a revolver.

When he ran out of ammunition, the lovers embraced each other in the face of death, accepting their fate as their fanatical killers impaled their bodies with 9 foot spears.

Meanwhile back on the Palmer River, James Mulligan's camp was attacked at the "Battle of Round Mountain".

The aborigines, in their determination to kill the whites, made 3 attempts to assail the camp, but were repulsed each time by gun fire.

Finally, their savage instincts forced them into making a screaming suicidal charge, only to be halted by a massive barrage of rifle fire.

Faced with this impenetrable wall of resistance they retreated back into the protective forest, dragging their wounded with them.

Throughout this savage attack 3 of the defenders were struck by spears, but fortunately, they all recovered from their wounds.

The primitive aborigines had still not come to terms with the reality that spears were no match for guns, and that their "tradition" of using violence against their fellow man, would be repaid with violence.

They sincerely believed that they had every right to kill any person outside their tribe.

Yet, they considered it a terrible injustice for anyone to strike back and kill them in return.

Whilst they continued their indiscriminate slaughter of men, women and children, then they must inevitably pay a high price, from their proposed victims, who retaliated by right of defence.

One of the most colourful characters on the Palmer was Dr Jack Hamilton. Although a medico he was also an adventurer and at one time was said to have been involved in a war in South America. Prior to his arrival at the Palmer River the miners had to wait for a visiting doctor who arrived only once in 3 months. [Dr Picho]

He had no shortage of customers as malaria, dysentery and other diseases were rampant along the river. Behind his scrub clinic was a graveyard where scores of patients lay buried.

Hamilton would often work all night trying to save his patients, but still the death toll mounted.

Although most of these had died from Dysentery, which far exceeded deaths from malaria, many also died from spear wounds inflicted during aboriginal attacks on their camps.

As well as being a "bush doctor", Hamilton was also a champion pistol shooter and in earlier years of competition he beat Colonel Withans, the American champion.

He excelled at whatever he tried, for he was also an excellent athlete, boxer and swimmer.

When a miner was seriously wounded after an aboriginal attack, he immediately saddled up and galloped into the dark rainy night to help him. When he tried to cross the flooded Palmer River he ended up with his horse back on the bank.

His athletic prowess as a champion swimmer, was now to his advantage. Leaving his horse on the bank he swam the river, fighting against the fast current and emerged on the opposite side with his medical bag intact.

He walked the remaining distance through mud and rain and finally reached the wounded man, saving his life.

Throughout that night he had travelled over 20 miles on his mission of mercy.

By the end of 1874 over 500,000 ounces of gold had been extracted from the field, by thousands of miners who scrummaged through every creek and gully running into the Palmer.

At this time there were 3 major settlements along the river, complete with shacks made from bark and saplings.

"Byerstown" was upriver from Palmerville [east] and between these 2 communities was "Maytown" the thriving hub of the Palmer.

The reefs here were extremely rich, assaying at 5 to 10 ounces to the ton, bringing untold wealth to their owners.

Within a short time 3 banks were operating at Maytown, and like most buildings were made of split bush timber, but with the addition of tin roofs for security.

Each evening the diggers congregated in the numerous bark shanties that passed for hotels, swapping tales and drinking to each others wealth.

Some of the wealthiest people on the Palmer were the butchers and storekeepers, who charged up to 5 times the normal price of their goods.

At times when meat was scarce, bullocks would be killed and the meat rationed out under an armed guard, at exorbitant prices.

Once reef mining commenced, Maytown prospered enormously as bags of gold were deposited each week at the gold assayers hut.

Yet, with its increased wealth, came tragedy, as casualties rose enormously, when scores of men were killed or seriously injured from terrible mining accidents.

Jack Hamilton moved to Maytown, where he built a small bush hospital from the usual split timber and bark.

He was both nurse and doctor and saved dozens of lives as he worked long hours repairing torn and broken bodies, curing Malarial fever and Dysentery, and removing spear heads from miners wounded from aboriginal attacks.

Doc Hamilton had a reputation for riding out at any time of the day or night, through flooded rivers and tropical storms to reach a wounded or dying man.

He often put his own life on the line, totally oblivious to the warring aborigines, who could so easily put a spear in his back as he rode to aid the sick.

On some of these "missions of Mercy" he would ride over 50 miles to treat a patient.

When large numbers of Chinese arrived on the Palmer in 1874, they were seen as a serious threat to the industry, by a number of businessmen at Maytown.

It was assumed that the Chinese would send any gold they found to China, where they would receive a higher price. Australia, would therefore be the loser. This was later proved to be correct.

However, many of the white miners were under the false impression, that most of the good gold had already been extracted and they wouldn't get much anyway.

In fact the richest deposits, amounting to several million ounces, had not been discovered at this time.

Meanwhile, Howard St George, [the Gold Commissioner], had observed hundreds of Chinese mining along the Palmer, and realised that if they continued to arrive unchecked, they must eventually outnumber the whites.

He therefore, called a meeting with the diggers, allowing them to decide whether the Chinese should be removed from the field, or allowed to stay.

Many of those present had had enough of Aboriginal attacks, fever and starvation diets and were convinced that the river was running out of gold.

As they did not realise, the enormous wealth that lay secreted in hidden reefs, along the creeks and river banks, they yelled out:

"Let 'em have it, Boss. It's only a Chinamans field anyhow."

In their ignorance, the diggers had thrown away a fortune in gold by allowing the industrious Chinese onto the field.

Within months, thousands of them were scouring every nook and cranny along the river, like an army of ants.

By early 1875, large fleets of junks, sailed from Chinese ports, jampacked with thousands of coolies, destined for the Palmer River.

Most of them were simple peasants, held to ransom, by wealthy merchants in China and Hong Kong. In many cases their families would be held as security, to make sure they repaid the highly inflated cost of their sea journey to Australia, plus interest.

By now, thousands were being packed into the hot and rancid holds of steamers heading for Cooktown whilst international liners were also hired to transport thousands more.

Many of these were not connected with the merchants, but had instead formed their own syndicates and were paying their own way.

Upon arrival at Cooktown, they set up large camps along the Endeavour River, preparing for the gruelling trip ahead of them.

The residents of Cooktown were so incensed at what they considered was a "Chinese Invasion", that they chased and stoned hundreds of them out of town.

At a large public rally over the Chinese issue, a miner stated:

"That, the diggers, who had protected themselves from the aborigines, would do so with the Chinkies, and that the Government, when too late, might discover, that more than the men of Lambing Flat, could do a roll up, when their interests were touched."

Among those, whose "interests were touched" were the packers [carrying supplies on pack-horses] and the teamsters [who carted supplies on horse drawn wagons].

They usually charged over £100 a ton and some were known to make between £400 to £1000 a trip, from Cooktown to the Palmer.

In comparison, it only took 15 Chinese coolies to carry a ton of supplies, for a minimum outlay of a few bags of rice.

The whites, naturally considered the use of slave labour by the Chinese as unfair competition, and it wasn't long before a number of coolies were found shot.

The Chinese often burnt the long grass on either side of the track, as a protection against being ambushed by the aborigines.

This infuriated the packers and teamsters who needed the grass to feed their horses. This no doubt, contributed to even more violence between the whites and their competitors.

Meanwhile, the aborigines had observed the increased movement along the Palmer track. They had spied out the Chinese columns from their hidden lairs, overlooking the route. The large overnight campsites, holding up to 400 coolies were also under observation.

They could at any time attack these crowded camps, but to do so could mean taking heavy casualties. They had learnt from past experience that it did not pay to attack such large groups.

Even a big mob of Chinese running amok with knives and axes, could wreak havoc amongst the attacking aborigines if they got close enough to them.

The savages simply watched and waited till the Chinese walked into one of their many ambush sites along the track. In this manner scores of them were massacred during these aggressive aboriginal attacks.

In one of these assaults, over 30 Chinese were slaughtered at "Hell's Gates."

Although many of the Chinese casualties were from aboriginal attacks, others also died from exhaustion and illness. Those who collapsed and could go no further, were left to die where they fell. [Cooktown Courier]

Upon arrival at the Palmer, they soon came into conflict with the white miners, who naturally resented them encroaching on their ground.

Signs soon appeared nailed to trees, warning the Chinese, that they would be hanged if they were caught near the diggings.

In reference to one of these signs at Sandy Creek the "Cooktown Courier" stated:
"Any Chinaman found higher up this creek will be instantly seized and hanged until he is dead."

The Chinese were far more meticulous in their search for gold, than were the whites. When the diggers abandoned a site for better ground, the Chinese moved in and in some cases made a fortune, from the old ground.

They used a unique system of mining, by cutting out a spiral stairway from the earth and rock, leading down into the mine.

This system permitted the workers to carry out their loads from the mine at a faster rate than the winch system.

They soon built their own towns along the Palmer, populated entirely by Chinese. They also operated stores in the white communities of Maytown, Palmerville and Byerstown.

Although, rarely violent towards Europeans, they often locked horns with each other. Their habit of jumping each others claims, often resulted in violent confrontations in which they attacked an opponent with any weapon that was available, such as, knives, axes, pick handles and meat choppers.

They generally mixed only with their own dialectual groupings. It was rare, for example, to see a Cantonese associate with a Macao, hokkien or any others, and vice versa.

In mid 1878, large quantities of alluvial gold was discovered at Lukinville, about 40 miles down the river from Palmerville. Within days thousands of miners rushed to the new field.

The population soon swelled to over 9000 of which most were Chinese. In their rush to claim the best ground, heavy fighting broke out amongst them.

The battle involved thousands of Macaos fighting several thousand more Cantonese. Some were armed with Snider rifles and old carbines, but the majority simply fought with iron bars, axes etc.

The casualties inflicted at the "Battle of Lukinville", included over 200 who were seriously wounded. Over 30 of these later died from the effects of their wounds, such as crushed skulls and axe wounds.

During the conflict, the whites stayed under cover as stray bullets occasionally ricocheted off metal objects.

A Chinese was seen poking his head from behind a tree and upon seeing his enemy, duck back and fire the gun in the approximate direction without aiming properly, then, stick his head out to see if he had hit his target.

Warden Sellheim and his police finally stopped the fighting, by arresting the ring leaders from both sides and peace was finally restored as they agreed to keep to their own defined areas.

The Chinese were generally despised by the whites and a large number were forced away from one area at gunpoint.

Others were murdered along the Palmer track as they carried their gold to Cooktown.

The hostility towards the Chinese was extremely volatile and in some cases explosive.

In order to appease the diggers and hopefully prevent an outbreak of racial violence, the Queensland Government finally passed a law, in which all Chinese arriving in Queensland must pay an entry tax of £10.

As this law was not passed until the 20th August 1877, then it was really a case of too little too late, as most of the good gold had already been extracted by that time.

However, another law was passed, which prevented any Chinese from prospecting on any new gold field for 3 years, after it was found.

This pleased the diggers more than any tax could, as it meant the real winners were the Australians, and the profits from the gold would benefit Queensland, rather than China and Hong Kong.

The total amount of gold extracted from the Palmer River, must have been phenomenal.

As only a small portion of the gold was ever declared to the Cooktown Customs, then the official figures are misleading.

According to the Queensland Department of Minerals and Energy, a total of 1,333,893 ounces of gold from the Palmer River was declared to the Authorities, between 1873-1878. This amounts to 7.5% of all gold declared in Queensland.

However, to avoid paying any tax on the gold at Cooktown, most people smuggled out their gold.

The Chinese are known to have smuggled out millions of ounces of gold, onto waiting vessels on the Endeavour River and taken to China, where they received a higher rate for it.

For this reason a more accurate figure could be closer to five million [5,000,000] ounces of gold.

Although thousands of Chinese worked and prospected along the Palmer River, their population was never as high as some writers have claimed. One source claimed there were 40,000 Chinese on the river.

This figure may apply to the total number of Chinese who worked along the Palmer between 1873-1880 and not necessarily at any one time.

Even in those days it was common for officials to carry out a census on horse back, past every camp, shanty and bush dwelling from Cooktown to the Palmer.

The highest number of Chinese recorded along the Palmer River was 17,000 in 1877.

The population of Cooktown has also been highly exaggerated with figures in excess of 30,000 being mentioned.

The total white male population of North Queensland in 1877 was only 17,042, and according to a document held by the Australian Bureau of Statistics, a census taken in 1876, showed the population of Cooktown to be only 2185 permanent residents.

A considerable number of Chinese had settled in Cooktown after working on the Palmer. They started their own businesses, such as Tailors, Launderers, Barbers and Storekeepers. It is very possible that they may not have been classified as permanent residents and not counted in the census.

Cooktown is said to have had as many as 60 hotels during the days of the Palmer gold rush. This must be a case of overkill.

Any dilapidated shack or lean-too selling sly grog could be classified as a drinking house. Many of these shanties were often called hotels.

In 1876, Cooktown became a municipality and all hotels and shanties as far as the Palmer were counted as part of the Cooktown Municipality. This may explain the rumour of Cooktown's 60 hotels.

By 1880 the Palmer rush was over and the miners moved to other areas to seek their fortunes.

Today, the Palmer River still flows majestically across Cape York during the wet season. When the rains are gone, the rusted relics of a bygone era can still be found.

The remains of wagon wheels, horse shoes, picks and shovels are the final tribute to the thousands of people who lived and fought along this River of Gold.

Chapter 13
"THURSDAY ISLAND"

Although Somerset failed to become the "New Singapore" of Australia, it was still a success when viewed as a "Refuge for Castaways".

During its short history of 13 years it had sheltered survivors from 14 officially recorded shipwrecks.

At one time Frank Jardine had sheltered 93 castaways from 3 different shipwrecks.

Somerset was slowly dying due to its position being too far south of the main shipping channels. The settlers never came because of the constant violence between the native tribes. Many of the buildings had been eaten out by white ants and the shallow anchorage could only handle 3 ships at any one time due to the gusty south east winds that swept through Albany Pass.

For the past decade talks had been held on the possibility of moving the settlement to a more suitable location.

There were various sites within the Prince of Wales group of islands that could be acceptable, but in most cases they were either too exposed to the North West Monsoons or lacked sufficient water.

The Authorities finally settled for Thursday Island which was protected by the surrounding Prince of Wales islands.

From here, one can look straight down Boat Channel which separates the eastern side of Prince of Wales from Horn Island.

One of the major reasons for choosing Thursday was the strategic position of Goode Island, several miles to the west of Thursday.

A signalling station was built here that could observe all ships passing through the Strait via the Prince of Wales Channel.

An added bonus was that a closer watch could be kept on the islanders who used to congregate behind Friday Island waiting for the opportunity to attack crippled ships.

The native name for Thursday Island is "Waiben" meaning dry or no water.

It may seem strange that a small island that is inundated with extremely heavy rainfall during the wet season was said to be a dry island by the Kauraregas.

When a native searches for water he may only dig a few feet with his simple implements of wood and bone. If he fails to strike it then he will search elsewhere. Whereas, European man used metal tools such as shovels and drills which permitted him to tap large reserves stored in deep rocky basins.

Because the Kauraregas had difficulty in finding water they concluded that it was dry and did not camp on the island other than for short visits.

On the 17th September 1877, Henry Chester was appointed Police Magistrate of the new settlement and commenced his duties at Thursday Island on the 25th September 1877.

With the transfer of the Establishment to Thursday Island, the Government sold the remaining equipment and buildings at Somerset plus cattle, horses and equipment from Vallack Point Station to Frank Jardine for £150 on the 24th November 1877.

Thursday Island was now the Administrative centre for Cape York and the Torres Strait Islands. It is situated 23 miles North West of Cape York.

Initially it was to be only a Government outpost and under the reign of Chester. Any Pearlers attempting to set up operations from the island were quickly removed.

It was not until 1885, that John Douglas [a previous Premier of Queensland] succeeded Chester as Police Magistrate that things began to change.

Thursday Island, became the major base of the pearling fleets operating throughout the Torres Strait Islands and the top end of Cape York.

Pearl Shell, [Maximus Pinctadus] had an unlimited market last century. The ladies of Europe wore footwear adorned with pearl shell, whilst knives of every description had handles decorated with pearl shell. Even American gunfighters occasionally fought it out with pearl handled revolvers.

Anyone not familiar with the Pearling Industry may naturally assume that pearlers searched for pearls amongst the shallow oyster beds.

In fact, the real wealth was in the inside layer of the shell.

Although pearls were always sought after, they were difficult to find, for on average only one shell in a hundred may have an acceptable pearl.

Pearling companies generally operated from a station on one of the islands. At the pearling grounds a mother ship often accompanied the luggers to keep them supplied with their weekly necessities.

When a diver surfaced, he would pass the shell to the small swimming boats that coasted above them. They would later transfer their load to the luggers where the oyster flesh was removed, and occasionally a lucky pearl was found. In some cases the tough little pearling luggers also operated alone.

These small luggers were only 30 feet in length with pointed bow and stern alike. Although they weighed less than 8 ton they could carry 4 ton of shell. They were ideal for the shallow waters of the Strait and could take quite a hiding in blustery weather [Large luggers were also used].

Although any pearls found were the property of the Company, they were often smuggled ashore by crew members and sold on Thursday Island to a "Chinese Gardener", who would then sell them to passengers on the visiting mail steamers.

During the early 1890's a fort was constructed on a grassy hill overlooking the picturesque bay of Port Kennedy. It was feared at the time that there could be a Russian invasion, and from its commanding position the large 6 inch guns [150mm] could soon zero in on any seaborne invader.

By 1892 there were over 500 people living on the Island, and with the signing of the Anglo-Japanese Alliance, the Strait was inundated with Japanese divers.

Many of the pearlers had now switched to Apparatus Boats which were fitted with compressors to feed oxygen to divers in suits and helmets.

This permitted them to stay down for a longer period of time and at greater depths.

As the pearl beds were fished out, new beds would be sought and found. Some of these were at the "Darnley Deeps", where Japanese divers went down as far as 60 fathoms [360 feet] in search of shell.

At these depths the pressure causes nitrogen bubbles to enter the bloodstream from the oxygen supplied by the compressor.

If a diver surfaced too fast he would suffer the "Bends". Those who survived would be crippled for life, with their knees bent outwards, and thus the term "Bends".

The "Darnley Deeps" are in the Eastern Torres Strait and were often called the divers graveyard due to the large number of divers who perished there. Because of so many casualties, it was decided to close the area to diving in 1897.

Later, a system that was to save many lives was used called "Staging". This method was simply a natural form of decompression.

When a diver surfaced suffering from the "Bends", he would be taken back down to the bottom and slowly brought up to a higher level and remain there for up to an hour. He would then be brought to another level and the same process repeated till he was finally brought to the surface.

The whole operation could take over 5 hours and certainly saved the lives of many divers.

Eventually it was to be normal practice for divers to be hauled up slowly and allowed to stage along the way up.

Many divers who had survived the "Bends" became virtual skeletons from the waist down, whilst others, who died were so twisted and crushed in their suits that they were buried in them.

The Thursday Island cemetery is a mute testimony to the large number of divers who perished from the "Bends".

When 2 hotels were built to cater for the thirsty lugger crews, the Island was aptly called "Thirsty Island".

It soon became a rollicking port as other hotels were built. The "Grand" was on the waterfront whilst the "Metropole" stood on a nearby hill. Other pubs took names applicable to the region such as the "Thursday Island" and the "Torres Strait".

The huge empty bottle heaps behind the pubs were an ample testimony to the pearlers thirsts.

In the meantime, back on Cape York, Frank Jardine now had a good market for his cattle.

With its rising population, Thursday Island needed plenty of fresh meat and who better to get it from than Frank Jardine.

The cattle were rounded up from Lockerbie Station, 11 miles South West of Somerset and herded to the holding yards at Galloway, on the western side of Cape York, where they were then inspected. From here they were taken the last 2 miles to the Red Island Point slaughter yards [now Seisia] where they were butchered and the beef shipped to Thursday Island.

By 1893 there were over 200 pearling vessels operating throughout the Torres Strait and the population of Thursday Island had soared to 1400, of which only half were whites. The remaining 700 were from all over the world including, Chinese, Japanese, Malays, West Indians, American Negroes, Singalese and many others from Mauritius, Zanzibar and the Sudan, as well as Torres Strait Islanders. Even the grandson of Fletcher Christian of "Mutiny on the Bounty" fame was pearling in the Strait.

The Chinese, were well known for their culinary skills and could soon prepare a sumptuous dinner of turtle and dugong steaks.

Whilst the Japanese, not to be out done, opened a brothel, much to the disgust of the respectable inhabitants of Thursday Island.

On some occasions when a prize pearl was found, the skipper would shout his crew to a champagne party.

In such an environment, crime and violence was to be expected and only the valiant few dared to walk the streets late at night.

Although pearling had contributed enormously to the success of Thursday Island, it could not continue indefinitely. In 1897 over 1200 ton of shell was collected and valued at £126,000.

As one area was depleted of shell, so the search would continue for new pearl beds. It had continued like this for decades until it became more difficult to locate and was becoming a scarce commodity.

During the 1920's various experiments were conducted to try to cultivate pearls artificially. This had shown only minor success until the Japanese company "Mikimoto" finally perfected it. Now the pearl replaced the shell as the more valued item.

For the success of cultured pearl farming it is essential to have calm water where a raft must float supported by water proof containers such as oil drums.

From this raft, baskets of shell containing healthy oysters are supported so as to allow the oysters to feed on healthy plankton.

In order that a pearl can be formed a culture must be placed into the oyster so as to provoke the oyster into retaliation.

The oyster senses the culture as an invader and attacks it by secreting a fluid over it. This fluid solidifies into a smooth solid ball, which becomes the pearl.

POEM WRITTEN BY AN UNKNOWN AUTHOR

*A saga from the tropical northern sea
of danger and death and black treachery
A too true tale that stirs the land
From Otway's Cape to Port Darwin Strand,
Out on the Lizard, with two Chinese,
Waiting and watching the friendly breeze.
which would bring back him whom she loved to please,
One love coming and one on her knees.
Every passing sail was a mark in the life
of the lonely fond mother, the loving wife;
and the murmuring wind and the dashing spray
Whispered hopeful tales of a happier day.
Out in the dusk on the "brown ribbed" strand'
came crawling and stealing, the murderous band;
one after another her servants fell,
and who can the thoughts of that woman tell?
Surrounded, cut off from hope or relief,
Yet never sinking in womanly grief;
Rising bold and true – like a spartan mother;
Fears and tears brave hearts should smother.
Sleep little babe! Let your mother fight
Through the sunny day and the lowering night
Holding at bay that demon score,
too often recruited from mainland shore.
Hold the fort indeed! her fort was here;
It held a mother her jewel most dear.
With a firm hand and a steady eye,
she sent a few devils to curse and die;
But nature must always claim its share,
and she sank at last in unanswered prayer.
Draw the veil! Wrap it o'er the closing scene –
The spear, the waddy, the tomahawk keen!
Would to God their work had been short and sharp,
But her last few words were devilish and dark.
Where was the guardian angel, then,
Who rescues women and saves brave men?
Why not strike with his flaming sword
The whole of that black and bloody horde!
Let us hope that she is dead and her soul at rest;
God knoweth and judgeth, aye, for the best,
But his judgements sometimes are hard to bear,
And I wish he had managed that woman to spare –
Not to be! But her life and end shall not die;
Bards with better pens, lift her memory high.*

CHAPTER 14
"LIZZIE WATSON"

Among the many small vessels sailing up the Endeavour River to Cooktown, were the Slug Boats, whose owners operated stations on the off-shore islands.

Many were hard bitten men, who often fought off attacks by mainland aborigines, who tried to ambush them at their lonely island outposts.

They spent their time collecting the ugly, fat, sea slugs along the beaches and shallow waters on the reef.

The slugs, known as "Sea Cucumbers", Trepang and Beche De Mer", were boiled in a large tank and sun dried, when they would shrink from as long as 3 feet down to 12 inches.

To the Chinese they were a delicacy and could fetch as much as £50 a ton in Canton, China.

Bob Watson was a tough Scotsman who operated his slug station with his mate Fuller on Lizard Island about 50 miles north of Cooktown.

They had built a stone cottage on a flat overlooking the beach, with a well and vegetable garden nearby.

On one of his visits to Cooktown, he met a shy 21 year old English school teacher in early 1880.

Her name was Mary Beatrice Phillips, who had recently arrived as a Governess for the family of a French Businessman, named Charles Bouel, who owned a hotel and restaurant.

She soon fell in love with Watson and they were married on the 30th May 1880 and left that same day for Lizard Island.

Watson had nicknamed her "Lizzie" after the island, which they also called "The Lizard".

When the sea slugs became scarce around the island, the men had to search further afield. On many occasions she waited long nights for their return.

In June 1881, she returned to Cooktown and gave birth to a boy, whom they named "Ferrier" [George Ferrier Watson].

Now back on the "Lizard" she continued her lonely vigil for weeks at a time waiting for their return.

By late 1881, the sea slugs were fished out and the 2 men sailed 150 miles north to Nights Island to start up a new curing operation.

Lizzie and baby Ferrier were left behind with 2 Chinese servants. Ah Sam was the house boy and Ah Leong, was the gardener.

Watson considered that it would be too dangerous to take Lizzie and the baby through reef infested waters, where hundreds of ships had been wrecked.

For this reason he felt they would be safer staying on the island which was amply supplied with food and water.

As the weeks slowly went by, no news came out of Lizard Island. Something was terribly wrong.

When Captain Frier was passing the island [Monday 17th October] he noted large bush fires and observed something suspicious through his telescope. He moved in closer and signalled the cottage but there was no reply.

The front door of the cottage was wide open, but no whites or Chinese could be seen. Instead, he saw 2 naked black men around the house.

Presuming the station must have been closed, he sailed on to Cooktown and reported what he had seen [Wednesday 19th October].

The following day another report came into Cooktown. The cutter "Neptune" had passed the Lizard and the crew saw 10 canoes and 40 armed natives on the beach near the cottage.

With this latest information, a police party boarded the Government schooner "Conflict" [H.M. Schooner Conflict] and set out for Lizard Island the next day [Friday 21st October].

Bartley Fahey [Sub-Collector of Customs], Lieutenant Izatt of the "Conflict", a white police officer and 5 native police, landed on the island and were shocked at what they found.

As they entered the cottage, it appeared as if a cyclone had struck it. Furniture was wrecked and thrown upside down, whilst papers, books and journals were ripped to pieces and scattered throughout the rooms.

The 2 rifles left for Lizzie's defence, had their barrels bent and the butts broken, whilst the sewing machine was smashed to pieces.

Fahey, now found her diary and learnt that Ah Leong had been brutally murdered by the blacks at the garden.

The searchers all pondered the same unanswerable question. "WHERE IS LIZZIE?"

In desperation they searched the entire island, but no trace could be found of Lizzie, her baby or the surviving Chinese Ah Sam.

They returned to Cooktown with her diary [Sunday 23rd October].

A search commenced along the coastline, to the north of Cooktown. In a short time some women's clothing was found at an abandoned aboriginal campsite.

Nearby they found a woman's long blonde hair, and concluded that it may have been Lizzie's, for by now it was accepted that she had been killed and eaten by the aborigines.

The hair and clothing was taken back to Cooktown, where Bob Watson had now arrived.

When shown the hair he stated clearly that it was not Lizzie's hair, for she had dark hair, not blonde.

With additional re-inforcements the search continued on the mainland opposite Lizard Island.

When a native camp was located, it was quietly surrounded and the Native Police moved in preventing anyone from escaping.

During questioning of captured natives, all kinds of explanations were given, which only made her fate more confusing.

Some aborigines claimed she was captured and clubbed to death when she struggled too violently, almost upsetting a canoe.

Yet, at another camp, a native claimed that, after killing Ah Leong in the garden, they attacked the house, whence she shot one of them, but was soon captured and then killed.

The police soon realised that the aborigines were simply lying, for no mention was ever made about her baby.

Meanwhile, as the search continued for Lizzie, the same natives who had murdered Ah Leong attacked other islands, where whites were living.

In most cases they were driven back by gun fire, when they retreated to their canoes, with the exception of one station, which was over run and the Islander, caretaking it was murdered.

The Authorities now had little hope of ever finding Lizzie alive, and the search was finally abandoned.

The blonde hair and clothing obviously belonged to a white girl, and this was probably the girl who was clubbed to death for struggling too much. She may have been a castaway from one of the many shipwrecks that dotted the coastline, or even the wife of a slug skipper, murdered at an isolated camp.

Nearly 4 months after Lizzie's disappearance the "Kate Kearney" arrived in Cooktown on the 22nd January 1882. She had been pearling in the Torres Strait and was heading south with her load of pearl shell.

The Kate's skipper, Captain Bremner, reported how he had arrived at the 'Howick' group of islands and anchored at number 5 Howick, which is a waterless coral cay, about 30 miles north east of Lizard Island.

His native crew of Islanders went ashore to cook some fish, which they had recently caught. One of them wandered away in search of bird eggs, when he came rushing back to the beach with a countenance of horror and fear emblazoned across his face.

After calming him down it was learnt that he had found a body of "um dead white feller". He nervously led Bremner and the Mate, William Scott to the remains of Lizzie's faithful servant 'Ah Sam', on the south east beach, near the mangroves.

Searching the area, the mate found a ships square water tank which had been cut in half and used for boiling the sea slugs. Such a tank was reported missing from Lizard Island.

As he looked into the murky water he saw a strange blurred image on the bottom of the half filled tank.

To drain the water out he fired a snider bullet into the bottom and sliced through the iron with an axe.

As the water emptied itself, he was stunned by this haunting discovery.

Lizzie had finally been found. She lay on her back with her baby nestled on her badly decomposed arm. Near her side was a loaded revolver, fully cocked, with a number of cartridges next to it. A trunk lay beside her and when opened, revealed her baby's clothes and tinned food, rice and condensed milk.

He picked up some sodden note paper with writing on them and let them dry. It was Lizzie's diary.

Although the papers were water damaged, the writing was in lead pencil and still legible.

Now at last the full story could be told ——

When the aborigines landed on Lizard Island in September 1881, it was their intention to kill Lizzie and the 2 Chinese servants.

They had paid earlier visits, watching the movements of the men [Watson, Fuller and crew]. When they saw the boat sail for Nights Island, they prepared to attack the cottage.

Their observations indicated that one of the Chinese went to the spring each day to fetch water and here they waited in ambush for their unsuspecting prey.

The freshwater spring was about 600 yards from the house and close to the garden where 'Ah Leong' worked.

As they waited patiently to carry out their murderous intentions, the weather changed to a gale and it was 3 days before they saw 'Ah Leong' approaching the garden, whence they killed and ate him.

When he failed to return with water, 'Ah Sam' searched for him and found his hat near the garden where he had been murdered.

The next evening at 7pm, Lizzie saw the natives on the beach and fired several shots to warn them away, as it was clear they were preparing to attack the cottage.

When 'Ah Sam' went for water in the morning he was speared 7 times before he reached the door and Lizzie opened fire hitting at least one of them. She defended herself so defiantly that they quickly retreated back to the protective mangroves leaving a number of spears on the ground.

In her diary found by Fahey at the cottage she wrote:
29TH SEPTEMBER:
'Ah Leong', killed by the blacks over at the farm [garden].
'Ah Sam', found his hat which is the only proof.
30TH SEPTEMBER:
Natives down on the beach at 7pm. Fired off the rifle and revolver and they went away.
1ST OCTOBER:
Natives (four) speared 'Ah Sam' four places in the right side and three in the shoulder.

Lizzie decided, that, as the aborigines were still lurking in the mangroves, waiting for the right opportunity to attack the cottage, she would be better off trying to escape from the island.

She was now in a precarious position. The spring was a considerable distance away and the wounded 'Ah Sam' would almost certainly be killed if he went for water.

Once he was eliminated they could again attack the cottage and sooner or later she must run out of water and ammunition.

As she had no boat for any emergency, the only alternative was the bi-sected ships water tank used for boiling the sea slugs, which she somehow managed to drag into the sea and with one oar, she rowed from the island with Ah-Sam and her baby.

Although she had escaped from the aborigines, her real battle for survival was only just beginning.

When they left the "Lizard", on Sunday 2nd October, she only had a small container of water, which she shared with her baby and 'Ah Sam'.

By the 6th October they had run out of water, and no matter where they landed on at least 2 islands, they could not find even a single drop of fresh water.

Whilst drifting in this ubiquitous iron tank, with the south east wind behind them, they were pushed further to the north west, away from civilisation.

Her faithful Chinese servant 'Ah Sam', although wounded 7 times by aboriginal spears, continued to search for water, whenever they beached the tank amid the Howick Islands.

With parched lips and sunburnt faces they landed on number 5 Howick and remained here, hoping to be rescued by a passing ship.

When a steamer passed by [7th October], she waved frantically with the baby's wrapper trying to signal it unsuccessfully.

Their immediate joy at seeing the ship now turned to despair as it continued heading north, totally unaware of the tragedy taking place on the island.

By the 9th October, 'Ah Sam', still suffering from his spear wounds and near death, from dehydration, stumbled away to die.

She was now alone, suffering the torment of a mothers anguish at watching her baby suffer in the torrid heat, unable to even produce milk to feed him.

Lizzie continued to write her diary each day until finally weakened by thirst, this brave young mother lost the battle to live. She had survived for at least 6 days without any water.

Her last sentence was "No water, nearly dead with thirst".

No better epitaph could she have left behind than her own diary, which is reproduced here. [She mistakenly wrote the month as September when it was October].

THE DIARY OF LIZZIE WATSON

SEPTEMBER 3	*Left Lizard Island Sunday afternoon in the pot that the Beche De Mer are boiled in. Got about three or four miles from the Lizard.*
SEPTEMBER 4	*Made for the island north of the Lizard, could not, and got on a reef, but do not know which one. Squally weather.*
SEPTEMBER 5	*Remained on the reef all day, looking out for a boat. Saw none.*
SEPTEMBER 6	*Very calm morning, able to pull the tank up on an island with three small mountains on it. 'Ah Sam' went on shore to try and get water as ours was done. There were natives camped there, so were afraid to go very far away. We had to wait the turn of the tide, Anchored under the mangroves, got in the reef, very calm.*
SEPTEMBER 7	*Made for an island about four or five miles from the one spoken of yesterday, ashore at last. Could not find any water. Cooked some rice and clawfish. Moderate S.E. breeze. Stayed here all night. Saw a steamer bound north, hoisted Ferrier's pink and white wrapper, but did not answer me.*
SEPTEMBER 8	*Changed the anchorage of the boat as the wind was freshening. Went down to a kind of little lake on the same island (This done last night). Remained here all day looking out for a boat. Did not see any. Very cold night, blowing very hard. No water.*
SEPTEMBER 9	*Brought the tank ashore as far as possible with the morning tide, made camp all day under the trees. Blowing very hard. No water. Gave Ferrier a dip in the sea, he is showing symptoms of thirst. Took a dip myself. 'Ah Sam' and myself parched with thirst. Ferrier showing symptoms.*
SEPTEMBER 10	*Still all alive. Ferrier much better this morning. Still feeling very weak. I think it will rain today. Clouds very heavy, wind not so high.*
HER LAST ENTRY HAD NO DATE	*No rain, every sign of fine weather. 'Ah Sam' gone away to die. Have not seen him since the 9th. Ferrier is more cheerful, self not feeling at all well. Have not seen any boat of any description. No water, nearly dead with thirst.*

Bob Watson first heard of Lizzie's disappearance at the end of October when he was at Cape Melville near Princess Charlotte Bay about 150 miles north of Cooktown.

He instantly sailed south checking all along the coast and offshore islands for his wife and baby. At one stage he had actually sailed around No. 5 Howick Island in his desperate search for them, never realising that they were already dead in the mangroves only a short distance away.

In Cooktown, he boarded the government schooner "Spitfire" and accompanied the police to No. 5 Howick Island.

As be bent over the tank he held Lizzie's skeletal hand and overcome with grief, burst into tears.

The remains of Lizzie, baby Ferrier and Ah Sam were taken aboard and returned to Cooktown.

The funeral was set for Sunday 29th January 1882 and it was to be the largest ever held in North Queensland up to that time.

A number of women felt that Lizzie should be buried with a special dignity and dressed her in her white wedding dress with her baby nestled beside her breast under her right arm.

The coffins were removed to the Town Hall on Saturday evening, where Bob Watson had one last moment with her. As he held her hand, he tried desperately to contain his grief within himself and finally broke down in tears as the ladies helped him away and the lid was closed.

At 2.30pm the next day, the hall was packed to capacity as the funeral service was held, whilst 67 school children formed a Guard of Honour around the coffin of Lizzie and her baby.

The procession of over 600 people followed the hearse containing Lizzie and her baby to the cemetery and was represented by all elements of Cooktown society.

The cortege was led by the band and followed by the fire brigade, The Hearse, mourners, school children, pedestrians and horsemen. From the Police Magistrate to the humble Chinese they all came to pay their last respects to this brave young woman and her baby.

Many of the mourners were visibly affected and tried to hide their tears behind their wreaths.

After Lizzie's funeral was over, the band and Fire Brigade marched back to the Hall and led the Chinese procession for the funeral of "Ah Sam".

Just as the Chinese had paid their respects to Lizzie by joining her funeral procession, so the whites also joined the Chinese procession for Ah Sam's funeral.

All along the route the Chinese let off fusillades of fire crackers and after burying Ah Sam they lit candles and incense and finally another burst of crackers was let loose around the grave.

With the funeral over everyone marched back to the Church gate where refreshments were passed round to the thirsty crowd, as the Chinese thanked the whites.

A senior fireman stepped before the large crowd and said:

> "Comrades, let us before separating, uncover in honour of the memory of a brave woman."

At that moment everyone removed their hats and bowed their heads in memory of Lizzie Watson.

Bob Watson never forgave himself for leaving his wife and baby on Lizard Island. At one time he walked out of a hotel in Cooktown with tears in his eyes as Lizzie's favourite tune was being played on the piano.

He died a broken man 13 years later on the 22nd October 1894 at 54 years of age.

They found him on an old mattress in his shack at Cooktown, where he lay down to die, with nothing to eat and not a penny to his name.

He was buried in a paupers grave in the Cooktown cemetery without so much as a headstone to be remembered by.

The island where Lizzie died [Howick No. 5] is now called "Watson Island" in memory of Lizzie Watson.

The bi-sected iron tank is "presently" held by the Queensland Museum in Townsville much to the anger of the residents of Cooktown, who rightly claim it belongs to Cooktown.

A portion of the stone cottage that was once her home on Lizard Island still stands as a memento to this courageous young woman, who braved the elements in an iron tank rather than be at the mercy of the aggressive aborigines.

When one walks down the main street of Cooktown [Charlotte Street] they are soon confronted by a memorial to the memory of Lizzie Watson, with the following verse taken from a poem written in the Sydney Bulletin.

> Five fearful days beneath
> The scorching glare,
> Her babe she nursed.
> God knows the pangs that
> Woman had to bear,
> Whose last sad entry showed
> A mother's care,
> then – "Nearly dead with thirst!"

THE FINAL PAGE OF "LIZZIE WATSON'S" DIARY [1881]

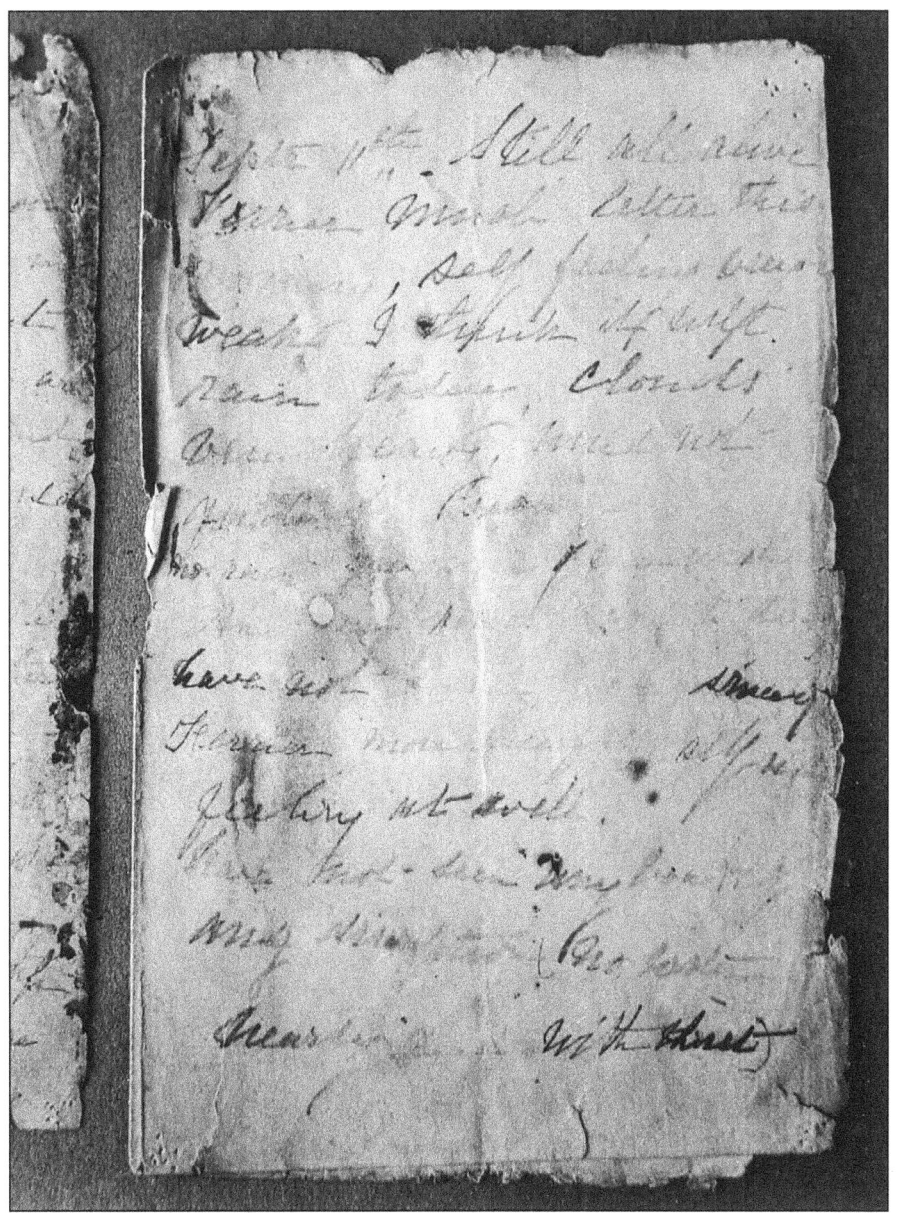

[Credit – John Oxley Library Brisbane]

A POEM FROM THE SYDNEY BULLETIN

"Dead With Thirst"

The drama's o'er, and we know the end,
    the bitter worst;
In droughty agony, with none to tend,
But with a fortitude that scorned to bend,
    to die of thirst!

For ever menaced by the savage spears,
    by night and day,
With nameless horrors threatened nameless fears,
No time for grieving, fainting, or for tears,
    but aye at bay.

She kept them off the black and devilish band,
    the fiends accurst;
And in her iron craft escaped the land –
Alas! upon the cruel, parching sand
    she died of thirst!

At death's worst anguish she could firmly look,
    and never quail:
Though wan and weak, her fingers never shook
As day by day she entered in the book
    her piteous tale.

From first to last, there is not one complaint;
    nor useless cry;
No sign of heroine's heart-strength waxing faint,
The while she watched – with pains no pen can paint –
    her baby die.

Five fearful days, beneath the scorching glare,
    her babe she nursed.
God knows the pangs that woman had to bear,
Whose last sad entry showed a mother's care,
    then – "Nearly dead with thirst!"

CHAPTER 15
"THE WRECK OF THE QUETTA"

Throughout the 1880's, Frank Jardine continued to operate his commercial ventures of cattle grazing and pearling.

Then, on the night of the 28th February 1890, the worst peace time single shipwreck in Queensland history took place on Somerset's doorstep.

The SS Quetta [3302 GRT] [Gross Registered Tonnage] was an iron hulled steamer belonging to the "British India Associated Steamers" [BIAS], an offshoot of the "British India Steam Navigation" Co. [BISN]. She was named after the town of Quetta in what was then Northern India but is now Pakistan. Like many ships of her time she was also rigged as a 3 masted sailing ship [Schooner].

The Royal Mail Ship "Quetta" in Brisbane. [Credit – John Oxley Library [Brisbane].

Among her crew of 120 were 92 native seamen from India and Ceylon [Sri-Lanka] known as "Laskars", supervised by 28 European officers. The ship also had it's own doctor [Dr Poland].

As the "BISN" had entered into a lucrative contract to carry the mail, then their 13 "BIAS" ships also had the title of "Royal Mail Steamers" [RMS]. This is why the SS Quetta was also known as the R.M.S. Quetta.

Due to the numerous shipwrecks along Queensland's reef strewn coastline, it was necessary for their ships to take on a "BISN" pilot to guide them through the maze of reefs and channels from Thursday Island to Brisbane, whence the pilot would later go aboard another ship and guide it to Thursday Island.

Eldridge Keatinge was the pilot assigned to guide the Quetta on its northern run of over 1500 miles to Thursday Island.

With Keatinge aboard, the Quetta left Brisbane under the command of 41 years old Captain Alfred Sanders on the 18th February 1890. On her journey up the coast she stopped at various ports [8] to pick up mail, cargo and passengers.

At Mourilyan, south of Cairns, 71 Javanese deck passengers came aboard. They had completed their 3 year contracts in the sugar cane fields around Innisfail and were heading home to Java, in the Dutch East Indies, [Indonesia] carrying their hard earnt money with them.

Because of their Islamic belief, a cowshed was erected on deck containing sheep and calves to be killed and eaten according to their religious custom of eating freshly killed meat.

The Quetta's last port of call along the Queensland coast was Cooktown, where she arrived on the 27th February at 10.30am and took on 4 more passengers.

She left Cooktown around 11.45am that same day and again headed north with a full compliment of 120 crew, the pilot [Keatinge] and 170 paid passengers. This amounted to 291 people.

The next 400 miles to Thursday Island was the most difficult and dangerous section as the ship negotiated hundreds of coral reefs, sandbanks and islands.

At 8.45pm on that last night of February [28th] the Quetta passed to the east of Albany Island only a few miles off Somerset. Had they been a few hours earlier they would have seen Jardine's paradise in the fading dusk.

A number of passengers were in the saloon writing letters to loved ones, which would be posted the next day at Thursday Island. Others were merrily singing in the music room, rehearsing for a concert.

By 9pm, most of the mothers had put their children to bed and would soon be joining them.

A small number of people remained on deck as the ship steamed through the 5 mile wide Adolphus Channel with Albany Island on one side [SW] and Mt Adolphus Island on the other [NE].

They enjoyed this enchanted scene of dark mystical islands amid a smooth glassy sea under a calm moonlit tropical night.

The Quetta was due to berth at Thursday Island only 30 miles away at midnight, but she never made it.

Directly in her path was a huge piece of granite that protruded from the sea floor like a giant dagger to within 16 feet of the surface on the high tide.

Although the waters had been surveyed and charts drawn showing the area clear of obstructions, this pinnacle of rock had miraculously gone undetected in spite of the fact that thousands of ships had used the channel.

At 9.14pm [28th February 1890] a shiver was felt and a strong grating sound could be heard throughout the ship. Some passengers later claimed it sounded like an empty water tank falling on its side.

The Quetta had struck the rock on its right side [starboard] near the keel.

At the time of impact she was travelling a little under full speed at 11 knots. As her own momentum pushed her forward, She tore and scraped her way over the rock, tearing out huge chunks of her hull that were from 3 to 12 feet wide.

In the engine room the floor was ripped open like cardboard, the crew down there were drowned in seconds as tons of sea water burst in.

Next to go were the boilers, which exploded as they were hit by a flood of seawater, sending a massive blast of steam up the funnel that was heard all over the ship.

Although the Quetta was mortally wounded, most passengers considered that the vibration they felt was simply the ship hitting a sandbar.

In the music room the singing stopped as the ladies looked at each other questioningly. For safety's sake they decided to go on deck.

Likewise, those in the saloon filed on deck when suddenly the alarm bells rang throughout the stricken vessel.

Down stairs, dozens of children were sleeping peacefully in their cabins, totally oblivious to the threat of the onrushing seawater about to engulf them.

A Steward, James Stallard realised there could be a danger to passengers in their cabins. He rushed down to alert them.

In the first cabin he observed a mother [Mrs Jackson] and her 4 children and now saw the salt water flooding through the cabin. He only had time to pick up one child and rushed up the alley when he saw another child of around 18 months and picked her up as well.

The water rose so fast he virtually floated up the stairwell onto the deck and was washed into the sea, still holding the 2 children.

Downstairs the flood of seawater surged through the cabins so fast that all the children and their mothers with them were drowned in seconds.

A number of mothers on deck realising their children were in danger, rushed down to rescue them, only to be drowned in the swirling waters.

By now the bow was well under water, and Captain Sanders yelled out to the passengers: *"Come aft for your lives"*.

A large number of people were on the foredeck trying desperately to pull themselves up the slanting deck as the bow sank deeper and the stern rose out of the water. Many never made it as the water overtook them and they were dragged under by the ships suction.

Whilst the crew were attempting to lower a lifeboat the Javanese rushed it without any consideration for other passengers.

One girl who was lucky to survive was a 17 year old, Miss Emily Lacy who stated:

> *"They were lowering one, but before it reached the water one could see black forms flying through the air to reach it, and in a second or two it was crowded with Cingalese, Javanese, etc, all blacks, I think."*

Whilst Pilot Keatinge and 3rd Officer Thomas Babb were busy casting out lifebelts the fore-hatch exploded from trapped air pressure blasting the wooden hatch cover into the air.

When the Quetta suddenly lurched to port [left] women started screaming and a panic ensued as they scurried around the deck looking for friends and relatives. Although half submerged the ship was still drifting half a mile north of the rock when the bow struck the bottom at only 70 feet.

By now over 150 passengers had reached the stern and were jampacked beneath one of the huge tarpaulins that normally sheltered them from the rain and harsh sunlight.

Many could not swim and were hoping in vain that the stern, sitting high out of the water would stay afloat long enough for them to be rescued.

A few people realised that the tarpaulin would be a death trap if the stern sank and jumped into the water.

Seconds later the stern slipped under amid the screams and cries of the helpless passengers until only a gurgling mass of air bubbles showed where the Quetta had once been.

Among those who survived the incredible suction as the ship went under was 16 years old Alice Nicklin who later said.

> *"I felt I was drawn into a dreadful pit. Time after time as I fought for the air and light, I was trodden under foot and forced downwards. I suffered all the agonies of a dozen deaths."*

Just before the ship went down, Emily Lacy realised that the canvas awning was a trap and made for the rail with her 13 year old sister May and their uncle, the Reverend Thomas Hall.

*An 1890 impression of the sinking of the "RMS QUETTA"
[Credit – John Oxley Library] [Brisbane].*

They managed to slide down the sloping hull into the sea only to be dragged under by the suction. She stated:

> "I felt myself being drawn down, down, down. It seemed a very long way. I got several blows on the head from people's boots, who like myself were struggling for life. I was nearly suffocated and this was the only time that I thought that I should be drowned."

When she tried to surface she had difficulty trying to "break through" the mass of people on the surface who were clinging to each other, grasping anyone within reach and dragging them down with them. She finally broke through, gasping for air and swam away from the crowd.

Her sister, May also survived the suction only to drown shortly after, as did the Reverend Hall.

The Quetta sank so fast that only 2 lifeboats could be released and these were still partially secured by rope to the ship when it went under, dragging them down with it.

Fortunately they freed themselves and bobbed to the surface. One of these was the gig that the Javanese had earlier swamped. When the Quetta's stern rose out of the water it dragged the boat into the air, spilling it's occupants into the sea.

The other boat was the large 30 foot lifeboat which surfaced amongst a large group of Javanese and Lascars. Within seconds they had crawled onto its upturned keel and were arguing with each other. The Lascars were ordering the panic stricken Javanese off the boat so that it could be turned over.

By now a number of the ships officers reached it and also ordered the Javanese off, but they still refused.

However, the upturned boat now being so top heavy from the number of people on it, caused it to suddenly flip over onto its keel when the cover was removed and 60 people were taken aboard.

Meanwhile, James Stallard had still managed to support one of the little children that he had rescued and passed her to a Lascar seaman named Clark. The other child had to be let go when she drowned.

When the gig also surfaced upside down it was boarded by some of the ship's officers after flipping it over and was found to be badly damaged but quite usable. About 40 Javanese and Lascars were taken aboard and shortly after Captain Sanders and other white crew members were rescued. Keatinge was also on board and yelled out to any women in the water to come to the boat to be rescued. There was no answer.

Fortunately the damaged boat still had 2 oars intact and was able to keep moving very slowly towards "Little Adolphus Island", about 4 miles to the north. On the way they were passed by the larger lifeboat and both vessels made it to shore.

Meanwhile back at the wreck site survivors had tried to cling to anything that was within reach, including other people.

Henry and Eliza Wrathall*, with their 7 month old baby "Fanny", had managed to swim clear of the Quetta when it sank, but now found themselves surrounded by Javanese who were grabbing at anyone for support.

Whilst Henry was trying to hold little "Fanny" above water, a Javanese grabbed him and refused to let go. By the time he finally fought him off his baby had drowned and his wife also disappeared and was probably dragged under in similar circumstances.

Among the items of debris floating around the wreck site was the cow shed with a live calf still tied to it. A number of people climbed onto it and cut the calf loose.

Throughout the night one could hear the constant cries of "Allah Allah" as the Javanese cried out for divine intervention.

When a dead sheep floated near Alice Nicklin, she used it for support. As her dress was too cumbersome she ripped it off as well as her shoes.

* A report later claimed Henry Wrathall went insane.

As a hatch cover floated by, she hauled herself onto it. This board had a large lifting ring at each end similar to a wrist bangle.

For security against falling into the water during the night, she put one arm through the ring, and exhausted waited for the dawn.

As the first rays of sunlight beckoned a new day she lifted her head and saw a small treeless island ahead. This was tiny "Acoineh Island" [Akone].

Her arm was now black with bruises from the shoulder to the wrist, from being secured in the ring.

As she paddled with her good arm towards the island she noticed dark shapes beneath her that appeared like sharks.

On the beach she saw a black man whom she thought was a Javanese, waving her away.

The sharks turned out to be logs rolling under the water and the Javanese was an Indian from Calcutta named Alick who was working as Captain Sander's cabin boy on the Quetta.

His signal of waving her away is the same as the English signal of welcome.

As she approached the beach he rushed into the water and helped her ashore.

Although safe from the sea, she was now faced with a new threat, for there was no water on the island. As the sun climbed higher, so the temperature soared.

To prevent sunstroke, she took off her blouse and wrapped it around her head and consequently suffered terribly from sunburn. Her only relief was to walk into the sea to cool off.

They were rescued late that afternoon.

Meanwhile, back on "Little Adolphus Island", Captain Sanders instructed several of his crew to take the good lifeboat and continue searching for survivors.

As they approached the site where the Quetta sank they saw the cow shed still floating with a number of people on it. After taking them aboard they continued the search for several hours passing numerous bodies of men, women and children and picking up the occasional survivors.

Unable to find any more survivors in the area, they returned to "Little Adolphus" at dawn.

There were now 98 people on "Little Adolphus", and many more were, no doubt, still struggling for survival over 30 square miles of sea and islands. It was clear they could not continue the search with a worn out crew who had no food or water.

Captain Sanders decided to take 9 men with him and seek help at Somerset. Taking the cutter they commenced the long haul of over 8 miles south to Somerset.

On the way they landed on the north western point of Albany Island where they found fresh water and quenched their thirst. They then entered Albany Pass, fighting hard against the tidal stream and finally reached Somerset Bay.

As the exhausted men struggled ashore, they were met on the beach by Frank Jardine, now almost 50 years old.

After Sanders quickly explained the situation to him, he took them up the jungle fringed cart track, to his house, on the hill, overlooking the bay.

As a number of them, including Sanders had no clothes except their underwear, Jardine quickly provided them with fresh clothing, while Sana prepared a sumptuous meal.

Whilst they chatted over their late breakfast, Frank mentioned that the steamer "Victoria" [AUSN] was due through Albany Pass in the afternoon and they could wave it down so as to assist in the search for survivors.

He also mentioned that the New-Guinea Government steamer "Merrie England" [250 ton GRT] and the Queensland Government steamer "Albatross" were at Thursday Island and could also help in the search and pick up the 98 survivors on "Little Adolphus".

Frank asked Sanders to write a note and he would send it to Thursday Island.

Jardine employed a number of Torres Strait and South Sea Islanders at Somerset in his cattle and pearling operations.

He instructed one of them to take the note and ride like hell to the Paterson Telegraph Station at Simpson Bay, 20 miles away on the west coast.

It would take several hours for his messenger to ride through scrub country to Paterson and several more before any search vessels could reach "Little Adolphus".

He therefore rounded up some of his Island crew and told them to take the Quetta's lifeboat and search for survivors.

Around 2 o'clock that afternoon, the most important message ever sent on the Overland Telegraph was received at Thursday Island. It stated:

Quetta struck an unknown rock nine last night, filled and sank within three minutes. About 100 souls rescued on Mount Adolphus. Anticipate appalling loss of life amongst European passengers. Islands in vicinity should be thoroughly searched for crew and passengers, will endeavour to stop Victoria to take food and water to North Adolphus Island. Send Albatross here to bring us on in case Victoria fails to have made arrangements. Sanders.

Half an hour later the "Albatross" left Thursday Island for the Adolphus Islands. Whilst the "Merrie England" loaded supplies of food and blankets and followed a little later.

Back at Somerset, the "Victoria" was waved down as it was steaming through Albany Pass. Keatinge had stood in a dingy in the centre of the pass signalling her to stop.

The "Victoria" joined the search for survivors after taking on Captain Sanders, Keatinge and three of their Lascar seamen.

Meanwhile, Jardine's men had found a number of survivors including William Gurvan, the Quetta's Purser. Also found nearby was the body of Doctor Poland.

His body was hauled aboard and taken to "Aconeih Island", for later burial when they met Alice Nicklin and Alick who were both terribly sunburnt and suffering from thirst. They were immediately given fresh water and taken aboard.

No sooner had they left the island and they sighted a cluster of rafts in the distance. As they approached they saw 18 Javanese, of which only 2 were women.

Only 3 were taken on board the crowded cutter [lifeboat] and the remaining 15 sat on the rafts as they were towed to "Aconeih", to be collected later.

Further north at "Little Adolphus", the "Albatross" arrived at dusk and all the 98 survivors were taken on board where they were given food and water.

The "Merrie England" arrived at around 7.30pm that night, and being a much larger vessel, the survivors were transferred to it where hot soup was waiting for them as well as blankets and clothing.

The little girl was wrapped in warm clothing and given to a young lady on board to nurse [Miss Brown]. She had boarded the ship at Thursday Island to volunteer her services to assist the survivors.

Also on board was Edmund Lechmere Brown who in earlier years was the Coxswain of the water police at Somerset, during the 1870's and now living on Thursday Island [there was no relationship between Miss Brown and Edmund Brown].

The little girl was seen as a miracle child to have survived so well.

When first washed off the ship with Stallard she almost drowned after swallowing sea water. Then when placed on top of one of the upturned lifeboats, she again went under when it righted itself. Once in the boat, a crew member hugged her to his chest [Clark- a Lascar seaman]. On "Little Adolphus", she was soon suffering from the effects of dehydration and he put his tongue into her mouth to give her some moisture.

That night the ships remained anchored at "Little Adolphus" and the following morning the "Merrie England" returned with the survivors to Thursday Island.

The little girl was doted on by many onlookers and was said by one person as being "the prettiest little girl I'd ever seen".

A number of people wanted to adopt the little orphan, whilst others felt she should be given to relatives if they could be found.

As Edmund and Marjorie Brown were unable to have children of their own, they were permitted to adopt the child and named her Cecilia.

However to the residents of Thursday Island she was always referred to as "Quetta Brown" whilst the Brown's generally called her "Cissy".

Meanwhile the boat sent out by Frank Jardine on the 1st March, arrived back at Somerset with a number of survivors, including Alice Nicklin who was terribly sunburnt.

As was normal at the Jardine household they were all given food and clothing regardless of their race and their wounds patched up by Sana [most were coloured].

The next day Jardine sent out 6 boats to continue the search for survivors. These boats were probably from one of his pearling operations further south.

Not all the survivors rescued by Jardine's men were taken to Somerset. Many were transferred to the "Albatross" where they could be looked after and given medical treatment.

Others were left on isolated islands to be collected later. For 24 hours, Jardine's boats scoured the sea as his men rescued scores of survivors.

By Sunday 2nd March, the chance of finding more survivors in the water was very minute.

Sharks had taken 2 Javanese and no doubt had feasted on many of the bodies at the wreck site.

On board the "Albatross" Capt David Reid, was searching to the south of "Little Adolphus" around the larger of the Adolphus Group known as "Mt Adolphus Island".

As he rounded the northern point, he scanned the area with his telescope and suddenly saw 4 Javanese on shore waving to attract his attention. He sent a boat ashore and brought them aboard.

When no more survivors could be found in the area he headed for the south of the island, and after rounding Cambridge Point, he spotted something strange in the water, around 9am.

His position was now about halfway between "Aconeih" and "Mt Adolphus" islands, or about 2 miles east of the wreck site.

At first, Reid, thought he could see a coconut in the water but on closer inspection, he realised it was a naked woman still swimming for her life.

When the boat was sent for her, she suddenly reacted in alarm, and swam away as fast as possible.

The crew finally caught her and calmed her down as she was helped into the boat.

She was none other than Emily Lacy, who had miraculously survived 2 cold nights and a very hot day in the water.

As they lifted her into the boat, her arms had to be gently held, for she was still moving them as if she were actually swimming.

She was clearly delirious and yelled out that she had come from a hotel at the bottom of the sea.

When lifted from the water, a crew member took off his shirt and covered her naked body. She had suffered terribly from sunburn with large blisters forming all over her, whilst her face had turned black and eventually her skin peeled off 4 times.

As she had by now fainted, she did not feel the agony of being lifted aboard the "Albatross", where she was attended to by Dr Salter and the Reverend Maclaren, who had both joined the ship to assist the survivors.

After regaining consciousness, she was able to give an accurate account of what happened after the ship sank.

Shortly after she made it to the surface, she lay on her back for about 10 minutes to regain her breath. As her clothing was too heavy with water, she decided to take most of them off, so as to give her more freedom to swim to one of the islands in the distance which was only 2 to 3 miles away.

She stated the following:

> "I rested, floating for about 10 minutes when, my dress getting heavy with water, I took it off. Then I took off my petticoat bodice, stays and petticoat, and lastly my shoes and stockings.
> There was a great noise of calling in all sorts of languages. One could hear cries of Allah!! Allah!! and see dark, indistinguishable masses on the surface of the glittering water. There was just enough moon to make everything look fearfully wild, weird and strange."

Unable to find her sister "May" and her Uncle she joined the Purser [Gurvan] and 3 Javanese on a wooden grating. They later found another "raft" and joined the 2 together.

Sometime later they saw some Javanese on a much larger "raft" with room for many more people, but they would not let any of them on it. Disappointed they drifted away and waited for the dawn.

As they could clearly see the Adolphus Islands in the distance they decided to manouver the rafts by using a large pole in which 2 of the Javanese sat on one end and rowed with their arms, whilst she got into the water on the other end and acted as a rudder to steer it.

The Javanese became too tired and gave up. They decided to separate and take the other raft on their own leaving Emily and Gurvan on the small grating.

At one time she thought she could see a boat with some people in it about 2 miles away and told Gurvan she would try to swim to it and come back to pick him up.

As Gurvan could not swim, he was very nervous about being left alone on the grating in shark infested waters. It was now 3 o'clock in the afternoon. All through the day she had been in the water towing him on his grating ever since the Javanese left them early that day.

Although she was now badly sunburnt, she felt their only chance was to reach that boat and once again she entered the water and swam for the "boat".

"Emily Lacy" was one of only 3 white females to survive the "Quetta" disaster of 1890. [Credit – John Hore-Lacy.]

One can imagine her disappointment when she reached it, to find that it was only another raft with 5, very aggressive Javanese on board [3 women and 2 men]. One of the men held a board in his hand and warned her to stay away.

They threatened that if she so much as touched the raft they would strike her with the heavy board. As only her head and shoulders were above the water then it was clear that their threat was to "belt her head in". She pleaded with them to no avail.

Totally exhausted she lay on her back to recoup her strength and swam back in search of Gurvan, but could not find him.

As darkness approached she became lost near the islands but was too delirious to find her direction and was fortunately found the next morning by the "Albatross".

The search for survivors continued all day and the 15 Javanese towed to

"Aconeih" were taken aboard. Some of these were the same people who had refused to help Emily Lacy and left her to drown.

Another Javanese was found on a hill on "Mt Adolphus Island". He had been with the 2 men who had been taken by a shark whilst all 3 were in the water clinging to a hatch cover.

Meanwhile the "Merrie England" had deposited her 98 survivors at Thursday Island. She then steamed back to the search area. Unable to find any more survivors she headed for Somerset and arrived there at 5pm.

All the survivors brought here were now in reasonable condition after being treated so well by the Jardines. After thanking them for their wonderful hospitality they were all ferried out to the "Merrie England", and taken aboard.

As the ship steamed north they all waved their last farewell to Somerset.

The "Merrie England" only went as far as the northern entrance of Albany Pass and anchored there, waiting, for the arrival of the "Albatross", which did not arrive till dark.

All the survivors on board the "Albatross" were transferred to the "Merrie England" except a Lascar crewman and Emily Lacy who were both too ill to be moved.

The next morning [3rd March] the "Merrie England" headed for Thursday Island where they were sheltered by the community.

When questioned by the Authorities over the disaster all the survivors who arrived at Somerset were unanimous in their praise for the Jardines and their boat crews.

Jardine's reputation for providing shelter to shipwrecked castaways was clearly evidenced by the Quetta disaster.

Meanwhile, back at Albany Pass, the "Albatross" continued the search for survivors and headed back to the Adolphus Islands, but all they found were decaying bodies which now had to be identified and buried.

As no more survivors were found they steamed back to the wreck site where the Quetta lay on her port side [left] with the starboard side [right] only 30 feet beneath the water.

In respect to those who perished, the Reverend MacLaren read the burial service over the Quetta.

As they headed back to Thursday Island they continued to search the water in the hope that there were more survivors but all they found was a rotting female corpse who was so bloated she could not be recognised. She was "Shotted" and sunk.

Upon arrival at Thursday Island, Emily was still in a serious condition. All over her face and back, blisters had burst and were in danger of infection and every movement was sheer agony. She was gently lifted in a cushion of blankets and lowered into a boat and taken ashore, to the Bowden Home.

Here she was looked after by Mrs Bowden until her parents arrived on the 13th March.

All the survivors were later shipped to their various destinations within several weeks of being rescued except Emily Lacy who was still too ill to travel.

The "QGSY Merrie England" [250 Ton GRT] rescued survivors of the "Quetta disaster" 1890.
[Credit – Arthur Tillett, Queensland Maritime Museum.]

When fully recovered she returned to St Helen's Station and 4 years later married Leslie Hore and they had 3 children. She later lost her husband to Malaria in New-Guinea in 1934 and moved to Moss Vale in NSW, where she died in 1951.*

The official statistics from the Quetta tragedy shows that 133 people died and 158 survived.

One author has claimed that there was a stowaway on board and the true figure should be 134. As I could not find any evidence to support this claim then the official figure still stands at 133. After all any writer could add a few more stowaways and raise the figure even higher.

When the death toll was published, Queenslanders were appalled at the large number of women and children who perished.

Of the 25 children on board, only one survived and of the 34 European women only 2 teenage girls survived.

At the time the Quetta sank it was reported that she went down in 3 minutes and this was why so many people drowned. Others have stated it was more like 5 minutes.

As the ship had been travelling close to 12 miles an hour, then it would take around 5 minutes to cover one mile.

However, once her bottom was opened, she would have slowed down dramatically when tons of sea water flooded in and she sank half a mile north of the rock.

Whether it took 3 minutes or as long as 6 minutes, it was incredibly fast for such a large liner to sink.

2 Weeks later the protruding piece of granite that caused it all was found. Its surface was over 30 feet wide and only 10 feet beneath the surface on the low tide or 16 feet on an average high tide.

As the bow of the Quetta is 19 feet deep, then one can imagine the starboard side being torn open only a few feet above the keel.

In April 1890, an inquiry into the "Quetta" was held in Brisbane and both Pilot Keatinge and Captain Sanders were absolved from all blame, since no one knew the rock existed and was therefore not on any charts.

The report of 2 divers [J Tolman and M Anderson] was also produced at the inquiry. They had inspected the wreck in March and found its starboard bottom to be severely damaged with huge dents over 3 feet deep and massive holes where hull plates had been torn from their rivets. This damage extended for most of the ships length.

The sinking of the Quetta was clearly the worst shipwreck along the Queensland coastline last century.

In memory of those who died, a church was constructed on Thursday Island and called the "Quetta Memorial Church" and later named "The Quetta All Souls Memorial Cathedral".

Although an Anglican Church it was opened to all Christian denominations. The foundation stone is said to have been laid by little "Quetta Brown". Considering she was the only child to survive, it is quite feasible that she may have been chosen to carry out this duty.

Numerous items from the "Quetta" are displayed in the church including a lifebuoy with "S.S. Quetta" stamped on it. Other nostalgic items are a brass lantern which still burns today, a port hole and most important, the ships brass bell.

In memory of the 133 people who died it rings 133 times on the 28th February at precisely 9.14pm, each year.

For many years after the Quetta tragedy, ships steaming through Albany Pass, would blow their whistle, raise a flag or even fire a gun as they passed Somerset as a tribute to Frank Jardine and his family in recognition of the incredible humanity they gave during the Quetta disaster.

* She was cremated and her ashes buried beside her husband at Kavieng – New Ireland, Papua New Guinea.

CYCLONE MAHINA 1899

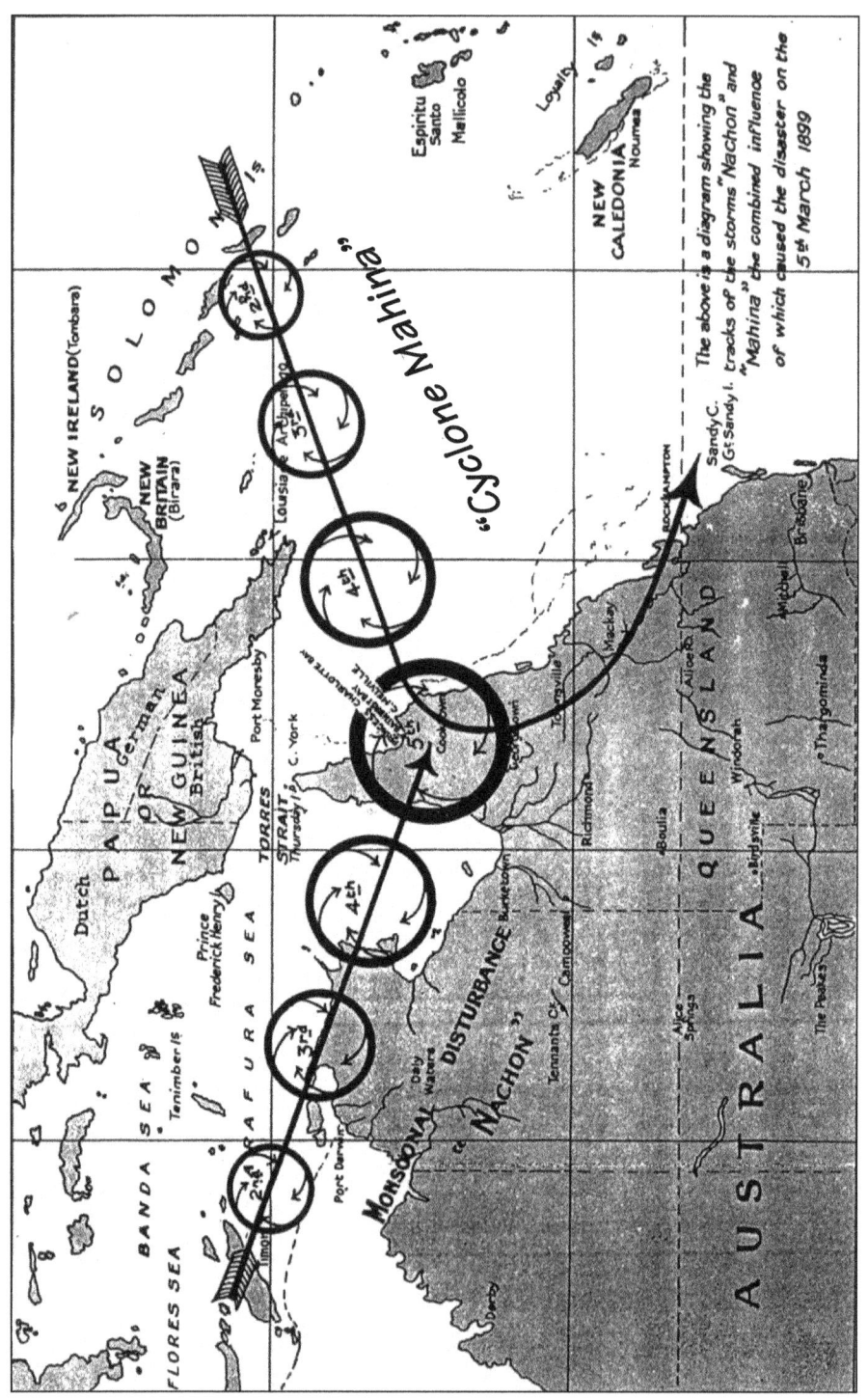

Chapter 16
"THE DEADLY CYCLONE"

With the scarcity of pearl shell in the Torres Strait the pearlers moved down the east coast of the peninsula in search of new pearling beds.

Within a short time a number of rich beds were found 200 miles south of Somerset and once again the crews went to work bringing the valuable shell to the surface. Here again, the swimming boats or dingys would constantly move in a set pattern among the "swimmers" who would pass the shell to a man in the boat as it passed.

On the 1st March 1899 a monsoonal depression was building up in the Arafura Sea off Timor, over 1100 miles North West of Cape York.

As it passed Darwin on the 3rd March it intensified and was moving towards Cape York.

On the 4th March it developed into a cyclone as it crossed the Gulf of Carpentaria and was named "Nachon".

At the same time that "Nachon" had developed off Timor [1st March] another monsoonal depression was building up in the Solomon Islands over 1000 miles North East of the Peninsula.

By the 3rd March it had also developed into a severe cyclone and was named "Mahina" which is a girl's name from Tahiti applied to a soft and gentle maiden.

It was also heading for the Cape York Peninsula and if both cyclones continued on their individual courses they would meet in the vicinity of "Princess Charlotte Bay" on the east coast of Cape York.

At this time there were 4 pearling fleets operating on the northern end of the bay near the Claremont Islands.

These fleets consisted of a Mother Ship from which the fleet was named and a number of luggers and swimming boats.

They were the "TARAWA", "MEG-MERRILEES", "OLIVE", and "ALADDIN".

These 4 fleets operated a total of 60 luggers.

About 45 miles away is the south east extremity of the bay with a promontory known as Bathurst Head from which Bathurst Bay curves east to Cape Melville.

3 additional fleets operated in this area with 39 luggers. They were "SAGITTA", "CREST OF THE WAVE" and "SILVERY WAVE".

Nearby was a "LIGHTSHIP" which was basically a floating lighthouse with its Captain [G O Fuhrman], the Mate, and 2 sailors on board to operate it.

She was anchored about 2 miles off Cape Melville near the "Channel Rocks", as a warning to shipping.

15 miles to the south, the lugger "NORTH WALES" operated at Noble Island off Barrow Point, whilst 6 cutters were operating among the Howick Islands 15 miles further south. These boats may have been a part of the small "North Wales" fleet.

It was normal that the weekends be free of pearling in order that the divers [both swimmers and apparatus] recuperate from a hard weeks work.

Occasionally, on Saturday mornings, luggers would be beached and their bottoms cleaned of barnacles etc.

This was also a time when the luggers would receive fresh stores such as food and water from their mother ship and deliver their pearl shell.

After midday Saturday they were free for the weekend when the crews could freely mix with dancing and laughter, enjoying the break from their monotonous and tiresome work.

As the 4th March was a Saturday, then it was normal for all the luggers to be together within distance of their mother ship.

That evening at around 7 o'clock a breeze came in from the east. Even now nobody in the area realised that 2 cyclones were hovering nearby.

At 10pm that night, "NACHON" and "MAHINA" joined together to form the most destructive cyclone ever recorded in Australian history.

Meanwhile a report had been received at Cooktown earlier in the week, that 2 native divers had absconded from their fleet and landed at Barrow Point where they were attacked by aborigines and one of them was murdered. The survivor escaped and reached Munburra when he reported the incident.

A police patrol consisting of Constable Kenny, 4 native troopers and 10 horses left Cooktown on the 28th February and arrived at Barrow Point on the 4th March to investigate the issue.

At 6pm they set up their camp on a ridge 40 feet above sea level and half a mile back from the beach. Between their camp and the beach was a high sand ridge.

Around 11.30pm that night the cyclone struck with incredible force and by midnight had blown away the troopers tent, they joined Kenny in his tent. 10 minutes later it was also destroyed as a branch fell onto it.

After extricating themselves they all made their way to an open space guided by the brilliant lightning flashes. The rain pelted down as hard as hail and they were forced to cover their face in a blanket as protection from the stinging rain.

Throughout the night they stayed in their open space as trees crashed around their camp as they waited for the dawn.

At 5am the wind changed to the north east and with it came a tidal wave that swept over the 40 foot ridge of the camp and stretched inland for over 2 miles. Fortunately they managed to wade through the waist deep water to safety.

Due to the heavy cloud, daylight was not fully visible till 10 o'clock that morning when they found that 4 of the horses had been killed by falling trees.

Whilst heading back to Munburra [50 miles away] they saw the beach was literally covered with piles of dead fish as well as dugong, sharks, porpoises, sea snakes, birds and wallabies. The stench of all this rotting flesh was unbearable and they moved inland, finally reaching Munburra on Friday.

Back near Princess Charlotte Bay "MAHINA" had wrecked havoc among the pearling fleets.

At the Claremont Islands, pearling crews had fought throughout the night to keep their ships afloat, only to have them smashed and sunk by heavy seas.

On board the mothership "Tarawa" the crew appeared to be winning with 2 anchors holding when suddenly the cables snapped and she was ashore on the only sandy beach on Pelican Island.

She also lost her tender, "Wai Weer" and 4 large luggers. These were "Xarifa", "Rosa", "Martha" and "Two Brothers".

Nearby was the largest of the motherships. This was the 143 ton "Meg Merrilees" with 14 luggers.

At 3am, the life boat was washed overboard as huge waves pounded her mercilessly. Unable to hold against the stormy tempest she dragged her anchors for 10 miles as crew members cut away her masts and rigging in a vain attempt to save her. Her doom was finally sealed when she struck a large reef and had to be abandoned without losing any of her crew.

Her luggers crews were not so fortunate, 9 of them were drowned. Four of her luggers were also wrecked during the night.

These were the "Giavarra Peres", "Sprig", "Jenny" and "Yamota", whilst all the others were seriously damaged.

When the cyclone struck, the mothership "Olive" was anchored on the north side of No. 1 Claremont Island. On board was Herbert Vidgen, [Frank Jardines son in law].

He released all the anchor chains available allowing the vessel to swing with the winds rather than be held rigid by a short chain.

Miraculously she survived with only deck damage, without losing any crew, although one of her luggers [Waratah] was sunk.

Not far from the "Olive" was the mothership "Aladdin" which dragged its anchors and was being pushed towards a large reef when they finally grabbed and held tight till the storm had passed.

She also had one lugger sunk [Pegasus] but all her crew were saved.

30 Miles away at Bathurst Bay, the "Lightship", anchored off Cape Melville, was sunk and her 4 crew drowned.

Closer to shore the "Silvery Wave" was anchored in shallow water near several other vessels. As the storm increased it became impossible to communicate amid the howling wind and the skippers fired a gun in the pitch darkness to let other vessels know their positions.

With waves crashing over her deck she had no chance and she was soon smashed to pieces and 3 of her white crew were drowned. Of her 15 luggers, 11 were wrecked and 108 of her coloured crew perished.

The "Admiral" was a small 25 ton schooner anchored to her north. She had only just arrived that morning from Thursday Island with more divers. She went down with all her 5 crew and passengers.

The 84 ton "Sagitta" was anchored to the north east of the "Silvery Wave" with 9 of her luggers anchored closer to shore.

When the winds increased she was pushed to the north into deeper water after colliding with the "Silvery Wave". Her crew of 4 whites and 14 coloureds were all drowned.

All of her 9 luggers were also sunk although 5 of these were later refloated and repaired. She also had 39 coloured crew from these luggers drowned.

As there were no survivors from the "Sagitta", the full story of her demise was never known. As only a small amount of her wreckage floated ashore she is believed to have sunk in deep water.

Of the 3 motherships anchored with the "Admiral" at Cape Melville, only one survived. This was the "Crest of the Wave".

On board was Captain William Porter, with his young wife and baby daughter of 18 months plus a crew of one white man [Tommy De Lange] and 16 coloured men.

All through the night they fought against the cyclone from a steady breeze early in the night increasing to an incredible storm. Whilst the intense wind and rain battered the ship, the crew cut away the main mast as huge waves crashed over her deck.

When the eye of "Mahina" passed over, there was a lull for 15 minutes. Now the wind suddenly came from the opposite direction, [N.W.] more powerful than ever as the giant waves washed away her boats.

As the storm intensified Porter and his crew battled against almost hopeless odds amid the stinging sheets of rain and vivid lightning flashes that occasionally illuminated the night, when they could see other vessels being tossed around like corks and slowly battered to death by horrendous seas.

Below decks Mrs Porter was comforting her little daughter when a huge wave crashed against the ship, knocking in the porthole windows and flooding the cabin, and her baby was washed away.

She searched desperately in the darkness and quickly found her little girl gasping for breath, when Tommy De Lange came down and helped her into another cabin, then he had to rush back on deck, and she was alone once again.

Throughout the night, Captain Porter would occasionally duck down stairs to check on her and then rush back on deck.

As the water rose higher in this cabin, she was forced to stand as the flooding water almost knocked her off her feet. Finally, too exhausted to stand, she was on the verge of collapsing, when her husband rushed in and helped her into the dining cabin and a dry seat.

He now told her that the ship was sinking and all the boats had been washed away by the storm. Yet she did not panic even though she was afraid for herself and their baby.

Captain Porter suspected that most of the water could be coming in from the bottom rather than through the broken port holes and soon found the rudder trunk was leaking.

It was sealed off with blankets and bags of flour and the pumps finally gained on the water in addition to the crew using buckets to help bail it out.

Of the 45 vessels anchored at Bathurst Bay, the only one to remain afloat was the "Crest of the Wave". All the others were either sunk or wrecked on shore.

When dawn finally emerged on Sunday 5th March, it revealed a scene of utter desolation. The sea was littered with debris from the sunken ships, whilst the shoreline was covered with numerous wrecks.

A number of luggers had been found smashed to pieces, a ¼ of a mile inland and were hardly recognisable as pearling luggers ["Pearl King", "Pearl Queen", "Zanoni", "Pert", "Leopold" and "Zoe"].

The most disheartening emotion, was the sight of 80 bodies, some of which were still floating in the water whilst many more had been washed ashore.

These were all collected and buried above the high water mark, with their tombstone, nothing more than a plank of wood from the wreckage standing upright in the sand to identify the victim.

Throughout that stormy night hundreds of crew members tried to swim for the shore as their ships sank beneath them. Only 32 made it and they had the painful task of burying their mates.

When inland aborigines arrived to plunder the wreckage, they thought better of it after seeing large numbers of Torres Strait Islanders among the survivors and were instead put to work helping to bury the dead. Some aborigines drowned helping survivors ashore. [The rumour that 100 aborigines drowned helping survivors is incorrect. The statement at the time said *"a number"* not 100.] [Possibly 4 or 5.]

Further south, the fleet of smaller luggers and swimming boats were also wrecked off Barrow Point. One group of 4 Islanders which included 2 women, [their wives] swam over 10 miles to the mainland and then walked to Bathurst Bay.

One of the saddest incidents concerned 2 Torres Strait Island women, who with their husbands had their swimming boat sink. Each of the women had a young child on their back and clinging to their hair for support.

They swam all night through the storm and landed on Flinders Island in the morning, only to find that their children were both dead.

The environmental destruction left in the wake of "Mahina" and "Nachon" was unbelievable. It was far greater than any damage ever caused by man to the area.

For hundreds of square miles the trees were thoroughly stripped of all their leaves whilst the giants of the forest had snapped from their trunks and in some cases had been totally uprooted. Overnight, the combined forces of "Nachon" and "Mahina", had destroyed the area so effectively that it now appeared as a desolate landscape reminiscent of an environmental holocaust.

By Sunday morning she had expelled her fury and after buffeting the coast on her way south, she headed back out to sea.

At 7pm that evening, [5th March] the steamer "Duke of Norfolk" was passing Bathurst Bay when it answered the distress signals from Captain Porter on the demasted "Crest of the Wave".

She anchored nearby and took on board Mrs Porter and her child and stayed for the night when Captain Jenkins received a full account of the cyclone. The next morning a boat was left with Captain Porter and the "Duke of Norfolk" headed south and in a short time she met the steamer "Duke of Portland' heading north. Mrs Porter and her daughter were put aboard and taken to Thursday Island.

Within days a number of rescue vessels arrived at Bathurst Bay and the Claremont Islands and took the survivors on board, whilst the "Crest of the Wave" was towed to Flinders Island for repairs. 2 luggers were also chartered to take additional survivors to Thursday Island.

The total death toll at the time of the disaster was 307 people drowned of which 12 were European and 295 coloured of Asiatic and Islander stock. These included: "Japanese, Malay, Pacific Islanders, Torres Strait Islanders, etc.

Several other reports claimed that 400 people had drowned. This may well have been the case due to the number of people swimming among the reefs and islands offshore several days after the tragedy.

Other vessels not connected with the pearling industry may also have been sunk with their crews and no one would be the wiser, if they were a long way off the coast.

Among the few European bodies on shore was a man by the name of Alfred St John Outridge from the "Sagitta".

He was highly respected by the pearling fraternity, including his own coloured crew. When his body was washed on shore several days later he was buried above the high tide with a 3 foot high paling fence, around the grave, made from shipwrecked debris that had floated ashore.

In memory of those who perished, a memorial was later erected by the "Outridge Family" who had lost 2 members of the family in the cyclone. For as well as Alfred, his nephew Harold also drowned.

The site chosen was about ½ a mile from Alfred's grave and here a large grave was dug by the crew of the "Olive" under the supervision of Herbert Vidgen and Captain Steve Clark.

A coffin was made from timber that floated ashore from Alfred's wrecked ship "Sagitta", as well as additional planks from the "Silvery Wave", "Lightship" and the lugger "Zoe".

It was felt that as he had been intimately connected with these ships in life then so it should be in death or at least parts of them.

His remains were removed from the original shallow grave and placed in the coffin which was lowered into the new grave as the crowd bowed their heads in reverence.

The next day a large area over the grave was cemented and the memorial monument was erected in place with the names of 11 of the 12 Europeans who died imprinted with leaded letters. The missing name was Captain William Powell which was mistakenly left out and not through any deliberate omission.

The names of the Europeans who perished are as follows:

NAME		SHIP
CAPTAIN R B MURRAY	36	SAGITTA
ALFRED ST JOHN OUTRIDGE	39	SAGITTA
HAROLD ARTHUR OUTRIDGE	23	SAGITTA
ROBERT CAMERON	23	SAGITTA
CAPTAIN EDWARD JEFFERSON	37	SILVERY WAVE
EDWARD CHARLES ATTHOW	21	SILVERY WAVE
JOHN NICHOLAS	20	SILVERY WAVE
WILLIAM POWELL		NORTH WALES [LUGGER]
CAPTAIN GUSTAV OSCAR FUHRMAN	46	LIGHTSHIP
DOUGLASS LEE	31	LIGHTSHIP
HENRY KARR [KASSUER]	28	LIGHTSHIP
DANIEL CROWLEY	62	LIGHTSHIP

VESSELS WRECKED BY CYCLONE MAHINA ON 4TH-5TH MARCH 1899

MOTHER SHIP & TENDERS	WHITE'S DROWNED	LUGGERS LOST	LUGGERS REFLOATED	COLOURED'S DROWNED
*"Sagitta"	4	Kathleen Estelle Zanoni Zoe	Zephyr Here's Luck Sea Breeze Nellie Sybil	51
*"Silvery Wave"	3	Pearl King Narellen Kirkham Vailele Ehime Flora Gipsy Endeavour Clara Merriman Daisy Jessamine	Boomerang Lily Johnny Enterprise	108
"Crest of the Wave"	0	Little Bill Pearl Queen Maggie Gitana Leopold Endymion Vision Pert North Star Carrie	Vera G.P.	88
*"Meg Merrilees"	0	Givarra Peres Sprig Jenny Yamota		9
*"Tarawa"	0	Xarifa Rosa Two Brothers Martha		0
"Aladdin"	0	Pegasus		0
*"Wai-Weer"	0			0
"Olive"	0		Waratah	0
*"Admiral" (Tender)	0			5+
*"Lightship"	4			0
*"North Wales" [Lugger]	1	19 Swimming Boats Cutters and Small Luggers		30
TOTAL 8	12	34 + 19 = 53 + 8 SHIPS = 61		295+

*Wrecked

IDENTIFYING WRECKAGE OF THE PEARLING FLEET

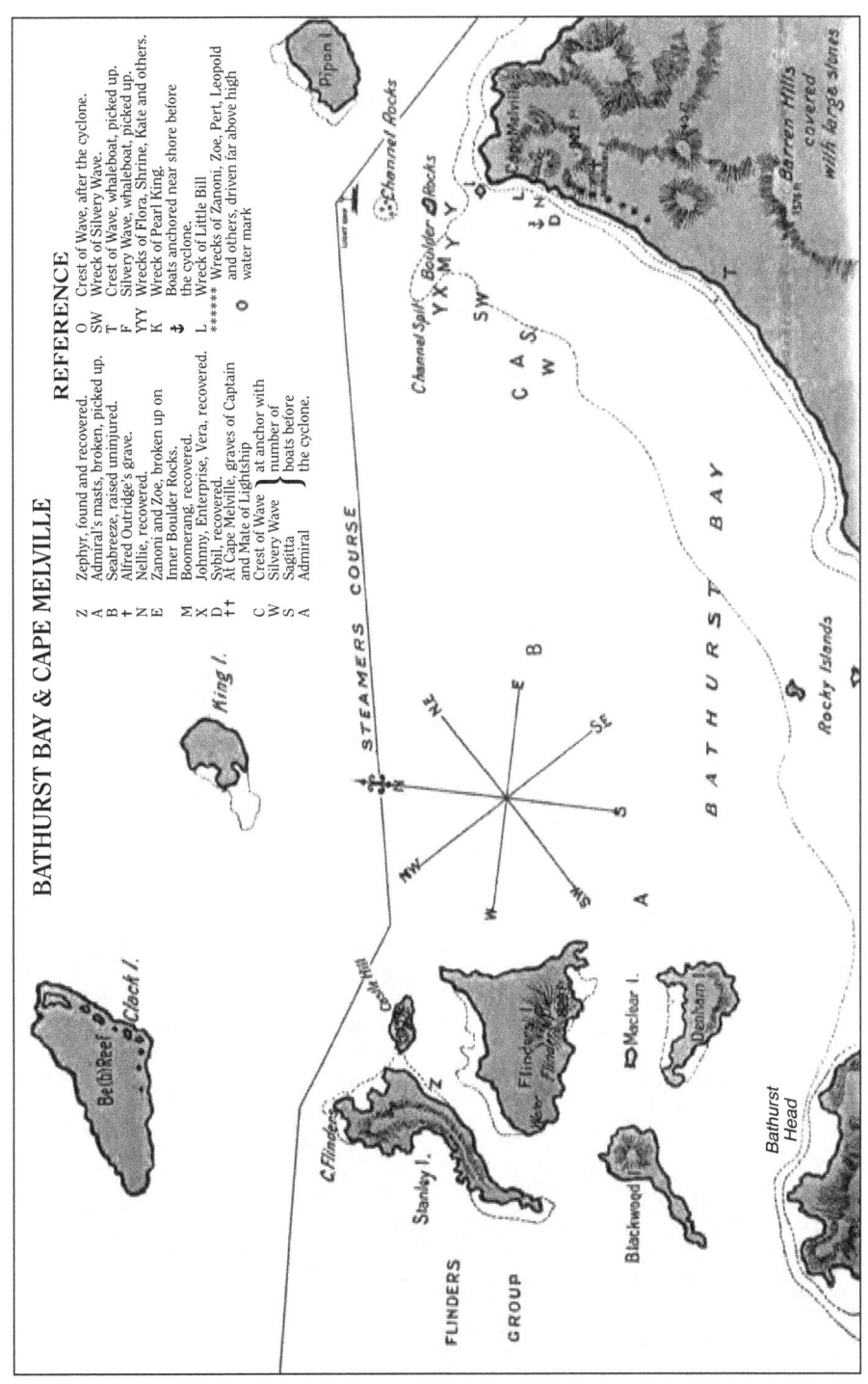

TELEGRAPH SENT BY HERBERT VIDGEN AFTER CYCLONE MAHINA DESTROYED THE PEARLING FLEETS [CREDIT GRAHAME JARDINE-VIDGEN].

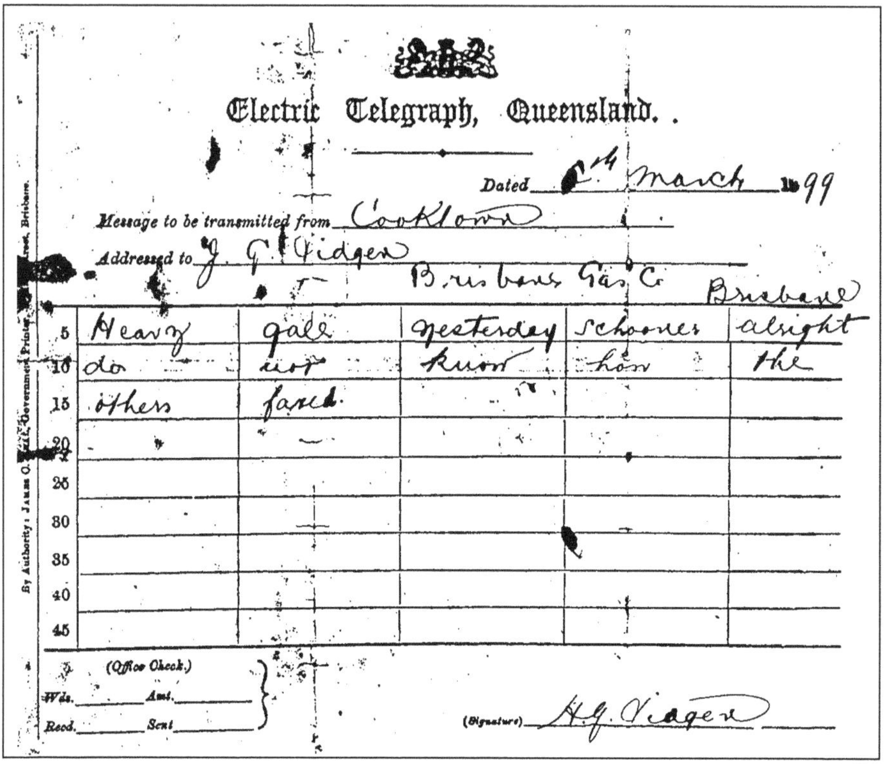

Electric Telegraph, Queensland.

Dated 6th March 1899

Message to be transmitted from Cooktown

Addressed to J. G. Vidgen
Brisbane Gas Co
Brisbane

Heavy	gale	yesterday	schooner	alright
do	not	know	how	the
others	fared.			

(Office Check.)
Wds. ______ Amt. ______
Recd. ______ Sent ______

(Signature) H.G. Vidgen

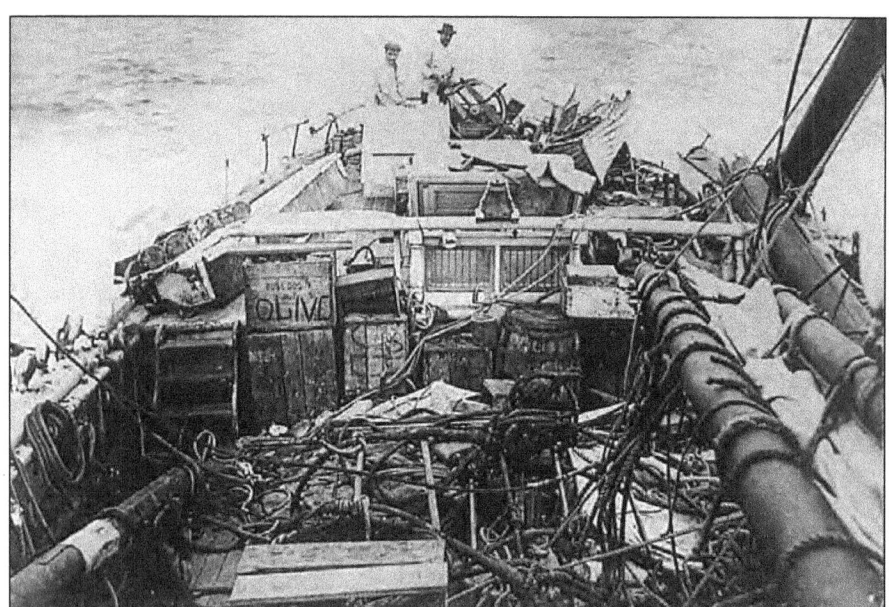

The pearling mother ship "Olive" after surviving cyclone "Mahina" in 1899.

Chapter 17
"OCCURRENCES ON CAPE YORK"

In early 1878, Frank Jardine transferred his pearling station from Nahgi [Mt Ernest Island] to Somerset, where he could operate both his cattle and pearling interests from the one base.

Upon arriving, he found the old Police Magistrates Residence was in urgent need of repair. The roof was leaking badly and the walls were heavily infested with white ants.

From the remains of the old Marine Camp on Somerset Hill he was able to extract enough timber and roofing iron to rebuild the Residency.

This large house, overlooking the picturesque beauty of Albany Pass, was now their home. Amid this tranquil setting the Jardines were to raise their 4 children of 2 boys and 2 girls.

The first to arrive was a daughter "Alice" born in 1878.

Next came a son "Cholmondeley" [pronounced Chumley] born in 1881. He would later grow up to become an olympic class swimmer.

The 3rd was also a son named "Bertie Bootle", born in 1884. Finally, the youngest was another daughter, born 11 years later in 1895.

Before she was born Frank was hoping for another son whom he intended to name "Jack Hamilton" after his personal friend, Dr Jack Hamilton of the Palmer River.

When the baby turned out to be a girl, she was named "Elizabeth Hamilton" but nicknamed "Jaki".

Over the years, the Jardines had earnt an excellent reputation for their humane assistance to travellers arriving at Somerset. Some of these were prospectors weakened by months of living on near starvation diets in the lonely bush.

The hospitality of the Jardines became their salvation, and after nursing them back to health they would continue on their way.

One such man was Dr Robert Logan Jack, a Government geologist. He had left Cooktown on the 26th November 1879 with a party of 7 other men to explore Cape York in search of auriferous country [gold bearing ore].

On the 16th February 1880, Jack found the wreck of the "Kate Connolly", half a mile south of Bolt Head [Temple Bay].

2 Years earlier the aborigines had been seen with a captured white woman who was believed to have come from this vessel. She was never seen again.

On the 9th March 1880 the expedition had reached False Orford Ness and saw a number of aborigines approaching along the beach. One of these wore a captains hat and Jack called him "Captain Billy".

As Billy came closer, Jack ordered him and his friends not to approach with their spears. Captain Billy tried to convince Jack that the aborigines were friendly, but he was not convinced. For years of dealing with aborigines had taught him to be very cautious.

He ordered the aborigines to leave, which they did, but later were found following them at a considerable distance along the beach.

That night the expedition made their 57th camp and shortly after going to sleep, the aborigines attacked.

A spear came flying through Jacks' tent and struck him in the right neck muscle. Within seconds the men fired round after round into the surrounding jungle at the treacherous perpetrators of this cowardly attack.

Faced with this determined resistance the aborigines retreated in the protective darkness of the night.

Jacks' wound was horrific. The spear had an iron barb that was 7 inches long. This had passed through the neck muscle and was followed by another 6 inches of the spear which was one inch thick. All told the spear had penetrated for 13 inches through his neck muscle.

As it could not be pulled out the only option was to cut open the flesh and remove it.

Although this bush operation was successful, it left him almost crippled.

Each day he would have to be lifted on and off his horse and at night he would also have to be laid gently down, like a mother supporting the neck of her baby.

Jack was amazed at the pain from what, he considered was just a flesh wound.

Finally, nearly a month later the party made it to Somerset on the 3rd April, where they were welcomed by Frank Jardine.

THE JARDINE TREASURE

During the late 1880's, Frank Jardine had an overdraft with the Thursday Island branch of the Queensland National Bank. He was described by the bank as:

"Pearl Sheller, Somerset. A respectable man of substantial character".

The bank held a mortgage over one of his pearling luggers the "Rattler", which was said to be in fair working order, of 6 tons with pump and diving gear.

Although he was a successful pearler, he was far from wealthy. Yet by June 1891, the overdraft was completely paid off.

Earlier that year [18 February 1891] the crew of one of his luggers the "Lancashire Lass' had discovered a mass of silver coins embedded in the coral, between the Portlock Shoals and Boot Reef, to the east of Murray Island.

The lugger is believed to have been caught in a storm and forced over a shallow reef into a small lagoon, where it was eventually anchored.

Once the storm had passed, they found themselves trapped by the receding tide. The native crew now attempted to cut an entrance through the shallow coral wall, when they struck over half a ton of silver coins near the remains of a sunken wreck.

The treasure was taken to Somerset where it was cleaned and weighed in at 1578 pounds. The coins were found to be Spanish silver dollars of the Don Carlos period plus a heavy gold Ferdinand. The dates on the coins clearly showed they were no later than 1833.

As a reward for his crew, the treasure was piled on the beach at Somerset and roughly divided down the middle. This gave the crew an amount weighing 657 pounds of coins whilst Frank Jardine kept the balance which weighed 921 pounds.

The coins were photographed on the beach and the photo kept by Alice Vidgen, Jardine's eldest daughter. A number of journalists had also seen the photo and wrote articles relating to this fabulous "Jardine Treasure".

When the Authorities at Thursday Island heard of the treasure, they demanded that it be handed over to the Queensland Government and came across to Somerset to seize it.

However, Jardine knew they were coming and buried the treasure before they arrived. He claimed that the treasure was found outside Queensland waters and therefore it was legally his.

In an attempt to pressure him into handing it over, they threatened to send him to gaol, much to Jardine's amusement. He now invited them to find it.

The authorities finally backed down and Frank Jardine was granted the right to the treasure.

Some of the silver was sent to London and fashioned into a silver service of cutlery, serviette bands, fish knives etc, and the balance sold by the Queensland National Bank on his behalf for £3700.

When favoured guests arrived at Somerset, the Jardines often entertained them to lavish tropical dinners prepared by Sana, set out on a table lined with expensive silver ware.

This was obviously the silver made from the Jardine Treasure.

The skipper of the "Lancashire Lass" was Captain Samuel Roe. He later purchased a lugger in partnership with an associate named Charles Bruce.

Captain Roe's share of the treasure may have been used to pay for his interest in the lugger.

In 1893, Bruce and Roe were murdered by their aboriginal crew at the Skardon River on the west coast of Cape York.

THE OVERLAND TELEGRAPH

Throughout the 1880's thousands of square miles of the northern Cape York Peninsula was turned into cattle stations.

With the end of the wet season large herds were driven north from the Coen country to Galloway where they could be fattened up after the hard overland journey.

They would later be butchered and dressed at the nearby Red Island Point slaughter yards, [Seisia] and shipped across to the Thursday Island Refrigerating Works of the Torres Strait Fresh Food and Ice Company.

At this time telegraphic communication only went as far as Cooktown and if a disaster took place, such as an aboriginal attack, then it could take several days of hard riding through swamp and flooded rivers before the news could reach Cooktown.

All this was now about to change as plans were made to extend the Overland Telegraph all the way to Cape York and then by submarine cable to Thursday Island.

In July 1883 a surveying expedition led by John Bradford left Cooktown to survey the route for the telegraph line.

Meanwhile in England thousands of galvanised iron telegraph poles were made known as "Steel Oppenheimer Poles". These were necessary due to the harsh environmental conditions of Cape York.

If wooden poles were used, they would soon be destroyed by termites and fire or if ungalvanised iron poles were used they would rust out due to the heavy wet season each year.

With the surveys completed in 1885, the construction teams moved in and cleared the scrub and jungle for one chain [22 yards] either side of the line, to prevent the vegetation from encroaching around it. All large trees on the fringe of the cleared track were also removed so they could not be a danger during cyclonic storms.

On the northern section, Frank Jardine acted as a guide for the construction crews and hauled supplies to their camps. It was during this time that he named a number of creeks after his children such as the North Alice and Bertie Creeks. He also founded another cattle station and named it Bertie Haugh after his son.

During the wet seasons, the work was halted due to the constant rain, flooded rivers and impassable swamps.

With the wet season over, the line was pushed further north through the humid jungle and finally completed in November 1887, when it reached Simpson Bay [Paterson] and was connected to the submarine cable.

Simpson Bay is only a few miles west of Cape York and from here the cable ran beneath the waters of the Torres Straits to Thursday Island via Boat Channel, between Prince of Wales and Horn Islands.

Now at last urgent messages that took days or even weeks could be sent in minutes.

Along the single wire route were seven repeater stations. Starting from the south, these were "Fairview", "Musgrave", "Coen", "Mein", "Moreton", "McDonnell" and "Paterson".

As a safeguard from aboriginal attack, many were fortified with turrets on the corners of the building from where they could fire down at the enemy. Even the water tanks were enclosed in a protective barrier to prevent them being punctured by iron barbed spears.

Although the overland telegraph was now completed, it could not function for long without regular maintenance.

The linesmen were that special breed of hardy individuals who patrolled the line from their isolated camps. It was their duty to make sure the line stayed open. If the jungle encroached too close, then they would clear it back from the line. Should the wire break during cyclonic storms, they would repair it.

THE NEW INVASION 1918

Ever since 1867, [when the "Yadagana" exterminated the "Gumukudin" and "Ambagana" tribes] the entire western side of Cape York, extending from the mouth of the Jardine River to Peak Point, [opposite Possession Island] became no mans land.

Occasionally the "Yadagana" would traverse the area feasting on Jardine's cattle. At other times they were known to spear stragglers from lugger crews, who often landed to collect wood.

A prime example was the murder of a sailor from the "Crinoline" which had anchored near Red Island Point on this western shore.

Captain Pennefather [of whom the Pennefather River is named], had sent 5 of his crew ashore to fetch wood and water when one of them was transfixed by 10 Yadagana spears on the 1st October 1875.

By the turn of the century most of the tribes living north of the Jardine had been decimated as a direct result of their incredible violence towards each other, in combination with disease. This included the Gudang who had suffered heavily at the hands of their enemies [the "Induyumu' and the "Yadagana'] and were reported as being totally extinct by Police Magistrate D'Oyley Aplin on the 1st September 1875 [Letter 90/75].

For many years now various tribes living south of the Jardine River had been interested in all that empty land at Cape York.

In 1911 John McLaren and his partner, [J Graham] commenced "Utingu Plantation', on which they planted thousands of coconut trees on 960 acres near the old abandoned Paterson Telegraph Station at Simpson Bay.

In 1918 McLaren learnt that various groups of aborigines had crossed the Jardine which was well north of their tribal boundaries. This was the new invasion of Cape York.

J W Bleakley [Chief Protector of Aborigines] later discovered a native camp on the northern side of the mouth of Cowal Creek situated between the Jardine River and Red Island Point [1920].

He noted thatched roof bark huts had been built, that were totally out of context to the normal "lean-too's" or native shelters that aborigines built.

As the huts were obviously not of any aboriginal design but were more akin to a type built by Islanders, it is more than probable that they were constructed by Islanders who had worked in the pearling industry.

If this was the case, then what was their fate? Did they invite the southern aborigines to join them and in the process take over the site, claiming it for themselves?

Bleakley, of course was totally unaware of events that had unfolded 2 years earlier. He did not realise that the aborigines he saw in this well laid out community had invaded the area from south of the Jardine River.

In a short time other groups joined them including some of the "Induyumu" and the savage "Yadagana", the very tribe that had slaughtered the traditional owners in the first place [Ambagana and Gumukudin].

Creeks and rivers often acted as borderlines between various tribal groups. In the case of Cowal Creek, the northern side had belonged to the "Gumukudin" and the southern side to the "Ambagana". As both these tribes were annihilated in 1867 then the new occupiers were clearly invaders and not traditional owners of the Cowal Creek region.

The power of the aborigines had now been neutralised and were no more a force to be reckoned with. They had lived for centuries under a code of violence, the likes of which the world had never witnessed. It is clear they had no parallel to equal their indiscriminate slaughter of the weak, be they aborigines, Islanders or Europeans.

When they attacked and murdered castaways from the numerous shipwrecks they unwittingly invited retaliation which naturally resulted in heavy casualties and untold suffering.

Finally, defeated and demoralised they acknowledged that their ancient weapons of wood and stone were no match for the superior fire power of the whites and ceased their hostility.

When the missionaries learnt of the various groups of aborigines living at Cowal Creek, they moved to the area and established a mission station on the site which was later referred to as the Cowal Creek Mission.

This was just one of the many mission stations established throughout the peninsula. Wherever communities of aborigines were living under the protection of the Government, the missionaries moved in to assist them. Some of the better known stations were the "Lockhart River Mission" on the east coast and "Mapoon Mission" on the west coast near what is now the mining town of Weipa.

Although, the missionaries main purpose was to bring Christianity to the aborigines, they also provided the natives with important health services. At times it was terribly frustrating as they tried to teach them personal hygeine only to witness the natives sitting in the waterholes they drank from.

At Mapoon, the missionaries could not believe that aborigines could ill treat their women so bad and stated:

> "The cruelty displayed towards women was at times almost fiendish. One man in a fit of rage seized his "Gin" by the head, and poked a red hot fire brand into her eye.
> If the mother tried to punish the children for anything, the men beat the mother and let the children abuse them.
> Telford speared Toby's dog. Therefore Toby speared Telford's sister.   [The Miracle of Mapoon. Page 96. A Ward.]

Although the missionaries are often condemned by today's academics, it is clear they did more good than harm. This applied especially to the custom, where aborigines killed their own children or in many cases abandoned them in the bush, knowing they would die.

It was left to the missionaries to raise abandoned children including babies. This was the major reason why the Government allowed the Whites to adopt neglected and ill treated native children and which today aborigines and academics have falsely claimed were kidnapped. As a result thousands of children being adopted by sympathetic whites, were prevented from dying due to abandonment and neglect by their native parents.

THE DEATH OF FRANK JARDINE

By 1913, the 4 children of Frank and Sana Jardine had all grown up and were leading their own lives. The eldest "Chum" had followed in his fathers footsteps, working in the pearling industry and later moved to the pearling grounds of Western Australia and from there to the Aru Islands off Dutch New Guinea [West Irian-Indonesia].

His brother Bertie Bootle stayed on and helped turn Somerset into a coconut plantation with his father. The eldest daughter "Alice" had married the pearler Herbert Vidgen and made their home at Muddy Bay [Paira] about 2 miles north of Somerset, whilst the youngest Elizabeth was a spritely 18 years old.

At this time Frank held the position of "Stock Inspector" and amazingly was still riding horses at 73 years of age. When a tall lanky stockman by the name of Cyril Holland arrived at Red Island Point with a herd of cattle, Jardine rode through the scrub for 20 miles to inspect them.

He took an instant liking to Holland, or "Ginger Dick" as he was often known and offered him a share in "Lockerbie Station", as he was now too old to work it himself.

Around the homestead the Jardines had turned the surrounding area into a paradise with lavish rocklined gardens growing all manner of herbs and vegetables.

Nearby, the jungle had been cleared and replaced with healthy crops of sugar cane, corn, tea, coffee and numerous tropical fruits, including a large plantation of mango trees, consisting of over 20 different varieties from around the world.

Holland gladly accepted the offer and worked the station till 1915, when he joined the army to fight in the Great War [World War I] as did Bertie Bootle Jardine who served with distinction in Palestine [Israel] and France.

At the end of the war Holland went to Scotland and married an attractive young lady and later brought her to Australia.

Back at Somerset Frank Jardine confided in a friend that he wanted to live long enough to see his son [Bertie Bootle] come home from the war. His wish came true and Bertie returned after being wounded in action in 1918.

Frank Jardine is said to have retained his vigour almost to the last.

In early March of 1919, Somerset was drenched by the continuous heavy rains of the wet season. Inside the house the humidity was extremely high as Sana continued to attend to her dying husband.

As each day passed he became weaker and finally Frank Jardine passed away on the 18th March 1919, at 78 years of age.

He was buried beneath the whispering palms on Somerset Beach, well above the high tide from where one can look down Albany Pass.

Throughout his chequered career, he had sheltered scores of castaways, during his 54 years on Cape York and the nearby islands, as well as protecting aborigines and Islanders from the blackbirders.

He was one of the most colourful characters ever to live on Cape York and was highly respected by all classes of society, including many of the aborigines.

Had he not put his own life on the line, by interceding on behalf of the warring tribes, they would have wiped each other out a lot earlier than they did.

Sana lived on for another 4 years when she also passed away on the 23rd September 1923 at the age of 67. She was also laid to rest on Somerset beach next to Frank.

The following year [1924] their son Bootle, erected a castle tombstone between the graves of his parents. It was now 5 years since Frank had died and 1 year since the death of Sana.

Contrary to statements made by various academics, authors and the media, the graves have never been disturbed.

For many years journalists and academics spread the myth "that after Frank Jardine died, aborigines sneaked into the grave yard and re-buried him upside down," whilst others claimed they buried him standing up. This has been totally refuted by the aborigines who knew nothing of such "Journalistic Fiction".

This fallacy was started by a journalist who thought he was buried under the tombstone and considered he must be buried standing up in order to fit beneath it. In fact he is not even buried under it but on the north side of it in the normal manner.

"Jaki"
Elizabeth Sheldon, the youngest daughter of Frank Jardine and wife of Major Sheldon.

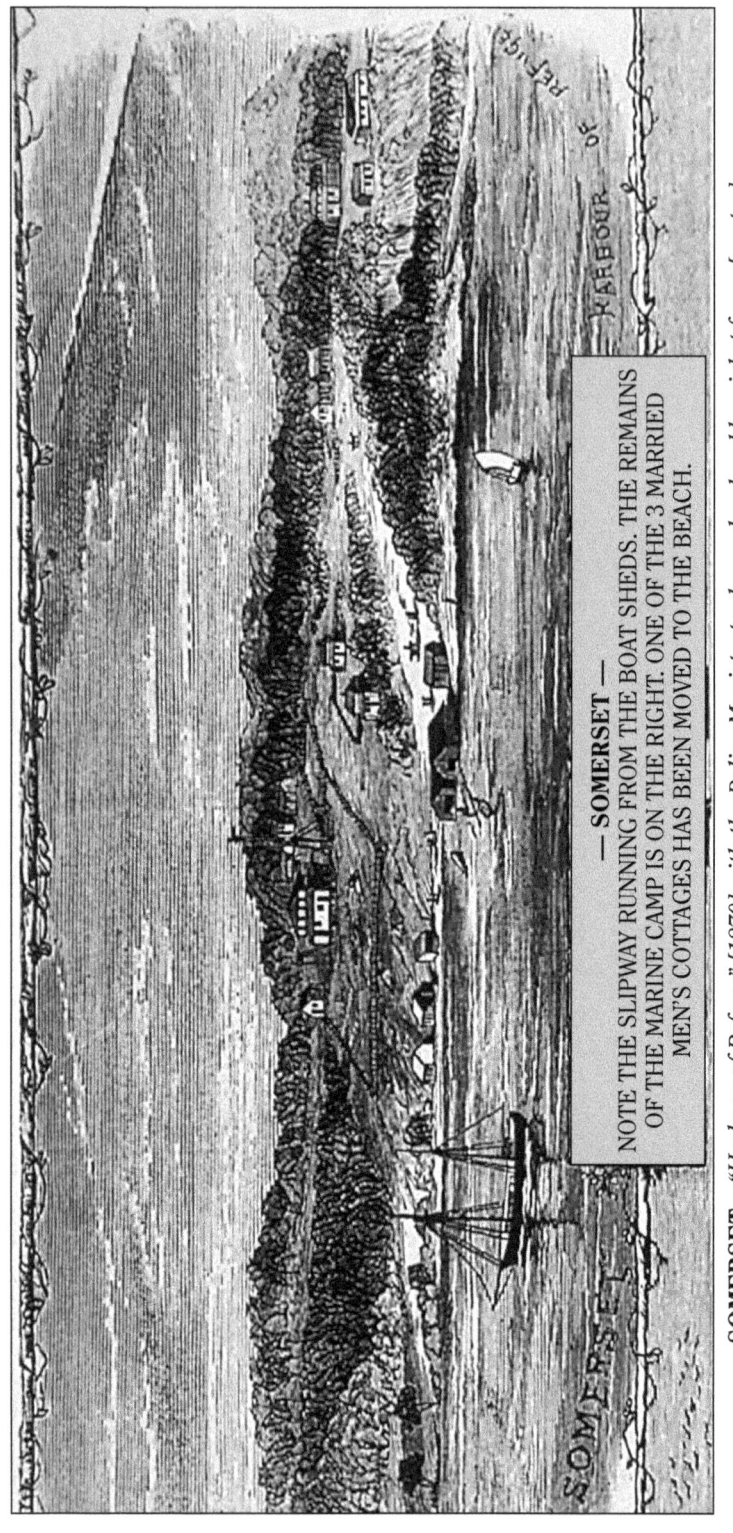

— SOMERSET —
NOTE THE SLIPWAY RUNNING FROM THE BOAT SHEDS. THE REMAINS OF THE MARINE CAMP IS ON THE RIGHT. ONE OF THE 3 MARRIED MEN'S COTTAGES HAS BEEN MOVED TO THE BEACH.

SOMERSET – *"Harbour of Refuge" [1870] with the Police Magistrates house bordered by picket fence [centre]. [John Oxley Library].*

SOMERSET – *Showing where the Police Magistrate's residence once stood [top]. Somerset Hill [Point] is bottom right where the British marines once guarded this "Harbour of Refuge".*

SOMERSET – *"Albany Pass" with Somerset left centre viewed from Vallack Point. This was also known as Port Albany where "Jackey" was rescued by the Ariel in 1848.*

SOMERSET – *The Jardine graveyard. Frank is buried in the large plot and his wife Sana in the small one with chain. The castle headstone was erected in 1924 by their son Bertie Bootle.*

SOMERSET – *The grave of Captain Archibald McAusland [1874].*

SOMERSET
The caretakers cottage at Somerset in 1971 [Credit John Gray].

SOMERSET
The same site after natives destroyed the cottage.

SOMERSET
The Lockerbie mango plantation was planted by Frank Jardine with 20 varieties from around the world.

SOMERSET
The remains of Sana Jardine's rocklined gardens at Lockerbie Homestead.

LIZZIE WATSON

Lizard Island: The Watson's cottage was at the far end of the beach (N.E.) whilst the well was at the other end [S.W.] [Credit Tom Moss].

LIZZIE WATSON – *The remains of Lizzie Watson's cottage on Lizard Island [Credit Tom Moss].*

LIZZIE WATSON – *Cooktown as it appears today, on the Endeavour River.*

LIZZIE WATSON
The memorial drinking fountain in Cooktown to the memory of "Lizzie and her baby".

QUETTA
The "Quetta" lies on its port side [left] exposing its mortal wound where it struck the rock [Credit H Hofer].

QUETTA
A 1920 portrait of Emily Lacy. She was one of the few European females to survive the "Quetta" disaster of 1890 [Credit John Hore-Lacy].

THURSDAY ISLAND – *Looking down Boat Channel from the Green Hill Fort on Thursday Island. Horn Island on the left, Prince of Wales Island on the right.*

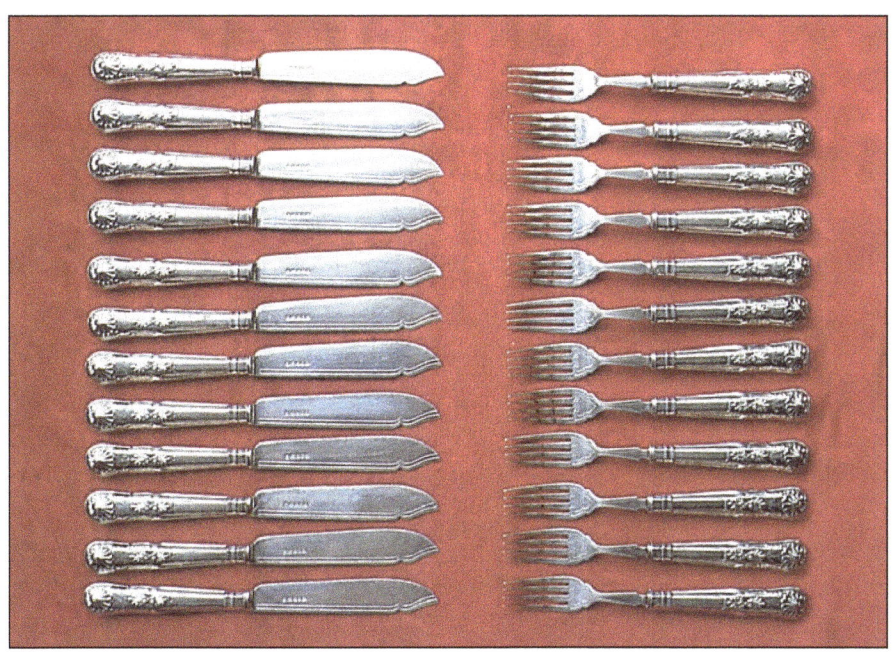

JARDINE'S DIARY
The silver fish knife set that was buried on Pulau Babi in 1942 and may be part of the Jardine treasure [Credit Pamela Ivey].

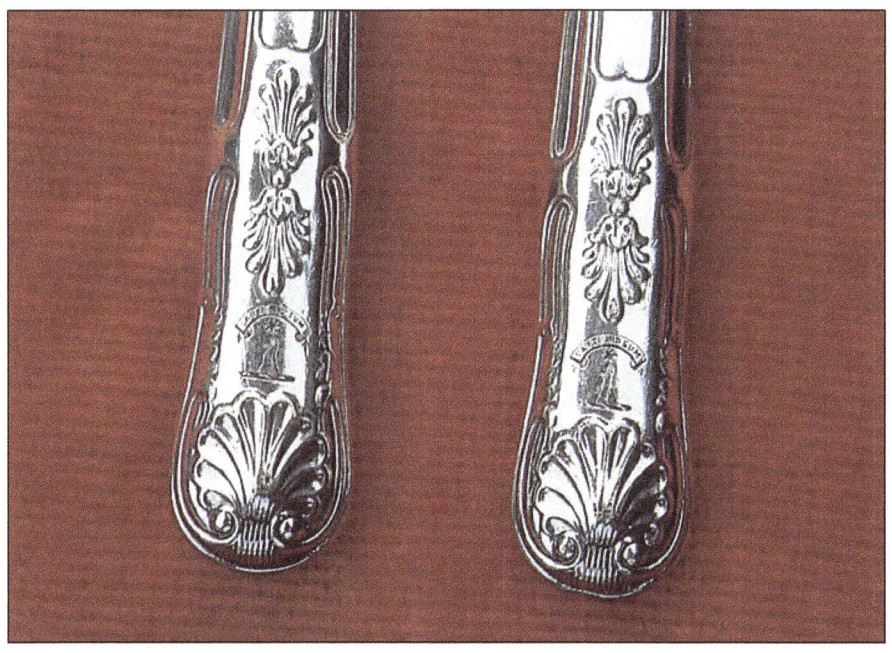

JARDINE'S DIARY
The Jardine motto "Cave Adsum" is engraved on the handles of every knife and fork [Credit Pamela Ivey].

POLITICAL AFTERMATH
Turtles towed alive up the beach with 4 wheel drives and caught with motorised boats and guns is not "traditional hunting".

POLITICAL AFTERMATH
The Jardine River Ferry costs an outrageous $80 return for non aborigines.

The "Cascades" on Canal Creek at Twin Falls is one of the most popular camping sites on the Cape York Peninsula.

SOMERSET – *Site where the Jardine coconut plantation once stood behind Somerset house [ex-Police Magistrate's residence]. The track to the left leads down to the beach.*

The Somerset Coconut Plantation planted in early 1914.

Sana overlooking the coconut plantation.

Alice Jardine [Vidgen] on her father's horse "Ramarar"

CHAPTER 18
"THE JARDINE-VIDGEN ERA"

After the death of Frank Jardine, the house was rebuilt by his eldest son "Chum".

With "Sana's" death, [1923] both Chum and Bertie Bootle became the leaseholders of Somerset. They also held title over 2 large lots of land behind the house of 320 acres each, on which the coconut plantation was grown [Portions 4 and 5 – 1913].

By 1928 Alice and Herbert Vidgen were living on Thursday Island after they purchased the spacious home of Mr Adams, an ex Burns Philp manager.

In that same year, Hector Macquarrie had completed the incredible journey of driving a "baby austin 7" car all the way through sand, creeks, rivers and scrub, where no road ever existed to Cape York.

Once they arrived at Red Island Point, the car was shipped across to Thursday Island and sold to Alice Jardine Vidgen.

Her joy was short lived however, when she learnt that the car's agents wanted it back to put on display down south and she reluctantly parted with it.

At this time Somerset was owned by her eldest son, 'Herbert Somerset "Boy" Vidgen. He had purchased it by paying Bootle one thousand pounds [£1000 = $2000] for his share and working for Chum on Pulau Babi [Aru Islands] over a 5 year period, alternating his time from 1925 to 1930 between Somerset and Pulau Babi, for the other share.

In 1931, "Ginger Dick Holland" returned to Cape York with his Scottish wife and five young children, who were generously accommodated by "Boy Vidgen" at Somerset for 6 weeks. During that time "Holland" was building their home from scrub timber, 12 miles away at Lockerbie.

During 1934 "Boy Vidgen" constructed an airfield on the mainland at "Fly Point", on the southern shore of Albany Pass.

He later received a letter of appreciation from Joseph Lyons, Prime Minister of Australia, for completing such a monumental task. [9th April, 1935].

Later that year [1934] when the new Nursing Sister arrived at Thursday Island on board the SS Taiping, Alice Vidgen asked "Boy" to welcome her ashore and escort her to the hospital.

Her name was Werna Reid and she had recently topped the Tropical Medical Examination at the Royal Brisbane Hospital. Within 6 weeks she was promoted to Matron of the Thursday Island Hospital.

That welcome on the wharf blossomed into romance and after resigning from the hospital, she married "Boy Vidgen" in 1936 and moved to Somerset.

Once a month they would go to Thursday Island in his launch also called "Somerset" and purchase the necessary supplies.

At this time many visitors from the south stayed at Somerset at £2 [$4] a week, where they could enjoy a tropical holiday amid the pristine surroundings of the area.

In between running Somerset as a coconut plantation, producing copra [coconut flesh] and mustering the wild cattle for the slaughter yards, "Boy Vidgen" also found time to join the local militia at Thursday Island, eventually rising to the rank of Sergeant.

With the outbreak of World War II, he was called up for active service in the Army, [AIF – Australian Imperial Forces], in 1940. A year later Werna gave birth to a son at Thursday Island and named him Grahame [November 1941].

When the Japanese invaded the Pacific, all European civilians at the top of Cape York and Thursday Island were evacuated to the south in early 1942.

Whilst based at Thursday Island, "Boy Vidgen" learnt that off duty soldiers on Cape York had broken into his Somerset residence, stealing his belongings. They also spent time shooting the tops off the coconut trees as well as shooting cattle to idle away their time.

To save his belongings he took the launch "Somerset" back to Albany Pass and removed all the remaining items of value from his home and stored them in a shed beside his airfield at Fly Point.

With the war over, the Vidgens were living in Brisbane where twin sons, John and Bruce were born.

"Boy Vidgen" had wanted to move back to Somerset with his family and give them the same exciting life that he enjoyed at beautiful Albany Pass. But it was not to be.

In 1948, the Queensland Government wanted Somerset as part of a reserve for aborigines. The Vidgens had little choice in the matter as their title to Somerset was relinquished and the site taken over by the Department of Native Affairs [DNA].

"Boy Vidgen" returned to Somerset to remove any of his personal property that was left. At Fly Point he found that the shed was completely overgrown with vines and creepers and everything inside was still intact.

Among the artifacts protected by this natural camouflage were valuable photographs and paintings, swords and telescopes as well as the famous "Somerset Visitors Book" with the names and comments of hundreds of guests who had visited this Northern paradise.

Most of the Jardine-Vidgen black and white photographs portrayed in this book were a part of that collection.

The DNA had by now become a law unto itself, answerable only to the top officials of the Government.

When they chose to seize large areas of private freehold land, they simply ordered the "Lands Department" to cancel the owners land title.

This was achieved under the "Acquisition of Land Act" in which the "Lands Department" advertised in the "Government Gazette" of their "NOTICE OF INTENTION TO RESUME" the land in question. [The lands department had no choice in the matter.]

Once the DNA took control of Somerset from the Jardine-Vidgens, the first act of desecration took place, with the total destruction and complete elimination of over 40 European graves on a rise at the rear of Somerset House.

Whether these graves were destroyed by the DNA or whether it was a personal vendetta by the new aborigines has never been explained and every attempt to expose this racist act was deliberately thwarted by the past Queensland Government [Goss Labor Government].

They refused to acknowledge the existence of the graves at this "Sacred European Site", simply because all trace of surface material such as gravestones and crosses were removed.

However, Author Frank Reid [Alex Vennard] was one of many people who had visited Somerset and had seen this graveyard during the 1930's and wrote the following:

> *"Situated on a hill at the rear of the old residence, and now hidden by dense shrubbery in which only a few faded and weather-beaten headstones can be seen, is one of the most historic Graveyards in Australia. Here are many graves, the last resting-places of those who died when Queensland was a young state. When I visited Somerset over twenty years ago I wandered amongst these burial mounds and read the inscriptions on stone or wooden crosses...*
>
> *Nearby is the resting place of Captain Archibald MacAusland, also the graves of several Burketown residents who were brought to Somerset to recover from fever, but who died soon after arriving there. I looked with feelings tinged with sadness at the*

> *well-kept grave of Madame Boisse, wife of a commandant at New Caledonia. She came to Somerset on the French transport L'Allierie, which lost over eighty men with fever on the way from Batavia, and she died just before the ship came in sight of the Jardine homestead. The dead woman was laid to rest during a heavy storm in a grave half filled with water. There are also scores of other graves in this historic old cemetery, some with no stone to tell who lies underneath, holding all that remains of early settlers, prospectors, sailors, shipwrecked people and pearl divers."*

[Romance of the Great Barrier Reef – Frank Reid – 1952]

Further evidence comes from Author George Farwell, who wrote of the Somerset graves:

> *"The headstones of those who died have been badly weathered by the rough caress of 90 wets."*

[Cape York to the Kimberleys – George Farwell – 1962]

By 1962, the "Department of Native Affairs", [DNA] was known as the "Department of Aboriginal and Island Affairs" [DAIA] under the control of P J Kiloran in Brisbane.

Meanwhile, at Bamaga, Cape York, native workers tried to pull down the old Residency [Vidgens home].

Unable to pull it down due to the heavy beams, they set it alight and burnt it to the ground.

This was the second major act of desecration of this historic site.

To replace the residency, a small caretaker's cottage was built where the residency had once stood.

When the DNA took control of Somerset, they mistakenly believed that it was all crown land under their control. What they failed to realise was that the lots sold in 1865 and 1866 were still freehold land owned by people down south.

It must have been quite a shock for them to learn that they only held control over the Jardine Vidgen land behind Somerset [portions 4 and 5] and not the 109 lots along the foreshore facing Albany Pass.

The only way they could have total control over all this land was to have the owners Titles cancelled, which was arranged through the Lands Department.

In January 1972, the Lands Department published a statement in the Government Gazette under the heading "NOTICE OF INTENTION TO RESUME" all land at Somerset [few people ever read the Government Gazette].

No mention was made in this statement that it was being seized so as to give it to the aborigines. This would have to be one of the most insidious acts of racism ever perpetrated against white land owners at that time, by the Queensland Government.

It was also stated that compensation would be payable. In my enquiries I have not found any of these landowners who were paid. As most land owners did not know that their land had been seized and were not contacted by the Government they obviously were not paid adequate compensation and under those circumstances, this act of "Legalised Land Theft" was in effect illegal.

On the 3rd June 1972, a statement under the title of "A PROCLAMATION" was published in the Government Gazette, to the effect that all Somerset Land was now the property of the Crown.

In 1974 the final act of destruction at Somerset was committed by a group of natives who dozed the caretakers cottage into the ground, wiping out all trace of its existence.

In 1986 Somerset was illegally given to the Injinoo community at Cowal Creek, even though they are not the traditional Land Owners of Somerset. It is ironic that some of the natives claiming Somerset as their traditional land are in effect, direct descendants of the very tribes who massacred the Gudang and now control their land [at least temporarily].

Prior to 1999 the aborigines of Injinoo had temporary control of Somerset with a title known as a Dogit [Deed of Grant in Trust]. This was later changed when they were allegedly given freehold title by the Queensland Government, which because of its illegality can be rescinded by a change of government so that all Australians can share in its colourful history.

Although tourists can still visit Somerset, many have been bullied and cajoled by local drunks demanding up to $40 per person as a camping fee.

From 1948 to 1972 the Goverment held illegal ownership of Somerset under the DNA-DAIA in which no lease fees to the owners was paid and therefore I have made available the names of all the land-owners up to the cancellation of their titles in 1972.

It is important to note that all these blocks of land were prime real estate that were classified as Town Lots and not rural under the title Town of Somerset. The fact that they all over-looked the beautiful Somerset Beach and the pristine waters of Albany Pass, made them expensive high class blocks valued in excess of $250,000 [¼ million] each on today's market.

I have therefore published the title holders names so that they may look into the possibility of taking legal action if they choose to on these 2 important violations.

A. That the Goverment took possession of their land whilst they still had freehold title to it, from 1948-1972, and no fees or compensation was paid.

B. That the Government took total possession of their land without the landowners knowledge and failed to pay adequate compensation to the landowner, after 1972.

It is also clear that the Government seized the land on "Racist Grounds". That is, the land was taken off the white land owners and given to the aborigines. This was clearly a case of "Racial Discrimination" and must be reversed.

As a result of the massive desecration of the buildings and graves at Somerset and the threat by aborigines to remove the Jardine graves from the area, I advised the Environment and Heritage Department of the Queensland Government by a series of letters [Comben and Robson] that Somerset was a Sacred and Historical Site of European settlement and that if Aborigines and Islanders could have their real or false Sacred Sites, then the White Australians are also entitled to their genuine Sacred Sites.

To fail to accept this fact is purely another flagrant violation of the Racial Discrimination Act.

During the separate rule of both these politicians, [Comben and Robson] the claim for a Sacred European Site was rejected.

I then submitted an original Claim Form for a Sacred Site through the Cairns Branch of the National Trust.

The last thing the Queensland Labor Government wanted was a mass of evidence that would prove that both Somerset and Albany Island were a "Sacred European Site".

To prevent the public from knowing about it they simply refused to correspond on the issue, believing that was the end of the whole affair.

I therefore formed a petition to be signed by thousands of people.

The most appropriate site was the Weipa Camp Ground where thousands of tourists camp each year on their stopover to Cape York.

In 1994, the petition was presented to the Queensland Parliament, which literally shocked the Labor Government, who quickly removed the petition to the Lands Department knowing they could not act upon it.

As word of the "Somerset Petition" spread all over Cape York, it wasn't long before tourists returning from Cape York, arrived at Weipa with the news that aborigines had told them that if I were caught north of the Jardine River they would kill me.

These death threats became the prized joke at Weipa and it wasn't long before tourists jokingly referred to me as "Salman", in reference to Salman Rushdie who was threatened by muslims over his book "Satanic Versus".

Although it would appear that the aborigines were the instigators of these threats, I am more inclined to believe that white do-gooders living in the area have been stirring up the aborigines and are the real culprits.

As things now stand, all the territory, that was once owned by the Gudang aborigines [East Coast – Cape York to Fly Point] is now controlled by aborigines at Cowal Creek [Injinoo], on the west coast of Cape York [their traditional enemies].

When one considers that large areas of land had been seized from white Australians and classified as Aboriginal Sacred Sites on the flimsiest of evidence, then likewise, land containing the graves of Europeans are clearly "Sacred European Sites" and must be returned to the total ownership and control of White Australians.

Both Somerset and Albany Island have scores of European graves of men, women and children and must therefore come under this criteria.

In addition to being a Sacred Burial Site of Europeans, it was also a major Historical Site of European Settlement and the term "Sacred and Historical Site of European Settlement" is also appropriate.

The following documentation includes:
1. Plan of Somerset Town Lots, sold by auction in Brisbane on the 4th April 1865 and the 2nd May 1866 and including Lots 4 and 5 leased by Frank Jardine in 1913 for the coconut plantation.
2. Names of 152 bidders of Somerset Town Lots auctioned in 1865 and 1866 and identifying 43 who failed to pay.
3. Final list of land owners of 109 Somerset Town Lots auctioned in 1865 and 1866.
4. Names of land owners of Somerset Town Lots whose land was seized by the Queensland Government in 1972 and given to aborigines.

The "Baby Austin" was the first car driven up the Cape York Peninsula by Hector McQuarrie and his partner – 1928.

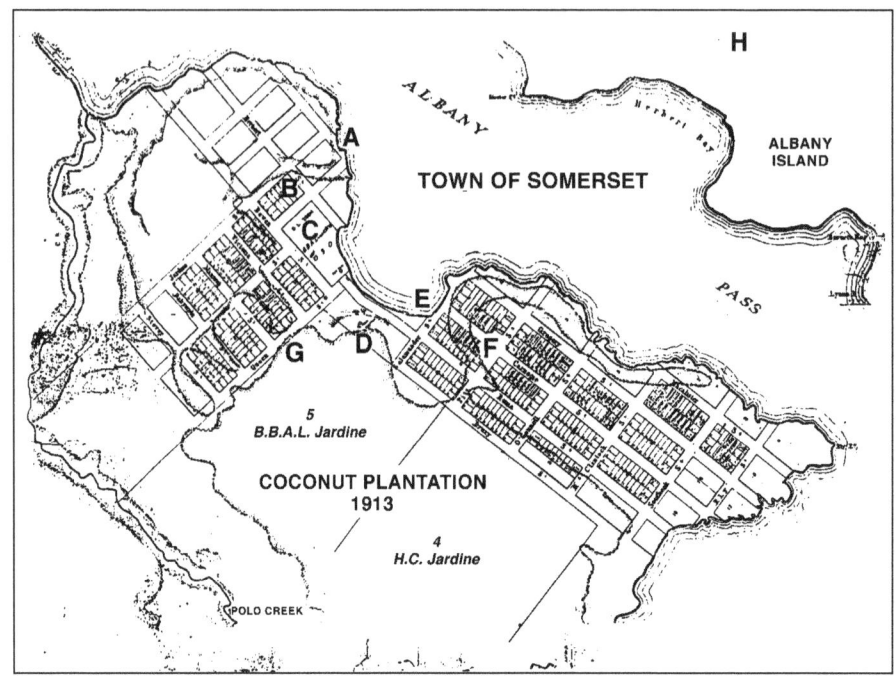

PLAN OF THE SOMERSET TOWN LOTS SOLD BY AUCTION IN BRISBANE IN 1865 & 1866 AND INCLUDING LOTS 4 AND 5 LEASED BY FRANK JARDINE IN 1913 FOR THE COCONUT PLANTATION FOR HIS SONS BERTIE BOOTLE AND HUGH CHOLMONDELEY [CHUM] JARDINE.

- **A.** New Aboriginal Paintings [1971]
- **B.** British Marine Camp [Somerset Hill]
- **C.** Jardine Family Graves
- **D.** Police Magistrates Residence [Jardine Homestead]
- **E.** Fresh Water Well
- **F.** Grave of Captain Archibald McAusland [22nd March 1874]
- **G.** Site of 40 European Graves
- **H.** Albany Island Graveyard

SOMERSET TOWN LOTS AUCTIONED ON THE 4TH APRIL 1865 AT MARTIN'S AUCTION ROOMS, BRISBANE

*BIDDERS WHO FAILED TO PAY.

	LOT	SECTION	AREA A.R.P.	PRICE £	NAME
	1	12	12	0.1.8	27	Thomas Birch
*	2	13	12	0.1.8	42	Charles William Brookes
	3	14	12	0.1.8	23	Benjamin Backhouse
*	4	15	12	0.1.8	24	Charles Gerard Campen
	5	16	12	0.1.8	24	Joshua Jeays
*	6	17	12	0.1.8	23	William Pettigrew
	7	18	12	0.1.8	24	Shepherd Smith
	8	19	12	0.1.8	25	Joshua Jeays
*	9	1	13	0.1.8	55	Charles Kumerer
	10	2	13	0.1.8	35	Robert Little
	11	3	13	0.1.8	31	Robert Little
	12	4	13	0.1.8	29	Joshua Jeays
	13	3	13	0.1.8	31	Abraham Hamilton Thompson
	14	6	13	0.1.8	33	George Harris
	15	7	13	0.1.8	36	Frederick R Rawlins
*	16	8	13	0.1.8	36	James Francis Garrick
*	17	9	13	0.1.8	37	Amos Braysher
*	18	10	13	0.1.8	50	Amos Braysher
	19	11	13	0.1.8	48	John Godfrey Cohen
*	20	24	13	0.1.8	52	Amos Braysher
*	21	1	21	0.1.0	57	James Collins
*	22	2	21	0.1.0	44	James Collins
	23	3	21	0.1.0	40	Shepherd Smith
	24	4	21	0.1.0	36	John Splain
	25	5	21	0.1.0	35	Shepherd Smith
	26	6	21	0.1.0	34	John Christian Heusler
	27	7	21	0.1.0	31	Shepherd Smith
	28	8	21	0.1.0	30	John Godfrey Cohen
	29	9	21	0.1.0	34	John Godfrey Cohen
*	30	10	21	0.1.0	61	Charles Kumerer
*	31	11	21	0.1.0	35	Amos Braysher
*	32	24	21	0.1.0	42	James Collins
	33	4	22	0.1.0	41	Allan McIntyre
	34	5	22	0.1.0	41	John Godfrey Cohen
	35	6	22	0.1.0	41	John Godfrey Cohen
	36	7	22	0.1.0	40	Shepherd Smith
	37	8	22	0.1.0	37	John Cadbury
	38	9	22	0.1.0	46	Edward Robert Drury
	39	10	22	0.1.0	71	Edward Robert Drury
	40	11	22	0.1.0	57	Edward Robert Drury
	41	10	34	0.1.0	45	Edward Robert Drury
	42	11	36	0.1.0	60	Edward Robert Drury
	43	12	36	0.1.0	42	Edward Robert Drury
*	44	13	34	0.1.0	42	George Harris
*	45	14	34	0.1.0	43	George Harris
	46	15	34	0.1.0	36	Shepherd Smith
*	47	16	34	0.1.0	40	Alexander Meyers
	48	17	34	0.1.0	40	James Ivory
*	49	18	34	0.1.0	45	Amos Braysher
*	50	19	34	0.1.0	47	Amos Braysher

	LOT	SECTION	AREA A.R.P.	PRICE £	NAME
*	51	1	44	0.1.8	65	Amos Braysher
	52	2	44	0.1.8	35	John Godfrey Cohen
	53	3	44	0.1.8	35	James Ivory
	54	4	44	0.1.8	36	E B Kennedy
	55	5	44	0.1.8	37	E B Kennedy
	56	6	44	0.1.8	36	E B Kennedy
*	57	7	44	0.1.8	37	Francis Murray
*	58	8	44	0.1.8	69	Amos Braysher
*	59	9	44	0.1.8	48	Amos Braysher
	60	20	44	0.1.8	44	Alexander Cameron
*	61	1	45	0.1.8	60	Amos Braysher
	62	2	45	0.1.8	34	James Warner
*	63	3	45	0.1.8	32	James Hargreaves Raffles
*	64	4	45	0.1.8	23	James Hargreaves Raffles
	65	5	45	0.1.8	32	William Clay Rush
	66	6	45	0.1.8	36	John Christian Heussler
	67	7	45	0.1.8	35	E B Kennedy
	68	8	45	0.1.8	65	John Christian Heussler
	69	9	45	0.1.8	46	E B Kennedy
*	70	20	45	0.1.8	38	Amos Braysher

SOMERSET TOWN LOTS AUCTIONED ON THE 2ND MAY 1866 AT MARTIN'S AUCTION ROOMS, BRISBANE

*BIDDERS WHO FAILED TO PAY.

	LOT	SECTION	AREA A.R.P.	PRICE £	NAME
	1	1	6	0.1.8	6.0.0	Hannah Alexander
	2	2	6	0.1.8	4.0.0	Hannah Alexander
	3	3	6	0.1.8	6.0.0	James Logan
	4	4	6	0.1.8	5.10.0	Robert Bailey
	5	5	6	0.1.8	4.18.0	Richard Ryan
	6	6	6	0.1.8	7.8.0	Richard Ryan
	7	7	6	0.1.8	4.7.0	John Gebbie
	8	8	6	0.1.8	4.15.0	John Gebbie
	9	9	6	0.1.8	7.10.0	Esther Theresa Thomas
	10	10	6	0.1.8	4.0.0	Leonard Mark Mendoza
	11	11	6	0.1.8	4.0.0	Solomon Edward Mendoza
	12	12	6	0.1.8	5.5.0	James Logan
	13	13	6	0.1.8	8.5.0	George Myers
*	14	14	6	0.1.8	7.5.0	George Myers
	15	1	7	0.1.8	8.15.0	George Myers
	16	2	7	0.1.8	5.10.0	Robert Fleming
	17	3	7	0.1.8	4.0.0	Aeneas Walker
	18	4	7	0.1.8	4.10.0	Aeneas Walker
	19	5	7	0.1.8	4.10.0	Aeneas Walker
*	20	6	7	0.1.8	3.15.0	Alexander Myers
*	21	7	7	0.1.8	5.0.0	Alexander Myers
	22	8	7	0.1.8	4.0.0	E H Booth
	23	9	7	0.1.8	6.5.0	Frank Grisbrook
	24	10	7	0.1.8	10.0.0	John Patrick Kelly
	25	11	7	0.1.8	5.5.0	John Patrick Kelly
*	26	12	7	0.1.8	4.15.0	Christopher Vincent Gorry
	27	13	7	0.1.8	12.10.0	Allan Ravenscroft Wettenhall
	28	14	7	0.1.8	4.0.0	Jane Daniell
	29	15	7	0.1.8	4.10.0	Jane Daniell

	30	16	7	0.1.8	4.5.0	Jane Daniell
	31	17	7	0.1.8	4.10.0	Peter Fleming
	32	18	7	0.1.8	4.10.0	Peter Fleming
*	33	19	7	0.1.8	4.0.0	Alfred Banfield
	34	20	7	0.1.8	4.10.0	Thomas Illidge
	35	21	7	0.1.8	5.15.0	Thomas Illidge
	36	22	7	0.1.8	13.10.0	James Francis Doyle
	37	23	7	0.1.8	5.10.0	John Patrick Kelly
	38	24	7	0.1.8	6.0.0	Nathan Levy
*	39	1	14	0.1.8	11.10.0	Louis Wittenstein
*	40	2	14	0.1.8	5.5.0	Louis Wittenstein
	41	3	14	0.1.8	4.0.0	Hannah Alexander
	42	4	14	0.1.8	4.0.0	Fanny Louven
	43	4	14	0.1.8	4.5.0	James Piper
	44	6	14	0.1.8	4.10.0	Mary Martin
	45	7	14	0.1.8	4.5.0	Henry William Turner
	46	8	14	0.1.8	4.10.0	Ann Taylor Burnett Illidge
	47	9	14	0.1.8	6.0.0	Francis Edward Johnson
	48	10	14	0.1.8	12.15.0	Francis Edward Johnson
	49	11	14	0.1.8	5.10.0	Thomas Illidge
*	50	12	14	0.1.8	5.15.0	Henry Parker
	51	13	14	0.1.8	7.10.0	James Robert Dickson
						James Duncan
	52	14	14	0.1.8	4.15.0	James Robert Dickson
						James Duncan
*	53	15	14	0.1.8	4.15.0	John Michael
*	54	16	14	0.1.8	4.10.0	George Myers
*	55	17	14	0.1.8	4.10.0	George Myers
*	56	18	14	0.1.8	4.10.0	George Myers
	57	19	14	0.1.8	4.10.0	George Spring
	58	20	14	0.1.8	4.15.0	Catherine Rielly
	59	21	14	0.1.8	4.15.0	Elizabeth Levy
	60	22	14	0.1.8	9.15.0	John Patrick Kelly
*	61	23	14	0.1.8	6.10.0	Sebastian Heussner
*	62	24	14	0.1.8	6.5.0	Louise Wittenstein
	63	1	13	0.1.8	10.5.0	James Ivory
	64	8	13	0.1.8	4.10.0	Hannah Alexander
	65	9	13	0.1.8	5.0.0	E H Booth
	66	10	13	0.1.8	13.0.0	Daniel Watts Sterling
	67	12	13	0.1.8	7.10.0	James Ivory
	68	13	13	0.1.8	4.0.0	James Ivory
*	69	14	13	0.1.8	5.0.0	Sebastian Heussner
	70	15	13	0.1.8	5.0.0	Hannah Alexander
	71	16	13	0.1.8	5.5.0	Hannah Alexander
	72	17	13	0.1.8	5.5.0	Charles Merkley
*	73	18	13	0.1.8	4.15.0	Walter Jour
	74	19	13	0.1.8	4.10.0	James Baker
	75	20	13	0.1.8	5.0.0	John Taylor Simmons
	76	21	13	0.1.8	6.0.0	James Ivory
	77	22	13	0.1.8	18.0.0	James Ivory
	78	23	13	0.1.8	7.0.0	James Ivory
	79	24	13	0.1.8	8.10.0	James Ivory
	80	13	12	0.1.8	15.0.0	James Hutchinson
*	81	15	12	0.1.8	7.0.0	Walter Jour
	82	17	12	0.1.8	7.15.0	John Patrick Kelly

LIST OF ORIGINAL SOMERSET LAND OWNERS OF APRIL 1865 AND MAY 1866

ADDITIONAL 1972 TITLE HOLDERS TYPED IN BRACKETS

LIST OF SOMERSET LAND OWNERS WHOSE TITLES WERE CANCELLED BY THE QUEENSLAND GOVERNMENT AND THEIR LAND GIVEN TO THE ABORIGINES

9 MAR 1972
SECTION

Acquisition of Land Act 1967–1969
NOTICE OF INTENTION TO RESUME

Department of Lands,
P.O. Box 168, North Quay.
Brisbane, 4000,
22nd December, 1971.

NOTICE is hereby given that, in pursuance of the provisions of the *Acquisition of Land Act* 1967–1969, it is intended to take for the purpose of being dealt with in any manner in which Crown land may be dealt with under the *Land Act* 1962–1971, the land described in the Schedule hereto.

Any objections may be set forth in writing, not having reference to compensation, to the taking of such land, stating therein the grounds of any such objection and the facts and circumstances relied on in support of those grounds. Such written objections must be served upon the Secretary, Land Administration Commission, at the above address on or before the 17th April, 1972.

If it is stated in the written objection referred to above that the objector desires to be heard in support of the grounds of his objection, the Land Agent, Cairns, will be at his office at 10 a.m. on 18th May, 1972, in order that the objector may appear and be heard accordingly.

This Authority is willing to negotiate to acquire the land by agreement, or, failing agreement and if the land is acquired, to treat with the registered proprietor as to the amount of compensation payable or negotiate any other matter arising out of the acquisition of the land.

Reference: L.A.B. 328.

C. CLAXTON,
Acting Secretary, Land Administration Commission,
the Delegate of the Minister for Lands.

SCHEDULE

THE TORRES LAND AGENT'S DISTRICT

County of Somerset, parish of Seymour, town of Somerset

Registered Proprietor	Area (A. R. P.)	Description	Parish	Town	Title	No.	Vol.	Fol.	Remarks
Hannah Alexander	0 1 8	Allotment 1 of section 6	Seymour	Somerset	D/G	15119	3	77	
Hannah Alexander	0 1 8	Allotment 2 of section 6	Seymour	Somerset	D/G	15120	3	78	
Archibald Anderson	0 1 8	Allotment 3 of section 6	Seymour	Somerset	D/G	15117	3	75	
Noel John Hughes	0 1 8	Allotment 4 of section 6	Seymour	Somerset	D/G	15127	3	85	
Richard Ryan	0 1 8	Allotment 5 of section 6	Seymour	Somerset	D/G	15094	3	54	
Richard Ryan	0 1 8	Allotment 6 of section 6	Seymour	Somerset	D/G	15095	3	55	
John Gebbie	0 1 8	Allotment 7 of section 6	Seymour	Somerset	D/G	15087	3	50	
John Gebbie	0 1 8	Allotment 8 of section 6	Seymour	Somerset	D/G	15088	3	51	
Esther Theresa Thomas	0 1 8	Allotment 9 of section 6	Seymour	Somerset	D/G	15126	3	84	
Leonard Mark Mendoza	0 1 8	Allotment 10 of section 6	Seymour	Somerset	D/G	15093	3	53	
Solomon Edward Mendoza	0 1 8	Allotment 11 of section 6	Seymour	Somerset	D/G	15092	3	52	
Archibald Anderson	0 1 8	Allotment 12 of section 6	Seymour	Somerset	D/G	15118	3	76	
George Myers	0 1 8	Allotment 13 of section 6	Seymour	Somerset	D/G	15115	3	73	
George Myers	0 1 8	Allotment 1 of section 7	Seymour	Somerset	D/G	15116	3	74	
Robert Fleming	0 1 8	Allotment 2 of section 7	Seymour	Somerset	D/G	15112	3	70	
Aeneas Walker	0 1 8	Allotment 3 of section 7	Seymour	Somerset	D/G	15098	3	58	
Aeneas Walker	0 1 8	Allotment 4 of section 7	Seymour	Somerset	D/G	15099	3	59	
Courtney Spry	0 1 8	Allotment 5 of section 7	Seymour	Somerset	C/T	N46208	15	78	
Victoria Booth, spinster	0 1 8	Allotment 8 of section 7	Seymour	Somerset	D/G	15096	3	56	
Frank Gribbrook	0 1 8	Allotment 9 of section 7	Seymour	Somerset	D/G	15128	3	86	
Council of the Shire of Cook	0 1 8	Allotment 10 of section 7	Seymour	Somerset	D/G	15101	3	60	
Council of the Shire of Cook	0 1 8	Allotment 11 of section 7	Seymour	Somerset	D/G	15102	3	61	
Allan Ravenscroft Wettenhall	0 1 8	Allotment 13 of section 7	Seymour	Somerset	D/G	15125	3	83	
William Ferguson and James Woodrow, as Executors with Power of Sale under the will of William Jerimiah Daniell, deceased	0 3 24	Allotments 14, 15 and 16 of section 7	Seymour	Somerset	C/T	104431	68	247	
Queensland Trustees Ltd., as trustee	0 1 8	Allotment 17 of section 7	Seymour	Somerset	D/G	15113	3	71	
Queensland Trustees Ltd., as trustee	0 1 8	Allotment 18 of section 7	Seymour	Somerset	D/G	15114	3	72	
Robert Blackall Lane	0 1 8	Allotment 20 of section 7	Seymour	Somerset	D/G	15111	3	69	
Robert Blackall Lane	0 1 8	Allotment 21 of section 7	Seymour	Somerset	D/G	15110	3	68	
Charles Baldwin	0 1 8	Allotment 22 of section 7	Seymour	Somerset	C/T	33800	10	54	
Council of the Shire of Cook	0 1 8	Allotment 23 of section 7	Seymour	Somerset	D/G	15103	3	62	
Nathan Levy	0 1 8	Allotment 24 of section 7	Seymour	Somerset	D/G	15130	3	87	
Henry Smart Cribb	0 1 8	Allotment 12 of section 12	Seymour	Somerset	C/T	18146	5	233	
Mary Ann Hutchison, widow of said deceased, as sole devisee under will of James Hutchison, deceased	0 1 8	Allotment 13 of section 12	Seymour	Somerset	D/G	15138	3	94	
Clive Norman Backhouse and Percy Maurice Hurbert Backhouse, as devisees in trust with power of sale under the will of Benjamin Backhouse, deceased	0 1 8	Allotment 14 of section 12	Seymour	Somerset	D/G	12101	2	40	
Hon. Daniel Foley Roberts, James Francis Garrick, Milliden Charles Belbridge, as trustees for Sarah Jane Lilley, wife of Hon. Charles Lilley, Attorney General under N/T No. 7806	0 1 8	Allotment 16 of section 12	Seymour	Somerset	D/G	12084	2	27	
Council of the Shire of Cook	0 1 8	Allotment 17 of section 12	Seymour	Somerset	D/G	15105	3	64	
Emily Smith, widow, and George Phillips, as devisees in trust under the will of Shepherd Smith, deceased	0 1 8	Allotment 18 of section 12	Seymour	Somerset	D/G	12088	2	28	
Emily Smith, widow, and George Phillips, as devisees in trust under the will of Shepherd Smith, deceased	0 1 8	Allotment 19 of section 12	Seymour	Somerset	D/G	12083	2	26	
Polet Loftus Cardent and William Alexander Laurie Ivory, as trustees under the will of James Ivory, deceased	0 1 8	Allotment 1 of section 13	Seymour	Somerset	D/G	15078	3	41	
George Selby Graham	0 1 8	Allotment 2 of section 13	Seymour	Somerset	D/G	12080	2	23	
George Selby Graham	0 1 8	Allotment 3 of section 13	Seymour	Somerset	D/G	12081	2	24	
George Selby Graham	0 1 8	Allotment 4 of section 13	Seymour	Somerset	D/G	12082	2	25	
Roseanne Joffurs, spinster	0 1 8	Allotment 5 of section 13	Seymour	Somerset	D/G	12102	2	41	
Alice Oxley, wife of Henry James Oxley	0 1 8	Allotment 6 of section 13	Seymour	Somerset	C/T	43892	14	88	
George Henry Newman, as trustee	0 1 8	Allotment 7 of section 13	Seymour	Somerset	D/G	12104	2	42	
Hannah Alexander	0 1 8	Allotment 8 of section 13	Seymour	Somerset	D/G	15122	3	80	
Ernestine Mary Booth, spinster	0 1 8	Allotment 9 of section 13	Seymour	Somerset	D/G	15097	3	57	
William Belither	0 1 8	Allotment 10 of section 13	Seymour	Somerset	C/T	12418	3	114	
William Neill	0 1 8	Allotment 11 of section 13	Seymour	Somerset	C/T	25612	8	149	
William Neill	0 1 8	Allotment 12 of section 13	Seymour	Somerset	D/G	15080	3	43	
William Neill	0 1 8	Allotment 13 of section 13	Seymour	Somerset	D/G	15079	3	42	
Hannah Alexander	0 1 8	Allotment 15 of section 13	Seymour	Somerset	D/G	15124	3	82	
Hannah Alexander	0 1 8	Allotment 16 of section 13	Seymour	Somerset	D/G	15123	3	81	
John George Cribb, as trustee	0 1 8	Allotment 17 of section 13	Seymour	Somerset	D/G	15140	3	96	
James Baker	0 1 8	Allotment 19 of section 13	Seymour	Somerset	D/G	15141	3	97	
John Taylor Simmons	0 1 8	Allotment 20 of section 13	Seymour	Somerset	D/G	15142	3	98	
John Taylor Simmons	0 1 8	Allotment 21 of section 13	Seymour	Somerset	D/G	15081	3	44	
John Taylor Simmons	0 1 8	Allotment 22 of section 13	Seymour	Somerset	D/G	15082	3	45	
John Taylor Simmons	0 1 8	Allotment 23 of section 13	Seymour	Somerset	D/G	15083	3	46	
John Taylor Simmons	0 1 8	Allotment 24 of section 13	Seymour	Somerset	D/G	15084	3	47	
Hannah Alexander	0 1 8	Allotment 3 of section 14	Seymour	Somerset	D/G	15121	3	79	
Fanny Loeven	0 1 8	Allotment 4 of section 14	Seymour	Somerset	D/G	15131	3	88	
James Piper	0 1 8	Allotment 5 of section 14	Seymour	Somerset	D/G	15132	3	89	
Mary Catherine Martin	0 1 8	Allotment 6 of section 14	Seymour	Somerset	D/G	15133	3	90	
William Castles	0 1 8	Allotment 7 of section 14	Seymour	Somerset	D/G	15134	3	91	
Ann Taylor Burnett Illidge	0 1 8	Allotment 8 of section 14	Seymour	Somerset	D/G	15108	3	66	
Francis Edward Johnson	0 1 8	Allotment 9 of section 14	Seymour	Somerset	D/G	15085	3	48	
Francis Edward Johnson	0 1 8	Allotment 10 of section 14	Seymour	Somerset	D/G	15086	3	49	
Robert Blackall Lane	0 1 8	Allotment 11 of section 14	Seymour	Somerset	D/G	15109	3	67	
James Robert Dickson, The Elder	0 1 8	Allotment 13 of section 14	Seymour	Somerset	C/T	104125	68	177	
James Robert Dickson and James Duncan	0 1 8	Allotment 14 of section 14	Seymour	Somerset	D/G	15106	3	65	
George Spring	0 1 8	Allotment 19 of section 14	Seymour	Somerset	D/G	15135	3	92	
Catherine Reilly	0 1 8	Allotment 20 of section 14	Seymour	Somerset	D/G	15136	3	93	
Elizabeth Levy	0 1 8	Allotment 21 of section 14	Seymour	Somerset	D/G	15139	3	95	
Council of the Shire of Cook	0 1 8	Allotment 22 of section 14	Seymour	Somerset	D/G	15104	3	63	
Emily Smith, widow, and George Phillips, as devisees in trust under the will of Shepherd Smith	0 1 0	Allotment 3 of section 21	Seymour	Somerset	D/G	12089	2	29	
John Splaine	0 1 0	Allotment 4 of section 21	Seymour	Somerset	D/G	12105	2	43	
John Splaine	0 1 0	Allotment 5 of section 21	Seymour	Somerset	D/G	12090	2	30	
John Splaine	0 1 0	Allotment 7 of section 21	Seymour	Somerset	D/G	12091	2	31	
William Neill	0 1 0	Allotment 8 of section 21	Seymour	Somerset	C/T	25614	8	151	
William Neill	0 1 0	Allotment 9 of section 21	Seymour	Somerset	C/T	25613	8	150	
Allan McIntyre	0 1 0	Allotment 4 of section 22	Seymour	Somerset	D/G	12106	2	44	
William Neill	0 1 0	Allotment 5 of section 22	Seymour	Somerset	C/T	25610	8	147	
William Neill	0 1 0	Allotment 6 of section 22	Seymour	Somerset	C/T	25611	8	148	
William Neill	0 1 0	Allotment 7 of section 22	Seymour	Somerset	D/G	12092	2	32	
John Cadbury	0 1 0	Allotment 8 of section 22	Seymour	Somerset	D/G	12099	2	39	
John Cadbury	0 1 0	Allotment 15 of section 34	Seymour	Somerset	D/G	12093	2	33	
John Cadbury	0 1 0	Allotment 17 of section 34	Seymour	Somerset	D/G	12072	2	21	
William Neill	0 1 8	Allotment 2 of section 44	Seymour	Somerset	C/T	25615	8	152	
William Neill	0 1 8	Allotment 3 of section 44	Seymour	Somerset	D/G	12073	2	22	
Edward Briggs Kennedy	0 1 8	Allotment 4 of section 44	Seymour	Somerset	D/G	12096	2	36	
Edward Briggs Kennedy	0 1 8	Allotment 5 of section 44	Seymour	Somerset	D/G	12095	2	35	
Edward Briggs Kennedy	0 1 8	Allotment 6 of section 44	Seymour	Somerset	D/G	12094	2	34	
Charles Christopher Cameron	0 1 8	Allotment 20 of section 44	Seymour	Somerset	D/G	12107	2	45	
James Warner	0 1 8	Allotment 2 of section 45	Seymour	Somerset	C/T	29270	7	70	
John Thomas Rush	0 1 8	Allotment 5 of section 45	Seymour	Somerset	C/T	68286	32	232	
Edward Briggs Kennedy	0 1 8	Allotment 7 of section 45	Seymour	Somerset	D/G	12098	2	38	
Edward Briggs Kennedy	0 1 8	Allotment 9 of section 45	Seymour	Somerset	D/G	12097	2	37	

Major C R Sheldon [beheaded by the Japanese in 1942].

CHAPTER 19
"JARDINE'S DIARY"

Frank Jardine lived on Cape York for over half a century. During that time he wrote volumes of information, compiled into a series of annual diaries relating to all the major incidents that occurred in the region of Cape York and the Torres Strait Islands.

This included the "bloody massacres" of ships crews by aborigines and Islanders. The failed rescue attempt of a white woman held captive by the Kauraregas [Sperwer], the savage tribal wars in which aborigines slaughtered their weaker opponents and even the names of pearlers known to have kidnapped Islanders.

The explorer, Robert Logan Jack made 2 references to the existence of these diaries, when he wrote:
> *"It is said that he kept a diary covering the whole of his northern life"*, and again ... *"It is hoped that the diary will be published without delay."* [Northmost Australia Pages 337 and 347]

The diaries remained at Somerset for many years after Frank Jardine died and various sections were quoted by a number of journalists and authors.

Because of their immense historical value, the Mitchell Library in Sydney, had offered to buy them off Frank Jardine in his later years, for a reputed £10,000.

The offer was rejected as he felt they should remain in the custody of his family [Elizabeth also declined many offers].

However, according to his grand daughter Pamela Ivey [Sheldon] a number of statements made could be construed as libellous against certain people and this may have been why he did not part with them.

The diary is often referred to as the "JARDINE JOURNALS". However, as this is easily confused with "JARDINE'S JOURNAL", I have used the term "JARDINE'S DIARY".

A. The term "JARDINE'S JOURNAL", relates to the book of that name about the cattle drive of 1864-1865.

B. The term "JARDINE JOURNALS" are the diaries he wrote during his life on Cape York [JARDINE'S DIARY].

At the end of World War 2, all the 41 Volumes of the Diary and the treasure of silver ware had mysteriously disappeared.

Rumour fed on rumour and men were actually diving in the waters off Cape York in search of the silver, after the war.

Frank Jardine's eldest son Chumley [spelt Cholmondeley] was as adventurous as his father. If something had to be done, regardless of the hardships involved then he did it.

With a wealth of pearling experience behind him, he left Somerset and settled at Dobo, on Wamar Island in the Aru group of Islands in the Dutch East Indies [Indonesia].

Although he was pearling with the Celebes Trading Co. he also saw a future in coconuts and soon purchased the small island of Pulau Babi for that purpose.

Pulau Babi [Pig Island] is 12 miles south of Dobo and is only 2 square miles in area with fresh water wells that never ran dry, even in the driest seasons.

At 6 foot 4 and 200 pounds, this gentle giant set to work, clearing the jungle and planting row after row of the best coconuts purchased from the Dutch Government Botanical Gardens at Buitenzorg in Djakarta [Batavia].

A house was soon built near the well amid the eastern plantation, and in order to be as independent as possible, he brought in goats and chickens as well as a herd of cattle that grazed on the southern part of the island, between the east and western plantations.

To run the plantation, he hired a Javanese overseer named Wongso and a number of labourers who kept the undergrowth clear and erected barriers around the tree trunks to prevent the rats eating the coconuts.

The labourers came from the island of Timor and were employed on a 3 year contract. During that time they would be given accommodation and food and be paid in full at the end of their 3 years. This permitted them to take home their full wages rather than waste it in Dobo.

Chum, later had 3 other plantations on the islands of Penambulai, Wokam and Wamar. As these were uneconomical due to distance and finance, they were abandoned and left to grow wild.

As it would take some years before he could harvest the coconuts, he decided to stop pearling and become a buyer and seller of the shell. He would now buy from the pearlers and sell the pearl shell to a company called "Schmid Jeandell" in New York. In this venture he was highly successful.

As well as dealing in pearl shell he was also the agent for B.P. [British Petroleum] and was known all through the Aru Islands as the "RAJAH", due to his habit of selling fuel to the locals on credit, who left him in debt when they failed to pay their bills.

"Chum Jardine has often been accused by his critics as being the person responsible for the disappearance of the Jardine silver treasure and diary from Somerset.

According to a number of writers he was supposed to have taken them to Pulau Babi after his fathers death and they have never been seen since World War II.

When the Japanese invaded the Aru Islands during the war the treasure and diary were said to have been buried on Pulau Babi in a steel trunk and to this day have not been found."

In order to find the truth surrounding their disappearance, it was necessary to find a reliable witness who could give an accurate account of events prior to the Japanese invasion of the Aru Islands.

The only person who lived in that era and who is still alive today, to give the full story is Pamela Ivey [Sheldon], the grand daughter of Frank Jardine. She is the daughter of Jardine's youngest daughter, Elizabeth Sheldon [Jardine].

The following information was related to me in 3 tape recorded interviews with her in 1994.

At the end of World War I [WWI] Lieut Charles Richard Sheldon had left the Army after receiving an honourable discharge.

He had been based on Thursday Island during the war [WWI] and had married Elizabeth Jardine shortly after his discharge. By early 1925 he had a wife and 2 young children to support [Pamela and Chumley].

It was a time of great hardship as he tried to survive by selling life insurance to farmers in the rural areas of Victoria.

Meanwhile back on Dobo, Chum Jardine had written to the Sheldons asking them to come up to the Aru Islands and look after the coconut plantations as he was now too heavily involved in buying and selling pearl shell.

The Sheldons needed little encouragement to move to the tropics and months later arrived at Dobo.

The family moved into a large house provided by Chum and adjusted well to their new life in the tropics in spite of the prevalence of malaria and other tropical diseases such as beri-beri.

To prevent this disease it was a simple matter of eating mung beans in the diet. In fact it was the law in the Aru's that any company issuing white rice to their employees, must also give them a ration of mung beans which are rich in the B vitamins, especially Vitamin B1.

It is the lack of the B vitamins that contributes so much to this crippling disease.

Above: Chum Jardine's home [X] and Sheldon's home [XX] Dobo.

Left: The faithful "Wongso" and a young Pam Sheldon [Pulau Babi].

Below: The Sheldon's home on Dobo with Elizabeth [Jaki] centre and her children Pam and Chum [taken 1931] Chum was beheaded by the Japanese, in 1942 for helping prisoners to escape from the Ambon Concentration Camp.

As a weight conscious teenager, Pamela stopped eating the beans and was soon suffering the effects of Beri-Beri.

She awoke one morning barely able to walk and spent the next 8 months in a Dutch Army hospital on Ambon.

In 1935, Chum Jardine died and Elizabeth Sheldon [Jardine] inherited Pulau Babi and other properties as well as Chums debts caused by his generosity to the locals.

Although the Sheldons were reasonably independent for food, such as beef, chicken, eggs, fruit and vegetables, they still needed other supplies.

Items such as, clothing, tinned food, stationery and medicines had to be imported from a company in Singapore called 'John Little's'.

A ship would arrive at Dobo twice a month and to the residents it was just like Christmas.

Like most people living in isolated areas, the small European community living in the Aru's created their own entertainment. When Elizabeth imported a piano, to Dobo, there were many nights of merriment as family and friends sang and danced to their favourite tunes.

Meanwhile, political storm clouds were moving across the Pacific as Japan geared for war.

During the late 1930's Sheldon realised that the Japanese were using the pearling industry as a front for their espionage activities in the Aru's.

Although it appeared to the untrained eye that they were engaged in pearling, they were also reconnoitring the area and drawing charts of the reefs and channels in case a future invasion would be necessary.

Sheldon wrote to the Authorities in Singapore and Australia on the issue.

For over a year correspondence went back and forth between Singapore, Australia and Dobo. Finally Sheldon offered to be a Consular Official in order to have some authority over the Japanese who were obviously spying out the region.

Although the issue was shelved, Sheldon continued to send out intelligence reports on the activities of the Japanese.

Meanwhile on Pulau Babi the coconuts were being harvested each year. After de-husking them they would be cut in 2 and smoked on racks, after which the flesh was extracted and exported as Copra for making glycerine.

With the outbreak of the Pacific War [WW2], the Japanese invaded the Dutch East Indies [Indonesia] in early February of 1942.

When Japanese aircraft attacked the Aru's, the Sheldons were on Pulau Babi and could see the indiscriminate bombing of Dobo.

As Pulau Babi was well stocked with cattle, pigs, goats, deer and chickens as well as fruit and vegetable gardens, then it wouldn't be long before the invading Japanese arrived.

Sheldon planned to evacuate his family and bluntly told his wife and daughter 'I don't want any women here when the Japs arrive'.

By now the Dutch oil company "Shell" had completed the total destruction of their operations in Dutch New-Guinea, including the "Scorched Earth Policy' of blowing up the refinery and support facilities and setting it ablaze to prevent the Japanese from refining oil which would then be used to power their war machine against the Allies.

It was arranged that Dobo would be the central evacuation point for the oil men and their families and that a Catalina flying boat would come in and evacuate them to Darwin from Dobo.

Meanwhile, Pamela's 18 year old brother Chum, had been working for the pearl shelling group called the Celebes Trading Company [CTC].

With the outbreak of war he started transporting supplies for the Dutch Navy and was later captured and sent to the notorious Japanese concentration camp at Ambon.

On the night of the 13th February 1942, the Sheldons left Pulau Babi and arrived in Dobo after the heaviest air raid so far and found their house still intact after the bombing.

The oil workers had arrived in the town and were waiting to be flown out. If they could get on that plane, they could be in Australia within hours.

When the Catalina arrived [18th February 1942] they were given only 15 minutes to get aboard the flying boat, due to the danger of being caught on the water in another air raid.

Outside the plane Sheldon stood in the dinghy saying his last goodbye to his wife and daughter, whilst in the town the locals were ransacking his house looking for money.

That night they were billeted in Darwin and the next day they were fortunate to fly south before the Jap bombers hit the town killing and wounding hundreds of civilians.

Meanwhile the Japs made several more air raids on Dobo and one bomb hit the Sheldons home but failed to explode.

Sheldon now removed items of value including documents and a number of items of silverware such as a fish knife set and 2 covered entre dishes. These were placed in a steel trunk with other valuables and put on the launch.

The bombers returned the next day and blew the house to bits and set it alight, destroying anything that was left inside including books, journals, furniture etc.

When the air raid was over Sheldon took the trunk to Pulau Babi and buried it in a secret location known only to 2 other men. These were his trusted overseer "Wongso" and a Danish friend, Carl Monsted, the Manager of the Celebes Trading Company [CTC].

After killing his 7 dogs he took the launch and travelled to Merauke on the Dutch New-Guinea coast and from there headed for Thursday Island.

As he was a reserve officer [Lieutenant] from World War I he rejoined the army to fight the invading Japanese.

Due to his knowledge of the Aru Islands he was transferred to a top secret commando intelligence gathering section of the I.A.S.D. [Inter-Allied-Services-Department], known as "Z" Force. The I.A.S.D. was later known as the "Allied Intelligence Bureau" or "A.I.B." which controlled a network of agents known as the "Coastwatchers", who were spread over 500,000 square miles of land and sea, from Singapore to Australia. Many were landed by submarines on enemy held beaches in the dead of night, forever cautious of betrayal by the natives.

From their dimly lit jungle camps, constantly plagued by tropical diseases they radioed valuable information of Japanese troop movements and equipment back to Australia.

With his previous military experience, Sheldon quickly moved up the ranks during the wartime emergency to Captain and in his capacity as the leader of 2 intelligence raids into enemy territory was generally known as Major Sheldon.

The plan to land agents in the Aru Islands was code named "Operation Walnut" and was divided into 3 stages.

WALNUT 1

This party consisted of Major C R Sheldon and his associate Lieutenant Neils Preben Monsted, the nephew of Carl Monsted of the Celebes Trading Company [CTC].

They brazenly sailed a schooner into the Aru's and were amazed to find that when they landed close to Dobo on the 7th July 1942, the Japanese had not arrived.

This all changed by the end of the month, when the Japs suddenly arrived in force and they now became the hunted and spent much of their time out-smarting the enemy.

With the help of the natives the Jap cordon was closing in and they finally managed to escape in a motorised lugger called the "Express" and made it to Thursday Island in September 1942. Lieutenant Monsted then sailed the "Express" to Darwin.

WALNUT 2

This party was again led by Major Sheldon in company with Lieutenant R W Feetum and Sergeant J McCandlish who were to carry out a reconnaissance of the islands and find out if the natives sympathised with the Japanese.

They were flown in to the Aru's in a Dutch flying boat and landed at Penambulai Island with rubber boats and equipment on the 15th February 1943.

For 3 weeks they reconnoitred the islands transmitting valuable information to Darwin. Their last message was sent on the 8th March stating that the natives were "hostile" and by now the Japs probably knew where they were and it would be very difficult to complete their task. Under these conditions they requested additional help, which never came. When they failed to transmit on their appointed time it was accepted that they may have been killed or captured.

WALNUT 3

This party was led by Lieutenant N P Monsted with 3 Sergeants, Plumridge, Dahlberg and Bloch, a man called Mr Mitchell and five national crew [Indonesians].

They left Darwin in the lugger "Express" and arrived at an island in the Aru's called Pulau Djeh [12th July 1943]. Their assignment was to reconnoitre the area around Dobo.

Their last message was transmitted on the 25th July, and after failing to come back on air it was accepted that they had also been killed or captured.

The mystery surrounding the disappearance of these men was only solved after the Japanese surrender in 1945 and with it came the horrifying conclusion of murder and torture by the Japanese against Prisoners of War.

When Australian soldiers started digging around the rear of the "Benteng Barracks" on Ambon, they found it to be a first class execution ground which was surrounded on 3 sides by a high wall. The other side faced the sea and in this way there could be no witnesses to their atrocities.

When Chum Sheldon [Maj Sheldon's son] was incarcerated into the Ambon Concentration Camp in 1942, he had somehow managed to smuggle in a pistol which he kept well hidden.

Due to his dark complexion [caused by being constantly exposed to the sun, during his pearling days] he was easily able to pass himself off as a native as he also spoke the language [Malay] fluently.

On a number of occasions he was able to sneak in and out of the camp and according to his sister [Pamela Ivey] he helped a number of Australians to escape.

On many of his escapades from the camp he was actually organising native resistance against the Japanese. He was finally betrayed and subsequently captured one night outside the compound armed with the pistol.

After being beaten and tortured by his captors he was executed. As the Japs were ordered to save ammunition he was be-headed with a single stroke of a Samurai sword, his grave has never been located.

THE FATE OF WALNUT 2

Major Sheldon was betrayed by the natives after moving his party to the island of "Djamboeal". At the time of his capture he had left the others at the camp whilst he carried out a reconnaissance on his own.

Natives led the Japanese to him and a battle soon erupted in which Major Sheldon was captured after running out of ammunition.

He was taken to Dobo and underwent torture and interrogation by the Japs for a month and then transferred to 'Toal' on "Kay Island" [originally "Kai Island"] and interrogated further. He was later sent to the same Concentration Camp at Ambon where his son Chum had been held before his execution.

20 Days after his capture, Feetum, McCandlish and 2 natives guides were also

betrayed and captured on a small island to the east of "Djamboeal". They were also taken to the Ambon Concentration Camp after suffering beatings and torture.

In mid August 1943, the Japs decided to execute Major Sheldon and a number of other prisoners. They considered him as a high priority prisoner and actually referred to him as the commander of the "Sheldon Special Suicide Unit" [Tokubetsu Keshitai]. "He secretly penetrated our occupied territory where the 5th Division was, in order to obtain information about our Army." [Japanese War Crimes Tribunal – Manus Island – 1950].

When Lieutenant Colonel Sumizu Junichiro [Judge Advocate] instructed Captain Kagiyama Kaneki [Ambon Camp Commander] that Major Sheldon was to be executed, the chief prison guard asked that he be permitted to decapitate him [Wagatsuma Junzaburo].

At the execution site a trench had been dug and Sumizu told Wagatsuma to carry out the execution.

Sumizu had a brand new sword that had never been tested and instructed Wagatsuma to use it in order that it be "Blooded".

On that same day, 2 RAAF personnel were also beheaded [Sgt Lee and Andrea]. Following them 30 natives suffered the same fate. They had revolted against the Japanese invaders.

The bodies were put in the trench with a space between the Prisoners of War and the natives, and then filled in.

Wagatsuma later boasted to other Japanese soldiers of beheading the P.O.Ws, and informed Sumizu that his sword was a good one [Japanese War Crimes Tribunal – Manus Island 1950].

2 Weeks later Sergeant McCandlish and Lieutenant Feetum were also beheaded behind the Benteng Barracks and later 2 airmen of the RAAF who were shot down whilst attacking the "Sugi-Maru" were beheaded. These were Sergeants Boanas and Graham.

One of them had a broken leg and had to be carried to the site of his execution on a stretcher.

The Japanese found guilty of war crimes received only light sentences of 7 to 14 years under the Australian Military Court, but fortunately, the Dutch had sentenced them to life imprisonment and the Australian sentences were suspended in favour of the Dutch.

THE FATE OF WALNUT 3

They were betrayed by natives at Pulau Djeh and ambushed by a party of 20 Japanese in the late afternoon whilst having a meal.

The battle continued for 3 hours when one of them who is believed to have been Lieutenant Preben Monsted covered the withdrawal of the others in the dark. He was finally shot and the Japanese buried him on the island.

Although the Japanese thoroughly searched Pulau Djeh and the surrounding islands, no trace was found of the other members of "Walnut 3".

As all their equipment was lost during the battle, it is suspected that they may have been taken by sharks or crocodiles whilst trying to reach another island.

During the war Pamela Sheldon married her fiance, Tom Ivey an oil man [Geo-Physicist] and in 1950 the steel trunk containing their valuables was dug up at Pulau Babi by Carl Monsted and sent to them at Palaembang where they now lived.

The stories of a trunk buried on Pulau Babi, containing the silver treasure and Jardine's Diary is clearly mistaken for the trunk that Major Sheldon buried containing the family valuables including the silver fish knife set and 2 entre dishes.

Pamela Ivey lived on Pulau Babi for 16 years and at no time did she see a treasure of silverware other than a few items that may have been part of the original service from Somerset.

However, she clearly remembers the large gold coin that was kept by her mother and which was probably the gold Ferdinand found with the treasure in 1891.

When Chum Jardine first went to Pulau Babi he purchased his own launch called No. 1. It is very possible that he may have sold off the silverware to pay for it. This however, can only be an assumption.

As for "Jardine's Diary," Pamela Ivey saw a lot of large books but cannot relate to any of the volumes of the Diary at Pulau Babi or Dobo.

However, her father wrote various articles for magazines before the war and this included an article in which he quoted from "Jardine's Diary". So they must have been with him in the Aru Islands, probably at his home on Dobo.

If this was the case then they would have been destroyed when the house was bombed by the Japanese in 1942 and everything went up in flames.

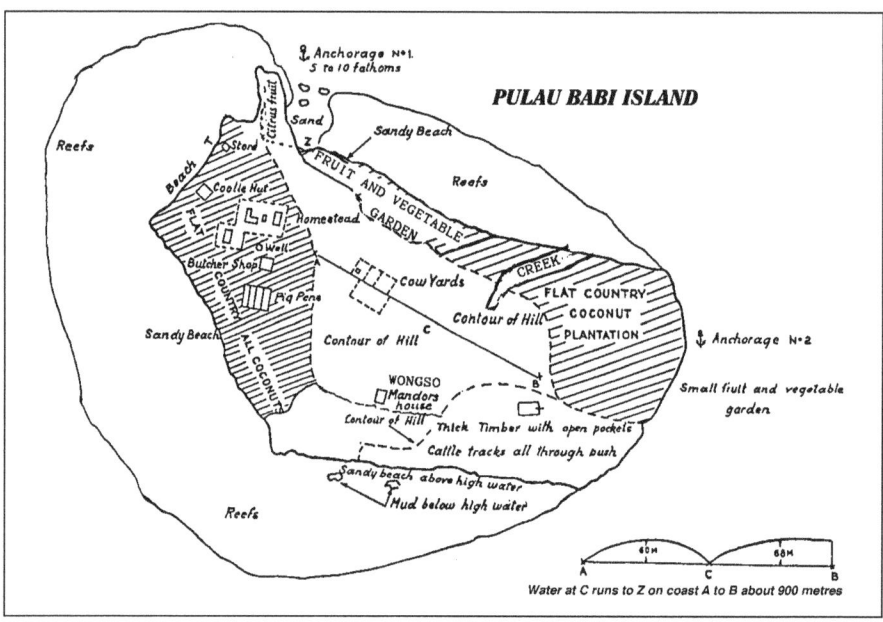

Pam Sheldon as a teenager in the Aru's.

Chum Sheldon, Tom Ivey and Elizabeth Sheldon [Jardine].

C R Sheldon reported Japanese Espionage activities. *C R Sheldon on his launch "No. 1" before the war.*

The Sheldon's home nestled amidst the coconut plantation on Pulau Babi Island.

Chum Sheldon, who was later beheaded by the Japanese [1942].

Pam Sheldon and Neils Preben Monsted before the war. He was killed in action.

The Sheldon's home on Pulau Babi.

CHAPTER 20
"ACADEMIC BLUNDERS"

When one considers the vast number of fallacies that have crept into Australian history, as a result of blundering academics, who failed to do their homework properly, it is understandable that they have become the butt of countless jokes.

Many of them are often referred to as "Educated Dunces" due to their inability to relate to the reality of the times. The reality was that aborigines were just as violent to their enemies as were other races around the world.

In the case of some anthropologists, their mental capacity to interpret violence between the native tribes, appears to have stagnated to the point of ignoring that it ever existed. They are somewhat akin to a child who has felt no fear and so concludes there is no danger.

Although they are amongst the most highly paid academics in the country, their contribution is almost negligible. In fact when one considers the millions of dollars they receive in grants to fund their "Imaginary Research Projects", plus their highly inflated salaries, they are more of a liability than an asset.

When a businessman questioned his anthropologist brother, on the lies and deceptions of "Australia's false aboriginality", he received the following answer:

"Look, I am paid a quarter of a million dollars a year, [$250,000] to promote aboriginality, I am not interested whether it is true or false, for this is how Universities get their funding."

When one considers that anthropologists judge one race against another, then many of them are in effect, the "silent manipulators of racial discrimination".

Some of them have been quietly working behind the scenes, pinpointing non existent sacred sites for future land claims in high priority areas such as tourist resorts and mining leases.

I am convinced that they are the greatest threat to racial co-existence in Australia.

The following section is just a small example of the large number of fallacies that have been written into history by various academics and later found to be wrong.

In some cases there were genuine mistakes whilst others were deliberate lies and deceptions concocted in an attempt to degrade our early pioneers.

NORMAN B TINDALE [ANTHROPOLOGIST]

In his book on the "Aboriginal Tribes of Australia", Tindale states "When dealing with any people, the basis of good reporting is accurate localisation". Yet this highly touted anthropologist actually used an ill informed aircraft pilot as one of his sources of information, which resulted in the wrong tribal names and their boundaries being stated.

He wrongly refers to all tribes from Punsand Bay, south to Vrilya Point as "Ankamuti" when they were the Gumukudin and Ambagana.

He refers to all tribes from Punsand Bay south to the Escape River as "Djagaraga" when there was no such tribe north of the Escape or Jardine Rivers. The tribe that lived in the region of the Escape was of course the "Yadagana".

In trying to identify the Induyumu he mistakenly calls them "Jathaikana" [Yadagana] and states that all tribes from Cape York to the Escape River were called "Djagaraga" when no such tribe existed in that region.

Incredibly, he refers to the 'Yegulle' as the name of a tribe when in fact it is a derogatory term for ugliness, meaning "big nose" of the kangaroo and was a name used by the Kauraregas to degrade their enemies, whether they be Yadagana, Gumukudin or any other tribe.

[Also pronounced – Yegille, Yegalla, Yegallie, Yegylie.]

He also claimed that Muralug was the native name of the tribe of Prince of Wales, when in reality it was the native name of Prince of Wales Island.

Even the lowly Gudang are insulted by calling them the "Jathaikana" [Yadagana] who were in fact their enemies.

When considering that so many mistakes were made on just that one section of Cape York, one wonders how many more must be made all over Australia.

This book is in 2 large volumes and believe it or not is used in Universities all over the world as an authoritative source of aboriginal tribes and their territorial boundaries!!!

"SOMERSET" – AN ACADEMIC DISASTER

In 1986, academics from the James Cook University in Townsville, visited Somerset on a grant assisted research project. Their tainted version of its history and site evaluation were recorded by Professor Barry Reynolds and David Lawrence. In their 2 separate manuscripts identified as Stage 1 and Stage 2, they made so many blunders, that I found it necessary to reject much of it as "Unreliable Research Material".

They appear also, to have gone to great lengths to falsely accuse Frank Jardine of offences he did not commit. In one section, they quote a statement from the missionary Jagg accusing the Police Magistrate in 1867 of shooting aborigines.

In their eagerness to degrade Jardine they have accused him of the offence instead of Police Magistrate Henry Simpson.

Frank Jardine did not become Police Magistrate until 1868. As it turned out the missionary Jagg was one of the instigators proposing "retaliatory violence" against the Yadagana, after the massacre of the Gudang at Albany Island.

I never cease to be amazed how academics continually condemn the whites for killing aborigines in self defence, but remain silent on the subject of massacres by aborigines against their own people in their tribal wars, in which dozens of people were often killed.

The following are just some of the incredible mistakes made by these academics in the "Somerset Fiasco".

MEAT-HOUSE:

On page 16, they refer to a 3 sided structure in bush some distance behind the Somerset house as a "Lock-up". This concrete structure is so small that a prisoner could not even lie down and as it only has a sandy floor, any prisoner could soon dig their way out.

It is more likely to have been a meat house where the beef may even have been smoked. Its distance from the house would also have kept the flies away.

SLIP-WAY:

On page 4 they mention that a wharf existed on the foreshore of Somerset Bay. No doubt, they believed this because of the rows of wooden stumps on the beach, which were the 4 rows of supports for the slipway, which ran from the boatsheds to the water. [There was no wharf at Somerset.]

LANDING STUMPS:

On page 18, they mention that another structure must have existed due to the finding of an isolated wooden stump near the mangroves and claim "there were no other stumps nearby".

When I inspected this area at the south east end of the beach in 1988, I found 3 of these large stumps of which 2 of them were surrounded by mangroves and a 3rd was almost covered by sand near the high tide mark.

A painting of this structure held by Graham Jardine-Vidgen, illustrates a small landing with a shed on it. This was one of the paintings salvaged from the airfield shed in 1948.

SHIP'S ANCHOR:
On pages 18-19 they refer to a large ship's anchor and claim that there is no documentary evidence on the origins of this anchor.

In fact a large anchor [ridge and warp] was lost by the German ship "Reichstag" when it became temporarily reefed in the Torres Strait, near Friday Island on the 9th June 1871.

Henry Chester later brought the anchor to Somerset. [See Page 225]

HOSPITAL:
On page 5, they state that the hospital was possibly transferred to Thursday Island in 1877.

This is just one of the many blunders made by them. Documentary evidence written by Police Magistrate Charles Beddome on the 22nd November 1873 [SLB-11-73] states the following:

> *"Mr Jardine has commenced to pull down the hospital to prevent it coming down. I have nearly completed the demolition."*

[See Page 225]

LAND SALES:
On page 12, they claim that the first Somerset Land Sale was on the 2nd May 1866, when in fact it was the 4th April 1865. Both Auctions were held at Martin's Auction Rooms in Brisbane. Because the listing of the amount of the Somerset Land sold was published in 1866, the academics presumed that the first land sale was also in that year when it was in 1865.

Both land sales were listed on the same sheets so as the lots would follow in sequence and the date sold printed next to it.

The allotments listed as the 4th April were sold in 1865 and those listed as the 2nd May, were sold in 1866.

THE SOMERSET PAINTINGS:
In 1971, several aborigines were seen accompanied by a white man, painting some "rock art" at an overhanging rock shelter near Somerset.

This site is less than a few hundred yards north west of Somerset Beach, on the shoreline below the old Marine Camp, facing Albany Pass.

Today, it has still not been established if they were simply painting over some old originals or if they were painting some new "originals" and hoping they would blend in with a few earlier ones.

When I photographed this site in 1988, I found there was a distinct colour difference between the paintings, clearly identifying the old from the new ones.

Yet, even the old ones may not be so old, for I have not found any documentation or reference to these paintings last century.

As far back as 1849, when the Rattlesnake was anchored at Evans Bay, no mention was made of any native paintings. At that time, the artist 'Brierly', was shown anything of cultural importance by the Gudang. If they had been there at that time, the natives would gladly have taken him there. Yet, in all his journals, there is no mention of any rock paintings.

The same applies to the Zoologist John Macgillivray, who also makes no mention of them.

When the Somerset Settlement was established in 1864, the British Marine camp was situated just above this rock shelter. If there had been any paintings there then, they would have been seen. Yet again, no mention is made of them.

Even Police Magistrate, John Jardine, in writing his voluminous report on the aborigines of the area, makes no mention of any paintings near Somerset.

In fact not one of the Police Magistrates wrote anything about "rock paintings" during the settlements 13 years existence, yet, these paintings were supposed to be only a few hundred yards north west of this establishment.

Any one passing the site would have seen the rock shelter and its little sandy beach and upon landing would have instantly seen the paintings, if they had been there.

All the available evidence appears to show that these paintings are of recent occurrence. That is, they were not there last century.

During 1971 and 1973, a particular anthropologist was seen lurking around the area and later wrote his distorted opinion of one of these paintings. He stated:

"In a cave near Somerset there is a faint painting of a white man in a hat, belt with revolver and breeches, flogging a dark crouching figure".

In fact, the faint image does not show any person being flogged, the dark painting portrays a creature with no discernible arms, face or belt.

This image is so indistinguishable, that anyone could apply their own interpretation to it. There is an amazing sequel, to this whole scenario and that is the weather patterns. This cave is flooded during the high tide and there is no way the Gudang would have painted these images, knowing they would be severely damaged by salt water.

As all the evidence clearly shows, there is no record of any paintings here last century, then these are obviously some of the many "new" ancient paintings that have suddenly appeared all over the continent.

A number of statements made by this anthropologist have been repeated by other academics, only to find out later that they were incorrect. This simply proves that if the initial statement is wrong, then those who repeat it are also wrong.

That applies to any author including myself, for the more fiction eliminated from history the better for us all.

CANNIBALISM

Recent statements made by various academics that aborigines were not cannibals is absolutely false. There is a mass of documentary evidence of cannabalism by aborigines, including the consumption of their own dead children.

One old aboriginal from Western Australia, stated to Jack Byham [The Murray River Man] that he ate his own 3 year old daughter who died in a drought.

Jack Byham lived with the desert aborigines over a 50 year period and claims that many ate more human flesh than kangaroo meat and that they often ate their own dead to be closer to them. He also knew of another aboriginal who shared in the consumption of 6 different people. He is one of the few real authorities on aborigines.

Jack Byham with the old aboriginal who ate his own deceased 3 year old daughter who died in a drought.

Chapter 21
"THE POLITICAL AFTERMATH"

In 1920, the explorer Robert Logan Jack, wrote the following statement:
"The future of the Australian aborigines may offer problems of its own to future generations." [of Australians]
[NMA – Vol 2 – Page 688 – R L Jack 1920]

This prophecy is now being fulfilled in such a deceitful manner, that few Australians would have believed it possible 20 years ago.

When the Labor Government came into power in 1983, one of the first objectives was to educate the public into accepting a "False aboriginality".

To do this they channelled millions of dollars to academics and universities to literally indoctrinate Australians into accepting an aboriginal pre-history that did not exist.

Although the anthropologists had all the evidence to prove that the original Australians were of Papuan decent, [Ulotrichi] and that the aborigines [Cymotrichi] were a recent invader, there was clearly no profit in promoting it.

On the other hand there were thousands of aborigines [Cymotrichi] in which academics could claim huge grants of $80,000 and more, in studying and promoting them as the original Australians, when they knew that their ancestors displaced the indigenous Papuans [Ulotrichi].

Political pressure was applied all over the country on issues relating to aborigines. Even the police had to ignore aborigines breaking the law, where whites under the same circumstances would be arrested.

This was the same government that was supposed to be non racist when in fact the evidence now portrays it as the most "anti-white racist government" in Australian history.

For many years, certain journalists continually degraded and falsely accused white Australians of racism, when they were openly flouting the law themselves, discriminating against anyone who was not a pro-aboriginal supporter.

A prime example is the "racist slander" against our early pioneers, who had little choice but to defend themselves against unprovoked attacks by aborigines.

Yet, because those same journalists consider themselves reasonably safe from legal action they feel they have free reign, and can paint the white man as a violent aggressor, even though they know that the reverse was more often the case.

Some journalists presenting documentaries on Australia's television stations have lied and distorted historical facts so often that most Australians now ignore them.

In 1994, I wrote to Channel 9, in Brisbane, informing them that certain statements made by one of their journalists in a documentary on Somerset was totally false.

The lies concerned the statement to the effect that "Frank Jardine was supposed to have shot a tribal chief, claiming it was a crocodile".

When I proved to Channel 9, that it was false I soon received a letter from the journalist concerned attempting to push the blame elsewhere when he wrote:
"I was the on-camera presenter of the documentary, but not the writer of the script.

The available evidence clearly showed that no one was shot, not even a crocodile and yet the public are continually swamped with these lies and deceptions that have been planted into Australian history by do-gooders unable to relate to the reality of the times.

In these days of discriminating laws enacted against the majority of Australians, many will be surprised to learn that prior to 1970 an incredibly racist sign confronted visitors at a public wharf only 20 miles south of the top of Cape York. It stated:

"CAUCASIANS ARE NOT PERMITTED ON THIS WHARF"

For the benefit of those who do not understand the meaning of "Caucasians", they are people of the European race, that is "White People".

That was the type of discrimination that whites had to put up with until recent times on Cape York.

Anti-white discrimination has become a favourite publishing theme of academics in recent years. They have clearly gone overboard in their false accusations against Australia's early pioneers knowing that people sympathetic to aborigines will believe it due to their own naivety.

A prime example was the publication of a book in 1992, in which the authoress has turned the hospitable Frank Jardine into some kind of ogre.

Although the book was published by the Aboriginal Studies Press in Canberra, it was virtually condemned in a scathing review [Australian Aboriginal Studies, 1992/No. 2].

The article clearly stated that her interpretation was:

"Coloured by her own political vision".

It further states that:

> *"I do not wish to imply that she has falsified the record, but I do suggest that oral accounts in non standard English, need more careful interpretation."*

It has now been alleged that her vindictive accusations against Frank Jardine were a mass of lies and distortions quoted by a local aboriginal.

In one section she quotes a story that Jardine shot aborigines at his coconut plantation at Somerset, prior to 1911 and that shortly after this incident John Mclaren arrived on the west coast and started to plant his own coconut plantation at Utingu [Simpson Bay].

If she had carried out any valid research she would have learnt that there was no coconut plantation at Somerset at that time whatsoever. The only plantation that was even commenced was Mclaren's at Utingu, when 550 seed coconuts had arrived at Somerset by ship and which Mclaren collected on the 17th March 1911. These were the nuclei of his plantation [Somerset visitors book 17th March 1911].

The Jardine's Somerset plantation did not commence until after 1913, when Jardine leased 2 large blocks of land behind Somerset from the Government. These were portions 4 and 5 which Jardine had purchased for his two sons Chum and Bertie Bootle on 30th December 1913.

As it takes many years for the trees to mature and bear fruit [5-7] then it is obvious that an old man in his late 70's could not have been hunting blacks in a coconut plantation.

The coconuts did not mature until mid 1919 after Frank Jardine had already been dead for 3 months. It is very clear therefore that the statement accusing him of shooting blacks for stealing his coconuts is just one of the many lies concocted by her native informer.

She also makes the same mistake as the anthropologist, Tindale in reference to the derogatory term of "Yegille". She states:

> *That the Gumukudin were a sub-clan of the Yadhaigana, [Yadagana] is suggested by the fact that the Kauraregas called them both "Yegille".*

After learning the real meaning of "Yegille" [Kangaroo face] she must be kicking herself to death by now. Indirectly she is acknowledging the racial discrimination that existed amongst the native tribes of the area.

In reference to the aboriginal attack on Somerset [November 1873] she claims:

> *Jardine led a raid on the Yadhaigana [Yadagana] camp thirty miles from Somerset which resulted in large-scale slaughter.*

The official documentation clearly shows that Jardine sent out police troopers and pearlers to confront the invading Yadagana. He did not lead any such raid but remained at Somerset [see page 226].

Here was another example of an academic mixing fiction with fact and thereby distorting the true history of the region.

Throughout the late 1980's, numerous academics were busy indoctrinating the aborigines at Cowal Creek, [Injinoo] into believing a false history.

As they were not traditional to Somerset many of them believed anything they were told. This applied especially to European occupation of the area.

Another major problem is the influx of white do-gooders into aboriginal communities. Many of them have used the pretence of equality to seduce young native girls and impregnate them. [Another is alledged to be a paedophile.]

One of these scoundrels had spent many years with the aborigines. Several allegations of paedophilia have been made against him to the police and the Queensland Government. However, it is alleged that he is protected by senior polititians of the Queensland Government and therfore nothing has been done about it. One source summed it up when he stated:

> *So long as Labor is in power in Queensland, there will be no investigation into the allegations against this man.*

A police officer was overhead to say: "He will probably get himself shot one day, we just don't know if it will be by a black man or a white man..."

He has since left the community, much to the satisfaction of the native women.

In 1991 the aborigines invaded the Cape York Wilderness Lodge in force and demanded that Australian Airlines [the legal owners] give it to them.

The whole scenario was covered by the invited press, who filmed the demonstrators at their best behaviour, but did not film several louts drinking the place dry and going on a drunken rampage, throwing the bins full of rubbish into the swimming pool.

Australian Airlines now realised that violence could erupt over the issue, due to the activities of a number of white do-gooders living with the aborigines at Cowal Creek.

In 1992, the resort was sold to the aborigines at a cost of 2.2 million dollars to the taxpayer. [A decade later it failed and was abandoned and trashed.]

The aborigines re-named the resort "Pajinka" after being told that was the correct Gudang name for the top of Cape York.

However, after checking the Gudang language which was written down in 1849 by John Macgillivray of "HMS Rattlesnake", I found there was no such word as "Pajinka".

The word appears to be coined from the English slang "By Jingo". In 1901, a Scotsman named Adam Black purchased "By Jingo" Station on the Campaspe River, to the south of Charters Towers.

His wife, Jane preferred a more native sounding name and called it "Pajingo" from which the local aborigines pronounced "Pajinka".

It has no relationship whatsoever with the Gudang language on Cape York.

When academics from the James Cook University attempted to translate the various dialects of Injinoo into a dictionary, it became the joke of Cape York.

I found 95% of the words were totally alien to the Gudang language. For example the Gudang world "Kaieeby" [Somerset] was wrongly written down as "Pulu", which happens to be a site in the Torres Strait, near Mabuiag Island, north of Badu.

In order to educate visitors to the area, on their particular version of history, a pamphlet was printed, which was practically the exact opposite to historical fact.

They even have the mild mannered Edmund Kennedy shooting aborigines all along the track, when in reality Kennedy was seen as an easy target because of his friendliness towards the aborigines, whence they brutally murdered him.

The academics are generally very silent on the testimony of the aboriginal "Jackey Jackey", for the last thing they want is for an aborigine to expose the murderous traditions of other aborigines.

Within this pamphlet is a page pertaining to be an extract of the native language. It may very well apply to native words south of the Jardine but certainly not to the Gudang language at Cape York.

Out of 125 words mentioned, only 6 had even the slightest resemblance to the traditional Gudang.

The correct word for "Rocky Place" is not Pajinka as claimed by academics, but "ULPA", from which the rocky outcrop of "Ulpha Rock" is derived [Macgillivray 1849].

The Gudang often used the suffix "Dinya" for important rocky points or capes. For example Evans Point, where Barbara Thompson was rescued was called "Mao-Dinya" and the north east point of Albany Island was known as "Tolo-Dinya".

The Gudang name of Cape York would almost certainly have had a special meaning and would probably also have ended in the word "Dinya" and not Pajinka.

The list of academic blunders is never ending, particularly anthropologists, of whom many are prepared to change history and language to suit their own beliefs, regardless of evidence to the contrary.

For many years "shell middens" were promoted as an example of ancient aboriginal occupation on Cape York extending back to thousands of years.

The oldest middens were known as the "Kwampter Mounds" near Weipa and if tested would no doubt prove an aboriginal occupation going back as far as 30,000 years or longer, or would it?

Therefore a series of tests were made from drilled samples from the top to the base of the mounds identified as numbers 1734-1737.

The results were devastating for the academics, as carbon dating only gave an average of 630-1000 years with an absolute maximum of only 1200 years. These results were similar to those taken at the top of Cape York in 1973.

This was more evidence that the aborigines were a very recent arrival and not an ancient inhabitant of Australia as is often portrayed by anthropologists.

The recent attempted cover up of the Hindmarsh Island Bridge affair in which a number of aborigines were claiming an area as a sacred women's site in South Australia [Adelaide] was finally exposed as a fraud by other aboriginal women much to the embarrassment of a number of anthropologists.

It is now very obvious that academics cannot be relied upon to give an unbiased non racist version of Australian history.

Yet many important sites have been given to various aboriginal groups who were clearly not the traditional owners. In many cases they had massacred the original tribes and seized their land. A prime example being Ayers Rock in central Australia. On the advice of anthropologists, it was given to the wrong tribe.

I am therefore of the conclusion that all grants to anthropologists should cease until they are prepared to pay at least 50% of the cost of their research projects. In addition any books written on their results should be paid for by the writer or a publisher and not at the expense of the tax payer, as has been the case on numerous occasions in the past.

Many Australians will be quite shocked to learn that some of those expensive hard cover books in brilliant colour purporting to portray "ancient paintings?" cost as much as a quarter of a million dollars to produce. They are not paid by the academics or the multi-national publishers, but by the tax payer.

One of the most accurate assessments of academic ignorance was written by the Author George Farwell in his excellent book, [Cape York to the Kimberleys, 1952].

Whilst interviewing George Darcy of Mallapunyah Station in the Northern Territory. He stated:

> *Darcy opposed the idea of turning them [aborigines] into exhibits on a reservation, or social pets, idling their lives away on government stations with no necessity to work for the "food handed freely to them".*
>
> *"He found some amusement in the way the dark mind of the stone age savage had found its way into national literature and painting, the romanticised notions of a watered-down Alcheringa being adopted by poets who had seen nothing more remote than a suburban bus-stop or a dairy farm."*

Darcy further stated:

> *"The savage is something very different from the romantic man of nature they dream about. I don't think any of us would like it, if we really had to go back there."*

George Farwell continues:

> *"George Darcy is a man I would like a great many people to meet. He would be good medicine for the theorists, the romantic poets, the do-gooders meeting on Sunday afternoon.*

What George Darcy was really saying is that the do-gooders including academics are dreamers who are unable to comprehend the savage lifestyle that the natives lived with.

When one discovers the numerous blunders, lies and distortions of history, promoted by academics, then unless they are prepared to start searching for truth, they cannot be taken seriously by the general public.

The question must be asked: If relatives could take them to court and sue them for falsely accusing our pioneers, would they still be prepared to write their distorted versions of history?

THE C.J.C. INQUIRY

During the early 1990's, numerous complaints had been received by the Queensland Government of blatant corruption amongst Aboriginal and Torres Strait Islander Councils on the Cape York Peninsula.

Finally, the Criminal Justice Commission, [CJC] was forced to carry out an investigation and their report was published in June 1994.

It was titled "Report on an Investigation into Complaints against 6 Aboriginal and Island Councils by the CJC."

The introduction of this document was clearly another example of an act of Anti-White racism when it states:

> *The report will be published in Anonymous Terms. The Commission has attempted as far as possible to "Couch the Report" in terms which will be "Effectively Anonymous" to members of the General Public.*

If the subjects of this investigation had been White Australians, then all the names of those involved in corruption, would have been made public, and flashed on the news of every television station, Yet, because they were aborigines and Islanders, the information was suppressed.

On Page 171 it states:

> **GRANTS IN AID**
> *Council had met debts of certain people by grants – Balance owed at 30th June 1989, amounted to $36,041.00.*
> *Council did not have power to give out loans.*

CANTEEN OPERATIONS
An audit on a canteen showed an unaccountable shortage of $35,418.

Although this corruption was bad enough it is peanuts when compared to the millions of dollars of the tax payers money that is said to have been sent out of the country by aborigines.

In 1992, I was informed, that $6 million had been sent through the Bamaga Post Office, to an organisation in Hawaii.

At first, I found it hard to believe, until 3 weeks later when I went to the Bamaga Post Office and stood behind an aboriginal woman, who stated to the cashier:

"I want to send $600 to Hawaii."

It was now very clear that money was being sent out of the country to Hawaii and that the statement of 6 million dollars might have some truth to it.

Of course aborigines have just as much right as anybody else to send money out of the country, providing it is not the taxpayers money.

If such a large sum of money was sent to Hawaii, then where did it come from.

Was it possible that the aboriginal communities on Cape York were funnelling their profits through the Bamaga Post Office and investing it in Hawaii?

Then again, could it be part of the millions that ATSIC receives from the taxpayer?

What about the huge profits that have been made from the "Jardine River Ferry", which is owned and operated by the aborigines. This is said to be the most expensive river ferry in Australia. It used to cost an enormous $40 return for each vehicle to cross less than 100 yards of water.

With ten thousand vehicles a year that amounts to an incredible $400,000 per annum [four hundred thousand dollars].

Because aboriginal business of this type operate under their own council, they may be exempt from paying tax.

In 1994, they pushed the price of the ferry crossing [return] to an outrageous $80.00 per vehicle.

The public were outraged by this incredible increase of an already outrageous fee, and a petition was soon circulating around Cape York and signed by thousands of people.

Here was a racist situation where aborigines did not pay this fee to cross. Instead, the very people who are heavily taxed to support the aborigines are themselves ordered by aborigines to pay outlandish sums of money to cross less than 100 yards of the Jardine River that is a public waterway and does not belong to the aborigines.

The last thing, the Labor Government wanted was more complaints against aborigines and particularly in reference to anti white discrimination by aborigines.

The easiest way out for the Government was simply to cover the issue up and hope it would go away. Alas, it was not to be and it cost them thousands of votes in the 1995 State Elections.

Although it is often assumed that the high cost of the Jardine River Ferry is aboriginal greed, there are many who believe the increased fee was planned by derelict academics living with the aborigines and that the natives are simply a pawn to be used by them to feather their own nests, such as receiving grants.

It is clear that the Jardine River Ferry has generated millions of dollars from the white tourists, but whether this is part of the millions supposed to have been sent to Hawaii cannot at this stage be confirmed.

However, the Taxation Department is now believed to be carrying out their own investigation into that issue as well as establishing the "real income" from the ferry.

I have often been asked, "What is the answer to the aboriginal question?" and it is clearly a case of "Work".

Over the years a number of industrial operations were established for the aborigines north of the Jardine River. These were centred mainly around the most northern Australian town of Bamaga.

They included, a "Brick Works", "Slaughter Yard", "Timber Mill" and an "Agricultural Farm" for fruit and vegetables.

In spite of the millions of dollars spent establishing these industries, they have been abandoned.

It is clear that if the aborigines want the respect of other Australians then they must also contribute as workers, who pay taxes, rather than idling away their lives at the expense of the taxpayer. For the day is fast approaching when the free handouts will dry up.

One day, at a coffee shop in Weipa, I was joined by a customer at my table who turned out to be a Social Security officer. She informed me that she had just handed out $780,000 worth of Social Security cheques to the aborigines.

As well as issuing these fortnightly cheques, she also inspected 7 new houses that had been built for the aborigines. One can imagine her disgust when she found that 3 of them had been burnt to the ground and the other 4 were total wrecks.

Is it any wonder that the majority of Australians condemn their own government for its incredible waste of the tax payers money in respect to aboriginal aid.

Must the Australian public be continually pressured into supporting a people who blatantly destroy millions of dollars worth of free handouts such as houses and motor vehicles.

By 1990, the Australian taxpayers had clearly had enough of political corruption and deceit by the major political parties, on a range of issues including the enormous waste of aboriginal financial assistance, which has cost the taxpayer over 25 billion dollars over the last 20 years.

There was at this time a large number of concerned Australians who had formed their own political groups. Some were against greed and corruption, others fought against illegal laws, and many more against anti-white racism, bank fees and a host of other issues.

As separate groups they could not achieve much against the giants of the political arena, such as the Labor, Liberal and National Parties.

So they joined together and formed the most dynamic political party that Australia had ever witnessed. As they were a confederation of various groups they called themselves the "Confederate Action Party" of Australia, [CAP] and within a short time thousands of people from all walks of life joined them.

The CAP made it very clear that any issue of importance to Australia, would be decided by the people and not the politicians. This would be achieved by a national referendum known as a "Citizens Initiated Referendum" [C.I.R.]

As this meant the politicians of the major parties would lose their power over the people, they were outraged and set in motion a plan to destroy the CAP.

One of the most important statements made in the CAP agenda was that all Australians would be treated on the same basis, and that the Aboriginal Affairs Department would be abolished. In this manner, all Australians would be equal before the law and thereby reject the present anti-white apartheid.

In order to degrade the CAP and hopefully prevent the public from supporting them, the major parties picked on this issue and advertised through the media that they were racist, when in fact the exact opposite was the case.

As it turned out, the CAP was the only registered, Federal Political Party that was prepared to treat the aborigines on the same basis as the whites. Rather than keep them on reservations, drinking themselves to death, the CAP opted for their right to work and live as ordinary Australians. When the racist slander failed to swerve the public, they were suddenly de-registered, although it was illegal to do so. Yet, even this, has failed to destroy the CAP. They are now known as "THE AUSTRALIANS" and although harassed by the major parties, for their equilibrium between the races ,they may very well be a vibrant political force in the future.

LAND RIGHTS

Some of the worst acts of anti white apartheid in Australia relates directly to the issue of Land Rights, in which more than half a million square miles has been taken from the legal land owners and lease holders and handed over to aborigines.

However, this is only temporary, as the Australian public can reverse the whole scenario, by a simple referendum to decide the land rights issue.

It is the people who must have the final say, not the politicians, and if the majority decide that all land must be returned to all Australians, then that is the way it will be.

"Mabo", is an example of how the public can be misled over land rights. This issue concerned Murray Island in the Torres Strait, and at that time the high court favoured the Murray Islanders in its controversial decision. It was clearly stated that the Mabo decision would not apply to land rights in Australia. It was only applicable to the Torres Strait.

Therefore any land claims made under the Mabo legislation in Australia, may be illegal and should be put to a referendum.

It is interesting to note that although, Murray Islanders can live and buy land in Australia, Australians, are not permitted to live or buy land on Murray Island [Mer] or for that matter most other areas of the Torres Strait. At present there are more Torres Strait Islanders living in Australia than there are in the Torres Strait.

As "Land Rights" is clearly, racial discrimination by one race against another, then it must be abolished.

When academics and politicians promote land rights, it is always somebody else's land they are giving away and not their own.

If they really believe that Australia belongs to the aborigines, then let them set an example of their sincerity, by giving away the land their homes are built on to the aborigines.

Throughout Australia's history, no issue has generated so much hatred amongst the races, than "Land Rights". If the politicians and supporters of "Land Rights" really believe in democracy, then they should let the people vote on it through a Citizens Initiated Referendum, throughout Australia.

"Land Rights" was described by an Australian magazine as "Legalised Land Theft" [4x4 Australia].

If left unchecked the freedom of the public to travel around the country may be very bleak indeed. Some aboriginal activists have already stated that highways around Australia will be another form of income for the aborigines by taxing all motorists who use them.

According to one newspaper they have already worked out the fee structure that motorists must pay who travel along inter-city and inter-state highways.

Most Australians are unaware of the incredible racist laws enacted against people of non-aboriginal backgrounds.

For example: White Australians must pay for the right to travel on many roads through land presently held by aborigines, but aborigines do not pay to travel on roads through land held by whites. This is clearly a racist situation and will be abolished if the majority of Australians vote against it in a referendum of the people, such as a "Citizens Initiated Referendum" [C.I.R.] previously mentioned by the Confederate Action Party. [THE AUSTRALIANS].

TRADITIONAL HUNTING

Another vital issue is the subject of traditional hunting by aborigines and Torres Strait Islanders. In the past it was traditional for natives to catch their prey with traditional weapons made from wood, stone, vines and bone.

However their habit of hunting with guns and outboard motor boats is certainly not traditional hunting. I have personally witnessed live turtles left to suffer on a hot beach for hours on end and then towed up the beach by 4 wheel drives and even then was not killed till the natives were ready to cook it whence it was cut open whilst still alive.

In one case a turtle was dragged on a corrugated road behind a 4 wheel drive for 5 miles because the natives were too lazy to lift it on to the back of the vehicle.

Whilst the world is trying to protect its wildlife in National Parks and water ways, Australia's present politicians blatantly allow its natives to slaughter them under the pretense of "Traditional Hunting".

If a white person were to commit such outrages they would be heavily fined and even gaoled. Should they have a turtle shell in their possession they can be fined as much as ten thousand dollars, [$10,000]. Such is the racial discrimination that exists under the present Government.

One of the most successful ploys used by academics and politicians is to brand those who dare to speak out against them as Neo-Nazi's. This is instantly advertised by the press all over Australia in an attempt to degrade them so as to appear as dangerous radicals, when their only crime was to expose the truth.

One of the major targets of these verbal onslaughts was the "Confederate Action Party" who had exposed a number of issues damaging to the major political parties, including aboriginal issues, particularly land rights.

Australia has reached a cross roads. It cannot continue under a system that favours one race against another. If all its citizens are to be equal then the same laws and conditions must be applied to everyone, otherwise the government will be guilty of anti-white apartheid.

When white Australians gave aborigines the right to vote, it was through a National Referendum of the people.

Therefore, "Land Rights" must also be put to a National Referendum and in this way it will be the people who will decide by a majority vote and not the politicians or academics.

REFERENDUM ON LAND-RIGHTS

PARLIAMENTARY LEGISLATION DOES NOT PROTECT THE PUBLIC FROM "LAND-RIGHTS – MABO – OR THE NATIVE TITLE ACT".

ANY GOVERNMENT COULD LATER REVERSE SUCH LEGISLATION.

ONLY A "NATIONAL REFERENDUM" RIGHT ACROSS AUSTRALIA WILL SOLVE THE LAND-RIGHTS ISSUE.

[SEE PAGE 276]

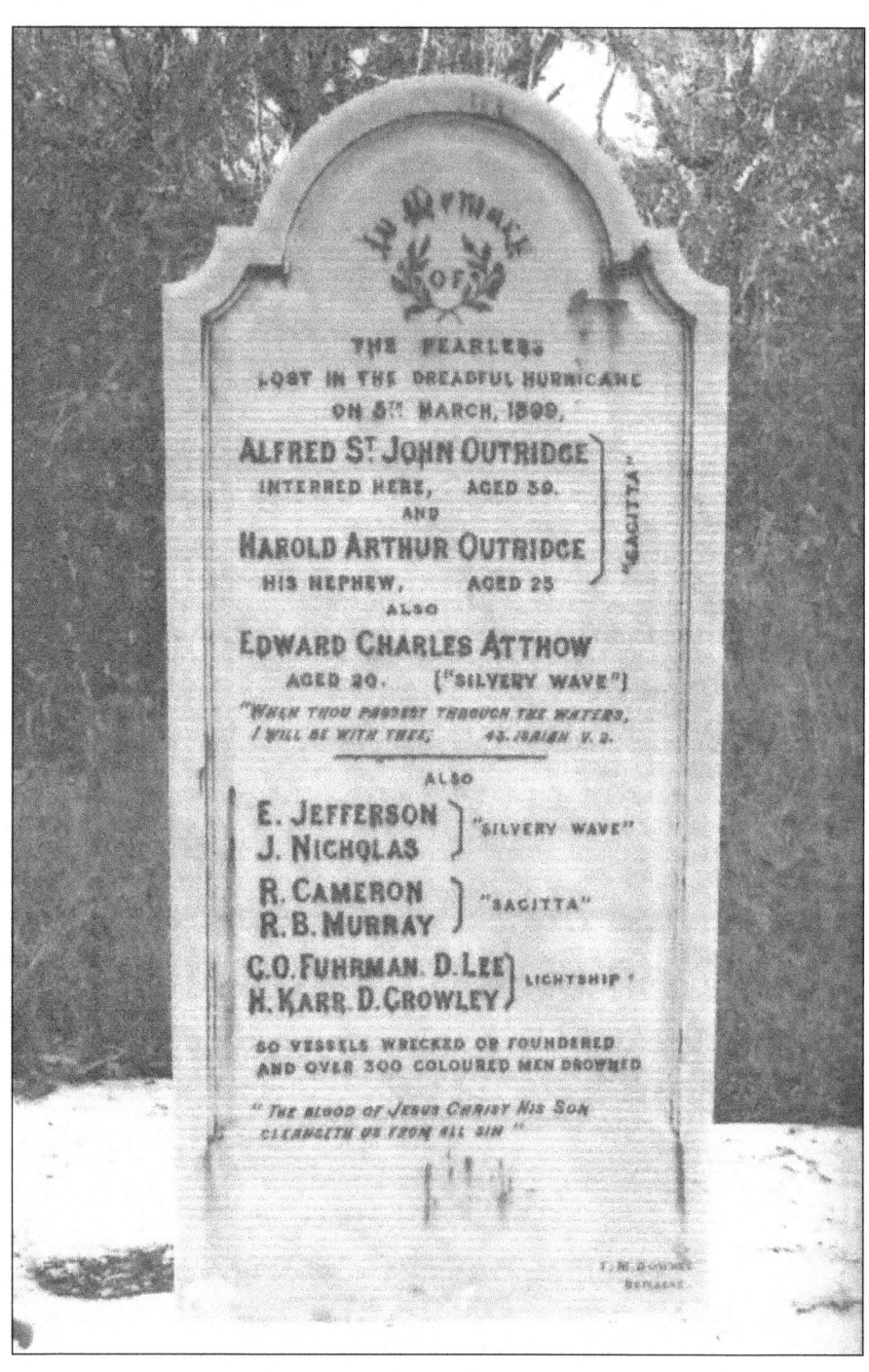

The Memorial at Bathurst Bay to the Europeans who perished from cyclone Mahina.

Chapter 22
"HISTORICAL STATEMENTS"

STATEMENTS MADE BY BARBARA THOMPSON ON BOARD HMS RATTLESNAKE AT EVANS BAY – CAPE YORK – 1849

WINI
There is a white man still among the blacks. He calls himself "Gienow" [White Pigeon]. The natives call him "Weenie" [Wini – The Dawn]. He was wrecked. I have seen him over at Morolaga [Muralug – POW] several times. I talked to him in the island language. He had quite forgotten his own. He is a tall middle aged man with light hair, marked with the smallpox, with lumps growing out of different parts of his body.

He lives with the natives of a small group of islands which the natives call Badu. He first came to the island in a small boat and had a small quantity of biscuit, one axe and one long knife.

He told the blacks that he killed a man who was in the boat with him and thrown him over-board. He has been there a long time. He was there at the time of the wreck of a vessel of which the crew was murdered by the natives.

He is connected with the murder of many white men.

WIFE BEATING
Sometimes when a man wants to beat his wife he will appear to be very friendly and go out with his wife. When they get into the scrub, he will beat her until she can hardly crawl.

The women are marriageable as soon as their breasts begin to show. They marry very young. Old men, grey haired, have sometimes very young gins. The men sometimes quarrel with the women and beat them.

The men are very lazy, except in the turtle season. They lie in the camp all day and the wives go out and get food for them. If the women do not bring in any, they beat them.

CHILD MURDER
All children born before marriage are "Marramatised" [buried alive], not by the freewill of the mother, but by the tribe. The other women take it away and do it.

They are fond of their children, but they are fonder of their own belly. They think more of the boys than they do of the girls. The female children are sometimes smothered at birth. They put them into a hole in the sand.

KENNEDY'S MURDER
The tribe who killed Kennedy were the Yegilie and were verra bad blacks – greedy blacks. They killed the poor man for the 'Domawaka', his shirt and bits of cloth he had on him.

ABORIGINAL DISCRIMINATION
There are some Yegilie (Big Nose) among the Angarkie. They are very ugly. They are called "Yegilie" because they are ugly.

ENVIRONMENTAL DESTRUCTION
There were no turtle caught here last year – or the year before. There might have been a few but they were both bad seasons.

But 3 years ago they were got in great numbers. We had more than we could eat. More than three hundred were caught.

SPIRIT DAUGHTER
Pequi said that I had his daughter's chin and eyes. Directly I was taken into the camp, when first I was wrecked, Pequi and his wives all jumped out and caught hold of me, calling me after his daughter.

HEAD HUNTING
I saw the men take the heads out of the canoes by the singers [head carriers] and carry them a little way up the beach, dash them down to the ground and make a circle round them.

EATING HUMAN HEADS
First they took the eyes out and cut the flesh from around the eyes, the men who cut it passing bits around to the rest ... They eat the eyes and fat first, then they cut the bits off the cheeks and hand them round.

Before they put the heads in the ovens, they cut the tongues out.

STATEMENTS MADE BY THE ZOOLOGIST JOHN MACGILLIVRAY AFTER QUESTIONING BARBARA THOMPSON ON BOARD HMS RATTLESNAKE AT EVANS BAY CAPE YORK – 1849

SPIRIT DAUGHTER
A curious circumstance secured for her the protection of one of the principal men of the tribe, a party from which had been the fortunate means of rescuing her and which she afterwards found to be the Kauraregas, chiefly inhabiting Muralug, or the western Prince of Wales Island. The person named "Piaquai", acting upon the belief (Universal throughout Australia and the islands of the Torres Strait so far as hitherto known) that white people are the ghosts of the aborigines, fancied that in the stranger, he recognised a long lost daughter of the name of "Gi(a)om", and at once admitted her to the relationship which he thought had formerly subsisted between them.

She was immediately acknowledged by the whole tribe as one of themselves, thus ensuring an extensive connection in relatives of all denominations.

From the headquarters of the tribe with which "Giom" thus became associated, being upon an island which all vessels passing through Torres Strait from the eastward, must approach within two or three miles, she had the mortification of seeing from twenty to thirty or more ships go through every summer, without anchoring in the neighbourhood, so as to afford the slightest opportunity of making her escape.

BOROTO'S THREAT
Giom was evidently a great favourite with the blacks, and hardly a day passed on which she was not obliged to hold a levee in her cabin, for the reception of friends from the shore. While other visitors less favoured, were content to talk to her through the port. They occasionally brought presents of fish and turtle, but always expected an equivalent of some kind.

Her friend "Boroto", the nature of the intimacy with whom was not at first understood, after in vain attempting by smooth words and fair promises to induce her to go back {to live with him}, left the ship in a rage and we were not sorry to get rid of so impudent and troublesome a visitor as he had become.

Previous to leaving, he had threatened that, should he or any of his friends ever catch her {his faithless spouse} on shore, they would take off her head to carry back with them to Muralug; and so likely to be fulfilled did she consider this threat, being in perfect accordance with their customs, that she never afterwards ventured on shore at Cape York.

NOTE: Statements in {brackets} were found to be incorrect. A medical examination on the ship showed she never had children. She was never married to any native.

HER ESCAPE

Last year she heard of our two vessels (described as two war canoes, a big and a little one) being at Cape York, only twenty miles distant – from some of the tribe who had communicated with us and been well treated, but they would not take her over, and even watched her more narrowly than before.

On our second and present visit, however, which the Cape York people immediately announced by smoke signals to their friends in Muralug, she was successful in persuading some of her more immediate friends to bring her across to the mainland to within short distance of where the vessels lay.

The blacks were credulous enough to believe that as she had been so long with them and had been so well treated, she did not intend to leave them, only she felt a strong desire to see the white people once more and shake hands with them, adding that she would be certain to procure some axes, knives, tobacco and other much prized articles. This appeal to their cupidity decided the question at once.

After landing at the sandy bay on the western side of Cape York, she hurried across to Evans Bay, as quickly as her lameness would allow, fearful that the blacks might change their mind.

HER RESCUE

When first seen on shore, our new shipmate presented so dirty and wretched an appearance, that some people who were out shooting, at first mistook her for a gin.

With the exception of a narrow fringe of leaves in front, she wore no clothing and her skin was tanned and blistered with the sun, and shewed the marks of several large burns which had been received from sleeping too near the fire on cold nights, besides, she was suffering from opthalmia, which had previously deprived her of the sight of one eye [right].

But good living and every comfort (for Captain Stanley kindly provided her with a cabin and a seat at his table) combined with medical attention, very soon restored her to health.

WINI

During the period of our stay at Cape York, the "Bramble", "Asp" and Rattle-snakes "Pinnace", were sent away to the western entrance of Torres Strait to finish the survey and returned after a months absence.

The boats had held no intercourse with any of the natives except a small party of Kowraregas.

The inhabitants of Mulgrave [Badu] and Banks [Moa] islands, having carefully avoided them.

Hopes had been entertained prior to starting, of seeing something of a white man of the name of "Wini", who had lived with the Badus. 'Giom' had seen and conversed with him during his visit to Muralug, which he had made in hopes of inducing her to share his fortunes.

She supposed him to be a foreigner, from his not appearing to understand the English she used, when asked by him to speak in her native tongue.

He had reached Mulgrave Island in a boat, after having by his own account, killed his companions, some three or four in number.

In the course of time he became the most important person in the tribe, having gained an ascendancy by procuring the death of his principal enemies and intimidating others, which led to the establishment of his fame as a warrior, and he became in consequence the possessor of several wives, a canoe and some property in land, the cultivation of which last he pays great attention to.

Wini's character appears from the accounts I have heard – for others corroborated part of 'Giom's' statement – to be a compound of villainy and cunning, in addition to the ferocity and headlong passions of a thorough savage.

It strikes me that he must have been a runaway convict, probably from Norfolk

Island. It is fortunate that his sphere of mischief is so limited, for a more dangerous ruffian could not easily be found.

As matters stand at present, it is probable that not only during his life, but for years afterwards, every European who falls into the hands of the Badu people will meet with certain death.

STATEMENT MADE BY THE ASSISTANT SURGEON THOMAS HUXLEY AFTER QUESTIONING BARBARA THOMPSON ON BOARD HMS RATTLESNAKE AT EVANS BAY CAPE YORK – 1849

KAURAREGA LANGUAGE

She speaks it fluently and at present, evidently thinks in it, having in talking to you, to translate her native thoughts into plain English.

Her manners present the most ludicrous graft of the gin upon the white woman.

CHILD MURDER

Child murder prevails to the most fearful extent. All illegitimate children are destroyed by burying them in a hole in the sand immediately on their birth, unless the father intends to marry the girl.

Mrs T [Barbara Thompson] gave us by name several natives, whom she knew to have destroyed child after child.

CHILD BRIDES

Girls are married as early as 10 to 11 years of age.

STATEMENT BY THE BOTANIST, WILLIAM CARRON FROM THE CAMP OF DEATH AT THE PASCOE RIVER WEYMOUTH BAY – 1848

NOVEMBER 21ST

About sixty natives came to the camp this morning … They were now closing round us in all directions, many of them with their spears in their throwing sticks, ready for use – pointing them to their own necks and sides, and shewing us by their postures how we should writhe with pain when they struck us … Eleven spears were thrown at us.

DECEMBER 26TH

We always divided whatever we got from the natives, be it what it might; but they brought us very little that was edible. I could easily perceive that their pretended good feeling toward us, was assumed for the sake of fulfiling their own designs upon us. Although they tried to make us believe they were doing all in their power to benefit us, their object was to obtain an opportunity of coming upon us by surprise and destroying us. They had at many times seen the fatal effect of our fire-arms, and I believe that it was only the dread of these, that prevented them from falling upon us at once and murdering us.

> "It would be almost impossible for any class of men to excel these fellows in the scheming and versatile cunning with which they strove to disguise their meditated treachery."

DECEMBER 28TH

About eleven o'clock as many as fifty natives, armed with spears, and some of them painted with a yellowish earth, made their appearance in the vicinity of our camp. There were natives of several strange tribes amongst them … This morning when I made signs to them to lay down their spears, they paid no attention, with the exception of two, who had been in the habit of coming very frequently to the camp. These two came running up quite close to us, without their spears, and endeavoured to persuade one of us to go across a small dry creek for a fish, which another of the rascals was holding up to tempt us.

They tried various methods to draw our attention from the rest, who were trailing their spears along the ground with their feet, closing gradually around us, and running from tree to tree, to hide their spears behind them.

Others lay on their backs on the long grass, and were working their way toward us, un-noticed as they supposed. Goddard and myself stood with our guns in readiness and our pistols by our sides for about two hours, when I fell from excessive weakness. When I got up we thought it best to send them away at once, or stand our chance of being speared in the attempt, both of us being unable to stand any longer. We presented our guns at the two by our side, making signs to them to send the others away, or we would shoot them immediately. This they did, and they ran off in all directions without a spear being thrown or a shot fired.

STATEMENT BY JACKEY-JACKEY [GALMARRA] MADE BY HIM ON BOARD THE "ARIEL", AND WRITTEN DOWN BY DR VALLACK.

Square brackets [ ] are Author's comments.

I started with Mr Kennedy from Weymouth Bay for Cape York, on the 13th November 1848, accompanied by Costigan, Dunn and Luff, leaving eight men at the camp, at Weymouth Bay. We went on till we came to a river which empties itself into Weymouth Bay. A little further north we crossed the river [Camp 1 – 13th November]. Next morning a lot of natives camped on the other side of the river. Mr Kennedy and the rest of us went on a very high hill and came to a flat on the other side and camped there [Camp 2 – 14th November]. I went on a good way next day [Camp 3 – 15th November]; a horse fell down a creek; the flour we took with us lasted three days; we had much trouble in getting the horse out of the creek; we went on, and came out, and camped on the ridges; we had no water [Camp 4 – 16th November]. Next morning went on and Luff was taken ill with a very bad knee; we left him behind, and Dunn went back again and brought him on [Camp 5 – 17th November]. Luff was riding a horse named Fiddler; then we went on and camped at a little creek [Camp 6 – 18th November]; the flour being out this day we commenced eating horse-flesh, which Carron gave to us when we left Weymouth Bay; as we went on we came on a small river, and saw no blacks there; as we proceeded we gathered nondas, and lived upon them and the meat; we stopped at a little creek and it came on raining, and Costigan shot himself; in putting his saddle under the tarpaulin, a string caught the trigger and the ball went in under the right arm and came out at his back under the shoulder; we went on this morning all of us, and stopped at another creek in the evening [Camp 7 – 19th November] and the next morning we killed a horse named Browney, smoked him that night [Camp 8 – 20th November] and went on next day, taking as much of the horse as we could with us, and went on about a mile and then turned back again to where we killed the horse, because Costigan was very bad and in much pain; we went back again because there was no water; then Mr Kennedy and I had dinner there, and went on in the afternoon leaving Dunn, Costigan and Luff at the creek. This was at Pudding-pan Hill, near Shelburne Bay. ["False Pudding-Pan Hill". It was mistaken by Kennedy for the real "Pudding-Pan Hill", 50 miles further north.] *Mr Kennedy called it Pudding-pan Hill. We left some horse meat with the three men at Pudding-pan Hill, and carried some with us on a pack horse. Mr Kennedy wanted to make great haste when he left this place, in order to get the doctor to go down to the men that were ill. This was about three weeks after leaving Weymouth Bay. One horse was left with the three men at Pudding-pan Hill and we (Kennedy and Myself) took with us three horses. The three men were to remain there until Mr Kennedy and myself had gone to and returned from Cape York for them. Mr Kennedy told Luff and Dunn when he left them if Costigan died they were to come along the beach till they saw the ship, and then to fire a gun; he told them he would not be long away, so it was not likely they would move from there for some time. They stopped to take care of the man that was shot, we (me and Mr Kennedy)* killed a horse for them before we came away; having left these three men we camped that night where there was no water; [Camp 9 – 21st November] next morning Mr Kennedy and me went on with the four horses, two pack horses, and two saddle horses; one horse got bogged in a swamp. We tried to get him out all day, but could not, we left him there and camped at another creek [Camp 10 – 22nd November], The next day Mr Kennedy and I went on again, and passed up a ridge very scrubby, and had to turn back again, and went along gulleys to get clear of the creek and scrub. Now it rained, and we camped; [Camp 11 – 23rd November] there were plenty of blacks here, but we did not see them, but plenty of fresh tracks, and camps, and smoke. Next morning we went on and camped at another creek, [Camp 12 – 24th November] and on the following morning we continued going on, and camped in the evening close to a scrub; [Camp 13 – 25th November] it rained in the night. Next day we went on in the scrub, but could not get through. I cut and cleared away, and it was near sundown before we got through the scrub – there we camped [Camp 14 – 26th November]. It was heavy rain next morning, and we went on in the rain, then I changed horses and rode a black colt, to spell the other, and rode him all day, and in the afternoon we got on clear ground, and the horse fell down, me and all; the horse lay upon my right hip. Here Mr Kennedy got off his horse and moved my horse from my thigh; we stopped there that night and could not get the horse up; [Camp 15 – 27th November] we looked to him in the morning and he was dead; we left him there; we had some horse meat left to eat, and went on that day and crossed a little river and camped [Camp 16 – 28th November]. The next day we went a good way; Mr Kennedy told me to go up a tree to see a sandy hill somewhere; I went up a tree, and saw a sandy hill a little way down from Port Albany. That day we camped near a swamp it was a very rain day [Camp 17 – 29th November]. The next morning we went on, and Mr Kennedy told me we should get round to Port Albany in a day; we travelled on all day till twelve o'clock (noon), and then we saw Port Albany; then he said, "There is Port Albany, Jackey – a ship is there – you see that island there," pointing to Albany Island; this was when we were at the mouth of Escape River; we stopped there a little while; all the meat was gone; I tried to get some fish but could not; we went on in the afternoon half a mile along the river side, and met a good lot of blacks, and we camped; [Camp 18 – 30th November] the blacks all cried out "Powad Powad," and rubbed their bellies; and we thought they were friendly, and Mr Kennedy gave them fish-hooks all round; everyone asked me if I had anything to give away, and I said, no; and Mr Kennedy said, give them your knife, Jackey; this fellow on board was the man I gave the knife to; I am sure of it; I know him well; the black that was shot in the canoe was the most active in urging all the others on to spear Mr Kennedy; I gave the man on board my knife; we went on this day, and I looked behind, and they were getting up their spears, and ran all round the camp which we had left; I told Mr Kennedy that very likely those black fellows would follow us, and he said, "No, Jackey, those blacks are very friendly;" I said to him "I know these black fellows well, they too much speak;" we went on some two or three miles and camped [Camp 19 – 1st December]. I and Mr Kennedy watched them that night, taking it in turns every hour all night; by-and-by I saw the black fellows; it was a moonlight night; and I walked up to Mr Kennedy, and said to him, there is plenty of black fellows now; this was in the middle of the night: Mr Kennedy told me to get my gun ready; the blacks did not know where we slept, as we did not make a fire; we both sat up all night; after this, daylight came and I fetched the horses and saddled them; then we went on a good way up the river, and then we sat down a little while, and we saw three black fellows coming along our track, and they saw us, and one fellow ran back as hard as he could run, and fetched up plenty more, like a flock of sheep almost; I told Mr Kennedy to put the saddles on the two horses and go on, and the blacks came up, and they followed us all day; all along it was raining, and I now told him to leave the horse and come on without them, that the horse made too much track. Mr Kennedy was too weak, and would not leave the horses. We went on this day till towards evening, raining hard, and the blacks followed us all the day, some behind, some planted before; in fact, blacks all around following us. Now we went on into a little bit of scrub, and I told Mr Kennedy to look behind always; sometimes he would do so, and sometimes he would not look behind to look out for the blacks. Then a good many black fellows came behind in the scrub, and threw plenty of spears, and hit Mr Kennedy in the back first. Mr Kennedy said to me, "Oh! Jackey, Jackey! shoot 'em, shoot 'em." Then I pulled out my gun and fired, and hit one fellow all over the face with buck shot; he tumbled down, and got up again and again and wheeled right around, and two black fellows picked him up and carried him away. They went away then a little way, and came back again, throwing spears all around, more than they did before; very large spears. I pulled out the spear at once from Mr Kennedy's back, and cut out the jag with Mr Kennedy's knife; then Mr Kennedy got his gun and snapped, but the gun would not go off. The blacks sneaked all along by the trees, and speared Mr Kennedy again in the right leg, above the knee a little, and I got speared over the eye, and the blacks were now throwing their spears all ways, never giving over, and shortly again speared Mr Kennedy in the right side; there were large jags to the spears, and I cut them out and put them into my pocket. At the same time we got speared, the horses got speared too, and jumped and bucked all about, and got into the swamp. I now told Mr Kennedy to sit down, while I looked after the saddle-bags, which I did; and when I came back again, I saw blacks along with Mr Kennedy; I then asked him if he saw the blacks with him, he was stupid with the spear wounds, and said "No;" then I asked where was his watch? I saw the blacks taking away watch and hat as I was returning to Mr Kennedy; then I carried Mr Kennedy into the scrub; he said, "Don't carry me a good way;" then Mr Kennedy looked this way, very bad (Jackey rolling his eyes). I said to him, "Don't look far away," as I thought he would be frightened; I asked him often "Are you well now?" and he said, "I don't care for the spear wound in my leg, Jackey, but for the other two spear wounds in my side and back," and said, "I am bad inside, Jackey." I told him blackfellow always die when he got spear in there (the back); he said, "I am out of wind, Jackey;" I asked him, "Mr Kennedy, are you going to leave me?" and he said, "Yes my boy, I am going to leave you;" he said, "I am very bad, Jackey; you take the books, Jackey, to the captain, but not the big ones, the Governor will give anything for them;" I then tied up the papers: he then said, "Jackey, give me paper and I will write;" I gave him paper and pencil, and he tried to write, and he then fell back and died, and I caught him as he fell back and held him, and I then turned round myself and cried: I was crying a good while until I got well; that was about an hour, and then I buried him; I digged up the ground with a tomahawk, and covered him over with logs, then grass, and my shirt and trousers; that night I left him near dark; [2nd December] I would go through the scrub, and the blacks threw spears at me, a good many, and I went back again into the scrub; then I went down the creek which runs into Escape River, and I walked along the water in the creek very easy, with my head only above water, to avoid the blacks, and get out of their way; in this way I went half a mile; then I got out of the creek, and got clear of them, and walked on all night nearly, and slept in the bush without a fire; [Camp 1]. I went on next morning, and felt very bad, and I spelled for two days; I lived upon nothing but salt water; [Camp 2 – 6th-7th December] next day I went on and camped one mile away from where I left, and ate one of the pandanus fruits; [Camp 3 – 8th December] next morning I went on two miles, and sat down there, and I wanted to spell a little there, and go on; but when I tried to get up, I could not, but fell down again very tired and cramped, and I spelled here two days, [Camp 4 – 9th-10th December] then I went on again one mile, and got nothing to eat but one nonda; and I went on that day and camped, [Camp 5 – 11th December] and on again next morning, about half a mile, and sat down where there was good water, and remained all day [Camp 6 – 12th December]. On the following morning, I went a good way, went round a great swamp and mangroves, and got a good way by sundown; [Camp 7 – 13th December] the next morning I went and saw a very large track of *blackfellows; I went clear of the track and of swamp or sandy ground; then I came to a very large river and a large lagoon; plenty of alligators in the lagoon, about ten miles from Port Albany. I now got into the ridges by sundown; and went up a tree and saw Albany Island; [Camp 8 – 14th December] then next morning at four o'clock, I went on as hard as I could go all the way down, over fine clear ground, fine iron bark timber, and plenty of good grass; I went on round the point (this was towards Cape York, north of Albany Island) and went on and followed a creek down, and went on top of the hill, and saw Cape York; I knew it was Cape York, because the sand did not go on further; I sat down then a good while; I said to myself this is Port Albany, I believe inside somewhere; Mr Kennedy also told me that the ship was inside, close up to the mainland; I went on a little way, and saw the ship and boat; I met close up here two black gins and a good many pickaninnies; one said to me "Powad, Powad;" then I asked her for eggs, she gave me turtle's eggs, and I gave her a burning glass; she pointed to the ship which I had seen before; I was very frightened of seeing the black men all along here, and when I was on the rock cooeying, and murry murry glad when the boat came for me [8am – 23rd December 1848].*

NOTE: At first glance, the dates shown would appear to identify Kennedy's death as being on the 2nd December. However, in Jackey's interview with the "Sydney Morning Herald", [6th March 1849], he stated that they rested for several days as Kennedy was too ill to be moved. This is not mentioned in Jackey's statement to Dr Vallack.

Therefore by adding these 3 days, then the more likely date is the 5th December 1848.

THE DATE OF KENNEDY'S MURDER

Ever since Kennedy was brutally murdered by the Yadagana, at the Escape River, the date of that offence has been stated as the 13th December 1848.

This date was only established from the information that was obtained from his faithful guide "Jackey" after being rescued at Albany Pass.

During questioning on board the schooner "Ariel", Jackey stated that on the night before Kennedy's death it was moonlight and he could see the aborigines searching for them. In his own words he stated:

I and Mr Kennedy watched them that night, taking it in turns every hour all night. By-and-by, I saw the black fellows; it was a moonlight night.

This was supposed to be the night of the 12th-13th of December 1848. But was it?

At this time the "Ariel" was still waiting for the Kennedy Expedition at Albany Pass, less than 20 miles away.

According to the log book of the "Ariel" the storms were so bad that crew members had to return on board at 4pm on account of the rain.

Thunder and lightning with hard squalls continued throughout the night and tapered off after midday on the 13th December.

The bad weather had spread all over Cape York and under these conditions there is no way moonlight would have been visible at the Escape River.

Secondly, Jackey gave a daily account of his journey with Kennedy after leaving the 3 men at the false Pudding-Pan Hill camp at Cape Grenville on the 21st November 1849.

From the 21st of November till Kennedy's death, they made 11 separate camps of one night each plus an additional camp where they rested for several days. This amounts to a total of 14 days.

If Jackey's account can be relied upon, then Kennedy's death was closer to the 5th December. Incidently, on that night there was also plenty of moonlight from a ¾ moon.

Chapter 23
"FACT VERSUS FICTION"

GIOM OF THE KAURAREGAS

	LEGEND	ANSWER
1.	The America was wrecked off Horn Island [Nurapai].	???????? The America was wrecked near a small island. Nurapai is the second largest island in the P.O.W. group. Entrance Island is the most likely site of the wreck [Juna].
2.	Barbara Thompson was rescued at Prince of Wales Island.	FALSE She was rescued at Cape York.
3.	Barbara Thompson was a survivor from a cannibal feast.	FALSE She witnessed the deaths of all 5 crew members, who had drowned. There was no cannibal feast.
4.	She was seen by the natives as the spirit of Chief Peaqui's dead daughter.	TRUE She was believed to be Giaoma [Giom] Peaqui's daughter, who had died several weeks earlier.
5.	She had good times as well as bad.	FALSE There were no good times amongst headhunters.
6.	She was forced to marry a native called Boroto.	FALSE She lived with Boroto's family.

WINI

	LEGEND	ANSWER
7.	He was a white man who ruled an island tribe called the Badus.	TRUE He was chief of the Badus.
8.	He tried to kidnap Barbara Thompson at Keriri. [Hammond Island]	TRUE He sent 16 war canoes and 200 warriors to capture her.
9.	He murdered any castaways from shipwrecks who landed near his island fortress.	TRUE Under his rule the Badu massacred entire boatloads of castaways.
10.	His nationality was never established.	TRUE Barbara Thompson was unable to identify his European language as he always spoke in the native tongue.
11.	He murdered his 3 companions before he landed at Badu.	TRUE The naturalist Macgillivray stated he killed the 3 men in the boat before he arrived at Badu.
12.	He was an escaped convict.	???????? This matter has never been resolved. Barbara Thompson stated he was shipwrecked. The naturalist, Macgillivray claimed he was probably an escaped convict from Norfolk Is.

	LEGEND	ANSWER
13.	He had his own harem of native girls.	TRUE He had fathered children to several Badu girls and had traded items of value in exchange for Gudang Aboriginal girls.
14.	He died in 1866	FALSE This rumour was started by a mission teacher at the Somerset Settlement. Wini was reported by Frank Jardine as being still alive after the massacre of the Kauraregas.
15.	Castaways massacred at Badu.	TRUE 18 castaways from a wrecked ship were beheaded by the Badus under Wini's rule in 1848.
16.	Wini was a "Good Man", which meant "Kopi Garki" in the native language.	FALSE This statement was made by the artist on board the Rattlesnake. The words "Kopi Garki" mean light coloured man as well as good man. In its true context it meant light coloured man.
17.	He may have been a Dutch or Indonesian sailor.	FALSE He may have been Dutch but certainly not Indonesian. Wini was European, not Asian.
18.	Wini was shot dead at Badu by Frank Jardine, in the early 1870's.	TRUE He is believed to have been shot by Frank Jardine, from a police boat anchored off shore. For obvious reasons it was not publicised.

LOST EXPEDITION

	LEGEND	ANSWER
19.	Kennedy was murdered because he entered an aboriginal burial ground.	FALSE The Yadagana Aborigines did not bury their dead in areas prone to heavy flooding such as the banks of the Escape River.
20.	The Yadagana killed him for his clothes.	TRUE Barbara Thompson stated after her rescue: *"They killed him for his Domawaka"* [clothes] She was the first white person to learn of his death
21.	Kennedy believed the Yadagana were friendly.	TRUE He was so convinced they were friendly that he gave them gifts and ordered Jackey to do likewise, even though Jackey warned him they were bad.
22.	The 3 men left at the camp at Cape Grenville were murdered by aborigines.	NOT ESTABLISHED Their bodies were never found although natives were seen wearing their clothes.

THE DEVIL OF CAPE YORK – Somerset

LEGEND	ANSWER
23. The 6 natives shot in a canoe, by the marines, were not involved in the earlier attack at Somerset.	FALSE Police Magistrate John Jardine identified them as being the same natives who attacked the marines in which Private Saich was seriously wounded.
24. The 6 aborigines shot in the canoe may have come from a different tribe and not the Gudang tribe.	???????? The Gudang tribe were surprised when the canoe was given to them as they had not missed any canoes or warriors.
25. A bora* ground was located near Somerset belonging to the Yadagana. [*Site of corroboree]	FALSE No aborigines had a bora ground on their enemies tribal land. Somerset was Gudang territory.
26. The Kauraregas from Prince of Wales Island, [Muralug] were always at war with the Gudang at Somerset.	FALSE The Kauraregas and Gudang were allies who traded with each other. The enemies were the Gumukudin to the west and the Yadagana to the south.

THE DEVIL OF CAPE YORK – Frank Lascelles Jardine

LEGEND	ANSWER
27. He deliberately shot dozens of aborigines during the cattle drive to Cape York.	FALSE Jardine instructed all the cattle men, they could only shoot at the aborigines if their lives were threatened. He always fired in self defence.
28. He fought an aboriginal warrior bare handed to death.	TRUE This incident took place in early 1866, at the Vallack Point cattle station.
29. Aborigines tried to kill him in his sleep.	TRUE The Yadagana aborigines threw 2 spears at him through the hut window on the 7th July 1866, whilst he was asleep.
30. Aborigines entered the hut at night to kill him and his brother in their beds.	TRUE After failing to spear him through the window, the Yadagana sneaked in to the hut one night but the Jardines were waiting. Only one Yadagana survived.
31. He shot 11 aborigines whilst digging a strainer post hole at Vallack Point.	TRUE He jumped into the hole and fired at 12 attacking warriors, 11 of them died.
32. The aborigines believed he was "A Markai Devil" or devil spirit who could read their minds.	TRUE After the Yadagana failed to kill him inside the 2 room hut he galloped his horse through their camp the next day. They believed it was the spirit of the man their warriors had supposedly killed. He was then "Debil Debil Jardine".

33.	He made peace between the Gudang and Yadagana tribes.	TRUE On the 27th July 1867 he rode into the Yadagana camp and made peace between these 2 tribes who celebrated with a grand corroboree.
34.	He reported kidnappers of islanders to his superiors in Brisbane.	TRUE 2 Of the kidnapping vessels captured by the Basilisk in 1873 were reported by Frank Jardine.
35.	He sheltered 93 shipwrecked castaways at Somerset and fed them at his cost.	TRUE These were survivors from the 3 ships wrecked at Raine Island. He was later re-imbursed the cost of feeding them.
36.	His closest friend was Black Eulah.	TRUE He shot the 3 police boys, Barney, Peter and Sambo who murdered Black Eulah.
37.	He shot aborigines on Albany Island from the beach at Somerset.	FALSE Jardines guns had a maximum range of 250 yards. Albany Island is 800 yards across the pass.
38.	He fired on ships in Albany Pass with the rusted cannons in front of Somerset Homestead.	FALSE The cannons were salvaged from a wreck and could not fire even if ammunition was available.
39.	He rescued missionary families scattered on isolated islands.	TRUE They were rescued by Jardine and the Reverend Murray with a police crew on Jardines instructions in November 1873.
40.	He was a racist who killed black babies.	FALSE He married a native woman from Samoa because he loved her. He then fathered 4 coloured children to her, and raised a family in the wilds of Cape York. He stood out against the racial prejudice of his day for Sana. He did not kill babies, black or white.
41.	He sent the telegraph that alerted the Authorities to the sinking of the R.M.S. Quetta on 28th February 1890.	TRUE After sending the telegraph he arranged for the rescue of the survivors.
42.	He sheltered survivors from the wrecked R.M.S. Quetta.	TRUE He nursed and fed the survivors at Somerset at his own cost, till they could be transferred.
43.	He led the rescue operation on Muralug to free a white woman captured by the Kauraregas.	TRUE When he found her she was already dead, killed as the attack commenced by the Kauraregas. He buried her on a hill outside the village.

44.	The woman held by the Kauraregas, was a Mrs Harriet Gasgoign, believed to have been captured from the Sperwer.	FALSE Mrs Harriet Gasgoign was later found to be alive in Melbourne. She may have been a Mrs Mathids captured from a previous massacre 3 months before the Sperwer massacre.
45.	Attacks against European ships ceased after the assault on Muralug. [P.O.W.]	TRUE The Islanders now knew that to attack any ship in future, they must expect retribution from Somerset.
46.	He had lavish parties in the residency with tropical dishes served on pure silverware to visiting officials and their ladies.	TRUE The silver dinnerware was formed from half a ton of silver coins found from a sunken wreck near Murray Is. in the Eastern Torres Strait.
47.	Upon his death, the aborigines sneaked into the grave yard and re-buried him upside down so his spirit would not haunt them.	FALSE The aborigines informed me that their people have never disturbed his grave. The Jardine family have stated: *"His grave has never been disturbed".*
48.	He is buried beneath the tombstone at the Somerset graveyard.	FALSE He is buried on the north side of the tombstone, whilst his wife, Sana, is buried on the south side. The tombstone was erected 5 years after his death, by their son, Bootle Lascelles Jardine in 1924, the year after Sana died.
49.	He shot aborigines at Somerset when they refused to rescue his 2 daughters as they were being eaten by sharks at Somerset Bay.	FALSE Both his daughters lived to a ripe old age. The eldest, Alice Jardine Vidgen died in 1961, whilst the younger Elizabeth Jardine Sheldon died in 1988 at 93 years of age.
50.	Ships passing through Albany Pass, saluted Jardine by firing a gun.	TRUE This salutation was in respect for the lives he saved and the people he sheltered when the R.M.S. Quetta was sunk on 28th February 1890.

CYCLONE MAHINA
STATEMENT BY MRS PORTER OF THE "CREST OF THE WAVE"

"...at about 10pm, I began to feel uneasy, and could not lie comfortably in my berth on account of the dreadful rolling of the schooner, so got up and put on a gown. My husband was out on deck then with all the men, doing what they could to try and save the boats and to keep things as well as possible. It began to sound very dreadful, and I too feel anxious. I stood beside the berth all the time to save baby from rolling out. She had wakened several times, but fell asleep again when finding I was with her. By that time the water was coming into the cabin very quickly through every little opening, and soon the bed and we were all very wet. While standing in my cabin trying to hold myself up and baby from falling, dreadful things seemed to be happening on deck, and I was always thankful if my husband made his appearance for only a second. My cabin got so full of water and everything into such disorder, that with Tommy De Lange's help, baby and I got into the next cabin, where we were much drier for a time. My poor little girl was very frightened, but did not cry very much, she clung to me and hid her face under my arm. She and I both got sea-sick, as the storm grew worse, and it was almost more than I could do to help her while being ill myself. Things were washing against my feet and nearly carrying me away I don't know how often. The worst of all for us in the cabins was when the windows were washed in with one sweep, and the cabins filled with water. Baby was washed away from me, and I groped in the dark until I found her dripping wet and gasping for breath. My heart ached for her. I couldn't stand with her in my arms, and was just falling when my husband rushed in just in time to help us to a seat in the dining cabin, where we remained until morning, clinging on to whatever would help us, the seas washing over us all the time. We had all given up hope long before daylight, as my husband had told me we were sinking fast, and in great danger. All the boats had gone, and the sea and storm were too fierce to allow of anything struggling long in them. I tried to feel resigned, but couldn't, to the thought of my little one being tossed into that dreadful sea. I clung to hope all through, and was rewarded when daylight came and we were still afloat. The leak was patched up and the water bailed out until we were out of danger, although all that day too was terribly rough. The 'Duke of Norfolk' passing, saw our signals of distress, and anchored near us for that night. I don't think any steamer looked so grand to us as she did with all her lights alongside our poor disabled schooner. They got baby and me on board, and were very kind indeed to us, lending us clothes, and doing all they could for our comfort. I was very stiff and ill through being in the water, although I had managed to change for a blanket and singlet, the only dry garments we could find; baby's attire being the same. I put on wet clothes to go on to the steamer in. The steamer seemed so comfortable after all we had gone through, but I couldn't sleep thinking of my husband and the others on board, and hoping for their safety. The next morning when leaving for Cooktown we met the 'Duke of Portland' coming to Thursday Island, so I transhipped into her, and arrived here the following afternoon.

I shall never in all my life forget the experience, and I am glad my little girl is too young to remember it for long. Her little nerves were upset for some time afterwards. We lost a great deal in the way of clothes and other belongings, but this is nothing since we ourselves were spared such a fate as befell so many others."

Chapter 24
"EXTRACTS OF OFFICIAL SOMERSET REPORTS"

The following documentation are extracts from the official reports of Somerset [1864-1877] and totally refute many statements made by various academics in their attempts to denigrate our early pioneers.

For the benefit of those who may find it difficult to read the hand written reports, I have typed them up so that they can read the reports word for word.

They are of course only a small fraction of the reports written by the various Police Magistrates, but at least they give a clearer insight into the reality of life last century rather than some of the fables emanating from many of our universities.

Frank Jardine has become a major target of our vindictive academics who are prepared to print the slightest rumour regardless of any evidence to the contrary.

Yet, a number of reports from at least 2 Police Magistrates show that Jardine was highly respected by both the aborigines and Torres Strait Islanders.

When Police Magistrate D'Oyley Aplin inspected Jardine's pearling station on Mt Ernest island [Nahgi], he was amazed at the good treatment and excellent living conditions that Jardine had provided for his 38 native workers. He had also provided food for 20 of their relatives.

[QSA–SLB–P.263–271–ACCESS NO. 13–5–CLASS NO.CPS–13C–G–1]

Additional evidence of the trust and friendship that Jardine had with the natives comes from Police Magistrate Henry Simpson, when Jardine lived at Vallack Point.

[GENERAL REPORT ON THE SETTLEMENT OF SOMERSET, etc.]
[H G SIMPSON, LATE POLICE MAGISTRATE, SOMERSET.]
[BRISBANE, 28TH JULY 1868.]

During the investigation in Brisbane, into the activities of the Reverend Jagg, Simpson wrote of the amicable friendship that Jardine had with the natives when he stated:

> "He [Jardine] *being the one of all others who is thoroughly acquainted with the habits of the aborigines, and whom they like and trust, and will do more for than any one else in the place.*"

The available evidence clearly shows Frank Jardine was very friendly with the aborigines and that certain academics have deliberately lied in their attempts to promote him as evil.

THE PEACE SETTLEMENT ARRANGED BY FRANK JARDINE BETWEEN THE GUDANG AND YADAGANA AND REPORTED BY POLICE MAGISTRATE HENRY SIMPSON ON THE 10TH OCTOBER 1867

The full report portraying violent aboriginal warfare was later presented to both houses of the Queensland Parliament in 1868 and read as a Parliamentary paper which was titled as: "General Report on the Settlement of Somerset, etc."

… I now repeat Mr Jardine's statement to me of what occurred. He started a day or two later, but, on arriving in the afternoon at his intended camping place he found 70 or 80 of the Gudang party there before him. They were just preparing to attack the Yardaigan camp, which they had ascertained to be only about half a mile off, the Yardaigans not being aware of their proximity. Mr Jardine would not allow them to make any attack, but said he would go with them and talk to the Yardaigans. He, therefore, sent the Gudangs in one direction, whilst he with his three boys took another, so as to come upon the camp from opposite sides. It was most fortunate for the Gudangs that Mr Jardine prevented them from attempting an attack, as the camp was found to contain nearly 400 men, all armed, who, if attacked, would in all probability have annihilated their assailants.

The Yardaigans were thoroughly surprised, and at first appeared to be half inclined to show fight, and half frightened; but, on Mr Jardine riding up to them without unslinging his carbines, and with no available arms except a revolver in his belt, they gathered confidence, and became quite friendly; and, after a time, the two parties of blacks made friends formally, embracing one another, and dancing and singing.

Mr Jardine and his boys camped close to the Yardaigans, who spent the whole night in dancing …

SPERWER MASSACRE – LETTER TO CAPTAIN McAUSLAND FROM FRANK JARDINE

82.69

Captain McAusland Somerset
Schooner Melanie June 21st 1869
Charo
Sir,
    I have been informed by the natives of this place, that a vessel has lately been captured by the "Prince of Wales" natives – The report is that "all hands" have been murdered and the vessel burned – I also have every reason to believe that the Captain's wife is still alive among the natives but as we have no means of getting over to the "Prince of Wales" island, will you be good enough to give me the use of two boats and their crews for a few days in order that I may search the island thoroughly for traces of the unfortunate vessel –
    I have the honour to be
    F.L.J.   P.M.
[Frank Lascelles Jardine – Police Magistrate]

SPERWER MASSACRE [FROM FRANK JARDINE]

83.69

The Honorable
The Colonial Secretary Somerset
Brisbane June 26th 1869
Sir,
    I do myself the honor to report for your information, the capture of the cutter "Sperwer" and murder of her crew, on or about the 14th April last by the "Prince of Wales" Islanders – James Gascoine Master, from Melbourne to New Guinea (See Log).
    As we are rather short handed here, I requested the use of two boats and their crews from Capt McAusland of the "Melanie" which I got and went over with Four N Troopers to the P of W Island, where we found the blacks camp full of ships gear, clothing & C but all property was totally destroyed. Such articles as watches, revolvers, gunlocks, and a quadrant having been taken asunder and portions worn by the natives as ornaments. The bodies of the murdered men have been put up into trees close to "Red Point" but cannot be recognised as their heads and clothing have been taken of, the Cutter has been run ashore and burned at the same place and I believe that there is still a large quantity of property lying about her ...

SPERWER MASSACRE
[EXTRACT OF REPORT BY HENRY CHESTER, POLICE MAGISTRATE]

3-1869
Somerset Aug. 10th
Sir,

At 10 AM, we weighed and stood for the islands, and passing through the boat channel between Horn and P. of W. Islands came to an anchor at 2.30 PM under the lee of Friday island, within a quarter of a mile of the wreck of the cutter. Landed the party and found that the vessel had been hauled up on the rocks, stripped of everything portable and burned down to the copper.

About 100 yards from the wreck we found the remains of two white men; a portion of the skin of the chest adhering to one of them exhibited marks of spear wounds, and sticking in the thigh bone of the other was about 5 inches of an iron barbed arrow. The skulls and arms of both, and the legs of one were missing, and had probably been devoured by the natives – The remainder of the crew appear to have been killed in the vessel and thrown over-board.

EVIDENCE TAKEN BEFORE POLICE MAGISTRATE BEDDOME PROVING FRANK JARDINE'S INNOCENCE – NOV 10TH 1873

By Mr Beddome.
Const Edmund Brown

Q1 Have you any complaints to make against Mr Jardine?
None.

2   Have you ever been employed in any boats pearl shelling?
Never whilst in government employ, except during my leave, when I was working on my own account.

3   Have the Government boats ever been employed in pearl shelling?
No.

4   Is this the licence the Vampire has been sailing under (licence produced)
Yes, she was used as a police boat and flew the blue ensign.

5   Do you certify that the log of the Vampire signed by you is correct?
Yes, as in the book.

Edmund L Brown
Coxswain

EVIDENCE THAT THE HOSPITAL WAS DEMOLISHED AND NOT TRANSFERRED TO THURSDAY ISLAND

11.73
To
    The Honorable Colonial Secretary   Somerset
    Brisbane   22nd November 1873

    The natives are in large force close to the settlement, I have been expecting an attack from them every night. If they come I am ready for them.
    I omitted to report in my last that Mr Jardine had commenced to pull down the hospital to prevent it coming down, I have nearly completed the demolition, the iron I have stowed in one of the cottages, the good timber I have stacked in a heap.

                             I have the honor
                                   CB.
                                   P.M.
                   [Charles Beddome – Police Magistrate]

THE MYSTERY ANCHOR ON SOMERSET BEACH IN WHICH ACADEMICS CLAIMED THAT THERE WAS NO DOCUMENTATION

114-71
The Hon'ble
The Col Sec Brisbane.

    "A 5 foot Ridge anchor and Warp abandoned by the Reichstag, has since been recovered by Mr Chester and landed here" …   I have the honor
                                 FLJ   PM
                           [Frank Lascelles Jardine]
                              [Police Magistrate]

THE ATTEMPTED ATTACK AGAINST SOMERSET BY THE YADAGANA ABORIGINES AND THE BATTLE THAT FOLLOWED REPORTED BY POLICE MAGISTRATE CHARLES BEDDOME

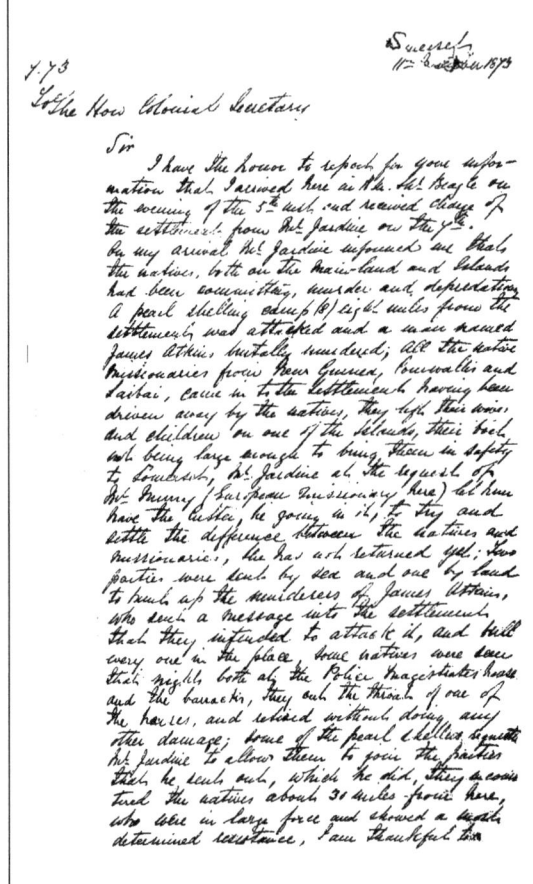

Somerset
7.73   11th November 1873
To The Hon Colonial Secretary
Sir

I have the honor to report for your information that I arrived here in the HMS Beagle on the evening of the 5th inst and received charge of the settlement from Mr Jardine on the 7th. On my arrival Mr Jardine informed me that the natives, both on the mainland and islands had been committing murder and depredations. A pearl shelling camp (8) eight miles from the settlement was attacked and a man named James Atkins brutally murdered; All the native Missionaries from New Guinea, Cornwallis and Saibai, came into the settlement having been driven away by the natives, they left their wives and children on one of the islands, their boat not being large enough to bring them in safety to Somerset. Mr Jardine at the request of Mr Murray (European missionary here) let him have the Cutter, he going in it, to try and settle the difference between the natives and missionaries, he has not returned yet; Two parties were sent by sea and one by land to haul up the murderers of James Atkins, who sent a message into the settlement that they intended to attack it, and kill every one in the place. Some natives were seen that night, both at the Police Magistrates house and the barracks, they cut the throat of one of the horses, and retired without doing any other damage; some of the pearl shellers requested Mr Jardine to allow them to join the parties that he sent out, which he did, they encountered the natives about 30 miles from here, who were in large force and showed a most determined resistance. I am thankful to report that they were properly dispersed;

EVIDENCE THAT THE GUDANG TRIBE WERE TOTALLY EXTINCT IN 1875 REPORTED BY POLICE MAGISTRATE D'OYLEY APLIN

Govt Offices, Somerset,
1st Sept – 1875

90/75

... We are obliged to keep a more vigilant look-out now that the quiet and friendly tribe of the Gudangs has become extinct.

Commissioner of Police
Brisbane

I have & C,
CDA, PM
Christopher D'Oyley Aplin
[Police Magistrate]

PORTION OF AN OFFICIAL REPORT SHOWING HOW WELL FRANK JARDINE TREATED HIS NATIVE EMPLOYEES
REPORT ON THE PEARL FISHERIES OF THE TORRES STRAIT BY POLICE MAGISTRATE CHRISTOPHER H D'OYLEY APLIN 18TH FEBRUARY 1875

Here the natives employed by him, who, with the exception of about 14 from Cape York belong to Mount Ernest, are comfortably housed in recently built huts of thatch, and judging from their condition, general appearance and exuberance of spirits must be as well cared for as could be desired. Indeed the Cape York natives offered a striking contrast with their relatives in camp at Somerset, showing the improvement effected in their condition by abundant & wholesome diet and regular employment. There were also about 20 relatives of the Mount Ernest natives – women old men & children – who are likewise supplied with food by Mr Jardine making altogether about 60 persons – This is also the usual custom with other employers.

THE WRECK OF THE QUETTA
EXTRACT OF THE STATEMENT MADE BY EMILY LACY AFTER SURVIVING THE QUETTA DISASTER – 1890

… but thought that it was best, he did not at all want me to go either; however, I went leaving him the raft and saying that I hoped to be back in about an hour. I reached what I thought was a boat but found it was only a raft with blacks on it, three women and two men but they would not let me touch it and tried to drown me by hitting out with a long board. I showed them my burnt arms and shoulders, but it was no use …

[Credit – Ian Hore Lacy]

CHAPTER 25
SEQUENCE OF EVENTS
"BRITISH SHIPS – SURVEYS"

FIRST NORTHERN SURVEY VOYAGE TO THE TORRES STRAIT OF "H.M.S. FLY" AND HER TENDER "BRAMBLE" 1843

19TH MAY - 1ST JUNE 1843 – Ships depart Sydney and anchor at Rockingham Bay.

31ST MAY 1843 – Crew share their fish with natives of Gould Island.
Later, natives attacked them with spears and rocks.
One black wounded as others retreat. One white injured by rock.

1ST JUNE 1843 – Ships depart Rockingham Bay for Lizard Island.

5TH JUNE 1843 – Party with Jukes and Evans [Fly] climbed hill on Lizard Island.

7TH - 17TH JUNE 1843 – "Fly" surveys Barrier Reef between Lizard Island and Cape Melville.

24TH JUNE 1843 – "Bramble" anchors at Cape Direction.

25TH JUNE 1843 – Sailor (Bayley) murdered by "Friendly Blacks" Mt Direction.

12TH JULY 1843 – Ships arrive at Sir Charles Hardy Islands.

18TH JULY 1843 – The "Fly's" Pinnace "Midge" [covered boat] arrives Cape Grenville.

29TH JULY 1843 – Ships visit Raine Island. Captain Blackwood and Jukes camp on it.

1ST AUGUST 1843 – Ships anchored at Pandora Entrance [Where HMS Pandora wrecked].

5TH AUGUST 1843 – Ships skirt the reef and anchor at Murray Island.

6TH AUGUST 1843 – Captain Blackwood from the "Fly" and Jukes land and trade.

11TH AUGUST 1843 – Ships arrive at Mt Adolphus Island near Cape York.

14TH AUGUST 1843 – Ships anchor at Booby Island and check "Post Office".
Ships leave Booby Island for Tasmania.

SECOND NORTHERN SURVEY VOYAGE TO THE TORRES STRAIT OF "H.M.S. FLY" AND HER TENDER "BRAMBLE" IN COMPANY WITH THE REVENUE CUTTER "PRINCE GEORGE" 1844 - 1845

22ND MARCH 1844 – The "Fly", "Bramble" and "Prince George" depart Sydney.

27TH MAY 1844 – Party lands on Raine Island to construct a beacon.

8TH AUGUST - 25TH SEPTEMBER 1844 – Ships survey north to Cape York and Endeavour Strait.

21ST SEPTEMBER 1844 – The "Fly" leaves for Port Essington [NT] ahead of other ships.

19TH OCTOBER 1844 – The "Fly" arrives at Java and is later joined by other 2 ships.

10TH FEBRUARY 1855 – Ships return to Booby Island with stores.

10TH FEBRUARY - 19TH APRIL 1845 – Ships survey and sound the north eastern Torres Strait.

28TH MARCH - 1ST APRIL 1845 – Ships anchored at Darnley Island [Erub].
11TH - 15TH APRIL 1845 – Ships anchored Murray Island [Mer].
19TH APRIL 1845 – The "Bramble" departs for Sydney via the east coast.
21ST APRIL 1845 – The "Fly" and "Prince George" leave Mer for New Guinea.
29TH APRIL 1845 – Captain Blackwood and Lieutenant Ince explore the Fly River [NG].
29TH APRIL - 1ST MAY 1845 – Upon landing on north bank attacked by 500 Papuans.
1ST MAY 1845 – Pursued all the way back to "Prince George" by 4 war canoes.
2ND MAY 1845 – 2 Boats and crews lost in bad weather off New Guinea coast.
6TH MAY 1845 – The "Fly" anchors at Bramble Cay in search for missing boats.
6TH - 7TH MAY 1845 – The "Fly" sails north to Airds Hill.
24TH MAY 1845 – The "Fly" returns to Treacherous Bay at Darnley Island [Erub].
25TH MAY 1845 – A civil war is on. No help available from the islanders.
27TH MAY 1845 – The "Fly" leaves Darnley and joins "Prince George" at Bramble Cay.
Captain Blackwood and Jukes board the "Prince George".
The "Prince George" sails up the Aird River, New Guinea.
29TH MAY 1845 – The "Prince George" attacked by Papuans.
2ND JUNE 1845 – The "Prince George" returns to Booby Island refuge.
3RD JUNE 1845 – The "Fly" returns to Darnley Island [Erub].
The Erubians are glad of the deaths of the hated Papuans.
4TH JUNE 1845 – The "Fly" leaves Darnley Island and anchors at Dove Island.
6TH - 8TH JUNE 1845 – The "Fly" arrives at Evans Bay, Cape York for water.
8TH JUNE 1845 – The "Fly" joins "Prince George" at Booby Island.
The "Fly" learns the lost boats crews are headed for Port Essington.
12TH JUNE 1845 – The "Fly" and "Prince George" arrive at Port Essington [NT].
25TH SEPTEMBER 1845 – The "Prince George" heads for Singapore, the "Fly" arrives Sydney. Both ships conveyed castaways from 2 shipwrecks.

FIRST NORTHERN SURVEY VOYAGE TO CAPE YORK AND THE TORRES STRAIT OF "H.M.S. RATTLESNAKE" AND HER TENDER "BRAMBLE" – 1848

29TH APRIL 1848 – The "Rattlesnake", "Bramble" and "Tam'o'shanter" leave Sydney.
23RD - 24TH MAY 1848 – The "Kennedy Expedition" landed at Rockingham Bay.
26TH JULY 1848 – The "Rattlesnake" visits Trinity Bay [future site of Cairns].
31ST JULY - 14TH AUGUST 1848 – The "Rattlesnake" spent 2 weeks at Lizard Island.
21ST AUGUST 1848 – The "Rattlesnake" reaches Cape Melville.
The watering party attacked on shore by aborigines.
22ND AUGUST 1848 – The "Rattlesnake" joins the "Bramble" at Pipon Islands.
28TH AUGUST 1848 – The "Rattlesnake" and "Bramble" reach Pelican Island.
31ST AUGUST 1848 – The ships separate. The "Rattlesnake" arrives Fife Island.
8TH SEPTEMBER 1848 – The "Rattlesnake" arrives Night Island.
29TH SEPTEMBER 1848 – The "Rattlesnake" joins the "Bramble" at Sunday Island.
3RD OCTOBER 1848 – The "Rattlesnake" and "Bramble" arrive at Cairncross Island.

7TH OCTOBER 1848 – The "Rattlesnake" and "Bramble" arrive at Albany Passage.

8TH OCTOBER 1848 – The "Rattlesnake" and "Bramble" arrive at Evans Bay.

2ND NOVEMBER 1848 – The "Rattlesnake" and "Bramble" leave Evans Bay.

4TH NOVEMBER 1848 – The "Rattlesnake" and "Bramble" arrive at Booby Island.

9TH NOVEMBER 1848 – The "Rattlesnake" sails off alone and arrives at Port Essington.

1ST DECEMBER 1848 – The "Bramble" continues the survey and arrives Weymouth Bay.

2ND DECEMBER 1848 – The "Bramble" leaves Weymouth Bay and sited by Kennedy Expedition as it heads south to Moreton Bay.

24TH JANUARY 1849 – The "Rattlesnake" arrives in Sydney.

SECOND NORTHERN SURVEY VOYAGE TO CAPE YORK AND THE TORRES STRAIT OF "H.M.S. RATTLESNAKE" AND HER TENDER "BRAMBLE" – 1849

8TH MAY 1849 – The "Rattlesnake" departs Sydney for Cape York.

26TH MAY 1849 – The "Rattlesnake" and "Bramble" depart Moreton Bay.

29TH SEPTEMBER 1849 – The ships survey Torres Strait and anchor at Marsden Island.

1ST OCTOBER 1849 – The "Rattlesnake" arrives at Evans Bay, Cape York.

13TH OCTOBER 1849 – The Kauraregas and Barbara Thompson leave Prince of Wales Island.

16TH OCTOBER 1849 – Barbara Thompson is rescued at Cape York.

5TH FEBRUARY 1850 – The "Rattlesnake" with Barbara Thompson arrives at Sydney.

THE FOLLOWING DOCUMENTATION IS FOR THE BENEFIT OF THOSE WHO WISH TO FOLLOW THE DAILY "SEQUENCE OF EVENTS" OF BOTH
"THE KENNEDY EXPEDITION 1848"
AND
"THE JARDINE CATTLE DRIVE"
1864 — 1865

CHAPTER 26
SEQUENCE OF EVENTS
"KENNEDY EXPEDITION"

THE FIRST OVERLAND EXPEDITION TO CAPE YORK UNDER THE COMMAND OF EDMUND BESLEY COURT KENNEDY – 1848

NOTE: [28] *Numerals in brackets signifies number of horses remaining.*

29TH APRIL 1848 – HMSS "Rattlesnake" and Barque "Tam'o'shanter" leave Sydney.

23RD MAY 1848 – The ships anchor at Rockingham Bay, to the north of Cardwell.

24TH - 25TH MAY 1848 – The party of 13 men and equipment landed.
One horse drowned [27].

24TH MAY 1848 – A group of aborigines approach and watch the landing.

30TH MAY 1848 – Kennedy and 3 others scout ahead.

3RD JUNE 1848 – They return to camp.

5TH JUNE 1848 – The expedition commences.

6TH JUNE 1848 – The Tully River reached and camped on the north bank.

7TH JUNE 1848 – The Tully River is crossed and a camp set up.

8TH JUNE 1848 – The remaining equipment crossed the next day.

9TH JUNE 1848 – Some friendly natives visit the camp.
Kennedy, Jackey and 3 others scout ahead.

10TH JUNE 1848 – They are halted by swamps and return to camp at dusk.

11TH JUNE 1848 – They travelled south for 4 miles. Found "Papuan" camp.

12TH JUNE 1848 – Crossed the Murray River.

13TH JUNE 1848 – The shepherd [Carpenter] is missing with tea, sugar and a damper.

14TH JUNE 1848 – Carpenter is found sharing the food with aborigines.
A crocodile surfaces in the river close to the camp.

15TH JUNE 1848 – The expedition advances 3 miles inland.

15TH - 17TH JUNE 1848 – They are held up by swamp.

17TH JUNE 1848 – They advanced 5 miles around the swamp.

18TH JUNE 1848 – Day of rest with prayers at 11am.

19TH - 22ND JUNE 1848 – Unable to advance through the swamps.

23RD JUNE 1848 – Moved south via the beach, turned inland. Camped at a creek.

24TH JUNE 1848 – Searched all day for a way out of the swamps.

25TH JUNE 1848 – Advanced 5 miles south close to the beach.

26TH JUNE 1848 – Supplies carried across creek as a cart sinks in the mud.
Aborigines [friendlies] seen stealing supplies.
A track is cut through half a mile of mangroves.
They passed within 2 miles of what is now the town of Cardwell.

27TH JUNE 1848 – The expedition advanced 5 miles west through dryer country.

28TH JUNE 1848 – A track is cut for 3 miles through the scrub.
Luff and Douglas ill with the Ague [Malaria].

29TH JUNE - 1ST JULY 1848 – Kennedy and 3 others explore ahead for 40 miles.

1ST - 4TH JULY 1848 – Remained camped due to illness of Luff and Douglas.

4TH JULY 1848 – Aborigines attack Kennedy and 3 others in nearby scrub. Kennedy shoots in defence, one is killed and 3 others hit.

5TH JULY 1848 – Rest in camp as horses and sheep regain their strength.

6TH JULY 1848 – Expedition heads west. Carts lowered by ropes into creek.

7TH JULY 1848 – Fallen trees slow the carts. Camped on a sandy creek.

8TH JULY 1848 – Most of this day spent cutting their way through thick scrub.

9TH JULY 1848 – Rest and prayers at 11am Sunday.

10TH - 13TH JULY 1848 – Several days spent cutting their way through scrub.

14TH JULY 1848 – One of the carts breaks down and is abandoned. The other 2 carts bog in a creek and abandoned at dusk. Their loads are finally carried to a dry camp by 10pm.

15TH JULY 1848 – Loads re-arranged on horses pack saddles. Many articles abandoned.

16TH JULY 1848 – Rest and prayers at 11am Sunday.

17TH JULY 1848 – Loads re-arranged on pack saddles. Heavy saws abandoned.

18TH JULY 1848 – Expedition covered 6 miles through open forest [26].

19TH - 22D JULY – Cutting their way through scrub and mountainous country.

23RD JULY 1848 – Rest and prayers at 11am Sunday.

24TH JULY 1848 – A lame horse is shot [25].

25TH JULY 1848 – Horses stumble and fall among granite boulders. Cutting scrub.

26TH JULY 1848 – Expedition continues cutting their way through dense scrub.

27TH JULY 1848 – Track cut to a grassy hill top. Horses feed and tethered at night.

28TH JULY 1848 – A horse is killed as he falls 30 feet down the hill [24].

29TH JULY 1848 – Kennedy scouts ahead and later returns to camp.

30TH JULY 1848 – Rest and prayers at 11am Sunday.

31ST JULY - 2ND AUGUST 1848 – Kennedy, Jackey and 4 other men cut a track.

3RD AUGUST 1848 – Expedition moves up the range via the cleared track and camp. A weak horse unable to climb the range is tied to a tree.

4TH AUGUST 1848 – The sheep and horses with the weak one are taken back to grass. Kennedy, Jackey and 4 men cut the scrub ahead of the camp. Niblett and 3 other men guard the stores at the main camp. Carron, Mitchell and Dunn camp with the horses and sheep.

5TH AUGUST 1848 – Kennedy's party continues to cut the track through the scrub.

7TH AUGUST 1848 – Carron moves the sheep and horses back along the track. One horse left abandoned at Carron's grazing camp [23].

8TH AUGUST 1848 – Carron and his men infested with leaches at their camp.

9TH AUGUST 1848 – Carron meets up with Kennedy. The expedition reaches the 2000 foot summit after 66 days of toil.

10TH AUGUST 1848 – Creek bridged by fallen trees. Supplies carried over it. Sheep and horses swim the creek [possibly Blunder Creek]. Niblett is suffering badly from the Ague [Malaria].

11TH AUGUST 1848 – Camped all day, allowing the sheep and horses to feed.

12TH AUGUST 1848 – The party camped near rocky waterholes after covering 5 miles.

13TH AUGUST 1848 – Rest and prayers at 11am Sunday.

14TH AUGUST 1848 – Niblett found to be stealing supplies, and making false returns.
Carron now in charge of stores.
Weekly rations to be weighed out.
Only 700Lbs of flour left from original 2240lbs.
The flour ration is now reduced from 1.7Lb to ½Lb a man a day.
Their weekly sugar is less than 1Lb and tea only a ¼Lb.
A sheep is eaten every 2nd day. They still have nearly 60 left.

15TH AUGUST 1848 – Cutting their way through thick scrub. Horse abandoned [22].
Camped on a creek with Casuarinas [possibly Wild River].

16TH AUGUST 1848 – A weak horse is killed and its flesh eaten [21].

17TH AUGUST 1848 – Only a short distance today allowing horses to feed and camp.

18TH AUGUST 1848 – Moved 4 miles N-W and camped near a river with steep banks.
Plenty of grass. A horse is injured as it falls into a gully.

19TH AUGUST 1848 – Substituted this day [Saturday] for the normal Sunday rest.
The injured horse dies [20].

20TH - 23 AUGUST 1848 – Travelled N-W through forest country, Emu Creek Valley.

23RD AUGUST 1848 – Friendly natives given a fish hook and a tin plate.
Goddard becomes lost whilst hunting wallabies with Jackey.
A party searches for Goddard unsuccessfully.

24TH AUGUST 1848 – Goddard finally reaches camp late in the afternoon.

25TH - 26TH AUGUST 1848 – The journey continues north.
They suffer from eating figs.

27TH AUGUST 1848 – Rest and prayers at 11am Sunday.

28TH AUGUST 1848 – A weak horse is shot and the flesh eaten [19].

29TH AUGUST 1848 – Camped on the Hodgkinson. A weak horse is left behind [18].

31ST AUGUST - 1ST SEPTEMBER 1848 – Traversed steep forested gullies down the valley.

2ND SEPTEMBER 1848 – Left the river and headed N-W and reached the Mitchell River.

3RD SEPTEMBER 1848 – Rest and prayers at 11am Sunday.
Some fish are caught and an emu and kangaroo are shot for food.

4TH - 9TH SEPTEMBER 1848 – For the next 6 days they followed the Mitchell River.

9TH SEPTEMBER 1848 – They were now about 90 miles west of Cape Tribulation.

10TH SEPTEMBER 1848 – Prayers at 11am Sunday. This day they continued moving north. Blacks attack the camp at 11pm, whites fire into the dark bush.

11TH SEPTEMBER 1848 – Headed north over poor country. Horses stumble on grass hillocks.

11TH - 14TH SEPTEMBER 1848 – Exchanged fish hooks for pandanus at native camp.

15TH SEPTEMBER 1848 – The expedition reached the Palmer River and made camp.
Several men catch a few fish in the river. Aborigines [8] threaten to attack the camp with spears raised. The whites offer friendship which the blacks interpret as fear.

15TH SEPTEMBER 1848 – As the blacks advance warning shots are fired, and they retreat. The blacks now attack the men fishing, they retreat when fired on.

16TH SEPTEMBER 1848 – The men remained in camp all day.
The aborigines try to burn the camp by setting the grass alight. The whites open fire and they retreat.

17TH - 21ST SEPTEMBER 1848 – The expedition moves north from the Palmer River. They forced their way over ironstone ridges.

22ND - 23RD SEPTEMBER 1848 – They have now crossed the range and are on pacific waters.

23RD SEPTEMBER 1848 – The midday shade temperature is 100 degrees fahr.

24TH SEPTEMBER 1848 – The expedition continues north over sandstone tablelands.

25TH SEPTEMBER 1848 – 3 Horses lost as expedition continues north.
4 Men left to search for missing horses.
Kennedy sets up camp at a large waterhole.
Only one man out of the searchers arrives in camp.
Carron goes back and brings the others to camp in the dark. Kangaroo Dog fails to arrive [Made it to camp on 28th and died].

26TH SEPTEMBER 1848 – The expedition arrived at Sandy Creek and camped [Station Creek].

27TH SEPTEMBER 1848 – They continue through marshy ground and sand ridges. They camped at a salt creek but found fresh water in a lagoon.

28TH SEPTEMBER 1848 – A large number of sheep are lost at this camp.

29TH SEPTEMBER 1848 – The search continues for the lost sheep unsuccessfully.

30TH SEPTEMBER 1848 – The expedition heads west only to find a dry waterhole. The remaining sheep are driven back to the previous camp.

1ST OCTOBER 1848 – Rest and prayers at 11am Sunday.

2ND OCTOBER 1848 – They again headed across the hot dry plain to the west.
They found water and camped.
A dying horse is bled and its blood is made into a pudding.

3RD OCTOBER 1848 – The horse died and its flesh is cut up and sun dried for food.
A guard was put near the meat to prevent any theft [17].

4TH OCTOBER 1848 – The expedition heads N-W and sighted a tableland [Janes].

5TH OCTOBER 1848 – The expedition continues north through hot dry country.

6TH OCTOBER 1848 – This day they camped at a salt water creek [Salt Water Creek]. They found 8 conical native huts, lined inside with woven bamboo.

7TH - 9TH OCTOBER 1848 – They continued N-N-W and struck a river [Annie].

10TH OCTOBER 1848 – Aborigines attack and spear a horse in the thigh, [not serious]. The blacks are repulsed with gunfire [No injuries either side].

11TH OCTOBER 1848 – Headed N-W and traded fish hooks to blacks for water in bark vessels.

12TH OCTOBER 1848 – The expedition heads N-N-W hugging the coast.

13TH OCTOBER 1848 – They failed to cut their way through mangroves to the beach.
14TH OCTOBER 1848 – They abandon the final try to cut through the mangroves to a beach.
15TH OCTOBER 1848 – Rest and prayers at 11am Sunday. The sugar is finished.
16TH OCTOBER 1848 – A horse falls into a rocky waterhole and is killed [16].
The flesh is sundried for food and guarded to prevent theft.
The horses are now too weak to carry heavy loads.
A tent and other heavy articles are abandoned.
17TH - 19TH OCTOBER 1848 – Crossed numerous creeks draining the McIlwraith Range.
19TH OCTOBER 1848 – Many horses are too weak to carry any more than their saddles.
20TH OCTOBER 1848 – Passed through cyclone damaged forest of uprooted trees. 2 Miles.
21ST OCTOBER 1848 – Forged a path through the valley between the ranges.
22ND OCTOBER 1848 – Costigan Douglas and Taylor are ill with diarrhoea.
These 3 men are permitted to ride their weak horses.
Blacks burn the grass to the south of them.
23RD - 28TH OCTOBER 1848 – Traversed rocky mountainous country.
Passed through deep gullies and creeks.
29TH OCTOBER 1848 – Rest and prayers at 11am Sunday. 3 Wallabies shot for food.
30TH OCTOBER 1848 – The last 2 round tents are burned to lighten the load.
Luff is too ill to walk and now rides the horse that carried them.
31ST OCTOBER 1848 – Remained camped enabling men and horses to recoup their energy.
1ST - 2ND NOVEMBER 1848 – A horse is killed and its flesh sundried for food [15].
The meat is guarded to prevent portions being stolen.
3RD NOVEMBER 1848 – They cut a track through scrub and gullies in the humid heat. They reach a river running to the south (Pascoe).
They cross the Pascoe and set up camp, in thick bamboo scrub. Horses are tied to trees to prevent them straying.
4TH NOVEMBER 1848 – Jackey shoots a cassowary for food and finds a grassy hill. Wall, fails to preserve the skin properly.
5TH NOVEMBER 1848 – The camp is moved to the site where Jackey saw the grassy hill. A horse is killed and its flesh sundried for food [14].
6TH NOVEMBER 1848 – 2 More dying horses are killed and the flesh sundried [12].
7TH NOVEMBER 1848 – Forged their way over rocky ground through dense forest.
8TH NOVEMBER 1848 – Continued through forest and gullies toward the head of the Pascoe.
9TH NOVEMBER 1848 – Followed a dry creek and found water by evening, then camped.
10TH NOVEMBER 1848 – Moved north for 3 miles and camped near myriads of pandanus trees.
11TH NOVEMBER 1848 – They headed 2 miles north and crossed the creek as it turned east. The only sheep to survive this far is now killed. Aborigines visit the camp and receive fish hooks and a tin plate. They are amazed at the power of the gun

11TH NOVEMBER 1848 – as 15 hawks are shot. A pup owned by the natives is killed by one of the dogs. The pup is eaten by Costigan, Dunn, Luff and Goddard. [3 Horses are unaccounted for and maybe the 3 lost on 25th September]

12TH NOVEMBER 1848 – Rest and prayers at 11am Sunday.
Carron and Jackey walk to the beach in search of salt [nil].

13TH NOVEMBER 1848 – The camp is moved to the south bank of the creek. It is erected at the base of a high bare hill.
There are now only 9 horses left [3 are unaccounted for] [9]. There is now only 46Lb flour, 1Lb tea and 75Lb of dried horseflesh. Kennedy leaves 2 horses at the Pascoe camp with Carron's party. He leaves 28Lb of flour, ½Lb of tea and the 2 horses [7}. He takes 18Lb of flour, ½Lb of tea and 75Lb of dried horseflesh. Kennedy, Jackey, Dunn, Luff and Costigan head for Cape York.
They cross the river [Pascoe] with the remaining 7 horses.

14TH NOVEMBER 1848 – Headed up a high range and camped on a flat behind it.

15TH NOVEMBER 1848 – Pushed their way north all day then camped.

16TH NOVEMBER 1848 – Spent much of this day extricating a bogged horse from the creek.

17TH NOVEMBER 1848 – Luff taken ill with a bad knee and left behind.

18TH NOVEMBER 1848 – Dunn goes back for him and helps him along. Camped at a small creek.

19TH NOVEMBER 1848 – The flour is all gone and they eat horseflesh and nondas. Costigan accidentally shoots himself under the right arm. They push north in the rain, mud and humidity.

20TH NOVEMBER 1848 – A horse called "Brownie" is killed and smoked in the evening [6].

21ST NOVEMBER 1848 – Continued north, Costigan in a lot of pain, returned to camp. As Costigan and Luff are ill then Dunn remains with them. A horse is killed for food and a live one is left with them [4]. Kennedy and Jackey leave this camp [False Pudding-pan Hill].

From the day they departed the "False Pudding-pan Hill" camp it is very difficult to identify their progress on a daily basis.

Although Jackey gave an excellent account of his journey to Cape York, he was unable to give dates.

We know that Costigan was shot on the first Sunday after leaving the "Pascoe Camp" and was therefore the "19th November".

2 Days later Jackey and Kennedy left for Cape York which would be the 21st November.

Although the official date for Kennedy's murder is given as the 13th December it is more likely to have occurred around the 5th December.

After burying Kennedy at the Escape River, he struggled north to the Kennedy Inlet and hid some of Kennedy's papers in a log and finally made it to Cape York where he was rescued by the "Ariel" at Port Albany, now known as Albany Pass.

22ND NOVEMBER 1848 – A horse is bogged in a swamp and finally abandoned.

23RD NOVEMBER 1848 – Pushed their way through gullies and scrub and camped in the rain.

24TH - 29TH NOVEMBER 1848 – They fought their way through jungle, mud and rain.

30TH NOVEMBER 1848 – Jackey's horse falls, trapping his right leg. Kennedy frees him.

1ST DECEMBER 1848 – In the morning Jackey's horse is dead [2].

2ND DECEMBER 1848 – Jackey climbs a tree and sights a sandy hill near Port Albany.

3RD DECEMBER 1848 – They arrive at the mouth of the Escape River and see Port Albany. Kennedy befriends the Yadagana aborigines at the Escape River. The Yadagana yell "Powad Powad" and rub their bellies. Their treachery is disguised by friendship as he trades with them.

4TH DECEMBER 1848 – The Yadagana hunt them all night.

5TH DECEMBER 1848 – As they head north the next day the blacks find them.
Jackey warns Kennedy to watch his back.
The Yadagana murder Kennedy with a spear in his back.
Jackey fires and hits a black with buckshot.
The horses are speared to death [0].
Jackey buries Kennedy and escapes from the Yadagana.

23RD DECEMBER 1848 – Jackey struggles north and is rescued at Port Albany by the "Ariel".

THE "CAMP OF DEATH" AT THE PASCOE RIVER UNDER THE COMMAND OF WILLIAM CARRON

13TH NOVEMBER 1848 – Kennedy's party leaves the Pascoe camp for Cape York.

14TH NOVEMBER 1848 – A horse is killed for food.

16TH NOVEMBER 1848 – John Douglas dies.
Aborigines spy out the camp on a pretext of friendship.

18TH NOVEMBER 1848 – Aborigines taunt the starving men by giving them rotten putrid fish.

19TH NOVEMBER 1848 – 60 Aborigines threaten to attack the camp.
They retreat when Carron threatens to shoot in self defence.

20TH NOVEMBER 1848 – Edward Taylor dies and is buried beside John Douglas.

21ST NOVEMBER 1848 – 60 Aborigines approach the camp heavily armed with barbed spears. They hold up fish to entice the starving men to come closer. They mimic agony with spears to their necks. The men are not fooled by their cowardly taunts and defy them. The aborigines surround the camp and attack, throwing 11 spears. The whites open fire wounding one black, then they retreat.

22ND - 25TH NOVEMBER 1848 – The aborigines watch the camp daily.

26TH NOVEMBER 1848 – Edward Carpenter, the shepherd dies. Carron reads the burial service.

27TH NOVEMBER 1848 – The last horse is killed for food.

28TH - 30TH NOVEMBER 1848 – The high heat and humidity turns the flesh putrid.
The horse flesh is eaten in its rotting state.
The starving survivors eat the hide of the horse.

1ST DECEMBER 1848 – Carron sights the "Bramble" heading south.
Carron hoists a flag on a hill to attract the ship's attention.
At dusk he lit a fire and fired 3 rockets and a pistol.

2ND DECEMBER 1848 – Carron packs his equipment as he sees a boat launched.
He climbs back up the hill only to see the "Bramble" sail away.

4TH DECEMBER 1848 – Carron and Goddard collect shellfish on the beach.

7TH DECEMBER 1848 – Carron and Mitchell collect shellfish on the beach.

9TH DECEMBER 1848 – Carron trades a knife and shirt for a few fish scraps and nondas from the aborigines. Goddard ill with Malaria.

10TH DECEMBER 1848 – All the survivors are suffering from Malaria. Prayers Sunday.

11TH DECEMBER 1848 – Aborigines trade turtle scraps for fish hooks.

13TH DECEMBER 1848 – Mitchell found dead in the morning with his feet in the creek.

15TH DECEMBER 1848 – The tent is flooded by heavy rain.
The thermometer breaks.

16TH DECEMBER 1848 – Heavy rain. Natives trade fish and turtle scraps.

21ST DECEMBER 1848 – The kangaroo dog is killed and eaten.
They drank its soup water.

24TH DECEMBER 1848 – Wall is so weak that a black steals a tin from out of his hand.

26TH DECEMBER 1848 – The blacks mock the whites by offering them rotten fish scraps.

28TH DECEMBER 1848 – Niblett and Wall died in the morning.
They are put in a gully and covered with branches.

29TH DECEMBER 1848 – Goddard shoots 3 pigeons. They eat one for dinner.

30TH DECEMBER 1848 – They eat the remaining 2 pigeons in the morning.
They boiled weak tea from the used tea leaves.
Goddard goes into the bush to find pigeons to shoot.
Carron fires a warning shot as natives approach the camp.
One of them gives Carron a note.
Carron is overjoyed and gives the native a shirt.
The natives do not realise the note is a "Message Leaf".
Carron writes a note in reply and gives it to the native.
The native suddenly realises the note is a message.
He throws the note and shirt to the ground in contempt.
He joins his tribe who are preparing to attack the camp.
Suddenly Jackey and the rescue party arrive.
Carron and Goddard are helped down to the beach.
They are put on board the "Ariel" and attended by Dr Vallack.

31ST DECEMBER 1848 – The "Ariel" departs for Sydney.

5TH MARCH 1849 – The "Ariel" arrives in Sydney over 2 months later.

I incline to the belief, founded on personal contact with the Australian aborigines, that their "Murderous Propensities" have no higher motive than mere sportsmanship, their instinct is to ambush and kill their game, and to a race of cannibals human strangers are big game, and nothing more ...

Unless the savages of three centuries ago were of milder manners than their descendants of today, I believe that they would have been tempted beyond their strength if ever they saw strangers at their mercy.

[Cape York Explorer – Robert Logan Jack. "Northmost Australia" Page 336 – 1920.]

THE VOYAGE OF THE SCHOONER "ARIEL" AND HER SEARCH FOR SURVIVORS OF THE ILL FATED KENNEDY EXPEDITION LEFT AT THE CAMPS AT SHELBURNE BAY AND WEYMOUTH BAY – 1848

2ND OCTOBER 1848 – The "Ariel" leaves Sydney to re-supply Kennedy at Cape York.

27TH OCTOBER 1848 – The "Ariel" arrives at Port Albany, Cape York.

23RD DECEMBER 1848 – Jackey is rescued at Port Albany, Cape York, by the "Ariel".

24TH DECEMBER 1848 – The "Ariel" leaves Port Albany and heads south. The "Ariel" anchors 5 miles south of Shadwell Point.

25TH DECEMBER 1848 – A native canoe approaches and an aborigine is allowed on board. Jackey identifies him as the one he gave his knife to. The longboat catches the canoe and Barratt is speared in the arm.

26TH DECEMBER 1848 – The "Ariel" anchors at Shelburne Bay. Near false Puddingpan Hill. Captain Dobson observes natives on the beach wearing blue shirts.

27TH DECEMBER 1848 – The searchers land at 3 different places but fail to find the camp. A part of a cloak found in a canoe belonging to the 3 lost men.

28TH DECEMBER 1848 – The search is abandoned and the "Ariel" leaves Shelburne Bay.

29TH DECEMBER 1848 – The "Ariel" anchors at the Pascoe River mouth at Weymouth Bay.

30TH DECEMBER 1848 – The rescue party arrives as aborigines prepare to attack the camp. Only 2 of the 8 men left at this camp are found alive. They are assisted to the beach and put on board the "Ariel".

31ST DECEMBER 1848 – The "Ariel" leaves Weymouth Bay and heads for Sydney.

5TH MARCH 1849 – The "Ariel" arrives in Sydney.

VOYAGE OF THE BRIG "FREAK" AND THE SEARCH FOR THE THREE MEN LEFT AT SHELBURNE BAY PLUS THE REMAINS OF EDMUND KENNEDY AND HIS JOURNALS – 1849

3RD MAY 1849 – The "Freak" anchors at Weymouth Bay at the Pascoe River. Searchers find the remains of Wall and Niblett, and taken aboard.

4TH MAY 1849 – The "Freak" anchors at Shelburne Bay.

5TH MAY 1849 – Coastline checked from Roundpoint to Helby Hill in a whaleboat. Pistol holster marked 34 found in a native canoe on the beach. Boat crew landed at 3 different places and fired a musket.

6TH MAY 1849 – Continued search. Met 30 natives on the beach.

7TH MAY 1849 – Captain Simpson boards Schooner "Coquette" and meets Captain Elliott.

8TH MAY 1849 – Captain Elliott lends additional boats to search for Kennedy's body.
2 Boatloads of searchers row up the Escape River for 11 miles.
The searchers land where the river tapers to a freshwater stream.
Jackey guides the searchers to the scrub where he buried Kennedy.
Searchers use ramrods attempting to find the body unsuccessfully.
Searchers return to river mouth and camp at Shadwell Point.

9TH MAY 1849 – Searchers find part of Kennedy's red cloak in a canoe.
Searchers return to the ships at 10am.
Ships leave the Escape River and arrive that night at Port Albany.

11TH MAY 1849 – Chief Officer McNate takes Jackey up the Kennedy Inlet.
Jackey finds Kennedy's "Papers" severely water damaged.

SUNDAY 13TH MAY 1849 – Remains of Wall and Niblett buried on Albany Island.

CHAPTER 27
SEQUENCE OF EVENTS
"THE JARDINE CATTLE DRIVE"

THE JARDINE CATTLE DRIVE FROM ROCKHAMPTON TO SOMERSET, CAPE YORK – 14TH MAY 1864 - 13TH MARCH 1865

NOTE: [1] *Numerals in brackets signifies the cattle camp.*

14TH MAY 1864
Alec Jardine leads 7 men and 31 horses from Rockhampton to Bowen.

17TH JUNE 1864
They arrive at Bowen.

16TH JULY 1864
Frank Jardine and Surveyor – A J Richardson arrive at Bowen by sea.
Frank Jardine purchases 6 additional horses.
Surveyor Richardson purchases 5 Government horses.

17TH AUGUST 1864
Alec Jardine leads advance party with horses to Carpentaria Downs Station.

30TH AUGUST 1864
They arrive with the horses at Carpentaria Downs Station.

3RD SEPTEMBER 1864
Alec and Eulah [aboriginal] explore the land ahead for 180 miles.
They are accompanied by Henry Bode looking for cattle country.

21ST SEPTEMBER 1864
They returned after covering 360 miles in 18 days.

6TH OCTOBER 1864
Frank Jardine arrives at Carpentaria Downs with the cattle [1].

7TH - 9TH OCTOBER 1864
Frank and Alec shoe the 41 horses and mule in 100° fahrenheit.

11TH OCTOBER
The expedition leaves Carpentaria Downs for Cape York.
The Jardines arrange to meet the cattle at the "Swamp".
The cattle do not arrive by 9pm and the Jardines camped alone.
The aboriginal guide "Eulah" has lost his direction.
The expedition is heading the wrong way. They halt and camp [2].

12TH OCTOBER 1864
The Jardines find them next day and camp near water [3].

13TH OCTOBER 1864
A packhorse called "Postman" falls upside down in a creek.
The pack is cut off as he lay with his feet kicking in the air.
They covered 11 miles today and camped near water [4].

14TH OCTOBER 1864
They arrived at the junction of Canal Creek [5].

15TH OCTOBER 1864
Arrived "Cawana Swamp" with plenty of grass for the stock.

16TH OCTOBER 1864
Whilst leaving "Cawana Swamp" they are tracked by aborigines.
* About 50 armed warriors painted for war threaten them.
The cattlemen turn on the "aggressors" who then retreat.
They camped at "Cowderoy's Bluff", named after one of the group [7].

17TH OCTOBER 1864
The cows begin calving. 2 Cows fell off the rocks and are killed.
The weak calves are killed. One cow lost. Camped at Parallel Creek [8].

18TH OCTOBER 1864
Continued N-W down Parallel Creek for 10 miles.
Saw some natives at a waterhole cooking fish.
They are described as puny, skinny creatures with 30 dogs [dingoes].
Lost one horse. Stock forced along villainous rocky bend.
Camped on the dry bed of Parallel Creek. No grass [9].

19TH OCTOBER 1864
Today they found the freshly cooked remains of a black man.
The body was chopped up near the fire and roasted for eating.
Camped near the Einasleigh River which was 700 yards wide [10].

20TH OCTOBER 1864
This river was mistaken for the "Lynd" by Richardson.
They crossed Galah Creek at its mouth [Martin Creek].
A tree marked V is found. This was Alec Jardines 5th camp [7th September].
The cattle are taken 5 miles further and camped at 9pm [11].
There is plenty of grass here and a large waterhole.
Whilst the stock feed, the men catch fish [cod, perch and lobster].

21ST OCTOBER 1864
They followed the river down for 10 miles [Einasleigh] W.N.W.
2 Blacks fishing, take to the river, howling as whites arrive.
One cow too weak to travel was abandoned down the track.
The camp is set up on the river bank and all went fishing [12].

22ND OCTOBER 1864
They followed the river for another 10 miles W.
Here they halt for several days to revive the cattle and horses.
The camp is erected near good grass and a narrow creek [13].
They had now travelled 120 miles from Carpentaria Downs.

23RD OCTOBER 1864
2 Calves are killed and jerked for food.
The cattlemen spend the day repairing saddles etc. [13].

24TH OCTOBER 1864
Frank, Alec and Eulah cover 28 miles exploring the route ahead.
They camped near a lagoon and caught some fish.
They are supposed to be on the Lynd River, but obviously are not.
They realise that the Surveyor, Richardson has made an error.
This day they have travelled over 30 miles exploring the area.

26TH OCTOBER 1864
At an abandoned native camp they found part of a saddle girth?

27TH OCTOBER 1864
Returned to the lagoons where they caught fish and shot pigeons.
They cut a tree line for 18 miles to guide the cattle on.
They return to the main cattle camp.
Frank Jardine confronts Richardson over his serious mistake.

Richardson refuses to admit to any error in his calculations.
From this day, the Jardines cease to consult Richardson.

28TH OCTOBER 1864
Remained in camp checking equipment for the next days trek [13].
Cattlemen told to move the herd on the 31st and camp at lagoons.

29TH OCTOBER 1864
Frank, Alec and Eulah head north to trace the Lynd [Red River].
They camp on the lagoons at the end of the marked tree line.

30TH OCTOBER 1864
They explored the land for over 40 miles to the north west.

31ST OCTOBER 1864
A large goanna was killed and eaten for dinner.
At 6.15 they headed N.W. crossing several creeks as horses tire.
They then head S.W. for 16 miles and camped without water.
The cattle were moved today and they camped halfway on cut [14].

1ST NOVEMBER 1864
The cattle are moved along the cut treeline to the lagoons.
The Jardines again moved S.W. and watered the horses in a creek.
They followed this creek for 8 miles N.W.
They left this creek and headed south for 16 miles.
They reached a dry creek and dug for water.
They camped and watered the horses after striking water.

2ND NOVEMBER 1864
They continued south for 18 miles and reach the Lynd [Red River].
They follow it for 16 miles to their camp of the 26th October.
Here they camped and caught a goanna, possum and 4 cod fish.

3RD NOVEMBER 1864
They followed the creek for another 16 miles to the lagoons.
Upon arrival at the camp they killed a calf and ate a good meal.
The cattlemen found to have "Sandy Blight" [Opthalmia].

4THE NOVEMBER 1864
Frank and Alec mark a line of trees for 5 miles to the next creek.
At this camp a horse "Belle" dies from snake bite [Belle Creek] [16].

5TH NOVEMBER 1864
This morning 16 horses were missing. One party searches for them.
Frank and Alec mark a tree line for 15 miles to Maroon Creek [17].
The cattle follow behind along the tree line.
The brothers dig for water unsuccessfully. It is a dry camp.
Frank and Alec are worried that there is something wrong at Camp 16.
By evening the packhorses and men have still not arrived.
The delay is caused by a grass fire that swept through Camp 16.
Most of their food and supplies are destroyed.
The Jardines spend the night watching the thirsty cattle.

6TH NOVEMBER 1864
The Jardines cut a tree line to a watered creek [Cockburn Creek[.
The thirsty cattle are moved north to Cockburn Creek [18].
The cattle feed on good grass and fresh water.
They catch several fish in the creek, their first meal in 24 hours.

7TH NOVEMBER 1864
They waited all day for the packhorses which failed to arrive.
That evening they caught 3 possums and some fish for dinner.

8TH NOVEMBER 1864
A calf is killed for food and portions eaten for breakfast.
About 30 cattle missing [no mention if they were found or not].

9TH NOVEMBER 1864
As the packhorses have not arrived Alec goes back to find them.
He meets them halfway to Camp 16 and learns of the fire.
"Maroon" a valuable horse dies from poison bush or snake bite.

10TH NOVEMBER 1864
Frank, Alec and Eulah leave the cattle party to mark the route.
They head N.W. down Cockburn Creek marking 3 camps 7 miles apart.
After 25 miles they found 2 small lagoons on the west bank.
A "Stop" sign is cut into trees on both sides of the creek.
They leave instructions for the cattlemen to halt here.
They continue for a mile down the creek and camp.
The cattlemen arrive at the first marked camp [19].

11TH NOVEMBER 1864
The Jardines check the route ahead for 13 miles down the creek.
They halt as one of their horses is too weak to continue.
They hunt for food, catching a goanna, a bandicoot and 3 possums.
They also find 3 nests of "Sugar Bag" [native honey].
The cattle arrive at the 2nd marked camp.

12TH NOVEMBER 1864
The Jardines now left the creek and headed N.N.W. for 9 miles.
They crossed 2 sandy watercourses ½ a mile apart running west.
Heading N.W. they noted floodmarks 4 feet up the tree trunks.
As they headed N.W. they saw there was no grass for 16 miles.
They finally reached a creek [Maramie Creek] and camped.
The cattle arrive at the 3rd marked camp [21].

13TH NOVEMBER 1864
The Jardines followed Maramie Creek west for 25 miles.
Found the fish poisoned by aborigines in different waterholes.
They camped at Maramie Creek and caught Maramie for dinner.
The cattle arrive at the "Stop" sign and camp [22].

14TH NOVEMBER 1864
The Jardines leave Maramie Creek and pass a swamp 8 miles south.
They continued for another 17 miles and saw blue lilies in a lagoon.
A mile further and they reached the Staaten River.
They were now 18 miles below the Cockburn Creek junction.
Aborigines seen at the lily lagoon now followed them.
The blacks followed the whites for 3 miles along the river bank.
* Suspecting an attack, the Jardines turned and confronted them.
The aborigines retreat and no one is hurt.
The Jardines followed the river for another 5 miles and camped.
They caught 2 turtles for dinner in the river.

15TH NOVEMBER 1864
They followed the river east, to the Cockburn Creek junction.
Headed up Cockburn Creek to the cattle camp at lagoon "Stop" sign.
The cross country route to Maramie Creek is abandoned.

16TH NOVEMBER 1864
The cattle are moved down Cockburn Creek.
A cow and steer are poisoned by a noxious week and abandoned.
A horse "Marion" is also poisoned but managed to keep up.
Continued 12 miles along the river and camped [23].

17TH NOVEMBER 1864
The dying horse "Marion" is abandoned as they follow Cockburn Creek.
Scrutton is bitten by a scorpion several times at this camp [24].
3 Cows that calved at Camp 22 escaped on Barney's watch.

18TH NOVEMBER 1864
The cattle are moved down Cockburn Creek to the Staaten junction.
The green tree ant is very numerous in this region.
Another sick cow is abandoned as they follow the Staaten west.
They camped this night in the dry bed of the Staaten [25].

19TH NOVEMBER 1864
Headed slightly inland parallel with the Staaten to avoid gullies.
Richardson [Surveyor] mistakenly believes they are on the "Mitchell".
Frank Jardine believes they are south of the "Mitchell River".
As they are definitely on the Staaten, Jardine is correct.
They cover 11 miles and camp at a lagoon [26].

20TH NOVEMBER 1864
Headed the cattle for 9 miles parallel with the Staaten.
They are forced to a halt in a thunderstorm.
The tents are pitched to protect the rations.
✷ Aborigines prepare to attack as the sun comes out.
As the Jardines are cutting out a "Sugar Bag" they hear a warning.
A man yells out "Here come the niggers" as they prepare a defence.
20 Aborigines send in a shower of spears from the setting sun.
The blacks retreat as the whites retaliate with gunfire.
There were no casualties among the cattlemen in this conflict.
The aborigines could be heard at night around the camp [27].

21ST NOVEMBER 1864
In the morning 13 horses are missing.
The aborigines had chased them around the countryside.
The cattle are headed further down the Staaten to a lagoon.
By 4pm the horses are still not found.
The saddles and packs are put on remaining horses.
These horses are walked to the cattle camp at the lagoon [28].

22ND NOVEMBER 1864
Throughout the day 5 of the missing horses were found.
Frank Jardine rides 6 miles ahead in search of a better route.
On his return he is attacked by a dozen aborigines.
As he turns he sees 6 spears thrown at him. He fires a warning.
As they still threaten him he fires and hits one of them.
They retreat in panic, dropping their spears.

23RD NOVEMBER 1864
The Jardine's best tracker "Sambo" finds the mule.
Peter finds aboriginal tracks where they chased the horses.
The cattle cannot proceed till the horses are found.
The blacks wait like hawks for an opportunity to kill the whites.

24TH NOVEMBER 1864
Frank and Eulah find 5 horse "Wild as hawks with broken hobbles".
The 2 best packhorses "Creamy and Cerebus" are still missing.
All 4 aboriginal stockmen continue searching for the 2 horses.

25TH NOVEMBER 1864
A steer shot the previous night is smoked in a tent with dung.
At this camp they all suffered heavily from mosquitoes and flies.
Crows and kites [hawks] steal the meat as it is cooking on the fire.
Many are killed with sticks and spears as they attack the fire.

26TH NOVEMBER 1864
During the night 15 cattle strayed from the camp.
Whilst searching for them Frank found "Creamy and Cerebus".
Only 7 of the missing cattle were found.
Aborigines could be heard around the camp throughout the night.

27TH NOVEMBER 1864
In the morning Frank rode ahead to mark the next camp.
He passed several lagoons and marked the camp site after 9 miles.
He now searched for the missing cattle near the Staaten River.
"Cerebus" was also missing this morning and never found.
* Whilst searching a gully a spear shot within 6 inches of his face.
He instantly fired at the man who threw it, killing him.
The natives retreated after observing the death of their comrade.
The cattlemen had also been attacked but repulsed the aggressors.
In this conflict they had killed several of their attackers.
The cattle were driven further down the Staaten and camped [29].

28TH NOVEMBER 1864
Thy now gave up all hope of finding the 8 lost cattle and "Cerebus".
The cattle were herded another 9 miles downriver and camped [30].

29TH NOVEMBER 1864
They continue to follow the river as the land improves slightly.
Another cow is lost and cannot be found.
A small terrier dog "Lottie " is also lost.
After travelling for 10 miles along the Staaten they camped [31].

30TH NOVEMBER 1864
The cattle continue west following the river, near the lagoons.
A native stockman "Peter" is sent back to search for "Lottie".
The termite mounds were up to 15 feet high in this area.
Frank shoots an emu for dinner.
Peter returns in the evening unable to find "Lottie".
The expedition camps within ½ a mile of Maramie Creek junction [32].

1ST DECEMBER 1864
The cattle are crossed through Maramie Creek junction.
They passed 2 parties of aborigines peacefully fishing.
After covering 10 miles down the north bank, they camped [33].

2ND DECEMBER 1864
Richardson finally admits this river [Staaten] is not the "Lynd".
He also acknowledges that the "Mitchell River" is to the north.
The Jardines name this river the "Ferguson" [Staaten] not accepted.
The expedition covered 11 miles and camped [34].

3RD DECEMBER 1864
Continued west down the river and halted by a thunder storm.
After the storm passed a steer is shot and cut up for jerking.
The surrounding area is a quagmire after the storm.
The horses bog in the mud, and pulled out.
A shovel nosed shark is caught and jerked with the beef.
Alec Jardine explores the river for 7 miles and sees crocodile tracks.
The river was salty and ½ a mile wide where he turned back.
The grass improved slightly at this camp [35].

4TH DECEMBER 1864
Continued jerking the beef, shark and a few cat fish.
The stores are unloaded and repacked for the northern trek.
They move 3 miles downriver to good grass near the mangroves.
This short journey allowed the stores to settle in the packs.
From this camp they prepared for the northern run [36].

5TH DECEMBER 1864
They finally turned their backs on the Staaten and head north.
The cattle are halted after 13 miles with plenty of grass.
A pool of slimy green water is found 2½ miles N.N.W. of the camp.
Enough water for dinner is brought back to the camp in billys.
As this is a dry camp the cattle must do without water [37].

6TH DECEMBER 1864
In the morning 28 horses are missing from the camp.
The cattle are moved to the green watercourse.
12 horses are found and brought to the watercourse.
The horses are taken back to Camp 37 to carry the packs.
The mule with his valuable pack wanders away unobserved.
The aboriginal "Sambo" sets out to track him.
Whilst searching for better water Frank and Alec find horse tracks.
After tracking them for 8 miles in 100 deg fahr they found 6 horses.
They followed more tracks back to Camp 35 and found 3 more.
Once again they camped on the Staaten waiting for the dawn.

7TH DECEMBER 1864
They searched up and down the Staaten for the other horses.
They returned to the cattle camp with the 9 horses found.
They now learn that only 2 other horses have been found.
"Sambo" returns delirious after not having water for 2 days.
He had tracked the mule to Camp 35 [it had been galloping].
"Eulah and Barney" continue searching for the 5 lost horses.

8TH DECEMBER 1864
Frank Jardine explores ahead for 18 miles looking for water.
Alec and "Sambo" continue the search for the mule.
They find 3 of the lost horses 14 miles from their camp [38].
The saw another horse "Lucifer" near Camp 35 galloping upriver.
They tracked him for 6 miles till dark forced them to camp.

9TH DECEMBER 1864
The next day they met "Eulah and Barney" who had also seen Lucifer.
"Sambo and Barney" to continue the search for the mule.
Alec takes "Eulah" to search for the mad horse "Lucifer".
The 3 recovered horses are left at last night's camp.
They found him, but could not catch him as he galloped away.
They were convinced he had gone mad from drinking salt water.
They returned with the 3 lost horses to the cattle camp.

10 DECEMBER 1864
Frank Jardine takes "Eulah" to search for the 2 lost horses.
They travel through 40 miles of desolate country and camp.

11TH DECEMBER 1864
They again found the tracks and followed them to Camp 33, at dusk.
They'd had no water in 2 days and now quenched their thirsts.
"Lucifer" is seen within 30 yards of where the horses are feeding.
Frank tries to catch him but he again gallops away, at sundown.
As it is now dark they let him go and camp for the night [Camp 33].
Meanwhile Alec has found water 8 miles N.N.W. of the cattle camp.
"Sambo and Barney" return to the cattle camp without the mule [38].

12TH DECEMBER 1864
"Lucifer" was again tracked and when found he was white with sweat.
His tracks showed he had galloped for 13 miles throughout the night.
As he was mad from drinking salt water he was finally abandoned.
They now searched for "Deceiver" the last of the lost horses.
Shortly after finding his tracks they found him dead from thirst.
"Lucifer and Deceiver" were their best riding horses.
The mule is also abandoned with its cargo of dried food etc.
The greatest loss is their only spade used to dig for water.
Scrutton and Cowderoy are ill from the water at the cattle camp [38].

13TH DECEMBER 1864
Whilst exploring ahead Frank finds a "Rocky Creek" [Leichardt ?].
The cattle are moved to "Rocky Creek", bypassing Alec's waterhole.
They are then taken a mile up the creek to clear fresh water.
After 13 miles they all drank and washed in clean water .
Birds, as dense as a flock of sheep stalk the marine plains.
A barramundi is caught and 6 whistling ducks shot for dinner [39].

14TH DECEMBER 1864
Headed the cattle north east and carried spare water, if needed.
After travelling 5 miles they crossed a small creek and waterhole.
They continued N.E. through gullies thick with pandanus palms.
After another 9 miles they camped at a creek [Dunbar Creek] [40].

15TH DECEMBER 1864
The cattle are headed N.E. in the early dawn under moonlight.
After 19 miles they camp without water, Eulah searches ahead.
He finds a beautiful creek with green grass and open country.
The cattle are moved the 3 miles to the creek and the camp erected.
It was named "Eulah Creek" [Magnificent Creek] [41].

16TH DECEMBER 1864
The cattle are headed 6 miles through dense scrub and creeks.
Frank and Alec cut a track through dense scrub for the cattle.
* The Aborigines arrive and threaten the Jardines.
With raised spears they dare the Jardines to come closer.
The Jardines oblige and force them back across the river.
The blacks return and surround the whites determined to kill them.
In their attempt to kill the Jardines, 9 of the attackers die.
The Jardines explore ahead for 7 miles and reach the Mitchell River
They observe native dams and weirs made of matted vines and palms.
They return to the cattle camp [42].

17TH DECEMBER 1864
The cattle are moved to the mainstream of the Mitchell River.
The cattle were crossed at this branch and headed 5 miles on.
They now crossed the 2nd branch which was 450 yards wide.
The cattle are headed another 2 miles and camped [43].
A fat cow dies from a poisonous herb. A wallaby is shot for dinner.

18TH DECEMBER 1864
The cattle were moved downstream for 9 miles to the main river.
They forged through ana-branches, gullies and vinescrub and rested.
Here the river was 30 yards wide, very deep and running too fast.
Frank, Alec and Eulah headed downriver to find a better crossing.
About 80 aborigines cross the river intending to kill them.
* The horseman cantered towards the camp as spears flew past them.
Unable to outrun their assailants, they turned and fired into them.
The cattlemen arrive and join the battle, repulsing the attackers.
Frank Jardine halts the firing and allows the aborigines to retreat.
Whilst heading back to the cattle, a spear almost hits Scrutton.
The native under the river bank, who threw it, is shot in reply.
Through their own violence the aborigines had lost 30 dead.
The Mitchell was finally crossed in safety and they camped [44].

19TH DECEMBER 1864
The surrounding country showed floodmarks from 5 to 15 feet high.
They estimate the river could be 8 miles wide in flood time.
The cattle were moved down the river for 13 miles and camped [45].

20TH DECEMBER 1864
Continued on a parallel with the river about 4 miles inland.
Headed through the tea tree flats with large melon holes.
Heavy wind and rain throughout the night. The ground is a quagmire.
They lost 2 more head of cattle [possibly by poison scrub].
After travelling 11 miles, W.N.W. they camped [46].

21ST DECEMBER 1864
The rain continued day and night almost unabated.
The cattle are moved down the river in pouring rain.
At sundown the blacks were seen stalking the whites at the camp.
They used green boughs for cover as they moved closer.
* The cattlemen approached them and they moved back.
Occasionally the men would give a spurt causing them to retreat.
This game of cat and mouse continued for 2 miles till dark was nigh.
They returned to camp laughing about their blank run.
The camp was situated near a lagoon a mile from the river [47].

22ND DECEMBER 1864
They finally left the Mitchell River and headed N.W.
After 15 miles they set up camp and a steer was shot for food.
It rained heavy throughout the night with a cold bitter wind.
The steer was cut up and partly jerked during the night [48].

23RD DECEMBER 1864
The cattle headed N.W. in the morning as the sun emerged.
Scrutton and Binney stay behind to finish jerking the beef.
After travelling 12 miles through wretched country they halt.
This is flat sandy country that absorbs the rain when it falls.
A little water is found in a creek 1½ miles ahead.
This is a dry camp and the cattle and horses are watched [49].

24TH DECEMBER 1864
The cattle were again moved to the N.W. for 7 miles.
At this point they would be a little south of the Edward River.
The camp was erected near a patch of course grass.
As the cattle had not had any grass in 2 days they ate it.

25TH DECEMBER 1864
Although this was Christmas Day they had to keep moving N.N.W.
The wet season had now well and truly settled in on this day.
After 4 miles they passed through a creek [Balourgah].
After another 7 miles they passed a similar creek [Christmas].
In pouring rain Frank Jardine wished them all "A Merry Christmas".
At this creek he cut into a tree "XMAS 1864" in a square.
After 15 miles they camped at a well watered creek [51].

26TH DECEMBER 1864
Today the cattle headed N.N.W. for about 14 miles.
On this day there was no water or creeks and the grass very poor.
They reached a well watered rocky creek 80 yards wide [Hearsey Creek].
This creek was named after W Hearsey Salmon [a friend of Jardine].
A number of fish were caught for dinner at this camp [52].

27TH DECEMBER 1864
The cattle headed N.W. for about 16 miles, through similar country.
They camped at a small creek. Only the horses and men have water.
The cattle have no water at this camp. This is a dry camp [53].

28TH DECEMBER 1864
The cattle headed north for 5 miles to a creek [Holroyd Creek].
Here the cattle had an abundance of fresh water.
Heading 2 miles further they crossed another [Dunsmuir Creek].
They headed another 4½ miles to a lotus lagoon and camped [Thalia].
With a thunder storm approaching they dig trenches around the camp.
✻ A native stockman warns the aborigines are running the horses.
Frank Jardine jumped on the bare back of his horse instantly.
Alec and Scrutton follow him to confront the attackers.
As spears whistle past them the cattlemen open fire.
The aborigines retreat after several are hit with gunfire.
The storm now broke with thunder and lightning scattering the cattle.
The horses were gathered up and brought back to camp [54].

29TH DECEMBER 1864
All the cattle were found except 10. They head N.N.E.
2 Of the native stockmen are left to find them and bring them on.
They return at night unable to find them.
After 11 miles they camped at a creek well watered with grass.
Frank Jardine decided to stay a full day to find the lost cattle.
They noticed the flood marks were 6 feet high at this camp.
Another heavy storm poured throughout the night [55].
Frank is nervous about staying too long in this flood prone area.

30TH DECEMBER 1864
The cattle remained here today with plenty of green grass.
Scrutton and Eulah go back to search for the lost cattle.
Frank and Alec go north to search for high ground unsuccessfully.
They claim "It must be one sea during the rains".
After 4 miles they found a creek [Macleod Creek].

They returned to camp and went hunting for "Sugar Bag" [honey].
They brought enough back to feed the whole camp.
Scrutton and Eulah return at night without the cattle.
A heavy wind and thunder storm hits the camp at night.
He states: *"The largest trees bent like whipsticks"*.

31ST DECEMBER 1864
The cattle head N.N.W. and crossed Macleod Creek.
They pushed the cattle through boggy tea tree flats.
They reached a flooded creek, [Kendall Creek] coming from the east.
This creeks is named after a friend of Richardson [Surveyor].
Several barramundi and perch are caught in the creek.
Frank Jardine rode ahead and found a crossing for tomorrow's march.
They camped on a rise after covering 12 miles to this spot [56].

1ST JANUARY 1865
The cattle head N.E. for 3 miles and cross Kendall Creek.
After 10 miles from camp they crossed another creek [Sinclair Creek].
They negotiate a devastated forest of fallen trees from the storm.
Several weak horses constantly fall over among the branches.
They reached a creek after 4 miles and camped [New Year's Creek].
This night a heavy thunderstorm broke over the camp [57].

2ND JANUARY 1865
The cattle were permitted to feed last night in the boggy soil.
Again, they are pushed N.E. through boggy ground and fallen forest.
They camped after 16 miles on a grassy rise [58].

3RD JANUARY 1865
Headed the cattle N.N.E. to a well watered creek [Kinloch Creek].
It is named after John Kinloch, Maths Master of Sydney College.
After 8 miles they had to "Bridge a Creek" to cross the cattle.
During the day they observed a variety of bird life and kangaroos.
After another 8 miles they camped on a small water course [59].

4TH JANUARY 1865
The cattle are headed north to a large creek for 5 miles.
They continued for 1½ miles past this creek and camped.
By camping early they were able to dry out the meat and packs.
The horses backs are also sore from carrying wet saddles [60].

5TH JANUARY 1865
For the past 2 nights they have experienced heavy thunderstorms.
The cattle are headed N.E. and reached a large river [Archer River].
This river is named after the "Archer Brothers" of Gracemere.
They crossed the Archer River and its ana-branches.
After travelling 15 miles through the rain they camped [61].

6TH JANUARY 1865
The cattle are headed north over rotten melon hole country.
The trek is hard on the horses as they push through the mud.
In pouring rain they crossed 9 waterless creeks.
After 17 miles they camped on one of these dry creeks [62].

7TH JANUARY 1865
Headed the cattle north across numerous small creeks, mostly dry.
Large termite mounds seen, 18-20 feet high.
After 15 miles they camped in a tea tree gully [63].

8TH JANUARY 1865
Headed the cattle north through undulating forest country.
The final 3 miles was as bad as the Staaten country.
2 More horses [Rasper and Nigress] were found knocked up.
After 18 miles they camped with heavy rain and high winds [64].

9TH JANUARY 1865
The cattle headed north and reach a large river after 10 miles.
A track was cut through the dense scrub to the crossing point.
The Jardines thought the river was the Coen.
Richardson believed, correctly that it was the Batavia [Wenlock].
The Jardines noticed their were crocodiles in the river.
The cattle and horses were crossed in safety.
After 16 miles they camped 6 miles north of the river [65].

10TH JANUARY 1865
Headed north through boggy tea tree flats.
Whilst crossing a small creek 40 cattle sink in the mud.
They bog to their bellies in the underlaying mire.
The horses cross successfully, their loads carried by the men.
They spent most of the day dragging out the cattle with horses.
5 Cows had to be abandoned with only their head and back visible.
4 Other cows refused to cross and were let go.
The total distance today was only 2½ miles.
They camped near the creek in heavy rain [66].

11TH JANUARY 1865
The cattle are headed north through the boggy mire and slush.
After 2 miles they came to a creek, 25 yards wide and flooded.
A track is cut through the vine scrub for the cattle to approach.
A large melaleuca is felled across the creek as a bridge.
The saddles, packs and stores are carried over this bridge.
The cattle swim across. One gets tangled in the vines and drowns.
2 Horses "Jack and Blokus" are swept away by the rapid current.
Both horses are tangled in vines in the middle of the creek.
The men try to pull them across by the ropes unsuccessfully.
Alec Jardine reaches the horses and tries to free them.
Whilst trying to untangle his horse "Jack" a log strikes his head.
Both horses are drowned.
With the cattle across they pushed through rain, bogs and swamp.
Unable to progress through the bogs and slime they turn back.
Several horses are left behind bogged in the mire.
As the creek is only a mile back they head toward it.
Leading their horses through heavy rain they camped on good grass.
This camp is ½ a mile from the creek [67].

12TH JANUARY 1865
This morning they went back to the bogged horses and got them out.
They return to camp and find 4 horses poisoned and one missing.
A yard was built for the horses and all herbs removed from it.
It was too late as 5 more horses die from the poison.
The missing horse "Rasper" is found dead in the creek from poison.
They have now lost 2 horses drowned and 10 poisoned leaving 21.
As there are insufficient horses left, supplies are buried.
The "Cache" included 25 sets of horse shoes and nails.
The site is marked "FJ OVER LXV11 OVER DIG IN HEART".
Frank Jardine writes in his diary "Nil Desperandum Black Thursday".

13TH JANUARY 1865
The cattle are headed N.E. as the men walk with the weak horses.
In some cases even the packs are carried by the party.
They now wear only a shirt and belt as their clothes rot away.
The cattle floundered and bogged every hundred yards.
The men carry the saddles and packs across the bogs, for a ¼ mile.
The weak horses bogged in the mud and were pulled out by the men.
Aborigines follow like wolves, waiting to slaughter their prey.
They camped 10 miles north of "Poison Creek" [68].

14TH JANUARY 1865
The cattle are headed N.E. through bogs and swamp.
With no rain in 24 hours a crust forms on the bogs.
The horses walking over the dry crust, break through and bog.
The slippery crust acts as a slide for the horses.
They are pulled out on their side and dragged along like a sled.
Another 2 horses died from poison, leaving 19.
* The camp is erected in heavy rain and the alarm "blacks" is given.
The "blacks" are unarmed and ordered to leave the area.
They later return heavily armed with spears and clubs.
As the blacks attack the whites open fire hitting 2 attackers.
The aborigines broke their ranks and fled.
On this day they travelled only 8 miles [69].

15TH JANUARY 1865
They remain here another day allowing men, cattle and horses to rest.
A cow is left bogged in the swamp, from the previous day.
A horse "Creamy" is suffering from eating the poison plant.
They spent the day removing pandanus thorns from each others legs.
Rain water runs through the tents 3 inches deep.

16TH JANUARY 1865
Jardine urges the men to cover longer distances each day.
2 Of them asked to camp another day, complaining of sore feet.
This was a life and death struggle and they must keep moving north.
After continued requests their guns were taken from them.
There was now no more grumbling as they all headed north.
Another horse "Combo" died from eating poisonous plants.
By now the men's legs were in a "frightful state".
They were horribly lacerated and infected by the thorny vines.
After 16 painful miles they crossed a large creek [Dalhunty].
Here they camped with a change of clear weather [70].

17TH JANUARY 1865
Headed the cattle north over stony ridges.
2 More horses "Rocket and Creamy" died from the poisonous plant.
As there is no transport for the saddles they are discarded.
The pitcher plant "Nepenthis Kennedya" is first seen today.
After 15½ miles they camp at the Skardon Creek [river] [71].

18TH JANUARY 1865
They push N.E. through the most abominable country imaginable.
They forged through low scrub thickly matted with prickly vine.
A horse was led through the heath creating a track.
The other horses and cattle followed in single file.
The foal of "Nell Gwynne" cannot keep up and is killed for food.
After 12 monotonous miles they camped [72].

19TH JANUARY 1865
The cattle are headed N.E. across the range.
They negotiate numerous boggy creeks.
Horses fall ending "Upside Down" in the creeks.
After 8 miles they reach the summit of the range.
From their camp they saw Shelburne Bay on the east coast [73].

20TH JANUARY 1865
The cattle headed north over scrubby range for 4 miles.
They are abruptly halted by a dense pine and vine scrub.
The Jardines check out a native track, which is too dense.
The cattle are taken back 2 miles and headed east.
They followed along the eastern slope and saw the sea, clearly.
They continued for another 4 miles and camped.
Throughout the day they had trekked only 9 miles.
The latitude was only 1½ miles from Camp 73 to this one [74].

21ST JANUARY 1865
Headed the cattle N.E. along the range [Richardson Range].
They cut their way through thick vine scrub on the creek banks.
They push the cattle through 7 of these scrubby creeks.
At one of these creeks it took 3 hours to cut their way through.
The cows horns were often tangled in the vines and cut free.
One enraged cow was cut free and galloped away and never seen again.
After 8 miles of hacking through this jungle they camped [75].

22ND JANUARY 1865
Headed the cattle N.W. through the same grassless country.
Continued hacking their way through dense vine scrubs.
A track is cut to each creek crossing for the cattle to follow.
After 10 miles they camped in heavy rain with no grass [76].

23RD JANUARY 1865
Headed the cattle N.W. through heavy rain and no grass.
They push through desert wastes of brush and tangled scrub.
Without leggings or boots their feet are torn by scrub and vines.
Their legs have the appearance of having been "curried by a machine".
After 9 miles they found good grass on a creek bank and camped [77].

24TH JANUARY 1865
Headed the cattle N.W. for 2 miles, then halted by a stream.
It had a clear sandy bed, 30 yards wide and running north.
The Jardines and Richardson conclude it must be the "Escape River".
They do not realise it is the head of an unknown river [Jardine].
They keep to the west bank [left] to avoid "the swamps" [presumed].
They cross numerous creeks that discharge into this river.
They continue to cut a track through dense jungle at the crossings.
After 6 hectic miles they were halted by a thunderstorm at a creek.
Whilst clearing a track, the creek flooded so they camped [78].

25TH JANUARY 1865
The cattle headed N.W. across the flooded creek, now almost dry.
Another thunder storm floods a small gutter a few feet wide.
The horses are so afraid of bogs and water, they are led over them.
After 10 miles they camped amid heath and brushwood.
This camp is described as "a miserable hole" [79].

26TH JANUARY 1865
The cattle are headed north west following the rivers course.
Tracks are cut through dense foliage at 4 creek crossings.
They pushed ahead through heavy rain all day for 10 miles.
They are suddenly halted by another large river [McHenry River].
This river joins the supposed "Escape" [Jardine] from the S.E.
It is named after Captain J McHenry of Arthur Downs, Isaac River.
The camp was erected and a crossing selected for tomorrow [80].

27TH JANUARY 1865
The cattle and horses crossed the McHenry in safety [50 yards wide].
The packs, saddles and supplies are carried on the swimmers heads.
The rain filled every creek and gutter mile after mile.
The "Escape River" [Jardine] had now increased to 100 yards wide.
It was 40-50 yards wide at the McHenry junction.
Due to the numerous creek crossings they only made 5 miles.
The country has improved slightly with better grass.
Several trees were marked at the McHenry crossing with a cross.
After pushing through rain most of the day, they camped [81].

28TH JANUARY 1865
Forced the cattle through rain and thick vine scrub for 2½ miles.
Unable to penetrate thick jungle and watercourses near the river.
Cattle constantly get their horns tangled in the hanging vines.
Several enraged cows take off upon being released and are lost.
The cattle are turned west to avoid the thick vine scrubs.
The head into a maze of scrub, heath, bogs and swamp.
They force their way back towards the river after 7 miles.
At this point the river was running north and 150 yards wide.
Through pouring rain they followed the river for another 4 miles.
2 Horses "Tabinga and Pussey" are left 3 miles back totally exhausted.
After 12 miles they killed a lame heifer for food and camped.
The camp was erected 9 miles N.N.E. of Camp 81 [82].

29TH JANUARY 1865
The day was devoted to jerking the beef of the heifer.
The 2 weak horses "Tabinga and Pussey" are brought into camp.
The packs and saddles are checked and found to be mostly rotted.
Richardson plots their position as 16 miles south of Somerset.
He also states they are 8 miles from the Escape River mouth.
Both Jardine and Richardson still believe they are on the "Escape".
The distances are incorrect as the sextant is out of order.

30TH JANUARY 1865
This camp [82] with the cattle was left in charge of Scrutton.
The Jardines and Eulah leave to search for Somerset.
They follow the river for 21 miles expecting it to turn to N.N.E.
They are amazed to find it flowing to the N.W.
Its width varies from 100-200 yards wide.
They followed its windings as it snaked through dense jungle.
This river is obviously on western waters and cannot be the "Escape".
Although they started in fine weather it poured all day after 11am.
After 21 miles they made a gunya and camped in pouring rain.

31ST JANUARY 1865
They continued to follow the river through bogs, creeks and swamps.
After 10 miles they were halted by a large stream.
It flowed from the S.E. and was as large as the McHenry.
Frank Jardine named it the "Eliot". Alec marks "A.J." on a tree.
It was traced back for 2 miles to find a crossing point.
They wade across carrying saddles and packs on their heads.
They head back to the main river [Jardine] through dense jungle.
After travelling all day for 17 miles they camped.

1ST FEBRUARY 1865
In the morning they continued following the river for 7 miles.
They had now followed the river for 45 miles [30 in a line] NW-SW.
They now turned back and camped at the gunya on their first night.
Here they slept after forging through bogs, swamp and pouring rain.

2ND FEBRUARY 1865
Continuing their course they returned to Camp 82 that morning.
Frank Jardine learns that there is a 30Lb deficiency of flour.
The cattlemen deny using and more than their daily rations.
Frank writes "Where it is gone to, I am never likely to know".

3RD FEBRUARY 1865
The brothers and their black boys search for a river crossing site.
They try several places unsuccessfully and return to camp.
Heavy rain pours throughout the day.
They decline to cross from Camp 82 and explore to the east coast.
As the river is still too high the crossing is postponed.

4TH FEBRUARY 1865
The river is still too high to cross and running strong.
The delay gives the horses time to recuperate.
Richardson manages to correct his sextant.
A raft is constructed using a dead nonda tree for its framework.
As the weather cleared a steer was killed for food.
The hide of the steer was stretched over the raft framework.

5TH FEBRUARY 1865
As the river had sunk considerably they attempted to cross.
The saddles and rations are floated across on the raft in safety.
With horses and equipment safely across they headed N.N.E.

6TH FEBRUARY 1865
The party comprising Frank, Alec and Eulah move through heavy rain.
Their purpose is to find the mouth of the Escape River.
After 15 miles they site Newcastle Bay on the east coast.
After 23 miles of mud, rain and jungle, they camped.

7TH FEBRUARY 1865
Today they forced themselves through boggy swamps and dense scrub.
After 8 miles they were halted by a large river ¾ of a mile wide.
They had found the "mouth of the Escape River".
Frank surmised, the river at Camp 82 and the Escape were the same?
He now decided to follow the "Escape".
Again they pushed through swamps, vine scrubs and swollen creeks.
Alec Jardine writes of this jungle maze "too bad to describe"
At one stage 3 hours were consumed cutting through vine scrub.
After 22 miles, they camped, plagued by mosquitoes and sandflies.

Fires burnt all night to keep away the hordes of mosquitoes.
Between the camp and the river are 3 miles of mangroves.

8TH FEBRUARY 1865
They follow the "Escape" outside the mangroves.
The horses are exhausted and are driven ahead of them.
They try 3 times to reach the river but are halted by mangroves.
They pass a black's camp and see heaps of shells and shark bones.
They continued along the crooked course of the river.
They camped and caught a goanna and turkeys eggs for dinner.

9TH FEBRUARY 1865
They followed the winding river through swamp and broken ridges.
From a tree on a ridge they saw Mt Adolphus Island off Cape York [east].
After following the horses for 7 miles they camped.
In their hunt for food they found more turkeys eggs and shellfish.
At this site the river was still salty and 300 yards wide.

10TH JANUARY 1865
Unable to penetrate the mangroves and cross the Escape River.
Turning their backs on the Escape they head for the cattle camp.
They forged through 4 miles of bogs, swamp and pouring rain. S.S.E.
The horses are bogged several times and dragged out by the men.
After 12 miles of bogs, swamps and bloodwood ridges they camped.

11TH FEBRUARY 1865
For the next 6 miles they pushed through more bogs and swamps.
Heavy thunder storms flood the creeks and they swim across.
For the next 6 miles they head through heath and brushwood.
They arrive at the crossing opposite Camp 82 in the evening.
Leaving their 4 horses on the north side they swam across.
During their absence a weak horse "Pussy" died from exhaustion.

12TH FEBRUARY 1865
The cattle are counted and several found to be missing.
The aboriginal stockmen are sent out to search for them.
As they are out of beef "jerky", a steer is killed for food.
As there is only 10Lb of flour left it is held for emergency use.
Due to the damp air the steer is smoked under a shelter.
The horses, saddles and swags are brought back from the north bank.

13TH FEBRUARY 1865
The smoking of the beef is completed.
Frank Jardine and Richardson still believe they are on the "Escape".
Frank believes it will "bend to the east" near the west coast.
They still do not realise they are on a completely different river.
They plan to push the cattle west and round the "non-existent" bend.
The missing cattle are found and brought back to the camp.
Much of today was spent preparing for tomorrow's journey.
4 Pack saddles, 2 police saddles and 2 Jardine saddles are abandoned.
Any equipment not needed is to be left behind.

14TH FEBRUARY 1865
The cattle were moved this morning along the south bank.
Cattle and horses continually bog down in the trench like creeks.
Another weak horse "Tabinga" is abandoned from exhaustion.
This now leaves only 13 horses.
Their loads are now reduced to jerked beef, ammunition and swags.
After 11 miles they camped. Direction N.W. [83].

15TH FEBRUARY 1865
Headed the cattle north west under light drizzly rain.
3 Hours spent pulling half the horses out of a boggy gully.
A weak horse "Lady Scott" cannot carry her pack. It is abandoned.
After 10 miles they camped near the gunya camp of January 30th [84].

16TH FEBRUARY 1865
Headed the cattle N.W. for 8 miles to Eliot Creek.
It had fallen a lot and was now 30 yards wide and 5 feet deep.
The cattle and horses are crossed in safety.
They head 2 miles up to the main river [Jardine] and camped [85].

17TH FEBRUARY 1865
Headed the cattle past the Jardines camp of February 1st.
After 8 miles they camped on the right bank of a large creek.
This broad deep creek joins the river [Jardine] from the S.W. [86].

18TH FEBRUARY 1865
The creek was crossed with cattle and horses a mile upstream.
The saddles and packs are carried across on the men's heads.
The weakened horses are constantly pulled out of bogs.
They negotiate around swamps and bogs running parallel to the river.
As the river turned N.E. they hoped it was the "bend to the east".
After 10 miles they halted and camped. They were also out of meat.
The weakest horse "Lady Scott" barely made it into camp.
A steer is killed for food [87].

19TH FEBRUARY 1865
Today they rested and cut up the beef for jerking it.
A gunya is built to smoke the beef.
The river here, has a rise and fall [tide] of 6 inches.
The river is about a ¼ of a mile wide.

20TH FEBRUARY 1865
Headed the cattle parallel to the river through pouring rain.
They are disappointed as the river turns westward.
After 9 miles they are halted by a large creek, 20 yards wide.
Unable to cross they camped in pouring rain [88].

21ST FEBRUARY 1865
In the morning, the Jardines and old Eulah swam across the creek.
They walked to a high ridge and Alec and Eulah climbed a high tree.
From their lofty perch they saw where the river entered the sea.
Only 3 miles away was the mouth of the river, 2 miles wide.
To the north they saw Prince of Wales Island and Endeavour Strait.
A small island near the river mouth was identified as Barn Island.
After taking a number of compass bearings they returned to camp.
The problem is finally solved. They are on an unknown river.
This is not the "Escape River" and there is no "bend to the east".
Twice they had been deceived in identifying this river.
They therefore, name the river the "Deception" [Jardine].
They arrived back at the cattle camp at sundown in heavy rain.

22ND FEBRUARY 1865
As the cattle cannot cross the flooded creek they return upriver.
After 6 miles the cattle are halted and they camped [89].

23RD FEBRUARY 1865
A steer is killed for food but cannot be "jerked" in the rain.
A bark gunya is erected to smoke the beef, in pouring rain.
The framework for a raft is made from a dead nonda tree.
The hide from the slaughtered steer is stretched over it.
Preparations are made for the 3rd attempt to find Somerset.
It rained heavily all through the day.
As protection against mosquitoes they rub beef fat on their skin.

24TH FEBRUARY 1865
3 Riding and one packhorse are taken across the Deception [Jardine].
The raft with saddles and rations on it is floated across.
Frank, Alec and old Eulah camp on the north bank of the "Deception".
A cold bitter wind forces them to the warmth of the fires.
They savour a concoction of bones and gristle. "Scruttons Soup".
Beef fat is again used against mosquitoes and the cold wind.

25TH FEBRUARY 1865
The brothers and Eulah head N.E. in search of Somerset.
They are halted after 2 miles by a flooded creek ½ a mile wide.
After searching for a crossing they failed to get across.
They tried several different places unsuccessfully.
They decided to wait it out and hope the flood would drop.
After searching the area they found a dry spot for the camp.

25TH - 27TH FEBRUARY 1865
They spent the next 2 days hunting food and a crossing spot.
They ate sweet, black wild grapes.
These grapes took the skin off the lips and tongue.
The creek is named "Cowal Creek" after "Cowal" in N.S.W.

28TH FEBRUARY 1865
This morning the creek has dropped sufficiently to cross it.
At the crossing point it was 15 yards wide with a rapid current.
The horses swim across with their saddles on their backs.
A rope is tied to a tree and the other end tied to the other bank.
The swags and rations are slid down the rope over the creek.
After travelling N.W. for 10 miles they camped.
Frank and Eulah walked to a conical hill and climbed a high tree.
They could now see Newcastle Bay and the "Escape" to the S.E.

1ST MARCH 1865
Again they headed N.E. through heavy rain for most of the day.
At 3pm they saw a group of blacks camped near a small creek.
They unslung their guns ready for any treachery.
As most of them bolted into the scrub, 3 natives stood unarmed.
They held their arms in the air yabbering at the cattlemen.
Eulah suddenly realises that they are saying some English words.
Eulah says: *"Hold on, you hearim that one bin yabber English"*.
Frank and Alec listen and distinctly make out several english names.
They hear: *"Alico, Franko, Dzoko, Johnie, Toby, Tobacco"*.
They point to Somerset and cry out "Kaieeby" [Somerset].
The aborigines [Gudang] guide the party N.E. towards Somerset.
After 7 miles they reached a salt water creek.
Here they met more unarmed aborigines of the same tribe.
The Jardines are given gifts of spears and woomeras.
Continuing N.E. with their black guides they again met the creek.

Here they saw 3 large canoes up to 28 feet long in the mangroves.
They were led for another 2 miles to the Gudang camp [temporary].
They camped with the Gudang and watched a corroboree in the night.
The Jardines kept watch all night in case of treachery.
At daylight they continued N.E. escorted by their "black guards".

2ND MARCH 1865
As only a few guides are needed the others were dismissed.
3 Horses too week to continue are left abandoned temporarily.
Just before midday they sight the settlement of Somerset.
Their black guides set up a yell of excitement.
Even in the heavy rain the commotion can be heard at the residency.
Police Magistrate, John Jardine suspects it is another attack.
With his son John they grab their guns and guard the residency.
They see 2 white men almost naked being escorted by the Gudang.
The men wear emu feather caps, trouser waistbands and moccasins.
Father and sons are finally reunited after 10 months.
After lunch the brothers rowed the whaleboat across Albany Pass.
They swim 3 horses from Albany Island back to Somerset.

3RD MARCH 1865
2 More horses are brought across the pass in the morning.

3RD - 4TH MARCH 1865
They search for a site for the cattle station for 2 days.
They choose Vallack Point which has plenty of grass and water.
The station is only 3 miles south of Somerset.

5TH MARCH 1865
With 5 fresh horses they head back towards the cattle camp.
They are accompanied by their brother John, Eulah and black guides.
They follow a tree line marked by their father in 1864.

6TH MARCH 1865
They arrive at the river near dark and camped on the north bank.
The black guides swim across the "Deception" [Jardine River].
They return with a shoulder of beef given to them by Scrutton.
The 2 guides then consumed the entire shoulder overnight.
Frank states: *"What a hungry native can consume is astounding"*.

7TH MARCH 1865
At first light the Jardines cross the river to the cattle camp.
Frank learns that a number of cattle and 2 horses are missing.
He also learns that the weak horse "Lady Scott" has died.
A steer is killed for food and the black guides feast again.
A raft frame is made from dead nonda and covered with the cowhide.
Several cattlemen search for the missing cattle and horses.

8TH MARCH 1865
The 2 horses and most of the cattle are found except 3.
They decide to wait another day and search for the 3 lost cattle.
The river is still 200 yards wide and flowing fast.

9TH MARCH 1865
As the 3 missing cattle cannot be found they decide to cross.
The nervous cattle are bunched into the river and forced across.
One cow refuses to face it and escapes in the scrub.
The horses were next crossed over in safety.
As "Alf Cowderoy" cannot swim he is left till last.

The raft with its cargo is floated across.
On its last trip he hangs onto the raft as it is taken across.
When only 30 yards from the north bank he upsets the raft.
It sinks with the packs etc.
Cowderoy is saved from drowning and helped ashore with difficulty.
Fortunately the cargo is recovered from the river bed.
The 2 aboriginal guides not wanting to work suddenly disappeared.
With everything safely across, they camped [90].

10TH MARCH 1865
The cattle are headed N.E. to Cowal Creek and crossed in safety.
A weak horse "Ginger" is bogged and pulled out.
She is too weak to continue and is abandoned.
After 11 miles they camped [91].

11TH MARCH 1865
The cattle are headed N.E. along the cut tree line.
It takes 2 hours to penetrate the scrub at Woomerah Creek.
3 Of the horses are totally exhausted.
After 10 miles they camped [92].

12TH MARCH 1865
30 Cattle were found to be missing in the scrub at Woomerah Creek.
2 Of their aboriginal stockmen went in search of them.
Frank and Alec move ahead to find a crossing over Ranura Creek.
Here they met some aborigines and traded for fish.
25 Of the lost cattle were recovered, the other 5 were not found.
They camped at Lake Chappagynyah which was teeming with crocodiles [93].

13TH MARCH 1865
Some of the horses were missing this morning.
They were rounded up and the cattle moved to Lake Baronto.
Here they were met by John Jardine [father].
From here the cattle were taken to Vallack Point, the last camp.
The cattle and men could at last rest at this camp [94].

✱ **ASTERISKS IDENTIFY ABORIGINAL ATTACKS OR THREATENED ATTACKS AGAINST THE CATTLE MEN.**

THE FOLLOWING IS AN EXTRACT FROM "FIGHT NEWSPAPER" 1992 [THE AUSTRALIANS]

The Aborigine Treaty

The ALP has promised a treaty with the aborigines before the end of this year. If you haven't seen what the ALP has on the drawing board you have about 17,000,000 mates. The ALP is keeping it as a surprise. It could be a good idea to have a quick read of the Draft Treaty written after consultation with the Sovereign Aboriginal Coalition at Alice Springs.

1. Recognition of Aboriginal ownership of Australia.
2. The establishment of a separate Aboriginal nation of states.
3. The immediate restoration of all inalienable crown lands, state and national parks, Aboriginal reserves and travelling stock routes of Australia.
4. Negotiation of Aboriginal state boundaries.
5. Recognition of Aboriginal sovereignty of all Aboriginal lands complete with inalienable title in perpetuity.
6. Agree to the requirement that 40% of the total land mass of each Australian state be transferred to permanent Aboriginal title.
7. Australians to pay the Aboriginal nation compensation for the balance of 60% of Australian land not available to aborigines to compensate for the social, physical, and psychological ravages that have been made upon the Aboriginal people. Compensation rates to equal not less than 7% of GDP for the first ten years, 5% for the following ten years and 2.5% of GDP inperpetuity.
8. The establishment of a treaty between Aborigine and non-Aboriginal Australians.
9. Aboriginals to retain soverignity over all land and islands presently known as Australia.
10. Aborigines to be given freedom to manage their own internal and external affairs as a separate nation of people.
11. Aborigines to be given freedom to make Treaties regarding land and sea corridors as would any independent nation.
12. The Aboriginal State to become a self governing state involving separate economic, social and cultural development combining traditional religions and practice.
13. The aboriginal nation to operate an independent legal system subject only to international law.
14. All State Governments will be required to return appropriated land unencumbered to the Aboriginal state.
15. Aboriginal states will impose entry restrictions in classified areas or those areas adjacent to nominated Aboriginal sacred sites.
16. The Aboriginal nation will require the release of all Aboriginal people from prisons and institutions plus the return to the Aboriginal state of all Aboriginal human remains residing in museums plus all Aboriginal artifacts.
17. Together with the total compensation package, the Australian Government will be required to pay a sum direct to the new Aboriginal nation equal to $1,000,000,000 within four weeks of the establishment of the Treaty.
18. The Aboriginal nation will require existing State and Federal Governments to provide permanently all social, political, educational and legal benefits currently enjoyed by other Australians to the Aboriginal people. These benefits will also include welfare payments, the provision of pensions and health benefits. These benefits are to be in addition to the total compensation package.
19. The Aboriginal Bureau of Aboriginal State Affairs will be established to take over the existing Department of Aboriginal Affairs and Aboriginal Development Corporation structures.
20. All towns and cities in the 60% of land mass ceded by Aborigines to the Federal and State Governments, shall, at municipal expense, provide and maintain for Aboriginal use special parklands of not less than twenty acres in area with appropriate sea and river frontages. These parklands will be utilised by Aborigines as centres for religious activities and camping. They will be available for general public use at other times.
21. In urban areas where crown land is not available, suitable land is to be returned to Aborigines on compensation and needs basis. The Aborigines families will occupy this land rate free.
22. Certain urban sections will become new Aboriginal domains involving their own Aboriginal administration and funding and political control.
23. All existing Aboriginal housing Australia-wide shall be transferred complete with deed title by the Australian Government to the new Aboriginal state as part of the compensation package.
24. Three percent of the revenue derived from all mineral and natural resources will be paid to the new Aboriginal nation.
25. Tollgates will be established and erected on all national freeways and highways interconnecting cities and states. One third of 1% of the total annual toll collected will be payable to the Aboriginal nation. Toll rates for consideration will be equal to $2 per car, $3 per vehicle with towing capacity, and 50 cents per motorbike. These tolls are all subject to variations in the consumer price index.

This is the treaty that Charles Perkins talked about on ABC radio AM on 13 March 1992.

SOLUTION

The black lobby and the ALP are dead serious about the treaty, and have already attracted tremendous International support. There are 200,000 aborigines in Australia as at March 1992 (1% of the total population). Is this the treaty Hawke promised before the end of 1992?

We need Citizens Initiated Referendum to sort this one out.

CHAPTER 28
SEQUENCE OF EVENTS
"CAPE YORK AND THE TORRES STRAITS"

Numbers in square brackets such as [11-22] are report numbers whilst dates such as [2nd February 1871] are the dates when the incidents occurred.

* *NAMED BY CAPTAIN WILLIAM BLIGH.*

1597 – A strait between New Guinea and Australia recorded by Cornelius Wyfleit.

1606 – A dutch sailor from the "Duyfken" is killed by aborigines at the Skardon River. This is the first recorded murder in Australia.
Another 9 dutch sailors from the "Duyfken" are murdered by aborigines at Cape Keerweer on the west coast of Cape York.
Luis Vaes De Torres "discovers" the Torres Strait.

18TH APRIL 1623 – An aborigine is captured by dutch sailors from the ship "Pera".

8TH MAY 1623 – Another aborigine is captured by the "Pera".

1644 – Abel Tasman in the "Limmen" explores the west coast of Cape York.

22ND AUGUST 1770 [21ST] – Captain James Cook, claims Australia at Possession Island.

29TH APRIL 1789 – Sailors mutiny on "HMS Bounty." Captain Bligh and 18 others are set adrift in an open boat at Tofua, the friendly islands [Tonga].

28TH MAY 1789 – Bligh reaches Australia and lands on "Direction Island".*

29TH MAY 1789 – Bligh lands on Restoration Island.*

31ST MAY 1789 – Bligh follows the coast north and lands on "Sunday Island".*

1ST JUNE 1789 – Bligh lands on "Lagoon Key".

2ND JUNE 1789 – Bligh passes the "Boydong Cays" and "Pudding-pan Hill".*

3RD JUNE 1789 – Bligh enters the Torres Strait passing Horn, "Wednesday"* and Booby Islands into the open sea.

14TH JUNE 1789 – Bligh reaches Kupang, Timor.

23RD MARCH 1791 – "HMS Pandora" arrives at Tahiti and captures 14 "Bounty" mutineers.

8TH MAY 1791 – "HMS Pandora" leaves Tahiti with her captives caged on deck.

26TH AUGUST 1791 – "HMS Pandora" reaches the northern Barrier Reef and Captain Edwards named the "Murray Islands".

29TH AUGUST 1791 – "HMS Pandora" moves south and strikes the reef, but stays afloat.

30TH AUGUST 1791 – "HMS Pandora" sinks with 31 crew and 4 mutineers [Pandora Entrance].

17TH-19TH SEPTEMBER 1791 – Captain Edwards, with crew and prisoners arrive at Timor.

5TH SEPTEMBER 1792 – "HMS Providence" commanded by William Bligh and her tender "Assistant" attacked by 3 war canoes at Darnley Island [Erub] in the eastern Torres Strait.

10TH SEPTEMBER 1792 – "HMS Providence" attacked by 8 war canoes and "Assistant" attacked by 4 canoes at Tutu [Warrior Island] Torres Strait.

3RD JULY 1793 – 5 Men murdered from the "Hormuzeer" and "Chesterfield" at Darnley Island [Erub].

15TH AUGUST 1834 – The "Charles Eaton" wrecked near Raine Island.

18TH SEPTEMBER 1835 – The "Mangles" commanded by Captain W Carr anchors at Murray Island and identifies a white boy [John Ireland] held captive.

19TH JUNE 1836 – The "HMCS Isabella" arrives at Murray Island.

19TH JUNE 1836 – Captain Lewis orders the natives to hand over John Ireland in exchange for axes, which they do.

20TH JUNE 1836 – The natives reluctantly trade 4 year old William D'Oyley in exchange for axes, under threat of violence.

26TH JUNE 1836 – The "Isabella" leaves Murray Island.

25TH JULY 1836 – The "Isabella" arrives at Aureed Island where Captain Lewis finds the skulls of Europeans from the "Charles Eaton".

12TH OCTOBER 1836 – The "Isabella" arrives in Sydney with the skull shield.

17TH NOVEMBER 1836 – The skulls are given a Christian burial at the Sydney Cemetery in Devonshire Street, now the central railway station.

1904 – The skulls were later re-buried at the Bunnerong Cemetery.

13TH JULY 1837 – Crawford family arrive in Sydney from Scotland as migrants.

20TH OCTOBER 1838 – Captain Bremer names Mt Bremer at Cape York and fires a 21 gun salute from HMS Alligator to commemorate the occasion.

1843 – Barbara Crawford elopes with William Thompson and marries at Moreton Bay.

SEPTEMBER 1844 – The "America" leaves Moreton Bay for the Torres Strait.

DECEMBER 1844 – The "America" is wrecked near Entrance Island, Torres Strait. Barbara Thompson [Crawford] is captured by the Kauraregas.

JUNE 1846 – 4 Sailors from the "Thomas Lord" are murdered by Wini's warriors on an island off Badu.

1846 – Wini's warriors try to kidnap Barbara Thompson at Keriri [Hammond Island].

1848 – Wini's warriors massacre 18 castaways near Badu.
Wini's warriors murder 2 sailors and a boy [castaways] near Badu.

24TH-25TH MAY 1848 – The "Kennedy Expedition" is landed at Rockingham Bay at Tam-o-shanter Point, 20 miles north of Cardwell at the base of Cape York Peninsula.

5TH DECEMBER 1848 – Kennedy is murdered by the Yadagana at the Escape River [13th?].

1848 – Barbara Thompson learns of Kennedy's murder whilst held captive on Prince of Wales Island. Barbara Thompson learns of the ships at Cape York and sends a native messenger pleading for help. He could not be understood.

23RD DECEMBER 1848 – Jackey is rescued at Port Albany by the "Ariel".

30TH DECEMBER 1848 – Carron and Goddard are rescued at the Pascoe River camp.

5TH MARCH 1849 – The "Ariel" with survivors arrives in Sydney.

13TH MAY 1849 – The bodies of Wall and Niblett are buried on Albany Island.

1ST OCTOBER 1849 – HMS Rattlesnake arrives at Cape York [Evans Bay].

13TH OCTOBER 1849 – Barbara Thompson tricks the Kauraregas into going to Cape York, they leave P.O.W. [Muralug] with her and arrive Cape York.

16TH OCTOBER 1849 – Barbara Thompson is rescued at Cape York by sailors from HMS Rattlesnake.

5TH FEBRUARY 1850 – HMS Rattlesnake arrives in Sydney and Barbara Thompson is re-united with her family.

27TH NOVEMBER 1850 – Barbara Thompson marries James Adams in Sydney.

23RD SEPTEMBER 1859 – The "Sapphire" is wrecked near Raine Island and 18 men are murdered by the Kauraregas.

10TH DECEMBER 1859 – Queensland separates from NSW as an independent state.

14TH MAY 1864 – The "Jardine Cattle Drive" starts from Rockhampton.

29TH JULY 1864 – HMS Salamander arrives at Albany Pass [Somerset].

1ST AUGUST 1864 – The Golden Eagle arrives at Albany Pass [Somerset].

21ST AUGUST 1864 – Official founding of the Somerset settlement.

30TH AUGUST 1864 – The Golden Eagle leaves Albany Pass.

7TH SEPTEMBER 1864 – HMS Salamander leaves Albany Pass.

13TH SEPTEMBER 1864 – Aborigines attack the marines wounding 2 [One Critically].

15TH OCTOBER 1864 – 6 Aborigines who speared the marines are killed in a fight with the marines off Albany Island.

22ND DECEMBER 1864 – HMS Salamander arrives at Somerset with stores.

2ND JANUARY 1865 – John Jardine puts a note in a bottle at the Kennedy River to instruct the cattlemen of the route to Somerset.

16TH JANUARY 1865 – Wounded marine [John Saich] departs on "HMS Salamander."

13TH MARCH 1865 – The cattle arrive at Vallack Point Station.

4TH APRIL 1865 – 70 Somerset town lots sold by auction in Brisbane [Final 42].

21ST APRIL 1865 – Wounded marine [John Saich] dies in Sydney.

2ND MAY 1866 – 82 Somerset town lots sold by auction in Brisbane [Final 67].

7TH JULY 1866 – Yadagana attempt to kill Frank Jardine whilst asleep.

1866 – Frank Jardine has a life and death struggle with an aborigine. Yadagana attempt to kill the Jardine brothers in the hut

20TH AUGUST 1866 – 24 Shipwrecked survivors taken south on HMS Salamander.

FEBRUARY 1867 – The Yadagana annihilate the Ambagana and Gumukudin tribes.

15TH MARCH 1867 – The Rev. Frederick Jagg arrives at Somerset.

1ST AUGUST 1867 – 7 White police arrive on HMS Salamander to replace marines.

7TH AUGUST 1867 – The British marines leave Somerset on HMS Salamander.

27TH AUGUST 1867 – Frank Jardine makes peace between the Yadagana and Gudang.

27TH JANUARY 1868 – Frank Jardine becomes Inspector of Police at Somerset.

1ST JUNE 1868 – Frank Jardine becomes Police Magistrate at Somerset.

1868 – School teacher William Kennett fined for obstructing police [45-68].

9TH MAY 1868 – Eulah murdered by Barney, Peter and Sambo, Jardines blackboys.

SEPTEMBER 1868 – Constable Ginivan found drunk on a ship [46-48].

9TH DECEMBER 1868 – HMS Virago arrives with stores and 3 native police [56-68].

1ST JANUARY 1869 – Queensland Government purchases Vallack Pt Station [61-69].

3RD JANUARY 1869 – Frank Jardine applies for leave [64-69].

APRIL 1869 – Kauraregas and Kulkalegas massacre crew of the "Sperwer".

1ST JUNE 1869 – Ex-marine John Smith becomes a Police constable [73-69].

21ST JUNE 1869 – Frank Jardine requests assistance from Captain McAusland to help find the victims of the Sperwer massacre [82-69].

26TH JUNE 1869 – Jardine finds the decapitated victims and reports to the Colonial Secretary about the "Sperwer" massacre [83-69].

28TH JULY 1869 – Jardine goes on leave. Henry Chester takes over [2-69].

10TH AUGUST 1869 – Police Magistrate Henry Chester visits the "Sperwer" wreck near Friday Island and buries 2 corpses [3-69].

25TH AUGUST 1869 – Induyumu aborigines rob the customs house [6-69].

30TH AUGUST 1869 – 10 Crew from the wrecked "Tynemouth" arrive at Somerset [5-69].

14TH SEPTEMBER 1869 – Chester reports supplies being stolen from "Booby Island" [13-69].

30TH NOVEMBER 1869 – Chester reports the kidnapping of natives [18-69].

1ST DECEMBER 1869 – Aborigines kill 2 crew of an 8 ton cutter [24-69].

4TH APRIL 1870 – HMS Blanche arrives at Somerset with stores.

14TH APRIL 1870 – 3 Kulkalegas are shot on Wednesday Island for their involvement in the "Sperwer" massacre [18-70] [6th April].

17TH AUGUST 1870 – Frank Jardine returns to Somerset.

23RD AUGUST 1870 – Frank Jardine takes over as Police Magistrate [40-70].

1ST NOVEMBER 1870 – Jardine builds cattle yards at 16,32 and 50 miles from Somerset with troopers help [50-70].
Frank Jardine reports on atrocities against natives [61-70]

3RD DECEMBER 1870 – 27 Castaways from the wrecked "Freak" arrive at Somerset including women and children [1st December 1870] [65-70].

1870 – Jardine assaults Muralug (POW) white woman hostage murdered.

31ST MARCH 1871 – 6 Native troopers desert from Somerset [2nd February 1871] [82-71].

1ST JULY 1871 – Anchor from the "Reichstag" brought to Somerset [114-71].

10TH AUGUST 1871 – Reverend Murray and McFarlane of the London Missionary Society arrive at Somerset in the "Surprise" [114-71] 11th July 1871.
Captain Banner dies at Warrior Island. Natives plunder the station in a drunken rort [114-71] 22nd July 1871.

MARCH 1872 – Jardine's 10 ton cutter arrives at Somerset [Vampyre].

27TH JUNE 1872 – The kidnapping act passed by the British Government.

24TH AUGUST 1872 – The Queensland border is pushed 60 miles north of Cape York.

11TH OCTOBER 1872 – 47 Missionaries of the London Missionary Society arrive at Somerset, including Sana Solia.

5TH JANUARY 1873 – Kidnapping vessel "Challenge" captured with 33 natives aboard.
Kidnapping vessel "Melanie" captured with 35 natives aboard.

8TH JANUARY 1873 – Kidnapping vessel "Woodbine" captured.
Kidnapping vessel "Chrishna" captured with 35 natives aboard.

25TH MAY 1873 – Government police boat "Lizzie Jardine" arrives at Somerset.

16TH OCTOBER 1873 – Frank and Sana are married by the Rev Murray at Somerset.

11TH NOVEMBER 1873 – James Atkins is murdered by the Yadagana [7-73] [October 1873]. Yadagana defeated as they march on Somerset. Missionaries wives and children rescued from islands [7-73].

NOVEMBER 1873 – Frank and Sana move to Nahgi to commence pearling.

7TH AUGUST 1874 – Kidnapping vessel "Margaret and Jane" seized and brought to Somerset by water police.

EARLY 1870's – Wini shot dead from a police boat off Badu.

APRIL 1875 – French castaway Narcisse Pelatier rescued from New Guinea after 22 years captivity and brought to Somerset.

1ST SEPTEMBER 1875 – Measles enters Somerset wiping out the Gudang [90-75].

9TH SEPTEMBER 1875 – Police Magistrate C D'Oyley Aplin dies at Somerset.

1ST OCTOBER 1875 – A crewman from the "Crinoline" murdered by the Yadagana.

JULY 1876 – Native troopers desert from Somerset.

17TH SEPTEMBER 1877 – Henry Chester appointed Police Magistrate at the new settlement of Thursday Island.

28TH NOVEMBER 1877 – Somerset is sold to Frank Jardine for £150.

24TH JUNE 1879 – All the Torres Strait Islands annexed to Queensland.

28TH FEBRUARY 1890 – RMS "Quetta" sunk off Albany Island. 133 Dead.

1ST MARCH 1890 – Frank Jardine sends the telegraph of the Quetta disaster.

MARCH 1890 – The Jardines shelter dozens of "Quetta" survivors.

18TH FEBRUARY 1891 – Silver treasure found by Lancashire Lass near Murray Island, Torres Strait.

4TH MARCH 1899 – Cyclone "Mahina" kills 300 people and wrecks 61 vessels at Princess Charlotte Bay.

17TH MARCH 1911 – John McLaren collects 550 seed coconuts to commence a coconut plantation at "Utingu" [Simpson Bay].

11TH MAY 1911 – Frank and Sana Jardine leave for "Apia Samoa".

23RD SEPTEMBER 1911 – The Jardines return from Samoa.

30TH DECEMBER 1913 – Frank Jardine purchases land for the Somerset coconut plantation.

1918 – Southern aborigines settle at Cowal Creek.

18TH MARCH 1919 – Frank Jardine dies.

21ST SEPTEMBER 1923 – Sana Jardine dies.

3RD JUNE 1972 – All Somerset land seized by the Queensland Government.

27TH OCTOBER 1986 – Somerset illegally given to the Cowal Creek aborigines as a deed of grant in trust [Dogit].

THE DATE OF THE PROCLAMATION OF AUSTRALIA

When Captain James Cook claimed Australia in the name of King George III, he stood on a small hill on Possession Island, off the west side of Cape York.

The official Date of Proclamation, was written down as the 22nd August 1770. "But was it?"

One of those in the party that landed with Cook was the botanist, Joseph Banks. In his own journal he wrote the date as the 21st August 1770. So who is right?

Although not well known, ships captains wrote the date in their log from midday on one day to midday the next rather than from midnight.

When Captain Cook and his party ascended the hill on Possession Island, it was four o'clock in the afternoon [4pm].

This would be the 4th hour of the 22nd of August in the captain's log but in reality it was the 16th hour of the 21st August as in any ordinary day.

There is another interesting point in relation to this date and that is the date of the official founding of Somerset.

The ships had been anchored in the bay for 3 weeks when it was officially founded as the Town of Somerset and a Port of Refuge on the 21st August 1864.

Why wait 3 weeks to proclaim the site unless a symbolic event of the past was to be commemorated.

I strongly suspect that the date chosen for the official Founding of Somerset of the 21st August was in memory of Cook's "Proclamation of Australia". 21st August 1770.

The date written in the Encyclopaedia Brittanica [P 413] by an academic as the 23rd August 1770, is obviously wrong.

JARDINE CATTLE DRIVE – MAJOR RIVERS AND CREEKS

THE MAJOR RIVERS AND CREEKS NEGOTIATED ALONG THE COURSE OF THE JARDINE CATTLE DRIVE TO CAPE YORK 11TH OCTOBER 1864 – 13TH MARCH 1865

EINNASLEIGH RIVER [CARPENTARIA DOWNS STATION] • PLUTO CREEK
• CANAL CREEK • JUNCTION CREEK • WARROUL CREEK [ELIZABETH CREEK]
• PARALLEL CREEK • GALAH CREEK [MARTIN CREEK] • COOROORA CREEK
• BYERLEY CREEK [RED RIVER] • BELLE CREEK • MAROON CREEK
• COCKBURN CREEK • MARAMIE CREEK • FERGUSON RIVER [STAATEN RIVER]
• ROCKY CREEK • DUNBAR CREEK • ARBOR CREEK • SCRUTTON CREEK
• EULAH CREEK [MAGNIFICENT CREEK] • MITCHELL RIVER
• CHRISTMAS CREEK • BALOURGAH CREEK • HEARSEY CREEK
• HOLROYD CREEK • DUNSMUIR CREEK • THALIA CREEK • MACLEOD CREEK
• KENDALL CREEK • SINCLAIR CREEK • NEW YEAR'S CREEK
• KINLOCK CREEK • ARCHER RIVER • BATAVIA RIVER [WENLOCK RIVER]
• POISON CREEK [NIMROD CREEK] • DALHUNTY CREEK • SKARDON CREEK
• MCHENRY RIVER • ELIOT CREEK • JARDINE RIVER • COWAL CREEK

ORIGIN OF PLACE NAMES

ALICE RIVER	Wife of Frank Johnson, Manager Koolata Station.
McHENRY RIVER	Captain J McHenry, McArthur Downs, Issac R. Station.
JARDINE RIVER	Frank and Alexander Jardine.
ESCAPE RIVER	Mermaid escaped being wrecked at river mouth 1819.
PASCOE RIVER	Lieutenant Pascoe of the British Marines, Somerset.
DUCIE RIVER	Earl of Ducie [ex-Palm Creek].
LOCKHART RIVER	Hugh Lockhart of Edinburgh. Friend of Frank Jardine.
LAURA RIVER	Wife of A C MacMillan.
DEIGHTON RIVER	Undersecretary of Mines.
TATE RIVER	Thomas Tate who survived the wreck of the Maria.
WALSH RIVER	W H Walsh, Minister for Mines.
HANN RIVER	William Hann – Explorer.
LYND RIVER	Robert Lynd of Sydney. Friend of Leichardt.
EMBLY RIVER	J T Embly, Surveyor of Cape York Telegraph.
NORMANBY RIVER	Lord Normanby – Governor of Queensland.
ARCHER RIVER	Archer Brothers of Gracemere Station.
STAATEN RIVER	Named by Dutch Navigator – Carstenzoon – 1623.
NASSAU RIVER	Named by Dutch Navigator – Carstenzoon – 1623.
MITCHELL RIVER	Sir Thomas Mitchell.
COEN RIVER	Named by Dutch Navigator – Carstenzoon – 1623.
BATAVIA RIVER	Named by Van Aschens – Dutch Navigator – 1756.
KENDALL CREEK	Friend of Surveyor Archibald Richardson.
CAMISADE CREEK	Explorer R L Jack speared by aborigines – 1880.
NORTH ALICE CREEK	Frank Jardine's daughter – Alice.
MARIA CREEK	Wreck of the Maria – 25th February – 1872.
STEWART CREEK	A member of the Hann Expedition.
CONN CREEK	Conn family massacred by aborigines.
POISON CREEK	Nimrod Creek – Jardine horses poisoned – 1865.
KINLOCK CREEK	Maths Master – John Kinlock – Sydney College.
COWAL CREEK	Town of Cowal in N.S.W.
HEARSEY CREEK	Friend of Frank Jardine – W Hearsey Salmon.
NOLAN'S BROOK	M J Nolan – Post and Telegraph.
SHADWELL POINT	Lieutenant Shadwell – HMS Fly.
VALLACK POINT	Dr Adoniah Vallack.
FLY POINT	HMS Fly.
YULE POINT	Lieutenant C B Yule of the Bramble.
CAPE MELVILLE	Harden S Melville – Artist on HMS Fly.
CAPE GRENVILLE	Lord Grenville of England.
WEYMOUTH BAY	Lord Weymouth of England.
RATTLESNAKE POINT	HMS Rattlesnake.
KENNEDY INLET	Explorer Edmund Kennedy.

PATERSON TEL ST	Thomas MacDonald Paterson – Postmaster General.
PANDORA ENTRANCE	HMS Pandora – Edwards.
EVANS BAY	Sailing master of the HMS Fly – F J Evans.
STAINER ISLAND	Lieutenant C E Stainer – HMS Dart – 1878.
POSSESSION ISLAND	Captain James Cook claimed Australia – 1770.
CAPE YORK	Duke of York.
SOMERSET	First Lord of the British Admiralty.
MT BREMER	Captain James Gordon Bremer.
MT BARTLEFRERE	President – Royal Geographic Society – 1873.
BERTIE HAUGH	Frank Jardine's son – Bertie Bootle.
MUSGRAVE STATION	Sir Anthony Musgrave – Governor of Queensland.
MEIN TELE STATION	C S Mein – Postmaster General – Queensland.
MT MULLIGAN	Explorer – James Venture Mulligan.
ATHERTON	John Atherton – Cattleman.
MOWBRAY	Warden – William Mowbray.
SMITHFIELD	William Smith-Trepang – Fisher and Packer.

THE NATIVE LANGUAGE

The various languages of the Torres Strait Islands and Cape York have proven to be extremely difficult to translate into English, even by experienced linguists.

The natives of Prince of Wales Island [Kaura-regas] often abbreviated their words and used the abbreviation as if it were the normal pronunciation.

To make matters more confusing, one word can have a host of meanings depending on how it is used.

For example: "Kopi" means a light colour as well as, thigh, good, seed and pretty. "Kopi" is also pronounced "Kapu", "Kappi" and "Kappa" according to the tribe of the individual speaking it.

The earliest recorded name of the inhabitants of Prince of Wales Island was "Kaura-rega" of which "Kaura" means soldier or warrior and "Rega" means people. It literally means "Soldier People".

When an amateur anthropologist wrote the name as "Kaurareg" others followed suit, never realising to this day that they are using abbreviated slang.

In fact, even the correct abbreviated form of "People" was recorded as "Raig" not "Reg", so that the correct abbreviated form of "Kaura-Rega" is "Kaura-Raig" and not "Kaura-Reg".

Further north at Badu, the natives were called "Badu-lega" which was abbreviated to "Badu-Laig". In this case the Badu word for people was "Lega" instead of "Rega".

Both "Lega and Rega" were also pronounced as "Laiga and Raiga", which explains why the abbreviated form was "Laig and Raig".

A similar academic misinterpretation also applies to the "Yadagana" on Cape York of whom anthropologists refer to as "Yadhaigana", "Jathaikana", etc.

As the aborigines used a repetitious vowel in their tribal names then these names have to be wrong. For example a repetitious "A" was used in "Yadagana" and "Ambagana" whilst a "U" was used in "Gumukudin" and "Induyumu" [Unduyumu].

Additional evidence also comes from the Somerset reports in which the abbreviated form of "Yadagana" is "Yadagan".

BIBLIOGRAPHY

THE FOLLOWING BOOKS, MAGAZINES AND NEWSPAPERS WERE SOME OF THE ITEMS RESEARCHED DURING THE WRITING OF THIS BOOK

– BOOKS –

Wreck of the Charles Eaton	Allan McInnes	1983
Narrative of an Expedition	W Carron	1850
The Australian Aborigines	A P Elkin	1938
The Races of Man	A C Haddon	1909
Head Hunters	A C Haddon	1901
Forty Eight Years with the Aborigines	E R Gribble	1930
Artists in Strings	K Rishbeth	1930
Endeavour Journal of Joseph Banks. [ED]	J C Beaglehole	1962
The Life of Captain James Cook. [ED]	J C Beaglehole	1974
Northmost Australia	R L Jack	1920
Owen Stanley R.N.	A Lubbock	1968
Scented Isles and Coral Gardens	C D Mackellar	1912
Voyage of H.M.S. Rattlesnake	J MacGillivray	1852
In Search of Survivors of Charles Eaton	W E Brockett	1836
Narrative of the Charles Eaton	T Wemyss	1884
T. H. Huxley's Diary [Rattlesnake]	J Huxley	1935
Romance of the Great Barrier Reef	F Reid	1954
Cape York to the Kimberleys	G Farwell	1962
Ships in the Coral	H Holthouse	1976
The Holland Family	A Hall	1990
From Spear to Pearl-Shell	P Prideaux	1988
Lizard Island	J Robertson	1981
We and the Baby	H MacQuarrie	1929
Jardine's Journal	F Byerley	1867
Reminiscences of Queensland	W Corfield	1921
The Rifle and the Spear	C Lack	1964
Queensland Frontier	G Pike	1988
The Torres Strait	J Singh	1979
Kennedy of Cape York	E Beale	1970
Myths and Legends of the Torres Strait	M Lawrie	1970
Romances of Gold Field and Bush	S Brown	1891
The Answers Book	K Ham	1993
The Answers Book	A Snelling	1993
The Answers Book	C Wieland	1993
Cambridge Anthropological Expedition to the Torres Strait [1901-1935 Printed]	A C Haddon	[Repr] 1971
Australian Shipwrecks	J Loney	1991
The Pearling Disaster – 1899	Outridge Family	1899

– NEWSPAPERS –

Australian Journal	Sydney	1846 [ML]
Sydney Morning Herald	Sydney	1850 [ML]
Palmer Chronicle	Maytown [Edwardstown]	1885-1889 [JOL]

The Golden Age	Maytown [Edwardstown]	1876 [JOL]
Cairns Post	Cairns	1884-1981 [JOL]
Brisbane Courier	Brisbane	1874-1924 [JOL]
Fight	Maryborough	1992 [CAP]

– MAGAZINES –

Geo Australasia Vol 15 No 4 The Date Debate		1993
Bone of Contention		
Carbon 14 Dating Exposed	S Baker	1981
Revised Quote Book	A Snelling [Ed]	1990
Steads Review	Jardine Treasure	1927
4 x 4 Australia	R Moon	1993
Underwater	H Hofer p 55-57	1990
Nautilus	Jardine Treasure	1955

– DOCUMENTATION –

The Brierly Journals	O W Brierly	1848-1850 [ML]
The Somerset Letter Book	Various Police Mag.	1864-1877 [QSA]
Somerset Land Sales	Brisbane	1865 & 1866 [QSA]
Wreck of the Quetta	E J Lacy	1890 [IL]
Log of the Ariel	Capt. Dobson	12th-13th Dec – 1848 [ML]
Lizzie Watson's Diary	Mary [Lizzie] Watson	1880 1881 [JOL]
Major C R Sheldon	Australian Military Forces	1943-1950 [CA]

ML	*MITCHELL LIBRARY*	*SYDNEY*
JOL	*JOHN OXLEY LIBRARY*	*BRISBANE*
QSA	*QUEENSLAND STATE ARCHIVES*	*BRISBANE*
IL	*IAN LACY*	*MELBOURNE*
CA	*COMMONWEALTH ARCHIVES*	*CANBERRA*
CAP	*CONFEDERATE ACTION PARTY*	*MARYBOROUGH*

DOCUMENTATION RELATIVE TO THE ABORIGINAL INVASION OF AUSTRALIA

PROFESSOR A P ELKIN
Emititus Professor of Anthropology, University of Sydney.
"THE AUSTRALIAN ABORIGINES"

Subject	PAGE
Aborigines identified as aboriginals of India.	4
Aboriginal invasion of Australia via Cape York.	6
Native dog [dingo] accompanied aboriginal invaders.	6
Aborigines identifed as invaders.	8
Papuans in Australia massacred by aboriginal invaders.	9

PROFESSOR A C HADDON – World famous Anthropologist.
Leader of the Cambridge Anthropological Expedition to the Torres Strait.
"THE RACES OF MAN"

Subject	PAGE
Aborigines identified as the "Pre-Dravidians" of India.	13
Aborigines identified as the "Aboriginals of India".	14
Papuans from New Guinea identified as original Australians.	20
Aborigines identified as invaders.	20

PROFESSOR A C HADDON
"THE RACES OF MAN"
(Oceania)

Subject	PAGE
Papuans living in Australia exterminated by aborigines.	122

KATHLEEN RISHBETH (HADDON)
Anthropologist.
"ARTISTS IN STRINGS"

Subject	PAGE
Aborigines identified as the "Pre-Dravidians of India".	96
Aborigines related to the Veddah of Ceylon and India.	96
Original Australians identified as a race from New Guinea.	96
Original Australians displaced by invading aborigines.	96
Tasmanian aborigines identified as Papuans from New Guinea	96

THE END